CIRCLE OF LIGHT

Circle of Light

The Autobiography of
KIRANJIT AHLUWALIA

———

Kiranjit Ahluwalia and
Rahila Gupta

HarperCollins*Publishers*

HarperCollins*Publishers*
77–85 Fulham Palace Road,
Hammersmith, London w6 8jb

Published by HarperCollins*Publishers* 1997
Copyright © Kiranjit Ahluwalia and Rahila Gupta 1997

The Author asserts the moral right to be
identified as the author of this work

A catalogue record for this book is
available from the British Library

ISBN 0 00 638329 7

Set in Minion by
Rowland Phototypesetting Ltd,
Bury St Edmunds, Suffolk

Printed and bound in Great Britain by
Caledonian International Book Manufacturing Ltd, Glasgow

*For all those women who have suffered at
the hands of men*

CONTENTS

ACKNOWLEDGEMENTS

MY SPECIAL THANKS TO: Southall Black Sisters, who campaigned so hard for my release and put in so much work over the custody of my children; Rohit Sanghvi, who took on my case without any prospect of legal aid and, along with Pragna Patel and Hannana Siddiqui, worked tirelessly to secure my release; Pragna, who visited me endlessly in prison to take my statement, and became my soul-sister in the process; my brother-in-law Sukhjit and my sisters Dev and Surinder, my brothers Billoo, Tommy and Bindhi who looked after my children and gave their unqualified support; Ranjit, Gurjit, Hansapur, Ajit and many others who helped me at various times; Joan Walsh, who wrote to me in prison and taught me how to write in English, took my children on outings and brought them to visit me, started a one-woman writing campaign to plead for my release, helped me settle down in my new home and was always on hand for help and comfort.

I would also like to thank: Crawley Women's Aid, Justice for Women and many other organisations who participated in my campaign; Julie Bindel and Harriet, who brought my children to visit me and lent their voices to the SBS campaign and demonstrations; all my supporters, including Maria Demi, who wrote to me in prison and gave me courage and strength; Miss Bott, my personal officer in prison; my probation officers in Holloway, Diana Bevin and John Michael; Rahila Gupta, whose writing skills and attention to detail speak for themselves.

Kiranjit Ahluwalia

IN THE PREPARATION of this book, I would like to thank the following: Kiranjit, of course, for her courage and determination, without which the book could not have been written; Pragna Patel, Hannana Siddiqui and Meena Patel, who provided detailed comments and proved that reality has many faces; Gita Sahgal, who wrote the concluding chapter on the role of Southall Black Sisters in the campaign; Rohit Sanghvi, for his impeccable attention to detail and logical inconsistencies; Robert Lacey, our editor at HarperCollins, for his efficiency, eye for detail and flexible deadlines; Michelle Brown and Donna Szombara for keeping my children at a safe distance when deadlines were looming; Rohan Thamotheram for reading the manuscript and pleading the case for balance.

Rahila Gupta

PREFACE

IRONICALLY, JUST AT the time Kiranjit Ahluwalia's case came to the attention of Southall Black Sisters, I was taking refuge from the shrapnel flying from the break-up of my own long-term relationship. I had asked to be excused from SBS work, and it was not until Kiranjit's campaign was in full swing in 1992 that I had recovered my sense of perspective enough to want to be involved again.

My main role was writing, designing and organising the printing of some of the publicity materials for the campaign – posters and leaflets – in the cheapest way possible. I also wrote a piece and read it on 'Comment', the slot after the Channel 4 seven o'clock news, in the heady days leading up to Kiranjit's appeal. All this while, the Kiran in my mind was the one in the only photo of her that seemed to be in circulation. But the Kiran I saw in the dock during the appeal – young and stylish and bent over with the weight of the entire world – was unexpected.

As luck would have it, on the day of her release, I was in bed with a bad back and my eyes streaming with tears because I couldn't be at court to share the joyful outcome of years of hard work. Nor at all the celebrations immediately after.

Southall Black Sisters, a group of Asian and African-Caribbean women, came together in 1979 to campaign on a variety of issues affecting black women – most famously against the virginity tests being carried out on Asian brides by the immigration authorities. In 1983 SBS became a funded organisation, opened a women's centre and started doing day-to-day casework – mainly with women fleeing domestic violence but also on other issues such as welfare benefits advice, housing and immigration problems. Until Kiranjit's case, SBS had run campaigns about women who had been killed by their husbands or pushed into committing suicide. Kiranjit seemed a natural extension – a woman who had escaped domestic violence in her own way.

At SBS we had been talking about a book to record the struggle, and perhaps another analysing the issues piggy-backing on Kiranjit's own story. Kiran herself was keen to participate, but first she had to sort out more important things like housing and the custody of her children. She was torn between wanting to inspire women trapped in brutal relationships and the pressure from her relatives to fade into obscurity and regain her status as ordinary citizen. We ourselves were galvanised into action only when Kiranjit met the Princess of Wales at the reopening of the Chiswick Refuge. The Princess advised her to write a book, all the press covered the story, and hacks of all shapes and sizes chased her to offer their services.

None of us wanted the story to be sensationalised. Besides, Kiran's English would not quite mould itself to the 'words from the heart' that were waiting to tumble out. I approached a number of publishers, quite a few of whom showed interest.

Kiranjit wavered from day to day, keenly interested in the book on one day and then, just as we thought we had an agreement, backing down again. Her newly acquired confidence, born of the campaign and successful appeal, was battling with the old uncertainties and nervousness. Finally, we were ready to go.

I started visiting Kiranjit once or twice a week. It was winter. She couldn't afford to heat her house all day, so I would huddle up in a blanket and overcoat and warm my hands on a regular supply of hot Indian tea (boiled with ginger, cardamoms and cloves). We would stop only for Kiran's delicious meals. We taped approximately eighty hours of conversation.

The pain of her memories had not been dulled by the endless repetition of her tale to psychiatrists, lawyers, probation officers, social workers and others. She would sob like a child as she relived the cruelty and humiliation of her life with Deepak. She would drag me into her pain and we would weep together. She would then brighten up and ask me half affectionately, half mockingly, if I was enjoying the Hindi film (known for their tear-jerking qualities).

There were many things that Kiran could not remember or did not understand – tantalising bits of information which could round off the picture for the reader. Some of them I picked up from the hundreds of files and letters I have waded through. At the risk of disrupting the flow, I have put these in as inserts, because I did not want to tamper with the image of Kiranjit which emerges through her story.

Kiran wanted me to visit Crawley with her, meet some of the friends and relatives she had talked about, see the houses she had lived in and get a sense of geography and atmosphere to help me locate the events. We had picked a day in February when the roads were encrusted with heavy layers of snow, so we couldn't make a quick getaway if Kiranjit was spotted by someone by whom she didn't want to be recognised. When we drove into Crawley police station so that Kiran could show me the cell where she had been kept before she was transferred to Holloway, a policeman walked past, waved and said, 'Hello, Mrs Ahluwalia. All right?' Kiran squirmed and tried to sink into oblivion. He was apparently one of the officers who had interviewed her immediately after the incident.

A gradual trust and friendship grew between us. We made jokes about killing and arson. She told me that her stock answer to the question about marital status on forms was 'self-made widow', and we hooted with laughter. On one occasion, when Kiranjit was relating how she felt haunted by Deepak after his death, the tape-recorder started sizzling ominously. Dissolving into nervous giggles, we switched it off and on in rapid succession, but were unable to get rid of the sizzle. Just as we were beginning to feel well and truly frightened, I turned the tape recorder upside down and a few drops of tea dripped out. The imbalance of power, in which she was obliged to confide the most intimate details of her life whereas I was under no such obligation, riled Kiranjit. She would want to trade information, refusing to continue until I had answered a personal question.

I was therapist, confidante, careers adviser and debt counsellor all rolled into one. Kiran would share her worries about her children, and would speculate about how her life might have been if she had done things differently at various turning points; she would feel consumed by guilt one day, thankful for her freedom on another. She needed to know that in one sense she could have done no differently, that she was brought to this point by the society which gave birth to her.

She has come a long way.

Rahila Gupta

Circle of Light

ONE

In the Bowels of Holloway

I WAS LYING IN A ROOM, barely conscious. I hardly knew
where I was – I knew only this, that the door was locked on
the outside. It was a small room with a wooden bunk, a filthy
mattress, a dirty, uncovered pillow stained with urine and a
torn military-green blanket. I was lying on this when the door
opened. A police officer was standing there. 'C'mon, let's go.'
Like an obedient child I emerged from the police cell and followed him quietly. A woman police officer was standing by a
van outside. It was probably five or six in the evening.

My head was exploding with pain, and my insides were quaking with fear. My arm was wrapped in a plastic bag, my hair,
which was permed at that time, was singed at the edges and
flying wild, my eyelashes were also singed, and there were burn
marks across my mouth and under my eyes. My face was pale,
my skin was dry. I was tired. So, so tired and depressed.

The van was dark and dirty, and the windows were covered
with an iron grille and could not be opened. I was alone. The
door was locked and the driver and the police officer – or prison
officer, I don't know which, I was so dazed – sat in the front.
I didn't even know that I was going to prison. If I was to serve
a sentence, so be it. My life was in their hands. I would have
to pay for what I had done as they saw fit. I had never imagined
that my life could come to this.

We started moving. I tried to cover my face so that no one
in Crawley would see me sitting in a police van. Only when we
reached the motorway did I lift my head. My eyes were full of

tears, but I could not cry. As we sped down the motorway, putting more and more distance between myself and Crawley, I felt my life and my children slipping irretrievably away from me.

I thought I was being taken to hospital for medical treatment and to await the outcome of my application for bail. My solicitor may have told me that Holloway was a remand prison, but in my confused state of mind the word 'hospital' would not be dislodged. I had been to hospital once already to be treated for my burns. The pathologist had taken a photo of my burnt arm and I had shouted, 'No, no, not until my solicitor gets here.' I thought they were taking my photograph to release to all the papers. Little did I know that the story was already out, that the world already knew.

I was starving, I was tired, I was feeling sick. The atmosphere in the van was smothering me. There was no ventilation, and I had been given three or four different kinds of medicines. I didn't know how to alert the officers that I was feeling sick. There was a little glass-covered aperture in the partition that separated me from the driver, but I don't think I even noticed it on that first trip. I had got so used to hiding my feelings from the eyes of the world that I drew upon that old habit and held my vomit in. I lay down, and within a few minutes I fell asleep.

When we arrived I saw the high walls, the iron gate, and a board with the words 'HM Holloway Women's Prison'. It sunk in then that they had brought me to a prison.

There was an eerie silence as I stood there, a carrier bag in one hand with one set of clothes, and a plastic bag tied around my other arm. I had asked my mother-in-law to send a change of clothes, and Deepak's younger brother Suresh had brought them to me in the police cell. The clothes I had been wearing had been sent off to the forensic department. I was lucky. The trousers Suresh had brought for me happened to be my new ones, and I found £70 in the pocket. In all my confusion and depression, I had had the presence of mind to say to Suresh when he visited me in the police cell, 'Give £20 to Mum to look after the kids for this week and I'll pay her the rest as soon as I come out.'

I was not handcuffed – they had seen from my demeanour that I was not going to be difficult. I did what they told me quietly and obediently. I had been in the police cell for thirty-six hours and had only occasionally disturbed them, to ask for a cup of tea or to go to the toilet.

The police officer spoke on an intercom, and they took me inside into a reception area. There was a small office with two prison officers, one of whom held a register in her hands. The walls were white and bare, there were no pictures, no carpet, and the floor was so ingrained with dirt that it never looked clean, even if it had just been swept. There were a few other women sitting in the room.

The officer asked me in a very loud voice, 'What is your name?' although she had the form in front of her on which all my details had been written down. 'How much money do you have? How many clothes? Any jewellery?' She took my earrings and my *kada*, a steel bangle. When I protested that it had a religious significance for me she said, 'Sorry, love. Those are the rules.' I felt intimidated by the tone of her voice. Would everyone in prison speak like that? I was told to go and wait in another room. There were fifteen or twenty tables and chairs. Women were chatting, smoking, rolling cigarettes, laughing, sitting with their legs apart, sitting on tables. There were all kinds of women, some young, some old. I had come into the midst of women with whom I had no connection. This was not my world. I was really frightened. In those days I was scared of everyone and everything. I thought the other prisoners would hit me. I had never had the opportunity to make friends with anyone, to talk to anyone. Fear, fear, fear, and it had kept growing. I went and sat in a corner. One of the women who worked in the kitchen asked me if I wanted anything to eat or drink. I asked for a cup of tea. When it came it was tasteless, like water, cold and without sugar. My head was being ripped apart, and cold tea was no cure for it. I felt as if I was going to be sick. There was some salt on the table, but I thought it was sugar and put some into my cold tea. I felt even worse when I took a sip.

One of the women came up to me and asked, 'What happened? What happened to your arm?' My life ebbed out of me. What was I to tell her? I froze, and tried to ignore her, hoping she would ask some other question. I wasn't in a mood to talk. What was I supposed to say? It wasn't that I didn't want to tell the truth. I had already given my statement in the police station. I said I had burnt myself and the woman didn't pursue it further, much to my relief.

Then I noticed that the women who had been sitting in reception were now coming out of another room, wearing dirty blue and brown towelling gowns, with naked legs. I realised it would be my turn soon, that I was going to be strip-searched. I had to wait an hour, an hour and a half. It was so slow. Every ten or fifteen minutes they would call out the names of women who were waiting. Holloway was like a railway station, with a constant coming and going of women. The officers jotted down every detail. They have to make sure that nothing is being stolen, nothing being brought in or taken out, no drugs, no needles – they even check your knickers.

When it was my turn, I pleaded with the officer not to strip-search me. I told her that I had never shown my naked legs in public before. She just said, 'Sorry, love, you have to do it.' In the corner was a pile of dirty gowns. I myself was filthy, I couldn't remember when I had last had a bath. There was fluid leaking from the blisters on my left arm, which the plastic bag was unable to contain. Slowly, with one hand, I undressed myself. I took my top off but left my jeans on. The officer asked why I wasn't undressed yet. I said, 'Please, Miss, I am too shy.' I felt like an insect whose wings had been trimmed and who couldn't fly away, no matter how hard it fluttered.

I asked the officer to check me in stages so that I wouldn't have to be completely naked. In the ten years of my married life I had never even undressed in front of my husband. Maybe the officer saw the tears in my eyes, maybe she saw my helplessness. She checked me from the waist up, and then slowly, with one hand, I put my top back on and pushed my trousers down. Then she said she needed to check my knickers. I had to walk naked and do a turn so that if I was hiding anything in my vagina, it would show up in the way I walked. Then I was asked to get dressed and wait in the next room.

It must have been nine o'clock by now. Already I had waited two hours at least. Everyone else had been taken away, and it seemed my turn would never come. My eyelids were drooping with tiredness. I was hungry, but at the same time I didn't want to eat. After about half an hour I was called again, and this time I was taken to the doctor. She asked me about my height and weight and how I had got the burns on my arm. I burst into tears and told her the whole story. Then I was asked by the nurse to go and wait outside. Oh my God, that was all I needed. I was dead tired.

I was given two sheets, a towel, two pairs of knickers, a nightie, toilet soap, a toothbrush and some tooth powder which tasted like soap powder for washing clothes.

A prison officer took hold of my arm and we began our long journey into the bowels of the prison. Clutching my carrier bag, I went up the stairs and down long, gloomy corridors with rooms leading off them. Every so often we came to a locked door, and the officer would unlock it with her big bunch of keys and then lock it behind us. The floors were brown, the lights were dim. Not a soul was in sight. The gloom and the isolation lay heavily on me. My voice escaped in a scream. I thought I would be taken into a cell and beaten to shreds, that they would lock me up in the darkness and leave me to starve. I broke down and sobbed uncontrollably. To my surprise, the officer held me and comforted me. 'Don't cry,' she said. 'Everyone who comes here for the first time cries. You're in safe hands now.' The warmth of her touch made me cry even more. I needed it so badly at that time. I kept sobbing, and she led me delicately, like a fragile child, by the shoulders, slowly down the corridor.

After four or five minutes we came to some stairs. These stairs led into hell, down into the underground depths of the prison. At the bottom was an office. The guard took me in and said, 'Officer, I have another one for you. This poor girl is very upset. Please look after her.' With every new face that I had to encounter, I felt an acute agony in reliving the shame of what I had done. The officer took me to my cell. I didn't know what to expect. I thought I would be locked up on my own in the dark, and that made me sob again. She opened a door and switched on the light. There were two women asleep, and two empty beds. When I saw the women, life flooded back into my veins. At least I wouldn't be alone. The one in the bed next to mine was white, and was aged between twenty and thirty. The officer said to her, 'Hi, Vicky, here's a new girl for you. Please look after her. Her name is Karen.' That was how I used to be known at work by those who couldn't manage my real name, Kiranjit.

The officer asked Vicky to help me make my bed, and she brought me a hot cup of tea and some toast. The tea was sweet and to my liking. I was given a nightie, a knee-length, thick cotton affair with blue and pink flowers. I was too shy to wear mine, I preferred track suits or pyjamas. So I tucked my nightie into my jeans and went to bed like that. Although it was uncomfortable, it stopped me feeling cold. It was summer, but I was too weak to feel warm. I was also given some medicine. I didn't know it included sleeping tablets. Within a few minutes of my head touching the pillow, I was fast asleep. I was too tired even to have the energy to think.

The next day, at about 7.30 a.m., Vicky woke me up and took me through the routine. 'Before the doors open,' she said, 'make sure you've made your bed and taken off your nightie.'

In daylight I could see the room for the first time. In one corner was a toilet without a lightbulb and a door that did not shut. I washed my face and changed and went with Vicky to join the queue for breakfast. She had not asked me any details about why I was there or what had happened to my arm, which was very comforting. I was given the regulation blue plastic cup and plate. Toast, jam and some tasteless porridge was what they called breakfast.

This was C1, the hospital wing, but it wasn't like other hospitals. The nurses carried great big bunches of keys and didn't speak gently. They shouted, 'Do this, ladies. Do that. Have you cleaned your rooms properly?' and were stricter than the prison officers. One of them, a big fat woman, talked to you as if you were a dog. She had no pity.

There were about twenty women, aged between seventeen and sixty-five, in the small dining room. Some of them had bandages and plasters on different parts of their bodies. One was on crutches, another had her leg in plaster. When breakfast was finished, a nurse called for the cleaning ladies. Another yelled 'Medicine!' Vicky showed me where to queue up. One woman was off for a bath, another picked up a broom, another a brush and started scrubbing. As I walked down the corridor I looked at everything carefully. Such a sad place, such sad walls.

God knows what the medicines were for – were they for my arm, for my blisters, for the pain, for sleep, for depression? I was like a statue, lifeless, a walking corpse. I was a robot, push whatever buttons you liked, and I would co-operate. Back in my cell the nurse locked the door, and after ten minutes I was again falling asleep. Lunch was at 11.30, and Vicky woke me up again. I was hungry, but the bitterness in my mouth was not relieved by the sight of prison food. Cold cabbage, potatoes and a piece of meat. It had no taste, and there was no salt, no pepper, nothing. Although the main kitchen was not far away, by the time the food was served on individual plates and wheeled in it was inedibly cold. The cabbage sometimes had worms in it, and once I found a tissue – had somebody blown their nose and dropped it in the food? Yukks! The bread was like rock.

As lunch finished, again the call of 'Medicine, ladies.' Then at 12 noon it was 'Lock-up time, ladies,' and I was back in the cell and falling asleep in no time at all. I kept wondering why I was always so sleepy. Was it aeons of fatigue that made me this way? At 1.30 p.m., after a roll-call, we were let out for 'exercise time'. I wondered what this exercise meant, what would I have to do? I found that you just walked around in the yard. I sat on a bench and watched. Some women were begging for cigarettes from the officers, one was talking to herself, another was kicking out in the air. No one approached me.

There was one tall, thin, sixty-year-old woman with a few grey hairs sprouting from her chin and two and a half hairs on her head, who used to make moaning noises. She would throw her head back and laugh in long 'ooo' sounds like a monkey. Sometimes she would ask for a cigarette. She would join her hands together and keep begging until the nurses relented and obliged with a roll-up or two. We got an allowance of £1.50 a week, and she would blow it all on cigarettes almost immediately and then hassle the nurses for the rest of the week. If they refused, she would get angry and kick an innocent bystander with a quick backwards movement of her leg. When she sat down she would spread her legs and treat us to a view of her grey hairs.

After thirty minutes the officers shouted, 'OK, ladies, go inside.' We were allowed to watch TV for an hour and a half before dinner was served at 4.30 p.m., and we were locked up again from five to six. At 6 o'clock it was, 'OK, ladies, association time.' Vicky told me that this meant that the television room was open for two hours. There we would have our supper, which was a biscuit and a cup of tea. After supper they gave us our medicine and locked us up. In fifteen minutes I was fast asleep again.

It might seem as if we had a lot of time out, but it was only the cell door that was open, not the prison gate. And if there was not enough staff, as happened quite frequently, we were locked up from 4.30 p.m. until 7.30 the next morning.

The next day at 12.30 p.m. the officer knocked on the door and said there was a telephone call for me, and that I was allowed to speak for a few minutes. It was my sister Surinder, who lived in Canada. She was calling from my brother Billoo praji's house. She asked me how I was. When I heard her voice I burst into tears. She started crying too and said, 'What have you done?'

I said through my sobs, 'What I did was right. I am very happy. I did the right thing.'

Billoo praji took the phone from her. The officer handed me a tissue and asked me to calm down as it was a long-distance call. Billoo said, 'I'm coming.' He told me my older brother, Bindhi (Bhupinder) praji, was also coming, from India. I didn't know whether they would be allowed to visit me – I didn't know that prisoners on remand were allowed daily visits.

I said, 'No need. Deepak deserved it. I don't regret anything. I don't want you to worry. I am so happy. Don't come.' I was afraid that if they came to see me they might hit me and shout at me. My brothers had never shouted at me before, but now I had stained their reputation, their *izzat*. The phone call lasted more than a few minutes. Maybe the officer took pity on me. That was the first time in prison that I wept heartbrokenly, remembering my children, Sandeep and Rajeev. When the nurses saw my grief, they told me that the probation officer, Diana Bevin, would be coming to visit soon. When she came, I could not stop crying. It was the mother in me crying. 'I want to see my children, I want to see my children,' I kept repeating. I was crying for Deepak, for my house, for my children. Diana asked me to tell her my story. I could speak English, but I had no confidence. I was afraid that people would laugh at my accent, that I might get a word wrong. In my broken English I told her about my marriage, about the years of torture, and what I had done. She offered me a cigarette, and asked for my mother-in-law's telephone number so that she could ring her and I could speak to my children. Normally making calls from prison is a complicated affair. You have to fill in a form giving the reasons for your call and hand it to your probation officer, who will question you to find out if it is necessary. She will then take you to the office and dial the number. Usually you are allowed to make calls only to your solicitor.

Manju, Deepak's sister, answered the phone. I asked for my mother-in-law. 'Mum, forgive me, forgive me. How are you?'

She said, 'I fell down the stairs, I am not well, I cannot look after the children.' I asked after Deepak. She said, 'Don't ask after his health. You doused him in fire, you gave him an *agni-ishnaan* [firebath]. He is lying in hospital covered in burns'.

'Forgive me, Mum, you know it wasn't my fault. You know how he used to treat me. Are Sandeep and Rajeev okay? Can I speak with them?'

'To what hell have you sentenced Deepak? You gave him a firebath.'

'Can I talk to my children?'

'They are playing. You have lost your husband, your children, your house.'

'Please,' I begged.

She shouted, 'Sandeep,' and then said, 'He is playing. He says he doesn't want to come.'

I said, 'Ask Suresh to organise a social worker to help you, as you cannot look after the children. I will come out quickly.'

'What makes you think you're coming out?' she mocked.

I knew from the tone of her voice that I was not going to be allowed to speak to my children. Although she was a mother herself, she could not hear a mother's desperate cry for her children. Diana comforted me, and I was taken back to my cell. Even though I had had my sleeping tablets, I could not sleep.

*   *   *

While on remand I was allowed to write four letters per week, the postage being paid for by the authorities. This included two specifically for my children. But I had to write in English so that the prison officers could understand it when they were censoring the mail. I picked up the pen and paper and started, 'Dearest Mum, Sandeep Rajeev,' writing in English to my mother-in-law for the first time. I could hardly write it, and she could hardly read it.

> Mum, Mum, sorry. Mum, Deepak did this. He did that. Yes, I gave him an agni-ishnaan, I am a papi [sinner]. I am paying for my sins by this jail yatra [pilgrimage]. But he is a sinner too. He has beaten and cheated me for the past ten years, cheated me on the insurance. I am sure he will be all right. Tell him not to pretend. The children need him. Tell him to go and look after them. He is probably still dreaming about his girlfriend.

I admitted that although my husband was God, I had hurt him. I didn't realise the impact this letter would have on my case. It was to prove to be my undoing, and was quoted again and again at my trial. But I had also written another letter a few months previously, to Deepak, committing myself to abject slavery in the hope of attracting him back to the family home, and that one was to help secure my release.

On the third day, the fat nurse said I could have a bath, but when I locked the door she yelled, 'What do you think you're doing?' I said I was too shy to take my clothes off in front of everyone. She said, 'Shy or not, I've got the same as you, love.' I thought, 'Big, fat woman. How dare she say there's no difference?' The nurses were worried about suicide, but with one hand I could only just take a bath, so how could I take my life? After my bath the water was almost black, and I felt much better. The only thing that spoilt it was having to wear someone

13

else's top and jumper because I had run out of clothes. I hadn't worn hand-me-downs since I was a child.

By the fourth day I was getting used to the routine. I thought I would be granted bail, get better and go home in four or five weeks. I didn't know how I would manage without seeing my children for that long.

At about 2.30 p.m. an officer came to the cell and said I had a visitor. I was shaking, my jeans were torn, my arm was in a bag. I thought, 'My brother will beat me. He will demand to know what I did and why.' I was searched in case I tried to smuggle something out. 'Sit at this table,' the officer said.

Billoo praji, Bindhi praji and my brother-in-law Sukhjit jijaji arrived. I couldn't even greet them. My brothers didn't hit me. Perhaps they were embarrassed in front of Sukhjit. I started crying, and Billoo and Bindhi praji followed suit. I had only ever seen my older brother cry at my mother's funeral and at my wedding. I told them through my sobs, 'He used to hit me every day, every day. He used to hit the children, he used to spit on me. Am I so dirty that my husband spat on me? I can't tell you how things are with me in here. I am fine.'

'Do they beat you? Do they keep you in solitary?' they wanted to know.

I said, 'No, no one beats me now. I have two other room-mates.'

'Are you eating? You look so thin.'

'Yes, English food.'

'Why didn't you tell us before things got so out of hand?' asked Bindhi praji.

I reminded him that I had phoned him just a few days before the incident. I was so deeply unhappy in those days, but when I rang him all I said was, 'I am so happy, so happy, you will not believe it.' I had planned to tell him everything that Deepak had done to me but when it came to the crunch, I couldn't make myself. Bindhi praji said that the tone of my voice had made him suspicious that there was something wrong with his

Poochi (my pet name). He said that if we had been in India he would have been able to organise everything, but here he was a nobody.

My mother-in-law had shown my brothers the letter I had written to her, saying, 'See, she has herself admitted to her crime, that she is washing away her sins in jail, that she gave Deepak a firebath.' They were angry: 'Do you know what a terrible sentence you could get as a result of that letter?' My eyes were opened by their words. I tried to defend myself by telling them that my mother-in-law had used the word 'firebath' in our phone conversation, and that I had merely repeated it. I had never heard it before. I was going to tell the truth anyway, so why not admit it to them?

'Don't worry,' Bindhi praji said. 'While I am alive, you have no need to worry.' I knew that my brothers would lay down their lives for me. They would run around and spend all the money they had to save me. They asked about my solicitor. I said that he had dealt with my case and had got me two injunctions before this. He knew my history. I told them how one day Deepak had followed me, caught hold of me on the street and dragged me home, where he had beaten me for a whole hour.

Bindhi praji was shocked by Deepak's cruelty. He told me that they had been to visit him in hospital, and that he was getting better. The children had also visited him. At one level I still believed my brothers would sort out my relationship with Deepak and reconcile us. At the very least, I thought they would take me out of prison. Instead, when their visit came to an end I was taken back to the dormitory by the officers. As I queued with the other women who had had visitors, I felt a strange peace settle on me. At least my brothers had not shouted at me.

On the fifth day I was taken to the doctor, who cut my blisters with scissors and took off my bandage. My arm and hand looked awful. Even my nails were burnt. The skin could not grow back until the water from the blisters had drained away. The doctor was Indian, and although she couldn't speak Hindi, I was very comforted to meet one of my own.

I told her, 'Doctor, I'm not mad, I remember everything. Why have I been kept here?' I was worried that I would not get my children back if they thought I was mad. A lot of other women on the wing were not normal. They screamed and kicked against the heavy wooden doors to their cells. During association time they would fight with each other, pulling each other's hair out. Even Vicky, who was so quiet, one day just tore up the pack of cards with which we used to play. I started getting scared of her too.

Women would suddenly stand up and press the emergency alarm, shrieking with pleasure as the prison officers came running, fell over or bumped into each other in their haste. One woman would start howling without rhyme or reason, another laughing. If they behaved badly or attempted suicide, women would be sent to solitary, and you could hear them all night swearing, kicking at the doors or just crying to be let out, 'Fucking bastards, I'll fucking kill you. You fucking kangaroos.' In solitary they would not even be given knickers, because prisoners had been known to attempt suicide with them. They were given a tunic made of such thick material that you couldn't tie a knot in it.

Holloway is a rectangular building built around an open space which is used as an exercise ground. The cell windows are tiny, to prevent anyone sticking their heads out. C1, the hospital wing, had been dubbed 'the Muppet wing' by the rest of the inmates. Sometimes they would throw food down to provoke the C1 'nutters'. We had an absolute plague of cockroaches in C1. From the first floor on the opposite side of the yard the other prisoners would egg on the screaming women in solitary by clapping, jeering and shouting: 'Yeah, come on, come on, you fucking bitch, louder, louder.' Associating with such women made me question my own sanity. Coming to this place directly after what I had done had blurred the certainties of my world.

As my arm healed, my routine was varied a bit. I was asked if I would like to enrol for education in the mornings. I was quite excited by the idea, but when I got there I was disappointed. It was like playschool. Some women were cutting up pictures, others were painting or drawing. On a white T-shirt I painted 'I love Sandeep and Rajeev', with a heart in the corner. I have kept it to this day. I thought that when I wore it I would feel that I had my children clasped closely to my heart, and that I would wear it when they came to visit for the first time. I would show them how close they were to me even though they were a million miles away.

The next morning, after I had my breakfast, the Indian doctor asked to see me in her office. I felt friendly enough with her to compliment her on her beautiful sari. The senior nurse, whom we all dreaded, was with her.

The doctor said she had bad news to give me. 'Your husband has died.'

I said with a smile, 'Doctor, don't joke with me.'

She said quietly, 'This is not a joke.'

I could not believe it. I had always thought it would be me who would die first, and I used to say, 'Deepak, don't come to my funeral, don't spend any money on it. I will pre-pay the expenses.' I would tell my mother-in-law, 'Mum, don't let him come to my funeral. I don't want to see his face as I am leaving this world.'

I let out a scream and started crying. I was sad for my children, who would have no one to call Daddy. I had never seen my own father, and now, because of me, my children would never see theirs, the word 'Daddy' would never pass their lips again. The doctor held me and said I had to be strong for the sake of my children. She made a gesture to the nurse, who brought some pink medicine in a big glass. The nurse took me to my room. I sat on my bed, unable to tell the other women what had happened. I tried to hide my sobs from them, and in a few minutes I fell asleep.

TWO

Let Him R.I.P.

THE NEXT DAY my sister Dev visited me for the first time. She said she had been to see Deepak in hospital, and that he had not had a single word of complaint against me. All he said was, 'Kiran and me, our paths have diverged.' I wonder if he had known that his death was imminent when he said this, or did he simply mean divorce? His condition had been improving when suddenly something went wrong. I think his kidneys packed up.

I didn't know, I didn't want to know, I still don't know the exact date of his death – it happened between the fifth and tenth day after I entered prison. I never verified it. I couldn't bring myself to do it. After the fire on 9 May 1990, no date had any significance for me.

[In the early hours of Monday 15 May 1990, Deepak Ahluwalia died of a heart attack after developing a number of complications as a result of 40 per cent burns to his body.]

I don't know whether it was the effect of the medicines or whether it was my inescapable depression, but I couldn't make myself feel anything. After Dev left my period started, and my left arm was shaking uncontrollably. For two or three days I didn't eat any food. The other inmates didn't know my story. All they knew was that my husband had died, and they said, 'Sorry, take it easy.'

I started having a recurrent vision that Deepak would get

18

better, and that he would be waiting for me at the prison gates with a bucket of petrol in his hands which he would throw at me in a final act of revenge, shouting, 'I want to kill her! I want to kill her!' Even if I shut my eyes for five minutes this image would haunt me and chase the sleep away from my eyes. My sleeping-tablet dosage was increased, but I still could not sleep properly. One night I was woken by what felt like a hard slap against my left ear. I was convinced it was Deepak, and I couldn't sleep all night after that. For days after, my left ear was buzzing with deafness. In the daytime, too, I was frightened. I used to pray all the time to God, 'Babaji, help me.' I couldn't tell anyone, because they would think I was going mad, and I didn't want to lose my children.

I had daily visits from a variety of relatives. My sister's brother-in-law, my aunt's son and daughter, friends, neighbours. Sometimes I would cry, but sometimes I could not, not even for their benefit. I had become a *tamasha*, a drama for them.

On Monday I was taken to Crawley Magistrates' Court to extend my detention in prison on remand. This happened fortnightly, I think. Deepak's entire family was gathered in the courtroom. I was asked my name, and told to sit down. The judge read something for two minutes. Deepak's brother Suresh said that there were two young children, that the elder one was very attached to his grandmother, and that they would look after them. That was also what I wanted. Suresh promised to bring them to prison to visit me. I was so naïve I thought I would be out in four or five weeks.

I was taken away to a police cell, where I was asked to sign some papers which apparently said that the charge of attempted murder had been upgraded to murder. I didn't know what 'attempted' meant, and refused to sign anything until my solicitor arrived.

Deepak's eldest sister Pummi had been in court, and she came to visit me in the police cell. I thought she would hit me, but instead she held out her arms, embraced me and burst into tears, saying, 'Kiran, what have you done?'

I started crying as well. I said, 'I have made a very big mistake. I cannot bring him back.'

My mother-in-law, Billoo praji and two other relatives also visited me in the police cell. My mother-in-law didn't say a word, but the others said I should be strong for the sake of my children. I was very weak. I had lost weight after years of a miserable marriage. I was a walking corpse. I had not been able to show my grief. I was tired of crying. They left after fifteen or twenty minutes.

After the shock of Deepak's death, I had another setback. Bail was refused. Earlier I had been physically beaten; now I felt mentally beaten. I didn't even want to know the reasons why bail had been refused. In some ways, I didn't want my freedom. Part of me wanted to stay in prison. Freedom scared me. What sort of a face would I show to the rest of the world? I was safe in prison, safe from my husband's family. No one could attack me there.

[According to Sukhjit, bail was refused on the grounds that Kiranjit was a danger to herself, on the basis of her earlier suicide attempt, and because she might abscond to India.]

Diana Bevin got in touch with an Asian women's group on my behalf. I can't remember their name. I talked to them for two hours, asking them to help me see my children. They said they would come back once they had thought it through. They never did.

I wanted to see my children very badly. Every time my brothers visited I'd ask them when they would bring the children. I didn't know that my mother-in-law was refusing to let them visit me. All my hopes were dying one by one. My solicitor's clerk came to see me and asked me to sign some papers to make the children wards of court. I didn't know what that meant until he explained it to me. I said, 'Look, I really want to see my children. Instead of doing anything about that, you're making me sign all these papers.' As I didn't understand much about legal matters, I didn't ask the right questions.

[In August, Kiranjit started wardship proceedings. Sukhjit and Gurdev applied for care and control and access to the children. In October the court ordered interim access so that Sukhjit could take the children to visit Kiran in prison.]

I had been in Holloway for three weeks, and I still hadn't seen the children. My husband had died. I had been refused bail. What was going on? I asked about my house. The clerk said that my in-laws had asked for the keys, as they wanted to pick up the children's clothes. I told him to go with them and to make sure that he returned the keys to me.

I had felt a great sadness when I had set the house alight, that house for which I had made such sacrifices, buying myself only cheap clothes in the sales. I had prayed to God for a small, beautiful house in which the four of us could be happy. I was careful with Deepak's money. Even when I felt like going to McDonald's I stopped myself, as I didn't want to waste £2 or £3. Now I was sitting in prison, powerless. My children were lost to me, and so was my house. I felt deserted by one and all – this God, this world, these jailors, these in-laws – they wanted to see how desperate I would become, they wanted me to have the maximum punishment. They were not satisfied yet.

I was seen by the prison psychiatrist, Dr Roderick Evans. I didn't know what 'psychiatry' meant; I thought he was going to test my memory. Quaking inside but trying hard to appear calm, I answered his questions carefully. I was not going to cry in front of him. If I did, they would take my children away. Afterwards, I kept repeating his questions and my answers to myself, in case next time he asked me the same questions to catch me out. This was my daily homework. What had I said to him? If I varied my answers, I was afraid he would say I was mad – and I used to consider myself an intelligent woman. I was putting on a façade, just as I had done for ten years with Deepak. It had become second nature to me. Laughing, putting on make-up, pretending. I was good at acting. I didn't want people to mock me. Everyone came to see the fire that had been lit in my heart and soul. It was a *tamasha*.

He came back after two or three weeks, and asked some more questions. He said that I had told him we had only one car. I said, 'No, I told you that we had two cars; one in the garage, a blue Datsun Sunny, and a blue Volkswagen outside. There was a third car, an XR3 which was being repaired. These were their registration numbers.' I gave precise answers to impress him with the power of my memory. I wanted to show that I could look after my children in the future. I did not dare show him my feelings, how hurt I was inside, how I cried on my pillow every night. I hid my arm from him so that he could not see it shaking. He asked me how I felt. I said I was heartbroken at having lost my children, and even Deepak. I missed Deepak. I couldn't help it.

After six or seven weeks, the social workers brought my children to visit me for the first time. I don't know how they persuaded my in-laws. The prison officer said to me sternly, 'Mrs Ahluwalia, if you cry like you're crying right now in front of your children, the social worker will not allow you to see them again.'

'Yes, madam, yes, madam. I won't cry in front of them,' I said, sobbing.

The day arrived. How would I explain to my children that their daddy had died because of me, that I had killed him? Sandeep was five years old, and Rajeev was only three and a half. I wore a new pair of jeans, the T-shirt I had painted, and a cardigan. I had to beg the officer to let me buy chocolates for my children. I kept looking at the door, waiting for them to come. Suddenly it opened and they came tearing in. I wanted to stand up and cry loudly. But I had to remind myself that only mad people did that, and I wasn't mad, I wasn't mad. I crouched to embrace them. They came like hurricanes, with such force that they knocked me over and we all collapsed in a heap on the floor, laughing and giggling.

We kissed and kissed like there was a worldwide shortage of kisses. I had found my gods. I gave them the chocolates. I had brought pens and paper with me (we were allowed to take these things for children's visits). I wanted them to do some drawings which I could put up in my cell. It was a one-hour visit, and they were too young to be able to talk for that long, so they would have to be kept busy. They sat in my lap. The social worker was Indian. She didn't speak Hindi but she understood me. I pleaded with her to bring my children every fortnight. She said she had heard a lot about me and that everyone in Crawley praised me. She gave me information about the outside world.

Thankfully, the children didn't ask me about their father. I asked the social worker for advice about what I should tell them if they did. She said, 'Say nothing. Just give them as much love as you can.' The children asked what had happened to my arm. I said I burnt it. Perhaps they knew. After all, Rajeev had seen the fire.

I was so hemmed in by problems at that time, I felt I was in a deathlike vice. My brothers would advise me to write letters in a particular way, but visiting rules were so strict that I was not even allowed to take a pen, so I had to memorise everything they were saying. I could hardly write in English, yet nothing could be done without my authority. If I had received a letter I would have to plead with the officers to let me show it to my brothers, saying, 'I don't understand this letter. I need to show it to my family so that they can sort it out for me.'

All my visitors would advise me. There were as many opinions as mouths. My family and I were confused. Who should we listen to? I wanted to tell them to let me die in prison, to leave me alone, but I didn't have the heart to hurt them after all they had done for me. I think they must have felt guilty too. They knew that they had done nothing when I had tried to kill myself, nor had they attempted to improve relations between my husband and me. 'Have children,' they had said. 'Maybe his attitude will change.' 'Deepak, send her out to work. Things will get better. You will have more money to spend.' Typical Indian advice.

My sister was also under a lot of pressure. After all, she was not in her own home, but her husband's. They had bought a new business, a newspaper shop which was supplemented by Sukhjit's job at the post office. They had to get up at 5.30 a.m. for Sukhjit to do a paper round. After breakfast he would go to the cash and carry to buy stocks for the shop, then work at the post office from 1 to 9 p.m. Because of me Dev and Sukhjit had numerous visitors. People came from miles around to witness this family drama. And this was some case. What I had done was a very big thing in our society, in any society. Where had all these people been before? Deepak had never hesitated to insult me in front of others. They had all seen it happening. Nobody had ever said to me, 'Sister, how are you managing to live with this man?'

All these people came to visit me in prison too. And when the prison officer came to get me I would obey like a child. When my husband had ordered me to do something, I had to do it; when the prison officer ordered me around, I had to do it. When had I ever been in control of my own destiny? I had always suppressed my own desires and aspirations. And now I wasn't bold enough to say to my visitors, 'Your sympathy comes too late.' I had been brought up to think of other people's happiness, not mine. I wanted to be loved by everyone, I wanted everybody's approval.

My brothers and sisters hid things from me, as they saw how devastated I was already. My weight had gone down to six and a half stone, and my body trembled involuntarily. Why beat a corpse?

The social worker brought my children to visit me about once a month. My second application for bail failed, although Sukhjit jijaji had put forward his house, his shop, everything as surety. I had had great hope, and my family had expected to take me home that day, but it was not to be.

During one visit at the end of June I could tell from Billoo praji's face that he had something important to tell me: they were going to hold Deepak's funeral. This was approximately six weeks after his death. The official pathologist's report had been done, but we needed to appoint an independent pathologist as well. I didn't know about all of these things. Billoo praji said I should write to my solicitors asking them stop the funeral.

The following Monday I had to go to the magistrates' court for my regular fortnightly visit. When I met my solicitor he said that he was doing his best. I was confused, and didn't understand the workings of the law. In my desperation, I wanted to get the solicitor off my case. He asked me to sign some papers. I refused. I was so angry. I had no other way of showing it.

The next shock was that Deepak's funeral could not be delayed. I asked the prison officer for permission to attend it. This was granted, but I had to be accompanied by an escort. On the one hand I was grieving for Deepak's death. I felt that as his wife I was within my rights to attend his funeral, touch his feet and ask for forgiveness. On the other hand, I hated him for having brought me to this – in prison, without support or friendship, while he himself was free of this world. I told the probation officer, Diana, that Deepak's funeral was going ahead despite my best efforts.

Diana was also upset. She offered to accompany me and support me on my solicitor's next visit to prison. When the time came, it was a different solicitor, an Indian one, who spoke

Hindi. Billoo praji had asked for a different solicitor from the same firm. I asked if he would take over my case, and he agreed.

The next day Billoo praji and Bindhi praji turned up, looking awful. One of Deepak's relatives had rung them and said they shouldn't attend his funeral. Fired by my anger, I talked back to my older brother for the first time in my life. 'There's no need to humiliate yourselves. I have already set fire to him, I have cremated him. What more needs to be done?' I had already dragged my family's reputation through the mud.

I said I wouldn't go to Deepak's funeral, and even if I did I would spit on him in front of the world so they would know how much I hated him. My escort would protect me, but would my brothers be able to watch me do that? After having the courage to do what I had done, surely I had the courage to face the disapproval of my community at my husband's funeral. I would show them how I was filled with hate, and how happy I was in jail. I had lost everything because of that man. Even in death he was causing me pain.

My brothers said that no matter what had happened, Deepak had been like a younger brother, the youngest son of the house, and that they too grieved for his death. They tried to reason with his family, saying that one household had already been uprooted, and that for the sake of the children it was important that the two families proceeded as cordially as possible. After this visit I wept uncontrollably. In the end my family didn't attend the funeral.

On the day of the funeral I was really upset. Anger on one side, and sadness for my children on the other. I asked Manjeet Singh Sali, a priest who is now dead, who used to come to prison to see me and comfort me, to conduct a service for Deepak's soul. I wanted to ask Deepak for forgiveness, I wanted his spirit to rest in peace. I wanted to ask Babaji for forgiveness. He agreed, but not only that, he decided he would ask the prison authorities for permission to conduct the ceremony in prison so that I could attend.

Manjeet Singh Sali brought two priests with him to read from the holy book, and two women who cooked all the langar (food blessed by God). When I said I didn't have the right clothes for the occasion, he even brought his daughter's Punjabi suit for me to wear. I gave him £11 as donation. As I sat in front of Babaji, I felt a deep peace enter my soul. For three days after that I felt no anger against Deepak. I felt so calm, I really believed that he had forgiven me.

After the funeral Deepak's uncle, Ranjit chachaji, came to visit me. Was he going to report on my plight to my in-laws? I wept when I met him, but I was also happy that someone from my husband's family had come to visit. He said he would help me because I had already suffered a lot. It was he who had stood and watched when, in the first week of our marriage, Deepak had pushed me down the stairs.

I felt guilty when I thought about the pain Deepak must have suffered in the days before he died. I was angry with myself for what I had done. I felt like banging my head against the wall to create vents for the anger to flow out of me. I hadn't understood the seriousness of his condition. I was a murderer. I had killed my husband. All the world would hate me. And for a woman like me who had spent so much time and energy to be praised and liked by others, especially my in-laws, the idea that people must hate me was very difficult to live with. Ten years of striving for approval had been wiped out by this one act. How would my children look upon me? What would they think of their mother? Why had my brothers left their jobs and families behind to come to my help?

THREE

A Kind of Freedom

ONE EVENING WHEN I returned to Holloway from the magistrates' court in Crawley and was sitting out the interminable time it takes to be readmitted, one of the prisoners came up to me and said, 'Karen, Karen, there is an Indian woman who is sharing your cell.' I was thrilled.

I had to go through seven sets of locked doors to get back to my cell. I sat on my bed and waited for her to come out of the toilet. I wondered who she was and what she was like. When she came out, we looked at each other. Versha. Her name was Versha. After a little while I asked her if she could speak Hindi. 'Yes,' she said, 'Yes.' I was so happy. She asked why I was in prison, so I replied in Hindi that I had a very long story and that I would tell her later. We asked the usual things: Are you married? Any children? I cannot explain the sheer pleasure of talking in my language. I could lay bare the contents of my soul in front of a sister. But I was also nervous that she might reject me when I told her my story. That fear rises to choke me even today when I meet someone for the first time.

After half an hour I asked her to come and sit on my bed. She told me that she had been charged with manslaughter. She ran a nursing home with her husband, and an old woman had died while in their care. They were accused of negligence. She was worried about her husband, who was also in prison, but hid her tears from me. Her older daughter was going to apply for bail.

Just as Vicky had taken me through the prison routine, it

28

was now my turn to introduce Vershaji. She was a business-woman. She had a house with a swimming pool, and her children had been educated in private schools. She was a clever, sensible woman. She was well versed in the ways of the world, she knew about legal matters, and her English was good. When I told my family about her, they asked why I didn't get her to write my letters for me. Vershaji agreed. She said I should copy the letters after she had written them and then tear them up – letters to my social worker, to my solicitors.

We became good friends. Wherever we went, we went together. To the canteen, during exercise time, to the library. She encouraged me to go swimming. I said I didn't know how, and I was shy about showing my legs. I had never worn a swimming costume. Because of her warmth, a smile returned to my face. I started eating. Vershaji was diabetic, so I used to give her all my fruit. She was given cheese toast at supper to supplement her diet, and she would often share it with me. When we were locked up we would talk or play cards or write letters.

Billoo said he wanted to meet Vershaji, and she agreed, as she also needed help. She had young children and was having financial problems, keeping up with school fees and sorting out bail. Vershaji became even closer to me after she met Billoo praji and Sukhjit jijaji. Billoo praji told her that I was insisting on telling the whole truth, and asked her to convince me that I should change my story to save my life. He and Sukhjit also went to visit her husband.

Versha told my story to other women in prison, and they would come up to me and say, 'Good, I don't blame you. He got what he deserved.' My fear that people would shun me or ridicule me when they knew why I was in prison started to evaporate.

Vershaji knew how to keep everyone happy. Soon she was friendly with the nurses, and I slipstreamed behind her, a guru and her disciple. Versha was my lifeline. When she went to court my heart would flap with nervousness. If she got bail she would leave me and go away. Of course she had young children who needed her, and I also wished for her sake that she would get bail.

Having your children snatched away from you is quite a different pain from being deprived of them through death. I felt the pain of separation from my family in every little material thing that I had in my house. I had invested all my energy and hopes for happiness in these things. I had wanted to be seen as a good wife, to show my mother-in-law what a sensible daughter-in-law I was, to show my husband that I was transforming our home into paradise, to be a good mother to my children. It was for their happiness that I had sweated. Vershaji would comfort me. She too was afraid for herself. How many years might she have to spend in jail? She would lose her business, her family, her home.

Vicky had left prison, and a number of different women shared our cell with us. At first there was a fat young white woman who had chronic asthma. She used to get loads of cards and flowers and visits, and she kept a framed photo of her son and daughter by her bedside. I wished I had my children's pictures too. She never told us what she had been charged with, but would cry a lot and say she didn't want to talk about her case. We were suspicious, and later we found out that she had been a childminder, and had killed the baby she was looking after. Inmates never leave such people alone. I read about her in a magazine. I had a famous person in the bed next to me. I didn't realise at the time that I too would have my pictures plastered all over the newspapers and television. She came to us after conviction, but was put into C1 wing because of her depression and asthma. She was moved to a different prison after a few weeks.

The three of us got on quite well, but one day a teenager, a real junkie, moved in. At night she would clear her throat noisily and spit on the floor. We all found it very difficult. She was intelligent, but she was very dirty, and she used to fart and burp as well as spit. We found it both funny and nauseating. Versha and I used to clean the room, and one day Versha's hand fell on the spit. I took one look at her face and couldn't stop laughing. We decided to complain to the senior nurse. When Versha started her complaint I suddenly had a vision of the druggie farting, and couldn't control my laughter. I was quite scared of the senior nurse, so I covered my face and tried to hold back my laughter. I thought that if she saw me laughing she might me put into solitary. When she turned to me and asked if I was all right, I was so frightened that my laughter turned to tears. She must have been impressed by my crying, because she agreed to move the girl.

Then another woman, Maggie, came and shared with us. She had not got on with her previous room-mate, and had spotted Versha during association time and thought she would get on better with her, so she asked to move in with us.

Versha said, 'Maggie is very cunning. She knows all about us, but when it comes to her she says she doesn't want to talk about it. I think her charges are serious. Let's check her letters when she's out of the room.' Maggie used to be out all day because she worked in the kitchen, washing dishes, ironing, doing the laundry (women who worked would get £3 or £4 a week, rather than the usual £1.50). The first time I saw her she was wearing a white overall, and I thought she was an officer. When she told me off for entering the kitchen to get a cup of tea I was quite intimidated.

Versha asked me to stand by the hatch and alert her if I saw anyone coming towards our dorm. She went to Maggie's cupboard – cupboards in prison cannot be locked – and found a letter from a social worker. Maggie had been charged with child abuse. She had held her young daughter's legs while her husband had sex with her. Maggie had pleaded ignorance at first, but when the daughter said that her parents had done this to her jointly, she maintained that she did it to educate her.

After a couple of weeks another woman came to occupy our cell's fourth bed. She had wanted a single room, and was told that she would be moved as soon as one was available. Because she was a drug addict suffering from withdrawal symptoms, she would become violent and look for excuses to fight. That evening I was writing a letter, and she asked to borrow my pen. I looked at Versha, who signalled 'no'. Versha said, 'Get another pen. Karen is using hers.' The woman picked up a plastic knife that Versha used to cut her fruit and crept up behind me to stab me. Versha called out and I ran and stood behind her. There was another woman in our dorm who suffered from a compulsion to set things on fire (no – I didn't share her obsession), and Versha shouted to her to alert the officers. But she was easily intimidated, and ran into the toilet and locked the door. Versha and I were both screaming. Versha held the woman at bay by asking her what we had done to her and why she wanted to kill us. I ran to the hatch and shouted for the officer. When the officer arrived, we all three burst into tears. Afterwards we couldn't stop laughing – the woman was only little, and the knife was made of plastic. The story spread everywhere.

This was a new experience. Before prison I had never known that people like this existed, that women took drugs, that they became violent. I had led such a protected life, I didn't even know what drugs were. Next day when my brother visited, I hesitantly told him the story. Although he eventually saw the funny side of it, I could see from his face that he was upset that I was living amongst such people and that my life was in danger. I had fallen from the well into the gutter.

A beautiful and moody young girl called Jane shared our cell for a few weeks. She was another druggie, and I felt real sympathy for her. Women suffering from withdrawal symptoms tend to be constantly hungry. Because I ate very little, I would often give Jane my bread roll or pudding. She also had tremendous problems with her periods, another side-effect of addiction. From my weekly allowance I would sometimes buy her a packet of biscuits or chocolates, and I would let her share my toothpaste and shampoo. She would tell us stories, like the time she had no money to buy drugs, so she sent her mother shopping and stole her video and sold it. Stealing her own mother's things! I was shocked, but we laughed as well.

As I got used to the prison food, I started getting hungrier, and on one occasion when Jane asked me for my bread roll I said, 'No, I'm hungry today.'

She said, 'You fucking bitch.' I was really upset by this. Not even the prison officers had sworn at me – and after all the things I had done for her.

After that I would throw my bread in the bin rather than give it to Jane. I laugh when I remember my pettiness.

After a few days, Jane was depressed again. She was screaming abuse at the officers, and because she had the runs she kept going to the loo. At one point she didn't emerge for nearly ten minutes. Our other cellmate opened the door and Jane fell forward, face on the floor. There was blood gushing from her wrists. We were given only plastic knives, but she had managed to burst open her veins by sawing hard. Women would use these knives to masturbate as well. I was stunned. I thought she was dead. I feared that I too might be driven to this one day by the desperation of having lost my children.

We raised the alarm and eight or ten prison officers came rushing in. For the first time I saw male officers. They told us later that if we had left Jane for another ten minutes she would have died. 'Thanks,' they said. 'You saved us extra paperwork.'

Versha and I were sent upstairs to another wing, because we were no longer sick enough to justify taking up beds needed by other inmates. We weren't terribly keen on going, because we had become friendly with all the officers and nurses and were feeling fairly settled, and Versha was afraid of the other inmates in case they treated granny-killers in the same way as child abusers. The officers said we would get better food – at least it would be hot, because the canteen was just by the kitchen. We were given separate cells, but we used to meet up during mealtimes, exercise times and association times. As it happened, it was even better upstairs, much livelier. We were not among depressed, schizophrenic types. The women would dance to music, make a lot of noise and have fun with the officers.

I was not unhappy in prison. The women laughed and joked, and I felt I was staying at a hostel. No one beat you. In those days on *EastEnders* there was a story about domestic violence. The way the man used to suspect his wife and beat her reminded me of Deepak, and I used to weep tears of anger and hopelessness at what women have to undergo.

I had to go to the magistrates' court again because my new solicitors, who had been recommended by a family friend, had to plead before a judge that I wanted to dismiss the other firm before they could take over my case. They argued that given the serious nature of the charges against me, no firm of solicitors could handle my case adequately if I was not co-operating with them and did not trust them. I would also be able to talk more freely with a woman solicitor. My brothers understood that there were areas of my life with Deepak that I could not discuss with them, or with any man for that matter. I needed to talk about the brutal sexual relations I had with Deepak.

My family didn't want me to tell the whole truth. I used to say, 'This is British justice, this is British law. I have all the evidence. I will tell them all that I did, and more importantly, why I did it. My husband must answer for it. I was not the kind of girl who would have taken a step like that. I was pushed. This is not India. I will get justice here. They will understand me here. This is a modern country. I have suffered for ten years. I have medical reports, court injunctions, witnesses. What more do I need?'

They said, 'Of course you must tell them what happened, but

just change the story a little bit.' They kept reminding me that my children were also serving a sentence while I was in prison. 'Change yourself, be strong. You can't go around writing letters about giving Deepak a firebath, these things will go against you. You will remain in prison for fifteen or twenty years, the boys will grow up and they won't want to know you. There is no point sitting in prison and crying. Save yourself.'

One of the other prisoners told me she was going to tell a few lies at her trial, if necessary, in order to save her family. 'This is not the time for telling the truth,' she said. 'That only happens in the films.' Other inmates, and even the nurses and doctors, would say to me, 'It is not your fault, be brave. Don't consider yourself guilty, that man pushed you to it.' Between them they managed to convince me that arson was more serious than murder – so to say that I had accidentally spilled the petrol during my row with Deepak would serve me better.

I agreed to tell the new story to the new solicitor when she came to visit. But telling lies is no easy matter. I felt no peace. Nor could I sleep. I would think day and night about the story I would tell my solicitor. It was like sitting a school examination. I didn't know if I would have the courage to lie – one lie calls forth a hundred new ones, and I could not keep track of them all. I knew that in court, in front of the prosecution, I would start stammering or weeping.

The solicitor came and took my statement. She gave me paper and pen and said, 'Take your time and tell us the story of your life in detail.' Every time I was locked up I would start in my broken English. In the end I wrote a thirty-five-page statement. My past and present – tenses, that is – were all mixed up.

During this time, Southall Black Sisters heard about my case from Crawley Women's Aid, who had learned about me through the papers. They contacted the probation officer, Diana, and asked if they could visit me and see if they could help. I agreed to see them when I heard the word 'help' – after my last experience with an Asian women's group I was reluctant, but my desperation was greater than my reluctance. I hoped the visit would not be seen as a social one, which would mean that I would have to forgo a visit from my family.

By the time Pragna Patel of SBS came with Lesley Clarke and Penny from Crawley Women's Aid, I was in a considerably better state. I didn't look like the wild, half-alive corpse of the early days. I had had my hair cut by a nurse in the hospital wing, and when I put my clean new clothes on everyone said I looked well. I felt self-confident. When I met Pragna I was very impressed by her personality – she is nothing to look at – and by the way she talked, although her Hindi was weak (it has improved dramatically since she took on my case). She would talk painfully slowly: 'We want to help you. Have you got a good solicitor? What are the facts of your case?' I said I was keen to sort out the affairs of my children, and that my murder charge was being handled by a reputable firm of solicitors. I was mindful of my family's warnings that I should choose my words carefully so as not to give anyone the wrong impression. Pragna told me about the centre and what it did, how they helped women like me with a history of domestic violence. I said that I wanted SBS's help, but that I couldn't accept it without my family's permission. Pragna asked if I was able to instruct my solicitors. I told her that I had difficulty explaining my deepest feelings in English. Pragna said I should ask my solicitors to allow her to act as an interpreter and help in any way she could.

When Pragna contacted my family, they said they were pleased with the new solicitors. Privately, they felt no confidence in a women's centre. What could they achieve in a case of such gravity? Billoo praji spoke to the solicitors, who also put him off SBS, saying they just handled insignificant little cases. 'They'll have leaflets printed and hold demonstrations and organise petitions. Everyone will get to know about Kiranjit. Do you really want that?'

I suggested to the solicitors that it might be useful to have

SBS women present during interviews to help with interpretation, but they felt my English was good enough for me not to need an interpreter. I was told by SBS that they had spoken to the solicitors and offered their help, but the solicitors were reluctant to take it.

My solicitor's clerk felt that my case was good. She and my barrister explained to me about provocation and diminished responsibility, and asked me how I would like to present my case. I didn't know, so I asked them to advise me. They explained that I could argue that I was provoked after years of suffering. I said all right. They felt they had a good chance of succeeding on the reduced plea of guilty to manslaughter. They wanted the names and addresses of all the people I knew who might come forward as witnesses. But I also gave them the false version of my story which I had been rehearsing in every waking moment.

Versha had got bail and gone, so I didn't even have her advice. I was alone amongst all these seemingly carefree girls, no one spoke to me and I spoke to no one. Holloway was like a holiday camp to them. You would see the same women coming back time and again.

When I went over the story again and again, I knew I wouldn't be able to sustain the lie. I would shout in court and tell the judge what Deepak had done to me, blow by blow, so that he could understand why I had done it. These thoughts would trouble me until my sleeping pills took effect. I was fed up with fighting with myself.

One day, about three months before my trial, my solicitor's clerk came to visit. I said I had something to tell her. And I told her the truth. I did not have the guts to lie. I had been momentarily misguided by the prospect of freedom, by the desire to save my home and be with my children. If someone so much as looked at me, I would cry and spill the beans. I remember once when I was living with my mother-in-law and I was cooking some *daal* in the pressure cooker. I fell asleep, because I hardly slept at night out of fear of Deepak. When I woke up I remembered the *daal*, dashed downstairs to the kitchen and found that I had burnt the *daal* and the saucepan beyond recognition. I was so afraid I went and confessed to my mother-in-law in tears. When I do something, I have to confess it, I cannot cover it up with a story.

I told the solicitor that my statement contained the full truth. 'Everything is true except for the petrol story. We had not made love that night nor the previous night, but he had forced himself on me for three nights running previous to that night. I had felt used and dirty and thrown aside like a banana skin once the flesh had been savoured. On that third night I had tried to refuse, saying I would get AIDS because he went with other women. He was infuriated by that.' The solicitor asked if that was now the truth. I said yes.

When my family came to visit I told them what I had done. They were very angry, but there was nothing they could do. They said I was foolish, but that it was my life. They could not beat me and make me say something against my will. Now they couldn't even use Versha as their ambassador, but they got her to write and try to make me understand the folly of my ways.

When I went for education in the mornings, I would stand by a window from where you could see a little bit of the road. I used to think, it is not in my destiny to walk those streets again. I would say to myself that if I ever came out of prison, I would never walk down Holloway Road for as long as I lived.

FOUR
=

Paradise Lost

BINDHI, MY OLDER BROTHER, stayed in England for three months; Billoo praji, who had taken extended unpaid leave from work in Canada, for seven. Billoo's wife was working overtime to pay the bills and look after their two young children. I used to say to him that he needn't come every day just to see me for fifteen or twenty minutes in the midst of all the other things he had to do. The legal system had not only sentenced me, but my children and my entire family.

I still remember the day Bindhi praji visited with Billoo just before he returned to India. He wept like a child. I sat there hard as a rock, convinced that he was crying because he had received bad news from India – perhaps his wife was seriously ill. They were hiding something from me. I kept saying, 'Praji, what's wrong?'

Only later did I realise that he was crying for my helplessness, for all the things I had kept hidden from them, all the things I couldn't talk to them about. I had not told them how I had started drinking in the three months before the incident. I had not told them how Deepak used my body. All they knew about was the beatings and the verbal abuse. Bindhi said that if I had been in India I would not have had to stay in prison even for one day. He would have exchanged places with me. He said he was proud of me, that despite everything that had happened, he had heard only good things about me. He knew how heartbroken I was to be dragging them through the dirt of prison.

A black prison officer was sitting nearby. When she noticed

us all crying like children, she came up to us and said gently to my brothers that she would have to ask them to finish the visit early. She said she understood their pain, but once they had left the real impact would be felt by me when I was locked up and had nothing but my sadness to confront. I quickly wiped away my tears and we promised to hold our emotions in check. We didn't want to cut the visit short because Bindhi praji was returning to India the following day. Billoo praji assured me that he would bring Bindhi praji back for one last visit before they went to the airport. Little did I know that he was lying to stop my tears.

The next day I got ready, but they didn't come. I understood the constraints on Bindhi praji. I knew he had to go, I knew he wouldn't have come from India if he didn't want to help me, I knew that he found it hard to leave his sister in prison. He was the only father I had known, and he commands so much respect among us that my younger brothers stand up when they are talking to him, even on the phone. My mother died when I was only sixteen, and I had never known my father, who died when I was only three or four months old. There was no photo that I could look at to satisfy my curiosity about his face, his features, his colouring. People used to say that he was a tall, fair, good-looking man with a great deal of personality and a lot of love for all his nine children. When we were born he gave us all funny nicknames – Tommy, Billoo, Poochi (that was mine), Bindhi.

One day, in 1956, he came home from the office (he worked as a court clerk in Bhiwanigarh, a small town in Punjab) and complained of a tummy-ache after lunch. The doctor was sent for, and without checking whether my father was allergic to penicillin, he gave him an injection. My father had an adverse reaction and died. He was only about forty. My mother was thirty-six, the same age at which I too lost my husband. She had been married when she was twelve or thirteen, and shortly after she had her first child. As there are no records, all the dates of birth, including my own, are provisional. My eldest brother, Raghvir, who was born in 1933, was taken by my Mama (mother's brother) to Ahmedabad to work in his restaurant when my father died. He would send us money from there. After a few years he had saved up enough to buy his own restaurant, and he paid for my second brother, Bindhi, to study engineering in Phagwara, a small town not far from our ancestral home in the village of Chak Kalal, in Punjab. When Bindhi qualified he joined Raghvir praji in Ahmedabad, and worked in the Public Works department. My sister Dev (Gurdev) married Sukhjit while she was in her early twenties, and has lived in London ever since. The next in line, Kuki (Mohan Singh), who I'm also very fond of, didn't do well academically, so Mother packed him off to Ahmedabad to work for Raghvir. He branched out on his own as a moneylender, then went into the construction business, and now he is rolling in money. Billoo (Amrik) went to Canada in 1972 after my mother's death, sponsored by my sister Surinder. He worked as a machine operator and now runs a shop selling ready-made clothes. In 1947 another brother, Tommy (Birjinder) was born. He came to Britain in 1978 to marry a British-born Asian girl. The marriage didn't work out, and he has since remarried twice. He is now in Canada, also running a shop. My favourite sister, Surinder, who was born in 1950, married an Indian settled in Canada in 1970, and joined him in 1971. She worked as a secretary and is now running a shop with her husband. I wrote long letters to her from prison. I have yet another sister, Gogi (Narinder), who is two years older than me and who lives in Miraj, near Bombay. By the time you take into account all the spouses, children and grandchildren, my immediate family must total around a hundred members.

My maternal uncles owned some fields just outside Chak Kalal. Wheat, corn, sugarcane, cauliflower, aubergines and spinach were grown by the tenants who tilled the land. They kept two-thirds of the produce, and the other third was given to us.

Bindhi praji, Kuki praji and Gurdev were living with my maternal aunt, who was also a widow. My uncles told my mother to go with her other children to Chak Kalal and look after the land, oversee the peasants, feed her children with the food grown there and, with a little bit of help from my brothers, make ends meet.

Although I was sorry about the fact that I could never use the word Daddy, I didn't really miss my father. How could I miss someone I had never known? My five brothers had so completely filled the vacuum. I was the youngest of four sisters, and I had been so pampered that even at the age of fifteen I didn't know how to plait my hair. My mother or my neighbours had to do it for me. I didn't even learn to cook. Although in our culture it was the norm to teach girls from the age of ten to cook, embroider and sew, my mother never taught me.

I used to play all day in Chak Kalal, which was a small village of forty or fifty houses, and was full of Ahluwalias, a sub-caste of Sikhs. We had one of the best houses in the village, a 'pukka' house with four or five bedrooms on two levels, a small verandah and some waste ground in front where I used to play. We didn't have electricity or 'pukka' roads until I was fourteen, so we used oil lamps. Nor did we have running water. There was a hand pump behind the house, and we used the fields as our toilet. But our lifestyle was quite comfortable, because my brothers who were working in Ahmedabad used to send money regularly. I used to sleep in the same bed as my mother. I didn't know or care how my mother made ends meet. If I wasn't given milk in the night, I would complain the next day. My mother would say that I had drunk it while I was half-asleep. We had a buffalo so that I always had home-made butter and fresh milk, and we also kept hens, so we had eggs.

I never became very close to my sister Dev because she lived with my aunt, and then got married when I was only five. I remember losing my tooth at her wedding while I was eating a ladoo (a sweetmeat). It was a strange wedding. She got married to a photograph. Sukhjit jijaji didn't even come to India to get married. Dev had never met her husband, and yet she is happily married to this day. Skin colour is very important in our society, and from that point of view it was not a suitable match. My sister is very fair, while Sukhjit jijaji is dark. My mother cried a lot at the wedding. I couldn't work out why at the time, but later I realised that this is the done thing at a daughter's wedding. I rarely saw my mother cry. She wasn't educated, but her life circumstances had made her strong. She could walk with her head held high because her sons had looked after her. Children could also raise your status. I remember once, when I was seven or eight, lying on my mother's stomach, and she said that she would get me married off one day, and that they would get me a nice bridegroom. We were considered one of the good-looking families in the village. My brothers were very handsome, and because of our fair skin it was thought that we were children of the British. Little did the other villagers know that we would be considered black in England.

As time passed, our living standards improved. We were the first family in the village to have a pressure cooker, an iron and a radio. We were also unusual in that we ate at a table instead of squatting on the kitchen floor. I started going to primary school, and my mother used to teach me sums and reading and writing on my slate.

When I went to high school at the age of eleven my mother bought me a bicycle and a winter coat. The school was in Banga, a small town a few miles from Chak Kalal. Our village had only a primary school. I used to get red cheeks when I cycled to school. When my teacher asked all the girls for their fathers' names, I realised to my embarassment that I didn't know mine. I had to ask my mother.

I was an average student, and I passed my exams. My mother was not a typical village woman; she was keen that I should do well at my studies, and wanted me to be a doctor. I too aspired to a career of some kind. I never realised that my brothers wouldn't let me work, that such things are not allowed in our society. My mother employed tutors to coach me in my weak subjects, maths and English, as I approached matriculation. When I had exams she never disturbed my studies with requests for help with the housework. In the evenings I would take the buffaloes out to the fields, and I would take my homework and study while they grazed. Sometimes I would go to the market to buy hay for them or to do the general household shopping or to get ground flour from the baker's. None of these were girls' activities, but my mother was liberal and my brother Tommy was lazy. I had a free mind, and wore trousers, which was frowned upon by the neighbours – in fact I used to wear Tommy's hand-me-downs. My mother never made me feel that because I was a girl I should always wear dresses or, when I grew older, *salwar kameez* – the Punjabi suit, a knee-length tunic with long baggy trousers gathered at the ankle. But she was a wonderful seamstress, and made the prettiest frocks. Her friends would say she shouldn't let her daughter wander around with naked legs, but she never paid any attention. It was because of pressure from my own friends, from feeling the odd one out, that I started wearing Punjabi suits at the age of twelve.

We used to call my sister Surinder 'Kalo' (dark-skinned). She was very shy, and did all the work in the house, while I used to run wild. I had been spoilt. I'd work if I was in the mood, otherwise I might just say no. When I was fourteen Surinder got married and went to live in Canada, where her husband was working. My brothers paid for the wedding. Tommy finished his BA in Banga and went off to Ahmedabad, so I was left alone with my mother except for Jyoti, a young niece of mine, Raghvir praji's daughter, who my mother brought back with her after a trip to Ahmedabad. Although there was eight years between us, and although I used to play with her, I started feeling jealous of her because I felt I was no longer receiving my mother's undivided attention. She would get new ready-made frocks whereas I was wearing *salwar kameez*. There was now no one

44

left to do the housework. I couldn't wash clothes, my hands would start bleeding, so my mother employed a servant.

One day my mother complained of pains in the stomach, and of constipation. For a few days she couldn't eat, and she felt giddy and weak. Although I was sixteen, I didn't realise the gravity of the situation. She went to Phagwara, about half an hour away, the town where Dev and Bindhi had studied, for a check-up. That was the first time I cried for my mother, the first time I had seen her ill. Some neighbours cooked for my niece and me. The doctors took X-rays, and said that my mother would have to be taken to Ludhiana, a city about an hour away by bus. The doctors there diagnosed cancer, and said she needed an operation. I wrote to Bindhi praji in Ahmedabad to tell him that our mother was seriously ill, and asked them to visit. Although Bindhi praji was not the eldest, he had assumed responsibility for all the family affairs.

At that time, 1971, there were terrible Hindu/Muslim riots going on, and there was a curfew, so it was difficult for Bindhi praji to get out of Ahmedabad. My mother's eldest sister came to stay and look after my niece and me. When I saw my mother after the operation, with tubes going in and out of her body, her skin the colour of parchment, her eyes open but not awake, I just stood there and wept.

After the operation she came home, but the doctor said she needed another one. Although she seemed to be recovering well and had regained her appetite, the cancer was still eating her away. After her second operation, she was considerably weakened. Bindhi and Kuki wanted to take her to Bombay or London or Canada for treatment, but she refused to leave Chak Kalal. Her doctor said that he had just completed his studies in England, and there was nothing more that they could do for her abroad. I was studying for my final school exams, and my mother didn't want me to fail. She said she would go to Ahmedabad when they were over.

Nobody told me she had cancer till much later. All I knew

was that she was ill and weak, but I thought she would recover. She had never been ill in her life, and she was only fifty-two. Billoo praji had come down from Ahmedabad, and he stayed with her night and day at the hospital in Ludhiana. He used to take her for blood and urine tests, buy her medicines and do all the chores.

One afternoon, two or three weeks after she came back from hospital, she fell down in the bathroom and lost consciousness. She appeared not to be breathing, and Billoo praji thought she had died. After ten minutes she opened her eyes, saw Billoo praji crying and asked him to hush. He took her back to bed. When I came back from school that day, where I had been sitting an exam, she said to me, 'I've come back because of you. I went up there and came back for you.'

On the day that I sat my last paper, I said to my mother that we would go to Ahmedabad. I was looking forward to the break after my exams. I felt a great load slip off my shoulders now that the continuous backbreaking study had come to an end. We were sitting on the verandah. Neighbours and friends were visiting and my mother was chatting away. I didn't realise why they were all assembling like that. This kind of family gathering usually happened only for my sisters' weddings. My aunt cooked the evening meal and I fed my mother. She ate better than usual, two chappatis instead of one. I felt encouraged, and believed that the illness had been defeated. Unknown to me, however, the doctor had told Billoo praji that if my mother slipped into unconsciousness again, as she had that day, it would be the end.

Because it was summer we normally slept on the verandah, but that night I decided to sleep inside. My mother wanted me to sleep with her, but I refused. I was in the habit of sleeping with my leg over her stomach, and I was afraid to lapse into that position unconsciously, because she had so many stitches in her stomach.

I gave her her medicine. She refused to take it at first, and we laughed and said we had other ways of giving it to her. We used to mix it in her milk. In the middle of the night, at about 2 a.m., she got up to go to the toilet. As she tried to stand she fell on my brother, whose bed was next to hers. Billoo praji ran to fetch the holy water he had got from Sai Baba, a religious and spiritual leader, some days earlier and gave it to her. But it was in vain.

Everyone said that my mother had willed herself to live until my exams finished. Tommy and Bindhi praji were still in Ahmedabad. The morning we sent the telegram, Tommy was tying his turban when the mirror broke. My sister-in-law said it was a bad omen. They managed to get as far as Delhi by plane. From Delhi they tried to take a taxi, but four times they were involved in accidents and had to change taxis. In our tradition we cremate our dead before the sun rises, and by the time they got to the village it was all over.

My mother was very popular, and large numbers of people had gathered at our house. It took another twelve days to finish all the ceremonies. I knew I would have to leave Chak Kalal and go and live in Ahmedabad. I had made so many plans about where I would study, but nothing that I have planned in all my life has come to pass. Every plan I have made has been shattered by events.

The day Jyoti and I left Chak Kalal a seven-year-old boy from the village who was like a younger brother to me burst into tears so loudly that he made us all cry. He said he would never come past our house again. I will never again feel the happiness I felt in that village, where we had so few modern conveniences, but where people cared for each other in a way that they don't anywhere else. There was a unity you don't see in our communities in Britain.

When I first arrived in Ahmedabad, I found it very difficult. I hardly knew my sisters-in-law, or my brothers for that matter, most of whom I had met only during holidays. I was also missing my mother. Everything was new, but my family was very caring. If I ever went to sit on my own in my room they would call me down because they knew I would be crying for my village, for my friends, for my mother. My brothers told their wives to see to it that I wanted for nothing – money, food, clothes. Even if I had had my dinner, they would insist that I ate with them again when they came home from work.

My brothers were fairly well-off. Bindhi praji was working as an engineer, and he had been given a jeep, a driver and a gardener by the government. He had three sons, and lived in a seven-bedroomed bungalow with Kuki praji, his wife and three children and Tommy. My eldest brother, Raghvir, lived with his wife and six children just down the road in a two-bedroomed house. We would always be in and out of each other's houses. There were never any major rows.

One day I had my period and was crying with the pain, but I wouldn't tell anyone why. When I had first started my periods, my mother had told me to keep it quiet. I didn't even know that other women also had them. My sister-in-law gave me two Anacins for the pain. When she told me that she also got periods, I asked why she hadn't told me earlier and put me out of my misery. I never found out anything about sex until I was eighteen, and that was from my niece. Before that I used to ask why children were born after marriage and not before. I thought the state of being married conferred children on you. I didn't realise that men and women had physical relations. When I first found about sex, I couldn't believe that my brothers slept with my sisters-in-law. I wish my mother had talked to me about these things as people do here.

My eldest sister-in-law, Leela, was very liberal-minded and fun to be with. She liked going to the cinema, and I would go with her. Bindhi praji's wife Gurudarshan, though, was religious, and would only go to films like *Jai Santoshi Ma*, which was about a female saint. She had converted an entire room in the house into a sort of a temple with a huge picture of Babaji.

Because of her I started praying morning, noon and night. I was the only woman in the house to read all 1400 pages of the *Granth Sahib* (the Sikh holy book) in very high-flown Gurmukhi. I even started it a second time, but only got halfway through.

I was very fashion-conscious. I always had a lot of pocket money – because it was an extended family, I could extract money from my various brothers and their wives. They never seemed to check with each other, so I was never found out.

I started getting used to Ahmedabad. My brothers agreed to my going to college to do a BA in sociology. The problem was that in Ahmedabad the medium of instruction was Gujarati, and I didn't know the language at all. I was only fluent in Punjabi. I wanted to go back to Punjab, live in a hostel and study in Punjabi to avoid having to translate all my subjects from Gujarati into Hindi. Although I could read Hindi, I could barely speak it, and my English was too weak to study in it. That is a regret I will always have. I could have made a good career if I had been better in English. Although Bindhi praji initially agreed to my studying in Punjab, Kuki praji refused on the grounds that I was a girl, and that if I were to do something wrong, it would be a question of their *izzat*. 'She cries here, she will cry there, there will be no family member to fall back on when she is lonely or ill. She has got used to a life of luxury here with servants to look after her. When she goes there she will have to fend for herself.' Of course, the real reason was that I might go astray. If I had been a boy, they would have let me go.

I went to the Swaminarayan college, a mixed college not far from home. My brothers said they would provide tuition in Gujarati. I could not disobey them, and when I agreed they were overjoyed. I had to learn the Gujarati ABC again, like when I was in primary school. I could never participate in class discussions. When the other students laughed I just sat there, uncomprehending and blank. The tutor would translate a couple of pages of history, sociology and psychology every night. I used to get very upset. I was afraid that I would fail. How could I sit an exam in a language I could not understand?

I was also weak in logic, so another tutor was employed to help me with that. It was costing my brothers as much as the hostel would have done, if not more. If I could have put in as much energy studying in Punjabi, I would have got a first class, whereas in Gujarati I might just about pass. But because my brothers had put so much money into my studies, I worked very hard. Gradually my Gujarati improved, especially my written language. At home we spoke mainly in a mixture of Punjabi and Hindi, so my spoken Gujarati remained poor.

I passed my first year's exams, whereas one of my nieces, born and bred in Ahmedabad, failed hers. My brothers were delighted, and told my niece she was stupid. They asked me what I wanted. I asked for a watch, and they bought me one. They took me to eat ice cream and bought sweetmeats. My results gave me a lot of confidence, and I didn't need a tutor to help with my Gujarati any more. A Punjabi girl with whom I had become very friendly would help out occasionally when I needed it.

My brothers bought me a scooter, which I used to go to college. Just next to my college Raghvir praji had opened a second restaurant which served delicious vegetarian and non-vegetarian snacks. My friends and I would often stop by and have free snacks to our hearts' delight. My memories of the village and my mother were receding.

My brothers said they would give me everything, even their lives, and in return I must do nothing to stain their reputation. I must not get so dizzy with freedom as to go to the cinema with boys or be seen in their company. I never went out with a boy, I never encouraged them, although there were some handsome boys from rich families at the college. They never had the courage to approach me. They never even teased me. They would all call me Punjabi sister. Perhaps because they knew that I was the sister of a sardar (a turbanned Sikh), they didn't dare come near me.

When my exams approached, I would study till 2 a.m. and wake up at five to begin studying again. No cinema, no outings, no fun, no food even. I survived mainly on tea. The rest of the year I had fun. I used to see a lot of Hindi films. I didn't copy their romantic value systems or their fashions, but I enjoyed them tremendously. One Sunday afternoon my niece and I decided to go to the cinema on our own. We asked Leela, our eldest sister-in-law, to tell my brothers that I had gone to my typing classes if they asked where we were. When my brothers came home for dinner, Leela said I had gone to college. They wanted to know which college was open on a Sunday. We were found out, and they shouted at Leela. We were scolded when we got home. My brothers would have preferred us to go in the company of one of the older women. It was a warning, and although they were not unkind, I cried a lot that night. I had only gone to the cinema, after all. I hadn't done anything wrong. Girls had no freedom. Boys could go anywhere they pleased, they didn't have to submit to a barrage of questions. I had to tell my brothers where I was going, what time I was returning, which friend I was visiting, what we were going to do, why we were going to do it. What was the point of having all that money if I couldn't spend it?

I learned to cook, and made chicken curry for the first time when my brothers had a big dinner party. Everyone praised my cooking. It was normally my duty to make tea. Being such a big family, and often having visitors, I might make twenty-five cups of tea several times a day.

My brothers were thrilled when I got my BA in 1976, in pass class. At least I didn't fail. I had also been ill: I used to have low blood pressure and had giddy spells. I wanted to go on to do a B.Ed and become a teacher, but I applied too late to get admission, despite Bindhi praji's influence (he was well-connected through his job). So I started a law degree, an LL.B.

My brother Tommy was also doing an LL.B. At the end of the first year I passed in the second class. I couldn't believe it. I began to see myself in a black gown.

One of my maternal aunts, Inder Kaur, came to visit from the Punjab. She thought I would look good in a salwar kameez, so she bought some material and took me to the tailor. I still remember the material, black silk with lots of little yellow stars. I used to wear mostly trousers and tops, but Punjabi suits had become very fashionable.

I kept wondering why the world seemed to be so interested in my Punjabi suit, and one day my aunt confessed that they were looking for a match for me. I was stunned. She swore me to secrecy, because she said my brothers would kill her if they knew that she had let the cat out of the bag. She said the boy's family was coming to view me. I felt a fire raging inside me. Here I was, dreaming of becoming a lawyer. Why was I born a girl? I thought of going away to a friend's for the day, but changed my mind. I could not embarrass my brothers, or get my aunt into trouble. I told her I didn't want to get married, as I thought there was more to life than having a string of children. She said that one day I would have to be bound by this commitment. For how many years could I be a burden to my brothers? My sisters-in-law advised me to go through with the visit and then just say that I didn't like the boy. I thought I would tell my brothers afterwards that I didn't want to get married, but I didn't have the courage to say to them outright that I would rather work than marry. For a woman to earn money and keep her husband would be scandalous. The man would be accused by society of wearing bangles.

On the day the boy's family came, I was shaking with nervousness. It was like sitting an exam. I would be examined like goods in a shop. The house was given a top-to-bottom clean. Food and sweetmeats arrived from the market. The boy's family were wealthy business people. Ten elders arrived to peer at me as if they were inspecting the engine and wheels of a second-hand car, or the teeth and milk-giving capacity of a buffalo. Would a man agree to being put on display like a showpiece? My make-up had to be just right. I had to show modesty by keeping my gaze lowered, and I had to show evidence of my domestic abilities. I was given the classic task of bringing in the tea which, true to cliché, I spilt in my nervousness. I then had to bring out the sweets. I sat there for ten minutes. It felt like ten hours. In the end the boy's family accepted me, but I rejected the offer.

Hardly had all of this turned cold than another aunt from Baroda came singing the praises of another boy. From the moment a girl in our society turns eighteen, everyone watches her like vultures. If you aren't married by twenty-five, everyone wants a run-down on your defects. My aunt had two marriage-able daughters, and I got so angry I said, 'If he is so wonderful, why don't you marry off one of your daughters to him?' That blew up into a huge family row, that I should have the cheek to talk back like that. My brothers had to speak to my aunt at length to pacify her. She said her own daughters were not good enough to marry this boy; they were outgoing, they had boyfriends. I was warned by my brothers not to talk like that again.

When I told my brothers I wanted to work, their response was, 'You want money, don't you? Tell us how much. We'll give it to you. You can't do a job.' For the first time I realised that they were letting me study only to help me pass the time. There was no question of a career. All my dreams lay in pieces. I wasn't ready to be a housewife. I went to my room, locked myself in and cried, and wrote a long letter to my sister Surinder in Canada.

I told her in confidence that my brothers were plotting to get me married. I asked her to arrange a visa for me to come to Canada, and told her to reply to my college address. Within a couple of weeks I got a letter from her saying she would help me to go to Canada. She had called Billoo praji to discuss it and they had agreed that they would find a match for me so that I could stay there after my visitor's visa had expired. It might seem odd that I was happy to get married in Canada, but I had heard that Canada wasn't like India, where if a married woman went to work it would destroy the family's reputation. My sisters-in-law had the keys to all the cupboards, they had control over all my brothers' earnings, but they were idle all day, sitting around and gossiping, eating and getting fat. That wasn't the life for me.

Billoo praji wrote to my brothers, and they agreed to send me to Canada. I was thrilled, but I was also apprehensive. I had now lived in Ahmedabad for five years. I had friends there, I felt settled. And now I was to be uprooted again. I lost interest in my studies. I knew that the legal system in Canada was different, so my Indian qualifications would be useless.

My brothers applied for a passport for me and started preparations for my trip. They were happy that I had agreed to get married, since that would mean the end of their responsibilities. Women are burdens to be got rid of at the earliest possible convenience. Men don't care about our dreams, our aspirations. It wasn't the fault of my brothers that they were trampling on my dreams. It was society which taught them that women should be treated in a particular way. They spent money on me like water, they cared about me, but their care was misdirected. Even after I was married I knew they would spare no expense. But that was not what I wanted.

It was 1977. As the day for going to Canada came closer, I was both happy and sad. My aunt Inder Kaur, Bindhi and Kuki praji came to Bombay to see me off. I was taking a flight to New York, and Billoo praji was coming down from Toronto to fetch me. My aunt told me later that after I had gone Kuki praji started sobbing and saying that this sister was his life.

FIVE

Looking for a Gilded Cage

BILLOO PRAJI MET ME at the airport and took me to a very posh hotel. I phoned Surinder and said, 'Cook for me, I've had hardly anything to eat. They served me tasteless boiled food in the plane.' I was used to eating spicy double-fried food.

When Surinder met us at Toronto airport she was very simply dressed, and her trousers were crumpled. I thought she must be poor. Even the houses in Canada failed to impress me. In Ahmedabad I lived in a three-storey house, and these wooden houses seemed very small. Apart from the carpet and the wall-paper, I wasn't impressed by the furnishings in Surinder's house at all. And to top it all, her poverty was so grinding that she used a wooden spoon (it was only later that I learned about non-stick surfaces). I thought that Canada must be very poor. Why couldn't they afford steel spoons? Of course they had TVs, big cars and telephones in the home. Their highways were something else, too.

In the evening, Billoo praji took me to the hospital to meet his wife Devinder and their newborn son. I had never met Devinder before, and she was very nice to me.

That first night I had real difficulties getting to sleep. I had come from a houseful of people, and I was cold and lonely. The next morning, Billoo praji went to work and said I would have to fend for myself. As local calls were free, I spent a lot of time talking to Surinder over the next few days, and I wrote long letters home. Sometimes I would be dropped off by Billoo praji at Surinder's house. Surinder was pregnant for the second time. After five days, Devinder and her son came home. She was on maternity leave, and we had a lot of fun together. We used to watch videos and laugh and joke.

Surinder used to work from three to 11 p.m., so I would spend the mornings with her. Gradually I picked up the courage to go for walks on my own, and as winter approached, I saw snow for the first time. We went to Niagara Falls and Montreal. Dinner parties and shopping trips also helped pass the time.

Surinder and Billoo praji were anxious about hitching me up with someone before my visa ran out. I wanted a man who was handsome, jolly and educated. I didn't care if he was poor. There were some Ahluwalia boys from the same caste as us, one in particular who was unfortunately a sardar – too traditional for me. We rejected each other. There was another boy I quite liked. He was educated, had a good job, and his own house and car. However, he was a Ramgarhia, and my brothers in India rejected him because he was of a lower caste. The thinking was that you could marry a lower-caste girl to an upper-caste boy and raise her status through the marriage, but if a girl married into a lower caste she would be dragged down by it.

I decided that if that was what would make my brothers happy, so be it. I would only marry an Ahluwalia, even if it meant going back to India if I didn't find anyone in Canada. Billoo praji said it was my decision and my life, and that if I wanted to marry the Ramgarhia boy I should. But I couldn't take the decision on my own. I needed support.

Billoo praji and Surinder placed an advertisement in the papers: 'Seeking a good-looking match for a good-looking, educated girl from India.' There were loads of phone calls, but no Ahluwalias. A Gill, a Kapoor, a Gupta. The Kapoor boy worked with computers and earned $25,000 a year, but he was dark-skinned and he chain-smoked. He accepted me, but I couldn't say yes. Billoo praji was angry. He tried to convince me about the importance of money, saying that I disdained it only because I had never experienced a shortage of it.

There was another boy, a Khanna, who had the cheek to say that he wanted to take me out before deciding. Did he think that, because he lived in Canada and I had come from India, he was superior to me, and that he could have relations with me before marriage and then pass or fail me? No, thank you! I have never been in love, despite the Hindi films I have seen. I have always hated the thought of having relationships because I felt men would just use your body and drop you. Anyway, no match was found.

Billoo praji and Surinder wrote to my sister Dev in London, saying that I was being stubborn about marrying an Ahluwalia boy. There were two or three Dev knew of, so she asked me to come to England. When I arrived, it turned out that two of the boys were over six feet tall – I would have needed a ladder to reach them. Fortunately they turned down the proposal, otherwise my family would have thought I was being incredibly picky.

One of Dev's friends, Kaushaliya, came to visit. She knew of an Ahluwalia family with an unmarried son, and I could tell from the way she looked at me that she liked me. She spoke to the boy's mother in Crawley, and showed us an old black-and-white photograph of the boy. His name was Deepak. He was good-looking, and Kaushaliya told us that he came from a good family, that he was a great devotee of the god Hanuman, that he fasted and didn't eat meat on Saturdays. My sister was uncomfortable with that. She said she was not agreeable to a match with a boy who was so religious, that he wouldn't fit in with us.

Dev's husband Sukhjit jijaji felt there was no harm in seeing the boy, but he was unable to persuade Dev, so nothing happened, and I returned to Canada. Devinder was due to return to work, and needed someone to look after the baby, so Billoo praji thought it would be a good idea to get me back on a visa as domestic help. He would give me a wage, and this appeared to be the best solution for all concerned.

I babysat for them, but I got very bored staying at home all day. I needed fresh air, but it was too cold to stir outside. I had been such a free bird in Ahmedabad that I found this life too restrictive. Devinder and Billoo praji noticed that I was looking depressed, and decided it would be good if I did a course. I started going to English classes twice a week. Unfortunately they didn't address my needs: I already knew my ABC. I unsuccessfully used the classes to try to get a student visa.

While I was in England I had met a family of Ahluwalias. The woman's brother was a doctor who lived in America, and she had thought I would be a good match for him. She suggested that I arrange to meet him when I returned to Canada. Billoo praji invited him to meet us, but when he arrived he confessed he was living with a woman. His family didn't know, so they were forever matchmaking.

Meanwhile, in London, Dev and Sukhjit jijaji went to Crawley to meet Deepak Ahluwalia because they were interested in him as a possible match for Sukhjit's niece. But when they showed him a photograph of her, he turned her down. Dev liked him very much, however, and thought maybe she could interest him in me. They got on well with Deepak's father, who was an easy-going man. They regretted not meeting him when I was in London.

Deepak had seen my photo on an earlier occasion and said that he was interested in me. He had heard that I had turned down a lot of suitors, that I was very snobbish, and he was a bit worried that I might turn him down too. Dev wrote and asked whether I would be interested in considering him. She sent us a more up-to-date picture, and I liked Deepak's looks. Tommy also met Deepak and his family, and really liked them. He felt that they were simple, good-natured and didn't show off. He rang and told me that Deepak was good-looking, was an Ahluwalia, the eldest son of six children, and was educated. He worked in a factory, but he had done electronic engineering. And after all, most of my family worked in factories. We had to in foreign countries.

I said that if Tommy thought Deepak was good enough, I would agree even without meeting him. For the first time, a suitor was being endorsed by my family. I couldn't take such a big decision on my own. I would never have left India in search of a suitor if I had known that I would be left to my own devices.

When my consent was reported to Deepak, he couldn't believe it. He thought my family must have pressurised me into saying yes, especially after what he had heard about me, and said he would travel to Canada to hear me say yes for himself. Tommy offered to pay for his ticket. Deepak said he would pay himself, because it was a question of his life. He came against his mother's wishes. The fact that he had paid for his own ticket especially irked her.

Deepak came to Canada for a week and stayed with us. Billoo praji fetched him from the airport. The entire family had gathered, and I was extremely nervous. I couldn't speak any English, and I was shy. Deepak was talking very quickly in English with my family, and I could barely understand him. After tea he asked me, 'Do you like Canada?' I said yes, hoping he wouldn't ask me another question. He got very friendly with Billoo, looking at photo albums and chatting. They were pulling each other's legs as if they were long-lost friends. My brother had a lodger, Guddi, who used to embarrass me by teasing me about Deepak, and Deepak joked with her as well.

Devinder told Deepak that Billoo praji was so handsome before he lost his hair that she used to call him Shammi Kapoor, after the Indian film star. So Deepak started calling him that too, as if he had known him for ages. My family really enjoyed his sense of humour. When Devinder said that the first thing she did on waking up was put on her make-up, and nobody had ever seen her without it, Deepak took up the challenge to catch her out. Next morning she got up, came out of her bedroom and yawned, unaware that Deepak was lying in wait with a camera. He took a picture and said he would show it to the world. He'd won the bet. He enjoyed the food we cooked because it was mildly spiced, the way he liked it. We took him touring to Montreal and Ottawa, to the seaside, to the park. I was still shy of him. I later discovered that he was still worried that I would reject him.

On the third day, when we were at the seaside, Billoo praji gestured to me that I should take Deepak to one side and ask about his plans. Billoo praji told me that it was silly to be shy, that in Canada women worked, went out, and that I shouldn't behave like a typical Indian woman. So I took my courage in my hands. Deepak was running his fingers through the water. I asked him how he liked Canada, and he said he liked it very much. I asked him what his thoughts were. He said that he had agreed before coming to Canada, but he wanted to know what I felt. I said that if he had agreed, then I would too. There were two other things that I wanted to say, and which also needed a lot of courage. I said that I would say yes if he agreed to me studying and working after marriage, and that I didn't want to wear a sari – I can't walk in them, nor do I know how to drape the six yards of cloth around me. Deepak said he didn't mind. I was thrilled that I had achieved what I had always wanted, to study and to work.

Billoo praji was extremely happy. He rang Surinder to tell her the good news. We also rang India, and Deepak rang his parents. The next day we sorted out a date in the registry office, met the priest at the Gurdwara, the Sikh temple, and ran a number of other errands. We went shopping, and Deepak asked me to choose a ring. I chose one of the cheapest, around $50, thinking it was not fair to burden him as he had already spent a lot of money coming to Canada and he only worked in a factory. Billoo praji bought a ring for Deepak, a gold one with a diamond in it. Just as we were signing at the register office, I said to Deepak, 'We have made the right decision, haven't we?' He said, 'If you think so, sign.' After I had signed and it was his turn, I said to him that he still had time to change his mind if he wished. He laughed, and later he told Billoo praji what I had said to him. That is how we became Mr and Mrs. It was 17 June 1979. Deepak was twenty-four and I was twenty-three.

We came home, exchanged rings and fed each other the traditional *mithai* (sweetmeats). That was our engagement, because we consider ourselves married only when we have walked four times around the *Granth Sahib*, the Sikh holy book. That night I wept for hours. I had never really wanted to marry, but I had no excuse to refuse Deepak, who had all the qualities I was seeking. I didn't want to be touched by a man, I didn't want sex, I didn't want to be seen naked. I was afraid of my first night with him. I felt the cage closing around me, I felt the door shutting.

The next day, Deepak and I were left alone. Billoo praji was out, and Devinder was busy. We were sitting in the corridor, and I asked Deepak about his family. I said I was very happy that he had a father and that for the first time in my life I would be able to say 'Daddy'. The family had emigrated to Britain from Kenya in 1977, sponsored by Deepak's paternal uncle Ranjit chachaji, who put them up until they found their feet. Ten people (Ranjit chacha had four children of his own) lived in a three-bedroom house for three months.

I asked Deepak why he hadn't brought any pictures of his family, and he said that he hadn't known whether things would work out. That was why he hadn't even bought me a ring. He said that his mother ruled the roost, and that his father never got his way. He was very different from his younger brothers Suresh, Raju (Rajesh) and Neelu (Anil), he told me, and of his sisters Pummi (Promila) and Manju, he liked only Manju. All his family were taller than me, which intimidated me too. Even his mother, who was the shortest, was 5'4". (When I got to England I discovered that she was the same height as me, 5'2", but liked to think of herself as taller.) I was a bit worried when he talked about his mother. She sounded very sharp. I thought,

'Oh, no, someone who will straighten me out, no doubt.' Deepak was honest, I must say.

The wedding was to take place in England in five weeks' time, on 21 July. Surinder and her husband would fly over for three weeks, the first week to prepare for the wedding, the second for the wedding itself, and the third to visit relatives. Billoo praji asked my future in-laws if they would like anything in particular as part of the dowry. Deepak's father said that they were happy to get a nice girl and didn't want any material goods.

Deepak took me to the immigration office and got my passport stamped. I was to follow him to England three weeks later. On Deepak's last day, we took him shopping, and bought him clothes, a gold watch, clothes for his brothers, a suit for his father, whatever he wanted. Deepak was going to buy gifts for his family, and didn't expect Billoo praji to pay for them. But, like me, Billoo praji felt that Deepak had already spent enough money on the trip. Billoo praji must have spent $500, but we had nothing for Deepak's mother. So Billoo praji went to an Indian shop and bought a chiffon sari in a light print, thinking that at her age Deepak's mother would not want a colourful sari. Deepak said he had never met such a loving family as mine. In fact, he started crying in the shopping centre. We were shocked. Deepak said it was the first time he had felt so much affection. Billoo praji put his arm around Deepak's shoulder as if he were his elder brother. Deepak didn't want to leave Canada. Billoo praji asked him to come and live there, and said he would help him open an electronic repair shop.

When Deepak was back in England he wrote to say that his mother didn't like the sari, which she thought was really meant for widows or much older women. She also didn't like the idea of me not wearing a sari after my marriage. I was rather worried. We hadn't even got married yet, and already my future mother-in-law was criticising me. Deepak had said that his family would make no demands, but the sari was not good enough, and instead of gratitude his letter was full of complaints. Deepak also had a further list of items that he wanted bought for him. Billoo praji tried to make light of it, but he too was hurt.

I wrote to Deepak with my flight details and asked him to meet me at the airport. I had to write in English, because he couldn't read any other language. That was very difficult for me. I was nervous at having to meet his family. In those three weeks Billoo praji bought me things for my trousseau – a heavily embroidered *gharara* (a full-length billowing skirt), Punjabi suits, two jewellery sets, one in silver and one in gold. For my mother-in-law I took a gold ring, a sari and a *salwar kameez*. For my father-in-law I took a three-piece suit, a shirt, a tie and a watch. For each of my brothers-in-law I took a pair of trousers and a shirt, a shirt each for Deepak's seven uncles, saris for their wives, and a suit for Deepak's grandfather and a sari for his grandmother. Billoo praji also gave me $1000 to give to my in-laws. Apart from all this expenditure, Billoo praji also had to buy my ticket to London. Deepak had offered to send me one, but when he got back his mother dissuaded him, saying that it was my family's responsibility. Deepak would phone from his factory every second or third day and complain to me about his mother.

On 7 July 1979 I arrived in England to get married. Deepak met me at the airport with a friend of his and his sixteen-year-old sister Manju. On the way to his home in Crawley, we stopped at the gates of a factory. Deepak explained that both his parents worked on the night shift here, making Hellermans cassettes, and that he had come to fetch them. He asked me to come in with him. It was the first time I had seen the inside of a factory. He introduced me to his mother, but she wasn't the tall and slim woman of Deepak's stories. To my embarrassment he told her that I refused to believe she was his mother. I greeted her nervously. At that moment I remembered overhearing, when I had been talking to Deepak on the phone from Canada, my mother-in-law screaming at someone, 'Do you want me to slap you?' Deepak's father was very tall and very nice, his eyes were full of love. I felt an immediate attachment to him. Perhaps it was the absence of the word 'Dad' in my life that made me feel that way. I also met Ranjit chachaji, who worked as a supervisor in the factory.

The house was a three-minute drive from the factory. Chachaji lived in the same road. Deepak's elder sister Pummi, who worked as a telephone operator, was waiting for us at the door. She was tall and slim, and very pale-looking, with puffy eyes as if she had been crying. Her face had sorrow written all over it. She was shabbily dressed. She gave me a hug as she took me inside.

In our culture we are not really allowed to step inside our in-laws' house before marriage, and because the traditional ceremony hadn't taken place, coming here was a break with tradition. But Dev's husband Sukhjit jijaji was working and was unable to fetch me from Heathrow, so Billoo praji had bought me a ticket for Gatwick because Deepak lived nearby.

The house was furnished very simply, and I resolved within a few minutes of stepping into it that I would gradually get the decor changed. My father-in-law was very chatty, asking me about my trip and my family while my mother-in-law busied herself in the kitchen making tea. He kept saying, 'This girl is like my daughter. She is a very nice girl, I love her.'

When Pummi brought the tea in, it was English-style tea, and I found it difficult to drink. But for the third round Deepak made Indian-style tea. I really enjoyed it, and told him it was the best cup of tea I had had. He was very pleased.

My mother-in-law asked me to have a wash and to change my clothes, as some other relatives would be visiting shortly to take a look at me. She thought I would change into a Punjabi suit or something more traditional, but I hardly had anything with me. Surinder was bringing all my good clothes with her from Canada the following week. I was so unaware of what was expected that I came down in a red silk shirt and black trousers which my mother-in-law, I found out later, did not approve of, although she didn't say anything at the time. Deepak wanted to know what I was carrying in my three suitcases and why I didn't have more appropriate clothes.

Ranjit chacha and his wife arrived. Just before lunch was served I was talking to my father-in-law when I heard a loud noise from the kitchen. I was later told that chachiji (aunty) and my mother-in-law were advising Deepak to behave more sensibly now that he was on the brink of getting married, that he had got a nice girl and should give up his old habit of fighting and shouting. He was angered by their advice and smashed a cup into the sink.

I offered to help with lunch, but my mother-in-law said she didn't expect me to do any work now and not for eight days after I married, but that one day the kitchen would become my domain and she would not even step into it. Although she said it as a joke, I got really nervous at this remark. I could hardly cook, and this family appeared to have such a large appetite. They would eat six or seven chappatis each. Would they like my style of cooking?

Deepak was sitting at the top of the stairs, and I went up to tell him to get ready so that we could all have lunch together. I tried to look at his room, but he wouldn't let me. I glimpsed items of *puja* (worship) and a picture of Hanuman. Women aren't allowed to worship Hanuman or to go into any area dedicated to his worship. When I asked Deepak to change into smarter clothes, I was shocked to find that he had nothing else, only one suit and another pair of trousers which were in the wash. He wouldn't go and get ready until the rest of us had actually sat down to eat. This was a peculiar habit of his – in all our ten years together, we must only have eaten together ten or fifteen times. He would always disappear around meal-times, and would eat before or after. I felt quite hurt that day. This was my first meal with the family, and he should have been by my side. The food was quite spicy, and Deepak later said that he didn't eat with us because he knew that I wasn't used to spicy food, and that he would have lost his temper with his mother if she had made it too hot when he had expressly asked her to make it mild. During my time in Canada I had lost the habit of eating such hot food, and although I enjoyed it, I found myself drinking a lot of orange juice to wash it down.

When my mother-in-law went into the kitchen, my father-in-law put kheema (mincemeat curry) on her plate, although she is a vegetarian. I thought this was very funny, but no one else appreciated the joke. He was trying to liven up the atmosphere, but my mother-in-law merely shouted at him for having a childish sense of humour.

At one point Deepak pinned me against the wall in the passage and, in what he thought was a gesture of fun, brought his fist down hard on my head. I felt faint, and told him not to do it again. In my childhood I was prone to nosebleeds, and this kind of blow could easily have brought one on. He then took off my very high heels and mocked me for wearing them in front of his family. All this really spoiled my mood. I thought he had a strange sense of fun.

I wanted to escape to my sister Dev's in London. This house felt oppressive – all the doors were shut, there was a lingering stale smell, the crockery was cheap, the carpets were old. I wondered how I would live there without the knowledge that it was only temporary.

When we were leaving, both of Deepak's sisters started arguing about which one would accompany us. There was only one car, and Deepak had just passed his driving test. He was nervous about driving on motorways and his friend, to whom the car belonged, was going to sit by his side. My in-laws were coming as well. Deepak just about managed to control his temper. I said we would all squeeze in somehow.

Dev was very pleased to see us. I went into the kitchen and quickly made tea. I knew where everything was from my previous trip, and I felt comfortable here. I had come home.

SIX

The Cage Closes

THE WEDDING HAD BEEN set for 21 July 1979. There was a lot to be done in two weeks. We had to get cards printed and posted, and in the end we ran out of cards. Nearly three hundred people came. Surinder arrived with Billoo praji, and Bindhi praji came from India. This was the first time he had been to England. It was the last wedding in the family, and he felt it was his duty to do it well. He brought a gold jewellery set and a wedding ring for me and a gold kada for Deepak.

Although I didn't like them, Surinder advised me that three or four richly-embroidered saris should be part of my trousseau. If I didn't want them, my mother-in-law could give them away for Pummi's wedding. I had a sharara suit (a top with a matching ankle-length full skirt) and some long dresses.

One day Deepak asked me to go with his family to see Kaushaliya, the matchmaker, from where they would take me shopping in Southall. The family took me to a jewellery shop. I didn't really want all this money spent on me, and Deepak was very quiet. He said later that he resented the amount of overtime he had had to put in to give his mother £700 or £800 to buy things for me. His sweat over many days and nights was being poured into gold jewellery for me. They bought me a heavily-embroidered sharara suit for £70.

I wanted Deepak to buy a suit for himself, and when my shopping was finished, he told his family that we would join them after he had bought one. As I was wearing very high heels, I got really tired. I was wearing such impractical shoes because when we went shopping in Canada we drove to a shopping mall, and there was not much walking to do. Even in Ahmedabad the car stopped just outside the shop we wanted to visit and then drove us to the next shop. I had never walked so much. Deepak didn't like any of the suits I chose – they were either too expensive or not to his taste. While we were roaming around we bumped into a friend of Deepak's family, who invited us to visit her. Out of politeness I said we would. But it is not done to visit people before you are married, and even afterwards I could only do it with my mother-in-law's permission.

Deepak wanted to visit the woman before we returned, but I refused because I was tired and because I wanted to go home and meet my family, who were arriving from Canada that day. When we got to Kaushaliya's Deepak lost his temper, shouting loudly, 'Take her back, I am not going to marry her. Who does she think she is? Is she special just because she has come from Canada? She is a spoilt little girl who lies. I don't want her airs and graces. She agrees to visit this friend we met in the street, and when I suggest we go, she says she's too tired. Who does she think she is? A princess?'

The anger he had suppressed in the street came spilling out now. I went upstairs and burst into tears. I had blisters on my feet. I couldn't very well have told the woman we wouldn't come. It was the first time I had met her.

Deepak's mother screamed at him, 'It's too early to show your true colours. What if she tells her family and they cancel the wedding? My *izzat* is at stake.' Kaushaliya was also angry. They told Deepak to apologise. He came upstairs and knocked on the bathroom door. I washed my face to hide my tears and emerged. He said he was sorry and we went downstairs. I tried to join in with the others, who were attempting to divert my attention, but I was in a state of shock. Was this the happy, friendly man I had seen in Canada? Kaushaliya tried to make light of it, saying Deepak was foolish, he would lose his temper for a minute and then he would be fine again. They were covering up for him. I felt like telling them I wanted to run away, but then my family would be caught up in the treadmill of finding me another husband. I would be a burden to them again. This was the third time Deepak had shown a nasty side, and I wasn't even married to him yet. Where could I run to? Too many walls had sprung up around me. I kept up a pretence that everything was all right, but my hopes had died within me.

When Bindhi praji arrived he asked if I was happy, and said I still had time to reconsider. He wanted to be sure that I had not been under any kind of pressure. I didn't want to hurt him, so I said everything was fine. Besides, I didn't want to go back to India – at least in England I would be free to work. Bindhi praji brought me lots of clothes, including a red silk suit for my wedding day. The long scarf, or *chunni*, had been specially embroidered by his wife.

Four or five days before the wedding there is a ritual called *kada kurdmai*, in which the bride's family takes a gold *kada* to the groom and puts it on his wrist. The men of the family take lots of presents: clothes, fruit and *mithai*. In the evening, when the men returned, there was dinner laid on for them at my sister's. I took Tommy to one side and asked him what Bindhi praji thought of Deepak and his family. He told me that the house was decorated with streamers and that they had laid on good food. The impression was favourable. I was pleased that they were pleased.

The day before my wedding we had *sangeet* and *mehndi* – women sing songs as intricate patterns of henna are etched on their hands and feet. Dev's husband Sukhjit jijaji and another relative sang songs and jollified the proceedings. This is usually a women-only event, but this was England. That evening I burnt my hand when I went into the kitchen to remove some deep-fried *muttis* from the hot oil because the woman who was cooking them had to change her baby's nappy. Was that an omen? Jijaji was angry with Dev for letting me go into the kitchen, because brides are not allowed to do any work. The henna cooled the burn down, and I didn't have any blisters or long-term scars. Now I have scars on that same hand from the other fire. Even during the wedding ceremony, when I shut my eyes to hide my tears, all I saw was fire, its flames lapping at my feet.

Deepak rang and told me that there was a lot of dancing in his house. It was the first wedding in the family. The next day I woke up early. A house full of people needed to have baths, and there was only one bathroom. We had put down mattresses on the floor of the living room and my sister and her family had slept over at her husband's family home. I got up at 5 a.m. and washed and curled my hair. Surinder helped me dress. In India there would have been many women dressing me, but here I would have to become a bride almost by myself. When I was dressed, I had my photo taken with Surinder and Dev. I thought I looked beautiful, and my young niece confirmed it.

We had booked a hall in Southall. Deepak was sitting in his car when I arrived, wearing a cream suit with a turban and a garland of flowers. Instead of behaving like a demure bride, I went prancing around introducing everyone to each other. Inside, my mother-in-law dressed me in the *chunni*, put *sindoor* (red powder, a sign of marriage) in my hair parting, put a ring on my finger and blessed me.

During the *phere* (walking four times around the *Granth Sahib*) I began to remember my parents, especially my father. I cried so much that I started Deepak and his father off. I tried to hide my face with my *chunni*. I couldn't even walk straight because I was so upset, and had to be led around by my brothers. When Surinder told me to shush because I was setting Deepak off, I nearly giggled. What sort of a man was he to cry? You could understand my tears, but why was he crying? Later, after the ceremony was over, I noticed that all my brothers had been crying. We are a very close family, and their sister was leaving home. At such times other sorrows come to mind, and further fuel your tears.

The phere have to be finished by midday. Then there was music and food. There had been a lot of argument about whether the food should be vegetarian or non-vegetarian. Being a Hindu, my mother-in-law was the only one to insist on vegetarian. In the end she got her way.

My brothers advised me for the second time in my life (the first was when I entered college) on how to conduct myself so that I did not bring shame to my family. I stood there in silence and wrapped myself in their advice. After all, my life was a gift from them. I could easily have been left to starve after the death of my parents. They said that they would stand by me if I was unhappy or if I needed anything. And when the mountain fell on me, they did all come to my rescue.

For the first and last time in my life, I changed into a sari for the *doli* (departure). My sisters had to persuade me to do this for the sake of propriety. During the *doli* my brothers sobbed out loud. When Deepak and I arrived at his house that evening, the car door banged hard against my forehead. I should have recognised that as a sign of my broken destiny.

There were further ceremonies to be completed on the home-coming. I had to sit Deepak's brother Suresh on my lap – I think this signifies the hope that I will give birth to sons. All the women were singing and dancing, and I wanted to sit and watch. They served tea and *pakoras*. I went upstairs to change. Deepak's room had been tidied up, and all the religious paraphernalia had disappeared. I was very tired so I stayed upstairs and rested. They were beating drums downstairs. I was tired from all the crying and I wanted to stay a while and see Deepak's family at play, but he wanted us to go to the hotel where we were booked in for two nights. He was worried that they wouldn't let us in after 9 p.m. When I didn't get up immediately, he went down to the kitchen and in low, angry tones said to his mother, 'What kind of a woman is this? When I ask her to get up, she won't budge.' I could see him spinning out of control.

We were driven to the George Hotel in Crawley town by

Suresh. The room was nice, and it had a television and a bath-room. We made some tea and Deepak switched on the TV. I changed into my nightie and he changed into his pyjamas. We didn't talk to each other, we just watched TV. I was feeling shy, and was also worried that Deepak would touch me sooner or later. We sat there till midnight. I wasn't ready, although I kept telling myself that, as my husband, Deepak had full rights over my body. He talked about other things, and then gradually broached the subject of sex. I told him frankly that I was scared. He said that as this was my first time, it would hurt. I hadn't known that. I asked him how he knew, but he didn't tell me that he had had girlfriends. As well as feeling shy, I was now scared of the pain.

The lights were dim. Deepak wanted to hold me, but the closer he got, the more rigid I became. As he started kissing and cuddling me I was torn by my shyness and the knowledge that it was my duty to make him happy. He said that it was getting late, and that we should sleep because his brother was coming to fetch us at eight o'clock the next morning. I was thrilled when I heard the word 'sleep', but it was only his cue to climb on top of me and have his way. I felt suffocated underneath his weight, and I was shrieking in agony. And he was moving. I kept asking him why he was moving, because it hurt me more. I didn't know that sex had to have a rhythm. It was just as well that we were in a hotel. Even there, Deepak kept telling me to lower my voice in case the people in the next room could hear us. He wanted to possess me, to satisfy his lust. He just went on and on until he had finished. I didn't even know what 'finished' meant. I didn't know there was a climax in which a man shot semen.

When Deepak got off me I felt relief, but I was engulfed by pain. I tidied my clothes and went to the bathroom where for some reason I passed gallons of water – my bladder must have been affected by all this. It was like the breaking of waters when a pregnancy ripens. I sat on the toilet weeping, wondering why sex was so highly rated. My thighs felt weak, my face was tear-stained. When I came out, the bedsheets were soaked in urine. There was no blood. Deepak folded the sheets and put them aside. I got into bed and turned my back on him. I couldn't face him in case it set him off again. The pain was incredible. I didn't want this kind of love, which brought so much pain. I couldn't talk to anyone about it, not even my sisters. Not only had I never shown my bare arms and legs, I had started walking hunched up when my breasts started growing at puberty because I wanted to hide them.

Next morning when I put my feet on the floor I felt my legs couldn't take my weight. I ached all over. I was worried that my in-laws would guess what had happened from the way I walked, and that would be so embarrassing. I wore one of my maxi skirts. When I met my father-in-law I couldn't look him in the eye. I was trying to walk as normally as possible instead of hobbling around with my legs apart as if I had just got off an elephant. My mother-in-law looked me up and down, critical and unsmiling. Later I heard that she was unhappy with the clothes I had chosen, when I should have worn a Punjabi suit. Even though I had told Deepak that I would not wear them, she had given me only saris, many of which were second-hand.

At Deepak's, Kaushaliya and Pummi were sitting in his brothers' room. Pummi said she liked my dress. I asked her to bring my suitcase in from the boxroom so I could show her some of my clothes and also give her the present I had brought for her from Canada. I was trying to be friendly. I was in a new family. I needed to forge links, and discussing clothes is often a way for young women to get together.

Deepak spotted her with the suitcase. 'Oi,' he said, 'what do you think you're doing?' Pummi started quivering. Deepak continued, 'You are nosy. You are fucking nosy, aren't you? Go and put this case back. Kiran doesn't know your habits. Why don't you mind your own business?' He started kicking the suitcase and the skirting board, which made a frighteningly loud noise. Pummi was in tears. I told Deepak that I had asked her to get the case. He told me to keep quiet, and said that he knew his sister better than I did.

The whole family went deadly quiet and tried to busy themselves with some other activity. Mamma shouted at Deepak, 'Keep your nose out of women's business. You're a man, go and sit downstairs.' He responded with, 'She's my wife. Don't try and dictate to her.' My mother-in-law went quiet. She didn't want the situation to run out of control. I was in shock. My respect for Deepak had diminished. How would he behave if there were more serious disagreements, which are inevitable in communal living? I couldn't say anything to him, not in the presence of elders. I had to respect them. I was now their *izzat*, and I couldn't do anything that would destroy that.

When we went back to the hotel that night, I told Deepak that I didn't want sex. I had pain in my legs and tears in my eyes. I told him I was going to be with him for life. What did it matter if we went without for one night? Although my legs had improved slightly during the day, I felt old every time I had to put weight on them. I was going to my sister's house the following day to meet my family from Canada, and I needed to feel well. What kind of act was this sex, when one partner enjoys himself and the other screams in pain? When I hear people talk about rape, that first night swims in front of my eyes. Though I wanted to be a good wife and not hurt my husband's feelings, I could not bring myself to have sex that second night. In the ten years of my married life, I never enjoyed sex. It was always painful, even after the birth of my children. It damaged me to such an extent that even today I have no sexual desires. I miss the good things about my husband when I see my children, but sex is definitely not one of them. Maybe God was on my side that night. Deepak said all right, but only on the condition that I agreed the following night.

The next morning, Tommy and Sukhjit jijaji came to fetch us. I was overjoyed. Deepak was on holiday for a week, so we both went to stay with Dev for five or six days. I was putting off living with my in-laws, which I was dreading. At least there was peace at my sister's. On the way there, Deepak warned me not to talk about his family.

When it was time to go to bed that night I asked my eight-year-old niece Kavita to insist that she wanted to sleep in the same bed as me, as she did in the old days. I had to take refuge in a child's presence. Dev and Sukhjit jijaji refused to allow it, but I kept saying, 'Let her.' Deepak knew why I wanted Kavita to sleep with me, and he wasn't very pleased. She fell asleep on our bed, but Dev and Sukhjit carried her downstairs. I didn't let Deepak touch me that night. I threatened that I would go and sleep with my sister if he tried anything. I allowed him to cuddle and kiss me, but not on my mouth. For the next few nights I got off scot-free. One night Deepak was beginning to get restless and I was taking some medicine. I said, half in jest, that I would drink the whole bottle if he touched me. Apart from Deepak's demands for sex, which frightened me and made me curl up with shyness, we talked about most things. I would try to explain to him that it hurt. He kept saying that it would not hurt the second time, but I couldn't bring myself to believe him.

When we returned to Crawley the following Sunday I pleaded with Deepak not to fight with anyone because it upset me. He agreed. That night his family were all watching a Hindi video in the living room. I wanted to sit and watch, but Deepak asked rudely if I had been invited. I said I didn't expect an invitation, as a family member. He went upstairs in a huff. Our bedroom was just above the living room. He took his shoes off and threw them against the skirting board, making a very loud noise. His mother asked me to go up and see if he was okay.

I asked if he was angry that I was sitting downstairs and watching the video. He denied it, and said he was no one to dictate to me what I should do, but I knew by his manner that it was annoying him. I said I would make him a cup of tea. When I went upstairs with it, he knocked the cup from my hands. The hot tea splashed my shirt, and I clutched at my chest and held the wet shirt away from my skin to stop the burning. Deepak ripped the shirt open, threw me on the bed, dragged my trousers down and climbed on top of me. What kind of fire was this, that he couldn't even ask me and I couldn't even object because I knew his family were awake? When he'd finished he said I could go down and watch the video. He had used my body to satisfy his lust and was now flinging it aside. I was sure that his family would have heard the bed creak. These English houses have no soundproofing. What face could I show to his family? How could I sit in their midst when I knew they would be thinking I was so thick-skinned that after making my husband happy I was now joining them? Deepak turned over and started snoring. I couldn't sleep. I couldn't refuse him. His family would say that I had failed as a wife if I couldn't meet his needs.

The next day he went to work. I waited all day for his return. At least he was someone to talk to. I was scared of my mother-in-law. There was no joy in that house. I was in the bedroom when Deepak returned. He had told me before he went to work in the morning that he wanted me to wait for him there, I don't know why. Maybe because he kissed me on the cheek when he came back and was too shy to do it in front of his family. Maybe he didn't want me to get friendly with the rest of the family and discuss him with them.

He asked me who had cooked the dinner. I said I didn't know. It could only have been Pummi or my mother-in-law. I was not supposed to enter the kitchen for eight days. He became very serious, and said I was lying. He said he had tasted the vegetable curry, and it had been cooked in oil. His mother only ever cooked in ghee, and when he had been in Canada he had noticed that my family cooked in oil. He flew into a rage when I denied cooking the meal. 'You are lying to me. You want to side with my family.' So saying, he slapped me, a great thundering whack on my face. I started crying. I was reeling from the shock – not the physical one, I could cope with that. It was as if someone had put a block of ice on my brain. I felt numb. I had never been slapped in my whole life, and in the second week of my married life I was undergoing this humiliation.

When Deepak's mother insisted that she had cooked the meal, he accused her of conspiring with me against him. He went out, after telling her that he had slapped me. My mother-in-law tried to comfort me, saying that the bastard didn't know the difference between ghee and oil. He came back half an hour later, apologised and asked me to get ready to go out. He wanted me to do my make-up well so that no one would spot any sign of tears. Before going out, we ate our dinner. Deepak insisted on feeding me the first mouthful of food from his plate. I felt shy because his parents were sitting at the table as well. He even washed our plates.

The next day passed peacefully, and when Deepak came back from work and asked how I was, I said I was happier without him. He didn't like that. He caught hold of my hair and shouted, 'I want you to cook *parathas* [Indian bread] for me.' I had never made *parathas* before, and I burst into tears. When you're in such a state, you forget what you know even. He dragged me into the kitchen by my hair. His family and his uncle were sitting in the living room. His mother shouted, '*Muya* [sod], leave the poor girl alone!' She tried to drag me out of the kitchen. He shouted, 'She is my wife. This is between me and her. Don't touch her.' He was banging on the door and on the wall, saying, 'Let's see what kind of *parathas* she makes.'

He tried to pull me up the stairs by my hair. 'I'll show her, coming here with her airs and graces.' I wouldn't go because I was afraid of what he would do to me when we were alone, so he picked me up and carried me upstairs. The rest of them just watched. It was as if the son of the family was simply torturing the family cat. Pummi started crying. I covered my eyes and my ears. I didn't want to hear his threats, I didn't want them to set my imagination alight. Where had my family dumped me, what kind of marriage was this? When we were upstairs, he apologised. If he hadn't frightened me, I might even have made the *parathas*. When I did start cooking in their house I would ask my mother-in-law to leave the kitchen, otherwise I wouldn't be able to make chappatis. Lack of confidence destroys everything. For ten whole years I lived with fear, fear, fear. It was only when I went into prison that I got my confidence, when Southall Black Sisters ran a campaign for me that I got to know what it was like to be free of fear.

When I lay in the bed next to him at night, I felt I was sleeping with a demon and that he would eat me up if I wasn't alert. And so I couldn't sleep at night. In the daytime I would become unconscious, so deep was my sleep, even deeper than those first days in prison when I was on sleeping tablets.

After Deepak went to work in the mornings, the first words uttered by his mother would be, 'Bastard, dog. How was he born of my blood? He brings this family into disrepute.' Before Deepak came home she would say to me, 'Go up to your room before that bastard gets home, otherwise he'll say we're setting you up against him.' Deepak had a tape of songs of prayer which used to bring me a deep sense of peace, and I would go up and listen to it while I waited for him to return.

On the third day, Deepak asked his youngest brother Anil, who was sixteen, to collect the wedding photos from the chemist. When Deepak came home and noticed that the photos had been looked at, he stormed at Anil, 'How dare you look at my photos? I gave you instructions to pick them up, not look at them. You've mixed them all up.' Anil replied, 'So what?' Deepak grabbed him by the neck and screamed, 'Who the hell do you think you are? They're my bloody photos, it's my bloody camera.' He was about to beat Anil up when his mother intervened. Then Deepak asked me to choose some photos to have copied for my family. I hardly dared look at them. They were my own wedding photos, and I was afraid to touch them. Nervously I picked up a few, making sure I didn't mix them up. When the copies arrived and I started sorting them out,

Deepak shouted at me for getting them out of order. I said it didn't matter what order they were in when they got to my family – it was the individual pictures that had meaning for them, not the order.

Such mountains Deepak built with incidents dug out of history. I used to cover my ears. I didn't want to hear anything that would enter my subconscious and keep me awake at nights. He had now erupted against almost every member of his family.

On the fourth day we had potato curry. Every day we had to make forty or more chappatis, and Pummi had made them on this day. I hadn't eaten all day – Deepak didn't want me to eat until he came home. When I got very hungry, I would have a couple of pieces of toast. I survived on black coffee, and that day I was starving. Deepak and I used to eat off one plate. That was his gesture of love towards me. I started eating, but Deepak found the curry too hot. He said 'Bloody hell,' and knocked a glass of water off the table. The glass shattered, and with it my composure. 'Bastards put so much chilli powder in the food. You don't find it hot?' he said to me. 'You're just trying to make my family happy by eating it. You're *my* wife. Mum,' he shouted, 'who cooked this meal?' Then the limelight was on me again. 'I know you sit and gossip about me all day. They're poisoning your mind against me. I know you want to make them happy.' I started crying. He said I couldn't eat this food, I could eat only what he ate.

He threatened to put water in the spice box, and threw the plateful of food into the sink. The plate broke. He came back with two slices of bread with margarine on them. My eyes swam when I thought of the cooked food that was not in my destiny and was going to waste. I was Deepak's property, not a human being. I had no desires of my own. I could eat only what he ordered. I had lost a lot of weight already.

In that first week we had another row one night when my parents-in-law were at work. Deepak wanted to write to some relatives in India. I was talking to Manju, his younger sister, in the parents' bedroom. We were exchanging stories about our families, when suddenly Deepak came thudding into the room and started shouting at us, accusing Manju of passing on family secrets to me. He caught hold of her and pushed her roughly against the wall. When I tried to explain what we had been doing he came towards me and pushed me into the boxroom, where he threw me on to the bed and started strangling me. He slapped me twice across the face, and sat on my chest so that I could hardly breathe. I was crying loudly but breathlessly. Deepak's brother Raju, who was about eighteen years old, came running in. He dragged Deepak off me and said he would beat him if he touched me again.

I cried bitterly. The marks of Deepak's fingers stayed on my neck for days. I couldn't even swallow without discomfort. The next morning Deepak phoned his mother from work and told her what he had done. She cursed him, saying, 'Bastard, is this some great deed for you to ring me and boast about it? Her brothers haven't even returned to India yet, the henna has not washed off her hands yet, and you've shown her your true nature already. Is this why you married her?'

I told my mother-in-law, 'I have never even been scolded by my brothers, let alone been beaten by them.' I started crying. She asked me to hush, saying she knew her son, and that she would straighten the bastard out.

If anyone stood up to Deepak, he would hold them by the neck. He also had a habit of keeping his index finger very rigid and poking you relentlessly on your chest, just under your neck, or on your forehead. That hurt more than slapping. I was so powerless. I couldn't even talk to anyone. I couldn't make friends with any of his family because it was an environment full of fear. His father would apologise to me for having trapped a nice girl like me. I could tell from his eyes that he felt love and sympathy for me.

Life seemed to have become one endless cycle of abuse,

beating, thumping, shouting, banging, screaming, breaking crockery. For twenty-one years I had lived such a sheltered existence that I thought these things happened only in Hindi films. On top of all this, I had to submit to Deepak's demand for sex. When I refused him he would point to his manhood and say, 'Shut up, or I'll put this in your mouth and piss into your body.' I had been humiliated enough. I dreaded him telling his mother that I didn't let him have sex with me.

Apart from blaming my problems on the fact that I was a woman, I started blaming my destiny, that I must have been evil in a past life. At one level I felt a strong impulse to tell my brothers everything, to ask them to take me away from here. They had pampered me so much – every whim of mine would be fulfilled – that this seemed like a journey from heaven to hell. I knew Bindhi praji's temper was such that he would beat Deepak in front of his entire family. But then I would become a burden on them again – after they had spent so much on my wedding – and that wouldn't solve anything. So I didn't tell my family what my life was like.

At the end of that first week in Crawley, Tommy rang and said that they would visit me the next day, before Billoo and Surinder left for Canada. I was thrilled. When Deepak heard that they were coming he apologised for what he had done, and made me promise not to tell them. He promised that he wouldn't hit me or shout at me ever again. He kept his promise for a few weeks.

SEVEN

Upstairs and Downstairs

WHEN MY FAMILY came to visit, I kept my hand around my neck in an attempt to hide the marks. Deepak was very quiet. He kept a watch on me to ensure my silence. I was going to keep up appearances anyway. After we'd finished eating, Deepak went into the kitchen and started washing up. 'Come on,' I said. 'Sit with the guests. It doesn't look good for you to be washing up like this.' I noticed that Surinder was looking at me curiously. I felt she suspected that all was not well. Both Pummi and my mother-in-law asked Deepak to join us, but he said he didn't want them to taunt him later about having to do the washing up left behind by his in-laws. They didn't press the point, knowing how he could fly off the handle in minutes.

I knew Deepak had gone into the kitchen to hide his guilt, but I felt disappointed that he couldn't even participate in ordinary conversation. I wanted so much to tell my brothers everything. If I had had the confidence then that I have today, I would have asked to leave that hell.

Daddy entertained them and covered up for the rest of his family. When my family left, Deepak started on Daddy, saying that he had felt humiliated when his father started talking about the price of vegetables with his in-laws. Mamma too launched in. Wasn't there a better topic of conversation? Well, I thought, why didn't Deepak contribute one instead of hiding in the kitchen?

On Sunday, Deepak decided to take me out for the day.

When he told his mother that we would probably eat out, she started yelling. 'If you're wining and dining this queen, who will do the housework? I work nights all week, then I do the housework at the weekends. What has she done all week? Don't you think I would like to go out as well?' My mood was completely soured by this. I didn't want to go out, and asked Deepak to forget it, but he started shouting at his mother, 'She's been sitting in the house all week. She's my wife. Doesn't she have the right to go out?' He told me to ignore his mother and to get ready.

We went by train to Gatwick airport, and spent the day there. Deepak insisted I have a glass of wine. He had noticed that we drank wine in Canada. I was reluctant, because he might later attack me for drinking. I was also worried that he might tell my mother-in-law. I made him promise to keep quiet about it.

On Monday I woke up late, as usual. I could sleep only after Deepak left in the morning, as I was too afraid to sleep next to him. After I made his cup of tea at seven I would go back to bed, and wouldn't be able to get up till eleven. Deepak's mother was infuriated by this. She would have liked me to make her and Daddy's breakfast when they came in from work at 6.30 a.m., touch their feet like a dutiful *bahu* (daughter-in-law) and keep my head covered, none of which I did. I respected them, but I could not show it in the traditional way.

Pummi said that my days of being a guest were over, and it was time for me to get involved in housework. I told her, to her complete disbelief, that I didn't know how to cook. I certainly couldn't cook like them. I could just about make vegetable curry in the way my family made it, but I couldn't make *rotis*. So Pummi taught me to cook. She taught me that Raju didn't like tomatoes and onions unless they were cut fine, and Deepak didn't like chillies – I'd learned that by then. They used to take his food out before putting in the chillies. This made him feel he was always being excluded by his family.

The first time I cooked, Daddy gave me some money. I joked that it would be great if I got paid regularly for working in the kitchen. The second time, I put a lot of chilli powder in the food because Raju liked it that way, but I didn't take any food out for Deepak. Everyone found it spicy, but they ate it. I confessed what I had done to Deepak, who started shouting that instead of wanting to please my husband, I wanted to please his family, that he had no place in the house.

One minute after a big argument, the family would be smiling and talking happily. But my mood would be spoilt for the whole day and my appetite would be killed. Either that or I would end up in the toilet, throwing up or letting go at the other end with nervousness.

Although Pummi and I were supposed to take it in turns to cook, we used to end up helping each other. It took so much dough to make forty *rotis* that I didn't have the strength to knead it. Sometimes Manju would give me a hand. I did all the cleaning. That first week, I tried to ensure that my mother-in-law did not have to do anything. Every time a family member came home she would shout, 'Kiran, Anil's home, make his tea.'

On Saturday, when Deepak wanted to take me into town, his mother lost her temper again. 'What has the queen been doing all week?' I couldn't believe it. Deepak told her he hadn't brought a servant for her, and that in any case he had spent his own money to get married. When we got back, his mother was sulking. She didn't talk at all. She had wanted me to stand up to Deepak and refuse to go out with him. She couldn't see that I went out of fear. I felt really bad, but Deepak said I should ignore her, there was worse to come, and I hadn't seen her true nature yet.

On Sunday morning I wanted to get up and do some work in the kitchen, but Deepak wouldn't let me. His mother was angry that I wasn't helping. She kept complaining loudly, 'That queen is lying around in bed without a care in the world. I kill myself working eight nights a week. But does she care? The mother is made of iron,' and so on. It wasn't as if there was that much work – only cooking and cleaning. They were all grown up. They washed their own dishes, ironed their own clothes and could even switch on the washing machine.

Mamma didn't realise that Deepak wasn't letting me help. He said, 'Don't you dare go downstairs. Let the bitch talk.' I was shocked. No matter what kind of mother she might be, it was not right to call her by that name. I felt really hurt that my husband could fall so low. He wanted complete control – to hit me, to have sex, to take me out, to keep me in, to take me upstairs. I couldn't watch TV, I couldn't eat or drink – not a thing could I do without his approval. Mother and son were tearing me apart in their struggle to be rulers of their petty fiefdoms.

When I was downstairs, I lived in fear of his mother; when I stayed upstairs, I lived in fear of him. In the day I feared the mother; at night I feared the son. I was Deepak's property, ready to dance when he said so, but his mother also felt that she had a right to my services because I was her eldest daughter-in-law, and everything that went on in the house should be by her say-so. In one of her rows with Deepak, she said that there was no way she would treat me like a daughter.

I used to sit on a corner of the bed in the boxroom, shrinking into the wall, rocking backwards and forwards nervously, expecting Deepak to come upstairs and drag me into some row which I could hear raging downstairs. Sometimes I would sit there with my hands over my ears to shut them out of my world.

They could vent their feelings on each other, but who could I show my feelings to? I had been forbidden by my husband to talk to anyone. Did they ever realise what impact their rantings had on an outsider? I had always wanted to be the good wife, the good daughter-in-law, but they weren't giving me a chance. Who could I respect, to whom could I show my love? I felt that

I had been brought into this house to give them an excuse to fight.

My in-laws used to go to bed after breakfast, get up at about 11.30 for lunch, then go back to bed. On Monday morning the phone rang. My mother-in-law answered it and then hung up. It rang again when she was in the kitchen, and this time I answered. It was Deepak for me. He said that I shouldn't be afraid of his mother, and that if I was I should sit in the boxroom all day. If anything happened, I should tell him. I realised that the previous call had also been from him for me. I felt very hurt that his mother's antagonism towards me ran so deep that she wouldn't even tell me that there was a call for me from my husband. And this was only the third week of my marriage.

After that I stayed out of her way. I used to sit in my room and listen to music when she was downstairs, and emerge only when she was asleep. I was afraid she would hit me. Deepak would tell me to be strong, that his mother would be all right if left to her own devices. This, I thought, must be real life. What I had lived through before was some kind of artificial heaven. It seemed to me that no one in this family cared for each other. They rarely ate together, or sat and chatted to each other. When they got home they'd just sit and watch TV, and even that was fraught with disagreement. Daddy, despite being the eldest, never got his way. Raju would hog the television when he got home.

That evening Deepak said that I must be getting fed up with sitting around the house all day, so I should come and meet him at the factory gate when he finished work. To his annoyance, I said I would ask his mother's permission. When I asked her, she said that she had no power in this house, and that if I wanted to go, I was hardly going to listen to her. Pummi said I should go, otherwise Deepak would lose his temper.

This became my daily routine, although I felt embarrassed by it – just like the acute embarrassment I felt when Deepak fed me the first mouthful from his plate. I wondered what

Deepak's family thought about a wife going to meet her husband at his workplace.

One evening after dinner Deepak suggested we go for a walk. While we were out, I said that we should have washed our dishes before leaving. He was so furious with me that he frog-marched me back to the house. When we got home he said to his mother, 'Take her. What kind of a woman is she? I want to take her out and she's being awkward about it.' Now his temper was spilling out on to the streets from within the four walls of the house. When I told Mamma the following day what had happened, she said, 'What can I do? Does he listen to anybody? You have to be strong. You have to be brave, like the Rani of Jhansi. He won't let you live or die.' The light had gone out of my eyes. I was withering away from inside. There was an ocean of tears building up within me. She asked me if I ever lost my temper. I said, 'When I lose my temper, I lose it very badly, but only once in ten years or so.' Fateful words. What made me choose the number ten? Ten years is how long my marriage lasted. I became such a Rani of Jhansi that I liberated my husband from this life on earth.

That week Deepak took me to his aunt's place without telling his family. They insisted we stay and have dinner with them. I told Deepak that it was not done to visit relatives after the wedding unless we were invited. I had bought a number of long dresses for the endless round of invitations that are always issued to a newly wedded couple, but I was shocked to find that no one invited us. Only Daddy's brother visited regularly, and he was not welcomed by most of the family. They had nicknamed him Chongo, because he blinked frequently.

When I told Deepak's mother about our visit, she couldn't vent her anger on him, so she vomited it out on me instead. 'Without an invitation, you go and visit our relatives. Have you become the head of this family? What right do you have to visit my relatives without my permission? You want to appear nice in their eyes, in Deepak's eyes. You will lower my reputation.'

She would not listen to my attempts to explain. Mother and son shared their words in common. The only difference so far had been that she had not lifted her hand against me. She knew I was not strong enough to stand up to Deepak, yet she continued her diatribe against me. I was being squashed between the two, being ground down into the earth.

I tried to do as much housework as possible to keep her happy, but that week Deepak tried to get me involved in another row with his mother. In our tradition, when you get married relatives come and bless you and give you money, which you then hand over to your mother-in-law. Deepak had his eye on this money, but his mother refused to return it to him. He argued that it was our money, that I had a right to it. She said she would not give it to him until I asked for it.

Deepak started shouting at me and banging the door to make me ask her for it, but I said I was too embarrassed, and pleaded with him to let it pass. He dragged me into his mother's presence and said, 'Open your mouth, let those words trip off your tongue.' He said he would beat me if I didn't talk. He screamed at his mother, 'She is standing like a deaf-mute. She can't ask for the money but she is asking for it by standing in front of you.' I was weeping like a child, and mumbling, 'Mum, give him the money.'

She gave it to him, but she was furious with me, and told me not to talk to her or to Daddy. Although I loved Daddy, I was angry with him. He saw everything, but he never intervened. He should have acted as the head of the household. What kind of man was he? Did his manhood stretch only to providing sperm?

Sometimes my mother-in-law would criticise my clothes. Why didn't I wear a Punjabi suit or a sari? Why was I always in trousers? Deepak would defend me, telling her that she had no right to dictate what I wore. The arguments would last two or three hours. The others got so fed up that all of them, including Daddy, rounded on Deepak's mother. 'If her husband doesn't mind what she wears, why are you interfering? She warned you before her marriage that she wouldn't wear a sari.' Of course, Deepak turned this to his advantage. He would say, 'Wear a sari, otherwise I'll tell my mother and she'll beat you.'

Then she would start on the fact that I had come empty-handed, with no dowry. When Deepak reminded her that I had brought £500 with me, she would ask what that could buy in this day and age. She knew that Deepak was irritated by her criticism of me. I felt so bad, especially when my brothers had bought so many presents for the family, as well as gold and silver jewellery sets for me, and my ticket. Deepak was so ignorant of Indian culture that he would turn on his mother in rage for not having given him a dowry.

Sometimes Deepak would protect me from his family. One day his brother Anil came in while I was cooking and said somewhat brusquely, 'Hurry up, Kiran, I need to use the kitchen.' Deepak said, 'Who the hell do you think you're talking to? She's my wife.' Only he was allowed to brutalise me.

Deepak opened a joint account with me, and I noticed that he had £900 in the building society. I was really upset that he had involved me in a fight with his mother over the wedding money, which only came to about £40, and which he didn't even need. When he told his mother about the joint account she was furious. He had been married only a month, and already he was trusting a stranger. Deepak said that as his wife I would share everything with him. His mother hated him doing any-thing for me, helping me in the kitchen or paying attention to me. She would say it was not a man's place to be in the kitchen.

Shortly after we got married, I told Deepak I wanted to take some classes, and he took me into Crawley and registered me for six-month courses in English and typing. He spent an entire week's wages, £80, on my fees, and explained the bus routes and roads to the college. In truth, I could not understand Deepak. I felt he must care for me if he was doing all this.

I had typing two mornings a week and two English classes

in the evenings. Deepak would come and fetch me from my English classes. I made friends with the only other Indian girl in the class, Kamlesh. It turned out that she knew my mother-in-law and didn't like her. Once when Kamlesh dropped me off at home and I invited her in she refused, so deep was her dislike of my mother-in-law. Despite that, I never told her about my problems. In Crawley the Indian circle is quite tightly knit, and I was never sure if things would get back to my in-laws. Besides, I was embarrassed. If I take my clothes off, it will be my naked body that I will be exposing, after all.

I found it impossible to concentrate in my classes. My eyes would fill with tears and the keyboard would swim in and out of reach of my fingers as the scenes of fighting and abuse flashed past like a film. I would try to hide my sorrow from Kamlesh and the teacher. I used to beg Deepak not to fight, at least not on the days of my classes, because I could not concentrate. The English classes were no good for me. I knew how to read and spell. What I needed was lessons in conversation. But then, classes were hardly going to tackle that. When the confidence is beaten out of a person, when she can't defend herself from abuse, how can she learn to talk in a foreign language? But at least the classes got me out of the house.

I wanted to work, and my sister Dev advised Deepak to let me. If I was earning money we would be able to buy our own house, and that might bring peace. But Deepak was adamant that no wife of his was going to work when he could provide, and certainly not in a factory. He said he wanted me to better myself, but the environment was not conducive to study. I was also in two minds. I didn't want to work in a factory either, because I was afraid that if I started I would be forever caught up in that treadmill. On the other hand, it would at least be an escape from my mother-in-law and her taunts.

Shortly afterwards it was the fast of *Karwa Chauth*, kept by women seeking a long life for their husbands. One would normally fast for a man who cared for you, not someone who treated you like his slippers. You would eat at dawn and then not again until the moon came out. However, at 4 p.m. your mother-in-law would give you a glass of sweet lassi (buttermilk). I thought Deepak's mother would insist that I keep the fast. I was so weak in those days, and so dependent on tea, that I didn't think I would last out for twelve hours without food or drink. I hesitantly said this to her, and was pleasantly surprised to hear her say that I needn't fast if I didn't want to. Besides, she articulated what I was thinking: 'What is the point of fasting for a man like him? I don't keep this fast either. Why should I, for a man who has given me no happiness, made me work long hours, used my money for gambling and drink and turned me into a production line with six children?' She just asked me to do the rituals and eat at sunset as if I had fasted. I was supposed to throw a glass of water when the moon rose, touch her feet, get her blessings and then eat.

When Deepak came home that evening he lost his temper over something, dragged me up to the boxroom and shouted that I was not to go to college any more, that he knew my real reasons for going, that I was telling Kamlesh all about his family. He was going to ask Kamlesh about what I had said. I pleaded with him not to. I was so full of anger that I threw the glass of water out before the moon rose.

Every time we had a major row, he would cut work on the pretext of being sick. He wanted to keep an eye on me, to make sure that I didn't run away, that I didn't ring my family and complain about him. Even when he had had a fight with his mother, he would stay at home to make sure that she didn't pick on me.

One evening when they had had a fight, his mother threatened to take it out on me. Deepak told her to leave me alone. She said, 'Your wife is also my daughter-in-law.' Deepak threatened to humiliate her at the factory if he found out that she had said a word to me while he was at work. When she went to work that evening, I told Deepak I was really scared at the prospect of what might happen the following day. Deepak got up, put on his outdoor clothes and said he was going to the factory. He warned his mother in front of all her colleagues that she must not ill-treat me under any circumstances. She didn't talk to me when she came home the next morning. She thought I had put him up to it. Did she not understand that I was frightened even of Deepak's shadow?

She complained loudly to Daddy that she had a savage son, and now she had a daughter-in-law who made matters even worse. Daddy tried to defend me by saying that I was really saintly, that I hardly said anything. My mother-in-law replied, 'She may be quiet, but she sharpens her knives behind the scenes. She's taken Deepak fully in hand.' When she went up to her bedroom, I went downstairs. My father-in-law put his hand on my head. With tears in his eyes he said he understood my grief and he was sorry. He was afraid that what his family were doing to me would rebound on him as a curse.

EIGHT

Thrown Out

A MONTH AFTER our wedding, Deepak started taking me to
Dev's house in London for the weekend. Irritated, my mother-
in-law would say, 'She's your sweetmeat, isn't she? Put her in
your mouth, put her in your pocket and take her everywhere.'
Her meaning was vulgar, and I would feel embarrassed by her
comments in front of my father-in-law and grown-up brothers-
in-law. Deepak would reply that he was taking me away from
the battlefield to rest. I was thrilled. Perhaps he cared for me
after all. I used to forget his beatings and anger at such times.

When we came back from one such weekend, we noticed
that the dishes had been piled up in the kitchen. Deepak,
between gritted teeth, forbade me to touch even one plate,
saying that I was not the family servant. I kept saying that
it wouldn't take very long, and that it would be best if
Deepak didn't make a huge issue of it. They were also my family.
Deepak felt it would set a bad precedent, and that they would
leave it for me all the time. In front of Deepak, his parents
wouldn't have the guts to ask me to make a cup of tea, but
when he was at work I was almost always in the kitchen.

He went into every bedroom, shouting, 'Why have you not
washed up after you? You've left it for my wife, haven't you?
She is not your servant, she will obey me and me only. If I find
out that Kiran washed even one plate, I will break every plate,
every cup in this house. Don't think that I won't find out
because l will be at work. Kiran will be beaten if she doesn't
tell me the truth.' He reinforced his point by banging on the

doors. The next morning when I went into the kitchen the washing up had been done. I don't know who did it.

One weekend when we were at Dev's I was sitting on the bed next to Deepak – Dev used to give up her bedroom for us. I don't know what got into him, but he got up and raped me. He wouldn't get off until the lustful devil which had hold of him had been satisfied. Why did he have to rip my shirt and trousers? He must have felt that was the only way around my regular refusals. If this was love, where were the playfulness and affection? I told him that the next time he tore my clothes, I would show them to his mother. I kept the shirt and trousers for just such an occasion. I extracted a promise that we would never have sex in my sister's house again.

Deepak didn't like me going into the kitchen to help Dev because he suspected me of telling her negative things about his family. Dev started resenting the fact that I didn't help out. In those days she worked hard in a factory all week, she went out of her way to cook a nice meal and entertain us generously at the weekends, and she couldn't even expect a little help from her sister. Because Deepak didn't eat meat on Saturdays, the day of Hanuman worship, Dev and Sukhjit jijaji used to wait up till midnight to have their evening meal so as to accommodate him.

On one occasion we took Manju with us to Dev's, thinking it would be a break for her. I was sitting on the floor in front of the television when Deepak rudely told me to get up. I ignored him. Sukhjit jijaji could see from my face that I was upset, and asked whether I had had a fight with Deepak. Deepak was furious that I had communicated my problems by sitting there with a long face. He shouted at me so much that Dev lost her temper with him. She asked why he squashed me flat for such petty things, why he had reduced me to a pale, thin, quivering mass in two months. Deepak said something rude to her and I asked her to keep quiet. I didn't want her to provoke him into saying something worse which would hurt her feelings.

A man who can abuse his own mother and catch his own father by the scruff of the neck can have no respect for his wife's sister. No one ate their meal.

I expected Deepak to take his revenge when we got back to Crawley. I sat quietly all the way back. On the way the car broke down. Manju and I got out and pushed the car while Deepak screamed abuse at us. Strangely, when we got home Deepak didn't utter a word.

On another occasion we took Ranjit chachaji with us. Dev had started matchmaking between the various young girls and boys in her circle, and chachaji talked about those who were available in his circle. Deepak lost his temper with both of them, asking his uncle what right he had to discuss their family with anyone else. Dev tried to defend their discussions, but Deepak started shouting. Everyone fell into a shocked silence. The next morning Dev had made breakfast for all of us. Deepak wouldn't let his uncle eat, but insisted on dragging him away there and then. 'These are my relatives. You have no right to talk to them,' he said. Dev asked Deepak why he had brought his uncle if he didn't want him to mix with them. Chachaji kept completely quiet.

Although by now Dev knew that I was unhappy, she couldn't do anything about it. Her hands were tied because she was in her husband's home, not her own. She was not about to advise me to divorce Deepak and live with her, but she told him, 'We haven't sold her to you, we have given her in marriage.' Deepak always shouted back when Sukhjit jijaji was not around. He said, 'Keep your sister, if you want her.' If I became single again, the old burden of being a burden to my family would come back to haunt me. I would be accused by my community of being a woman without character. These chains of character, divorce, *izzat*, family were tying me down. And because I had started believing that this was my destiny, I felt it was pointless trying to change things.

Chachaji didn't visit us for a few days, and after a bit Deepak went and apologised. But a leopard cannot hide his spots, and by the fifth or sixth weekend Deepak had upset Dev and Sukhjit jijaji to such an extent that they said they would welcome me on my own, but not with him. Their children, who were six and thirteen, asked that Deepak should never visit again. Even little children could see him for what he was. Deepak started taunting me that I liked going to my sister's so that I could gossip about him. He didn't believe my denials. He didn't realise how fear had scotched my mouth. After that, I told him I didn't want to go to London. I'd rather confine the battles to Crawley.

One Friday Dev phoned and said they would come and drive us down to London the next day because we hadn't visited for a few weekends. They felt that I needed a break from my miserable life in Crawley, so they ignored Deepak's recent behaviour. I couldn't refuse out of respect for Dev. Daddy asked what we should cook, and I said it would be nice to buy some meat and make *kheema*. I knew that Sukhjit jijaji liked beer, so I asked Deepak to buy some when they arrived. He lost his temper. 'Bitch!' he screamed. 'You know I don't drink, and yet you want me to buy booze. Why couldn't you ask Daddy? I'll break this rolling pin over your head.' He frogmarched me up to the box-room, picked up a half-open suitcase which had our clothes in for the weekend and threw it hard against the door. Unknown to us, my sister was in the toilet, and when she heard this commotion she came into the room to find out what was going on.

I was sitting there controlling my tears. Dev tried to placate Deepak, saying, 'Come on, let's go away for the weekend. You'll feel much better for it.' She was sixteen years older than him, but because he was the *jamai* (family's son-in-law) she was speaking with respect, adding 'ji' to his name every time she addressed him. Deepak kicked the door and said he was not coming. She persuaded him to join us downstairs anyway.

Deepak went out and bought the beer, but he had spoiled our mood. On the way to London I sat very quietly in the car, wiping away the tears. Sukhjit jijaji's remark, 'Poochi, which world are you lost in?' incurred Deepak's wrath. When we got to their house Deepak started on his mother, calling her a bitch and saying that she was giving me a hard time. I couldn't tell my sister that the son was no better. Dev admonished Deepak for showing no respect for his mother.

Deepak wanted us to live separately from the rest of his family. Dev advised him not to do it just yet, because we were newly married, and everyone, including his mother, would say that I had snatched their son from them. Dev felt I should start working so we could save money and buy a house. I wanted to move because I felt there would be more peace without my mother-in-law around. Deepak also felt there was a wall between him and his family, and that maybe a separation would make the wall less visible.

Within three months of my marriage, I became pregnant. I didn't realise it at first. The family rows would give me a runny tummy or bouts of vomiting, so when I started having morning sickness I didn't recognise it for what it was. I thought maybe the different style of cooking didn't suit me. I hadn't been keeping track of my periods, and I didn't really understand the connection between the two things. But I knew one thing – I did not want this monster's children. Deepak wouldn't let me take the pill because he said it would make me fat. I had no control over the use of condoms. He would buy them or not, use them or not, as he wished. I had no rights. We went to the doctor, who asked me to return with a urine sample the following day. I offered to give him one there and then, which amused Deepak no end.

One weekend I was feeling so sick and claustrophobic that I went into the garden to vomit. The kitchen window was open, and I overheard Deepak's mother and Pummi talking. His mother said, 'The world will know that she is pregnant if she goes into the garden to be sick.'

I was losing a lot of weight and feeling very weak. Deepak

had bought some medicine to curb my sickness, but the medicine itself made me ill. He used to force me to take it, and one day I just vomited it out in the corner of my bedroom. Then, during a family row, he threw all three bottles of the medicine against the wall, smashing them to smithereens and leaving sticky trails down the wall. The fight was over money. His mother wanted more than £20 a week from Deepak now that he was married. Deepak refused, saying that I hardly ate anything and that I didn't work, so he couldn't part with more. In everyone's hearing he ordered me not touch any food in the house again. There I was, feeling so ill, and these were Deepak's instructions. I knew that he wouldn't check up on me, but I didn't want to touch any food as a matter of principle and pride.

When Deepak calmed down he wiped all the surfaces clean, then demanded money from his mother to buy some more medicine. She refused, saying, 'I didn't ask you to break the bottles.'

In those days I wanted to commit suicide. I wanted to jump under a train. What kind of husband had I got? He would neither let me live nor die. Day and night he sucked my bones. Only at his will could I laugh or go out for fresh air. He was the hangman's noose that dangled forever in front of me.

I persuaded Deepak to let me have an abortion, saying that we could hardly bring up a child in a boxroom on the £80 a week that he brought home. When we had our own house, we would have children. He agreed, and we went to Brighton and had it done privately. Deepak made me swear that I would not tell his mother. He took the day off work and sat in the car while my womb gave up its contents. When we got home he sent me up to my room and made some excuse to his parents. They never had the courage to ask him anything anyway.

Moves were afoot to get Pummi married. One morning when I came downstairs I noticed that there was intense cleaning going on. Daddy told me that a man from India called Paul was coming to see Pummi. Paul was from Punjab, and we hit it off extremely well. Pummi and Paul agreed to marry within a week.

When I went to meet Deepak that evening at work, I told him the happy news. He asked if I had been with them. When I said yes, he erupted. 'How dare you participate without my permission? When we get home I'll crush that spirit out of you. That'll teach you.' I tried to defend myself, saying that it would have looked bad if I had just sat upstairs. Every step of mine became filled with lead. I didn't want to go home.

I went straight up to our room. Deepak yelled, 'Mamma, I am the eldest son. I should not only have been informed about today, you should have asked for my advice. You have always excluded me from family affairs. How did you dare to involve my wife then?' Deepak's parents tried to explain that they had had no idea that Pummi and Paul would agree to the marriage. It had only been a preliminary visit. Deepak said that neither he nor I would attend the wedding. Pummi started crying. All our happiness had turned to ash. Deepak warned me that if I partook in the festivities, or even said hello to the man or his family, he would break my legs. His mother said there was no need for either of us to be present. 'Bastard,' she said to Deepak. 'There is never a moment's peace when you are in the house. What example are you setting for your other brothers and sisters? Get out of this house, the both of you.' I was grateful to God that I didn't get beaten that day. Deepak's mother blamed me the next day for his anger. She said that I had put him up to it, that behind my silence I was a sharp operator.

Paul and his family were invited over for a meal before the registry office wedding. Deepak argued about this, and then took me into town to avoid the meal. We got back at 5 p.m. or so, and were sitting in the car when Paul came up and asked me to wind the window down, as he wanted to say something to Deepak. Deepak said, 'Don't you dare put that window down.' I was so embarrassed. I was caught between the two. I had to ignore a simple request from Paul, and I couldn't even explain why. Paul could see that Deepak was shouting at me. Deepak reversed the car and drove around the block.

The day before the wedding, I was worried about what people would think if I spent the entire day in my room. My mother-in-law had said to me, to the complete amazement of Narinder chachiji, Ranjit chacha's wife, that I should go away to Dev's for the day rather than hang around and embarrass her. I was petrified, because I didn't know how to get about in London and because Deepak would not approve of my going without his permission. Mamma spent the whole day trying to persuade me to go away before Deepak came home that night. Chachiji was shocked that Mamma should be saying such things to a new daughter-in-law. After that I went upstairs. I had been feeling feverish all day but I had not dared to go into the kitchen to make myself a cup of tea, although I was dying for one. Manju made me one when she came home from work, and I thanked her effusively, with tears welling up in my eyes.

On the day of the marriage Deepak took time off work, saying he was going to attend Pummi's wedding. Right up until the previous night he had warned me to keep away, that he would break my legs if I went, and then suddenly he decided that we were going. On the morning of the Sikh ceremony I wanted to get up and help, but Deepak wouldn't let me. He said that neither of us were going. All the relatives had gathered, the groom and his family arrived and the *milni*, the exchange of garlands between bride and groom, took place. I missed all of this. Suddenly Deepak barked an order at me to get dressed because we were going after all. In the photographs of the wedding he is smiling and dancing with Paul as if nothing had happened.

Pummi went to live with her husband, and the fighting caused by her presence decreased. But Deepak's fights with his mother more than made up for Pummi's departure. One day they had a huge row, and Deepak poked her repeatedly on the forehead with his index finger. She warned him to stop. Deepak told me to go upstairs unless I wanted to be beaten. I ran upstairs, but saw him going into the kitchen saying, 'Today, I will kill the bastard.' His mother told me that he picked up two kitchen knives. His trousers were rolled up and he was shifting his weight from foot to foot like a boxer ready to do battle. 'Come on,' he said, 'I won't let go of you today. I will kill you today.' Daddy tried to separate them, but Deepak pushed him aside. I could hear Mamma's cries. Through the boxroom window I saw her run out into the street, screaming for help. She had no shoes, no *chunni*, and her hair was dishevelled. She tried to get passing cars to stop, but none of them did. Then she banged on the neighbours' door, begging them to let her in and to call the police.

What kind of a son was this, and what kind of a mother? Knowing what an ogre he was, I couldn't understand why she provoked him. He was forcing his mother to run on the streets, barefooted. Little did I know that one day I would be doing the same. That day, for the first time, I saw Daddy lose his temper. He told Deepak to get out, that he would not tolerate him in the house for one minute longer. Deepak said, 'This is my house, too. Give me my share and I will get out.' Daddy said, 'I want the keys right now, otherwise I will call the police and have you arrested.'

Deepak told me to come down. He gave the keys to his father and we left. Where were we to go?

NINE

Nowhere to Run

DEEPAK AND I WENT to stay at Ranjit chachaji's house. I would sit there all day, but at night, when his parents were at work, Deepak would take me back to his house. His brothers or sisters would let us in, and we would leave early in the morning before his parents got home.

Deepak asked chachaji, who was a supervisor in the factory, to help us find a room. Chachaji had a good reputation and a wide network of contacts, and he found us a place behind my college within two days. Deepak told them that his mother was making life hell for me, and chachaji told him that he had to change his ways. He didn't want him to ruin their reputation by fighting with anyone.

On the day we moved, the car wouldn't start, and I had to push it. In India a daughter-in-law would never be expected to do work of this kind. Here I was, a woman who had lived in relative wealth, and today I was homeless and pushing my husband's second-hand car.

We didn't have a quilt, so Deepak asked his mother if he could borrow one. At first she refused, saying she didn't have any to spare. Deepak promised to return it as soon as we had bought our own. In fact, I have it to this day.

We paid £12 a week for our room, and shared the kitchen, toilet and bathroom. As we didn't have any utensils the landlady, who was a Gujarati, let us use hers temporarily. We went to Southall and bought pots and pans, some of which I still use today. It was an enjoyable day, buying things to set up house.

We were starting our life together. Deepak drew up a menu of what should be cooked on each day of the week. It featured all his favourite foods.

We spent a night at Dev's, and she stressed that we mustn't behave in a way that would spoil the family name. Tommy phoned from Newcastle. He wasn't very happy about us moving out, and Deepak didn't tell him what he had done to warrant the eviction. He just kept complaining about his mother. I told Deepak that we must live in peace, that life was too short for rows. I thought that there wouldn't be any fights when we lived on our own because I wouldn't let them happen, and there would be no third person to provoke Deepak.

Two weeks passed peacefully. Tommy phoned in the third week to find out how we were coping. When I told Deepak, he was annoyed. He thought I must be using such opportunities to complain about him, and said that from now on Tommy must phone only when he was at home. When Tommy rang next, I told him about Deepak's suspicions and gave him Deepak's times at work. Tommy never phoned again in his absence, such was his concern for my happiness. Deepak didn't like my family writing to me either, unless they wrote in English.

Our room was close to the library, and one afternoon Paul dropped by after returning a book. When Deepak heard about this, he was angry. 'He has no business coming here. He comes here because he likes you because you are good-looking and humorous. He shouldn't visit when the man is at work. Tell that *singha* [lion] not to visit unless I'm at home.' I was very upset by these allegations, but I relayed Deepak's message to Paul. He was shocked by Deepak's dirty thoughts. I told Paul I was very unhappy. On another occasion Deepak said, 'That *singha* was staring at your figure. I know he likes you and you like him.' I said, 'If that's what you believe, then don't allow him to come here again.'

Some days later we ran out of milk, so I went into Crawley town with our landlady to buy some. We bumped into two of

Deepak's aunts, and when I told him about this he was furious. 'Don't you dare go into Crawley again without me. You'll bump into my relatives and they'll set you against my family.' Apart from my classes, I never again went into town without Deepak. When I told my landlady that I couldn't accompany her any more, she couldn't understand why Deepak should object to me going out with another woman.

I was stuck in that one room all day for eight months. Even my prison cell was less confining than the days I spent there. In jail there were officers and other prisoners with whom I could talk and laugh, but in that room I was alone. We had no TV, and all day I would sit and listen to the radio. I had stopped writing to my family in India. I could not tell them my innermost feelings, and I couldn't write purely superficial letters. When Bindhi praji wrote, worried that they had not heard from me, Deepak was angry that I was showing them how unhappy I was by my silence. So on his instructions I wrote to them, pretending that all was well.

One day I told Deepak I would make rice and *daal* for lunch – he used to come home from work at lunchtime, and we would sit on the floor, spread out some newspapers and eat our meal. But the cauliflower was rotting, so I made a vegetable curry instead. Deepak asked why I had made this when I had promised something else. 'Are you making a fool of me? You eat this, I won't eat it,' he screamed. I burst into tears, and said I would make rice and *daal* in the evening.

He did the same again when I put too much chilli in something by mistake. 'Bitch, eat this. You like chillies, yes? Let's see how you put this in your mouth. I'll tear your mouth open if you don't.' When I started putting the food in my mouth he said, 'If you dare eat it, I'll break your legs.' I sat there with the food between my fingers, my hand shaking, hovering between my mouth and the plate, not knowing what would anger him more. Should I eat it or not? I was crying like a child. He didn't hit me, but he frightened me so much that I couldn't eat. He went back to work, and I spent the whole afternoon weeping. When he returned in the evening, he behaved as if nothing had happened. I had cried for five hours and he was behaving normally. He said I was mad to cry over such little things. Either he didn't realise the impact his words had on me or he was enjoying the torture in which I was trapped like an animal. From that day on I would start shaking just before he came home, in case he manufactured an argument. I used to make sure that his lunch was ready on time because he had only half an hour in which to drive home and eat. And yet I could not please him. When he arrived home I would beg him, 'Don't hit me.' Sometimes unpredictably he would give me a cuddle, saying, 'Don't be silly.' What did he want?

In the middle of another row, when I threatened to go to the police, Deepak behaved in his usual sadistic manner. I tried to put a foot outside the front door but he stood in front of me shouting, 'Let's see how you run, bitch. Run, go on, run.' As I took a step outside he said, 'If you go, I'll break this milk bottle and plunge it in your stomach.' When I withdrew he said, 'I'll cut your legs in half if you dare to come back inside.' He enjoyed keeping me dangling over a precipice. I said, 'If you want to kill me, go ahead, but don't leave me hovering between life and death. Finish the job. I don't want to live this dog's life.' I don't know whether this had an impact on him, but he became calm and we went inside.

One day he was criticising my brothers, which really annoyed me, so I asked him to stop. He hit me on the face with his *kada*, and within seconds my eye swelled up. As a reflex action I scratched his face and drew blood. That was the first time I had protected myself. I told him not to push me so far again. I was lucky that his *kada* came down a fraction of an inch away from my eye, otherwise my eye would have burst open with the impact. I told him I would leave him unless he took off his *kada*. He did, and I hid it. I was weeping with fear of what he would do to me for daring to lift my hand against him, but he backtracked. 'You've been saved today. Otherwise I would have ground your bones into a chutney.'

I said I would call the police next time. A woman I knew had called the police when her husband had beaten her, but the police hadn't really wanted to get involved, as it was a 'domestic'. The next time the husband gave his wife quite a thrashing, and there were marks on her face. She called the police again, and this time a policeman took the husband aside and said, 'You want to beat your wife without getting caught, hit her on the head like this, so as not to leave any marks.' Having heard that, I was too scared to call the police. I didn't think Deepak needed any further lessons in violence, invisible or otherwise.

The next day, we had a phone call that Pummi was in hospital. She had miscarried. We hadn't even known she was pregnant. Deepak said we should go to the hospital. I didn't want to go looking like I did, and we both tried unsuccessfully to hide the marks on our faces with cream. Deepak's mother asked what had happened, and I told her. She said, 'Now there's no mother to upset the apple cart. What's going wrong now? You see, he won't let anyone live in peace.' When she asked Deepak for his version, he said, 'Ask that timid, innocent little thing sitting next to you.' She said he must have provoked it. The family now knew that things were still much the same for me, even though we had moved out. Although I told Mamma that Deepak was beating me, I could not reveal my deepest feelings: how unhappy I was, how I wanted to leave him. My muteness used to make me very angry. I was trapped in this devil's clutches.

When we went shopping I was not allowed to pack the things, because I didn't do it well enough, nor would Deepak let me carry the bags. No matter how much shopping we did, he would carry all of it. I was only allowed to carry my handbag. Once when the shop was really busy I started packing to hurry things along, and Deepak told me off in Punjabi. I was embarrassed because people were fuming with impatience and wondering what kind of wife I was, just hanging around and not helping out. When we came out he flung one of the bags on the ground, and a bottle broke. Some young kids started laughing. I just stood there, helpless and immobile. Suddenly I saw a couple of policemen. As Deepak caught my eyes straying in their direction he quickly picked up the shopping and took me home.

My mother-in-law had arranged readings from the *Granth Sahib* over a weekend. This is usually arranged as a form of thanksgiving or to ask for the fulfilment of a wish or God's blessing for family plans. Some families hold it once a year. The reading of 1400 pages must be carried out uninterrupted over three days and two nights by four or five priests, reading in shifts of two hours. If the priest wants something done he bangs with a spoon and gestures, while carrying on reading. Family friends and relations come and go during the three days, and at the end of the reading everyone gathers for a big meal. I told Deepak I should help his mother out, as she was on her own. It was my duty. Besides, I had nothing to do, and I wanted to hear the readings. I asked him not to fight with his family when we went there because I was the one who would be upset.

That evening, when Deepak was getting ready to go home, I said that I would stay and help. The readings would go on all night, and his mother would need help in providing refreshments for the priests. She and I would stay up half the night each. Deepak was not pleased. In front of the visitors he started shouting, 'Keep her here!' Mamma said that prayers are supposed to bring peace to the house, and that he was destroying her honour by behaving like this. She asked me to go with him, but I insisted on helping her out. He banged the door as he left.

The next day I told Pummi that I would go home to have a bath and a change of clothes. Pummi advised me to take someone with me to protect me from Deepak's wrath. She was too scared herself, and Mamma was too busy, so I went on my own. Deepak's temperature was riding high. He started shouting, 'Why have you come back? Go and live with my mother. You obviously prefer them to me.' He started pushing me out of the room and threatened to beat me. I decided to go to the police. When I saw my chance I ran down the stairs and out on to the street. Deepak came running after me.

I ran for dear life, in fear that he would not let me live if he caught me, that he would beat me to a pulp. The police station was at least fifteen minutes away, and I was getting tired. Deepak caught up with me and grabbed me by the hair, then hit me on the head so hard that I fainted on the footpath. When my eyes opened, the first thing I saw was him looking at me. My head was in his lap and a white man was standing nearby. I didn't know that Deepak had already asked another white man to phone his parents. He stood me up and got me home. My feet were filled with lead. I was dreading the return. Our landlady would find out the true state of affairs between us. Deepak said, 'You were running to the police, weren't you? You want a divorce? Okay. My parents are coming. Today I will divorce you. I will grind you to a paste in front of them.' Mamma, Daddy and an uncle arrived at our room shortly after us. Their faces were lined with fear; they didn't know what Deepak had done to me when the man rang and said I was lying on the footpath. They asked how I was. I started crying. Deepak said I was running to the police. Because the uncle was there I couldn't talk freely and let the family secrets out. They were very angry that while prayers were going on at home, Deepak was doing his *tamasha* (drama).

A couple of days later Deepak took me out in the car. He was driving so fast and recklessly that I was quivering with fear. He didn't say anything. He took me down the motorway towards Brighton, the same road we had travelled for my abortion. Suddenly he pulled up on the hard shoulder, screamed 'Get out, get out, you bastard,' and whacked me one. 'You like running, don't you? Today I will make you run, I will kill you.' He was banging on the steering wheel. I didn't dare get out – there were woods out there, he might tear my clothes, he might humiliate me, he might kill me. I prayed for a police car to pass, but they're never around when you need them. I pleaded for mercy, and said I would never run to the police again.

I was sobbing loudly, like a child. I felt all the hopelessness of an animal being pursued by a hunter. That scene is embedded in my mind. I remember every second of it. Those woods still flash by in front of me, catching me unawares and ruining my happiness. This is one of the memories from my marriage which will haunt me all my life. After ten minutes of banging and shouting and my heartbroken pleas, Deepak calmed down and drove back to Crawley. When we got home, he made tea and behaved normally.

I had no way out. Divorce carried such a stigma. If I lived on my own, I would be condemned by society. If I lived with my family, I would be a burden to them. I was settling into a pattern: Deepak would be violent, I would cry in response, then after four or five days I would cool down, but I would remain depressed. Depression became a constant feature of my life. Only the degree varied. What had I done to deserve this? I could understand it if I had behaved immorally, smoked and drunk in pubs. But I was doing none of this. I hardly talked, and this was how I was being rewarded. I couldn't even behave freely with my husband's family without arousing his anger. I wanted to show my brothers, who went around proudly claiming that I was their *izzat*, how their *izzat* was being made to run in the jungle. At the time of our wedding my brothers had said to Deepak, 'This is our beloved sister. Look after her carefully. Don't let her be unhappy,' words which were forever flung in my face by Deepak's taunts.

After throwing me into the depths of depression, Deepak would force me to use make-up to hide my sadness from the world. It irritated him to see me sitting with a long face. He instructed me to laugh and be happy. Once we went to Ranjit chachaji's for a meal, and he warned me not to give them the faintest indication that I was unhappy. 'Remember,' he said, 'you have to return home with me after all.' When we arrived, it was obvious that we hadn't been invited. Deepak was just trying to get me out of the house. He couldn't take me home to his family because I'd spill the beans there. Tears were welling up in my eyes all the time. I was scared that my façade would crack. Chachiji looked at me and said, 'I know you're not happy. I can see that he is harassing you.' She started on Deepak, and when Ranjit chachaji told her to keep quiet she replied that she would not be silenced by fear. I sat there, breaking up inside and trying to keep a lid on my pain. She kept talking. The woods were flashing past in front of my eyes, the steering wheel was shuddering from the impact of his blows. I knew Deepak's eyes were bulging with ferocity in his attempt to control my actions.

When I went into the kitchen to help chachiji, my heart was crying out to say to her, 'Ring my brothers and tell them that I am unhappy.' But I couldn't. Even now I get so angry when I think how mad I was to suffer in silence. I couldn't sleep for fear, couldn't eat for fear, fear when my brothers or sisters phoned, fear of Deepak's return from work, fear of weekends – fear, fear, fear, it paralyses you beyond belief. I used to try and tell him when his mood seemed all right that he should not go on like a cassette, that I might become so immune to what he said that it would no longer have any impact on me, that I might lose all respect for him. I told him that he only had to say one word to get me to change my behaviour. How long could he control me? I could always run away while he was at work. I wanted to tell Deepak's parents that I was unable to uphold the family honour as a daughter-in-law should while all this was going on. I wanted to tear myself open, inside out, and reveal all that lay inside.

The cassette recorder used to be on endlessly, driving me crazy. Sometimes, like a child, Deepak would spend hours putting cassettes in and taking them out again, with loud clicking noises that hurt my head, unable to decide what he wanted to hear. When he drove his car he would let out loud yells of delight, 'Whoopee, wheye . . . eee . . . ee!' like a cowboy, driving recklessly and delighting in the speeds he could reach.

One afternoon we had to go to the council for our housing assessment interview, and Deepak was coming back early from work for this appointment. As chance would have it, that day my landlady wanted me to look after her children. She hardly ever asked, and I felt that I couldn't refuse because she was returning at least an hour before we had to leave. I told her to make sure that she returned on time, but despite all her assurances she was half an hour late. Deepak was furious. He wanted to know if I did babysitting on the side. We didn't owe her anything, we were paying rent, we weren't living off her charity. Why couldn't I have said no when he had told me ten times to be ready on time. It was my weakness that I said yes to everybody to please them, and yet I pleased nobody.

When the landlady returned, I told her that her lateness had led to a quarrel between Deepak and me. She was so upset that from that day on until the day we left, she never spoke to me again. Even my few sessions watching TV with her downstairs came to an end. Nor would she let her husband eat my *khichri* (rice and pulses cooked together), which he used to enjoy, any more. For the first time I had been assertive, and what a response I got. I couldn't explain to her what a devil of a husband I had.

At the assessment interview I was in tears because I so desperately hoped that, in the privacy of our own house, our battles might come to an end. We would be busy decorating, and that might be a focus for our energies. Those daily rows had left blisters across my brain. I felt like an open, throbbing wound which bled at the slightest touch.

I sat my English and typing tests, and failed them. I was scared that Deepak would get angry, but he joked about it. He rang my brother Tommy and informed him that I had got two diplomas. Although I laughed, I was upset that I could not pass such easy tests when I had passed my BA under such difficult circumstances. But then, I had failed in life too – as a wife and a daughter-in-law. The word failure was printed across my brain.

I was petrified of getting pregnant. I wanted to bring up children in a home full of happiness, to teach them manners and understanding of our culture and respect for their elders, none of which Deepak had. Ours is a culture that imprisons women, while allowing men the freedom to do what they like. They have neither the barrier of religion nor that of *izzat* standing in their way. Only women are made to suffer like this. There are hundreds of thousands of women who are tied down by these restrictions. I might have the label 'murderer' hanging around my neck, but I think I have escaped lightly compared to those women whose legs have been broken, whose bodies are scarred with burns and stab wounds. Why do men behave like this? I couldn't understand why I couldn't break these chains. I was educated. I could have stood on my own two feet. But these cultural restraints proved unbreakable. When a daughter is born in our society, it is a matter of grief. She is a drain, she will have to be fed and educated and clothed, and then a dowry will have to be found for her so that she can become an asset in someone else's home. And she is the vehicle for the *izzat* of the whole family, whether the one into which she was born or the one into which she marries. This *izzat* is the noose around her neck. It curtails her freedom to study, to work, to do what she wants, because family honour is always at stake. This *izzat* kills her off, bit by bit.

After the abortion, the nurse had told me about various methods of contraception. I couldn't understand anything.

Deepak didn't let me have a coil inserted. If he ran out of condoms, he didn't care. I would refuse him on these occasions. Sometimes he would catch me by the throat, and sometimes he would let me be. Once when I refused him he slapped himself, he was so angry. I couldn't work him out. He used to say that Hanuman came to him and made him lose control, just like women did when they got their periods.

Sometimes when I threatened to leave him he would kneel at my feet, take my hand and say, 'Go on, slap me, strangle me, get the frustration out of your system. Forgive me, please don't leave me, please don't tell anyone what happens beween us.' I couldn't hit him. That is not to say that I was not tempted. Some days I was so angry I wanted to accept his invitation. But fear of further beatings stayed my hand. I said I wanted us to achieve equality, not by me being as violent as him, but by him controlling his temper as well as I did.

Of course, there were days without fights. We would go for a walk every evening, and Deepak would tell me about the day's events. We drew up a budget for our household expenditure: insurance, food, rent, fares – and a little put by for a new place.

That year we decided to go to Newcastle to stay with Tommy and his family for Christmas. One night while we were there Deepak started on me, saying that he knew I told my brother everything. I swore that I hadn't, but he didn't believe me. He put his fingers around my neck and started squeezing the breath out of me. I felt a certain amount of confidence because I was in my brother's house, and I knew Tommy would sort him out. I grabbed his neck as well, and said, 'Come on, I'll show you how much it hurts.' As they say, even a dog is a tiger in his own street. Deepak's eyes popped open and he released his fingers – a woman who normally quivered when she set eyes on him was holding him by the neck. He apologised, then clambered on top of me. What kind of love was this, with sex following a near-strangulation? Deepak would sit fully dressed on my chest trying to persuade me to take him into my mouth. He would threaten to tie my hands behind my back and have sex with me if I didn't agree. I felt sick at the very thought of it. Once he brought a blue movie home and there was a woman giving a man a blow-job on it. I was violently ill.

Just before midnight on New Year's Eve, Deepak went up to our room. I followed because I wanted to be the first to wish him a happy new year, as this was our first New Year's Eve together. He was looking through our suitcase. I hugged him but, inexplicably, he flung me violently aside and I fell on the bed. I was so shocked that my eyes rattled in their sockets. He apologised, but my mood was completely destroyed. He then forced me to have sex with him. This was a good start to the new year.

As it was the first time I had visited Tommy, he wanted to buy me a present. I didn't want one, because I didn't think he could afford it on his bus conductor's wages. But he insisted, saying I would only get lumbered with something I didn't like if I didn't choose it myself. After consulting Deepak, I bought some maroon winter boots. I didn't know that a storm was gathering inside him. Later he shouted at me, 'You want to show your brother that I can't afford to buy you boots. You never asked your husband for those. Don't you think I can afford them?' Those boots proved to be a millstone around my neck. For the next ten years I was taunted about them: 'Yes, you are the pet sister who's been spoilt by her brothers.'

In the new year, we started applying to go to Canada. Billoo praji had said that he would help Deepak set up a business repairing TVs and hi-fis. He was lonely out there, and wanted more of his family to join him. I wanted to be near Billoo and Surinder, and away from Deepak's family. In order to get a Canadian visa, we had to show that we had money and assets in England. Billoo said that we should arrange a paper transfer of Deepak's parents' house into Deepak's name, so that we could show that with the sale of the house we could start a business in Canada. But Daddy wouldn't agree to the transfer. He said he didn't trust Deepak. Deepak said that Daddy could keep the papers with him and that he would write a letter disowning the house, but Daddy still wouldn't agree. When he heard Deepak's story, Ranjit chachaji took him to a solicitor and got the paperwork done. He has such a big heart. I didn't blame Daddy, although I was upset by his decision.

In October 1980, the council offered us a house. The first place we saw was old and dilapidated, and in a part of Crawley where Asians had suffered from the racism of white neighbours who used to throw eggs at their houses. We moved into the second place we were offered.

TEN

Turning the Tables

THE HOUSE WAS newly built, with large rooms. It had three bedrooms, an attached garage and a tiny patch of grass at the front and back. We had accepted it because there was a direct bus to Mamma's house and we did not have a car. For the first six months we did not have any money to furnish it, as we were saving to go to Canada. There were no carpets, and we did not bother to decorate. We were using a broken-down fridge as a dining table, and we had a bed which we had bought just after our marriage, a couple of second-hand chairs and a shabby settee.

A few days after we moved in, Paul turned up. He and Pummi were being thrown out of their lodgings, and would need somewhere to stay for a couple of months. Deepak invited them to stay with us. When Deepak asked my opinion I declined to give one, saying that Pummi was his sister, and it was up to him. Whichever way I answered I would get into trouble. Paul said he didn't want their arrival to affect our marriage, but alarm bells went off in my mind. Mamma had already warned us, saying that a dog and a stone can never be friends.

One afternoon while we were asleep, the doorbell rang and there stood Pummi with her bedding and pots and pans. They had come earlier than expected. We agreed to shop and eat together and share the bills. This arrangement lasted two or three weeks, but then Paul and Pummi's money dried up. They would fight over the smallest things, and money was always an issue between them. Although Paul was earning well in the Post

Office on night shift, he used to make Pummi pay for half their shopping. He also liked to eat lavishly, so my work in the kitchen increased. Deepak and Pummi would constantly monitor how I behaved with Paul, how I laughed and chatted with him. I felt very self-conscious, like a prisoner in my own house. Unless everybody else was there, I would make sure I was upstairs if Paul was in the living room. One day Paul and Pummi had such a huge fight that Pummi went to stay with her mother. This meant that when Deepak was at work I was on my own with Paul. We both felt very uncomfortable. Pummi told her family that I had Deepak under my thumb, and that I must be making Paul happy. She thought we must fancy each other, and hoped I would tell Paul to go. But it was not my place to kick him out. I still had to cook the same grand meals for Paul, but I no longer had Pummi's help.

At about this time Deepak gave up his job as a machine operator in a plastics factory and started working as a guard with British Rail. In September 1981 I got a job at Bale & Church, a caustic soda factory. Mamma was already working there, and she had told me about the vacancy and got me an application form. I was thrilled at the thought of making new friends and having a change from the drudgery of housework. But at the back of my mind I was conscious that I had been put to work in the same place as Mamma so that she could keep an eye on me. I found that she was very unpopular at work.

I had never worked in my life before, so when I got home I often fell asleep on the sofa. Deepak would cook and wake me up for dinner, or tell me to go upstairs and sleep. He would even wash up. I would offer to do the dishes but he would say that I was not a servant. Sometimes he would make delicious and complicated snacks like samosas, muthis and sev, which he would lay before me. Because I was a fanatic for cleanliness, he would clean the kitchen and air the place so thoroughly that I couldn't even smell the fruits of his labour. He would try to persuade me to have a child now that we had a house and two pay packets coming in, but I kept refusing. He would then embarrass me by telling his mother that I refused to have his children.

One of the supervisors at the factory would make the Asian women workers wash her lunch dishes. They were too timid and knew too little English to stand up to her. One day she asked me to do it, and I refused. I always stood up for my principles when I was outside the house. It was not my job to do her dishes. The manager called me in and shouted at me. 'I'm not deaf,' I said. 'There's no need to raise your voice.' When I went home I told Deepak about it. He paid a visit to the manager, who apologised to me and told the supervisor not to make the other women do her dishes. I was a bit of a star at the factory after that.

Pummi came back, and she and Paul lived with us for three or four months. The fights continued. Deepak and Pummi also fought. It was not in my destiny to live a peaceful life. After a fight with Paul one day, Pummi wouldn't join us for dinner. I went to call her down, but to no avail. Paul was sitting there, sucking his meat bones with great relish, when Pummi came down screaming that no one cared about her. She upturned Paul's plate with its pile of bones onto his turban. Out tumbled all the Punjabi swearwords – 'Sisterfucker, motherfucker' – from Paul's mouth (interestingly, Deepak never used these words with me because he had only been exposed to his mother's bad words, and so he knew only the foul language used by women and not that used by men). The three of them began wrestling with each other while I cowered in the kitchen. Deepak dragged me into the fray, saying that I was the cause of the fighting because I had gone to call Pummi instead of letting sleeping dogs lie. Paul shouted to Deepak to leave me alone. Of course, that only strengthened Deepak's suspicions about Paul and me. He was alway linking our names. I threatened to leave Deepak, and asked him why he had invited Paul and Pummi to live with us. He beat me and shouted at me. I said I was going to ring my family, so he phoned his parents and asked them to mediate. When they arrived I was sitting in my bedroom, crying. I told them I couldn't live with Deepak any more, that he was linking my name with Paul. Deepak took off his shoe and hit me repeatedly on the head with it. His parents tried to pull him off me. I was covering my face and head and crying loudly.

Paul heard my cries and came to find out what was going on, but none of us were prepared to tell him that he was the cause of our fighting. Deepak took me downstairs so that we could discuss our problems with his family. I sat there, eyes down and head throbbing. Deepak perched a hot cup of tea precariously on my knee. The heat was uncomfortable. I was so full of hatred that all I could think of was throwing the tea in his face and smashing the cup on his head so that he too could experience pain. But of course I wanted to be the good girl, so I didn't.

I said I wanted to phone my brother. Deepak dialled Canada, although he knew that he could have rung Tommy in Newcastle. It would have been cheaper, but Tommy was closer, and would have got on a train to rescue me. Billoo praji was preoccupied with a nephew's wedding, and I felt really bad for spoiling his day. Deepak didn't tell him the whole story. All he said was that we had fought and that I wanted to leave him – nothing about the beatings or his treatment of me. Naturally Billoo praji was worried, and asked to speak to me. I didn't say much. Then my mother-in-law spoke to him. She said that nothing much had happened – 'The children are fighting' – and that she was going to smooth things over.

Billoo praji phoned Dev and Tommy, who rang later, when Deepak was not at home. I told him everything. He got very angry, and asked whether he should come and sort Deepak out. I asked him to leave it for now.

Paul and Pummi moved into their own house shortly after-wards. Even that was delayed, because they couldn't decide which area to move to. Paul didn't want to be close to his mother-in-law, while Pummi wanted to be as close to her as possible. Pummi won. After they left we received a telephone bill for £400. While we were at work Paul had been making calls to India and America. I didn't know how we would pay it. Deepak's guard's salary from British Rail wasn't much. Our electricity bills were also high because Paul would put the fan heater on all day in the living room while he made his calls. I didn't show the phone bill to Deepak immediately on his return from work, but waited till after he had had his tea. That delay was the cause of another row between us because Paul was not around for Deepak to vent his anger on him. Paul refused to accept his liability. Deepak complained to his parents, but they had no sympathy. He went to Paul's and Paul tried to slam the door in his face. Deepak's foot was in the door, and he forced it open. They started fighting, and Deepak picked up the telephone and put the wire around Paul's neck. Pummi called the police and her parents. Both Paul and Deepak had marks on their faces and bodies. Things had cooled down by the time the police arrived, so no charges were preferred.

Within six months of moving into our council house, our application to emigrate to Canada was turned down because of me. There had been an attempt to get me entry to the country when I was sixteen which hadn't worked out, and this affected our application. We used the money we had been saving to go to Canada to furnish our house. We bought carpets in burgundy, my favourite colour, an expensive hi-fi and other furniture. Deepak decorated the house while I slept, and made a wonderful storage area for his tools.

It was five years since I had left India, and I wanted to go back there for a holiday. I had decided that while I was there I would tell my brothers about Deepak and see whether they would agree to a separation or divorce. If Deepak dared raise his hand against me in India, I would slap him really hard. We arranged that he would go for six weeks or so, while I would stay for six months. I don't know why he agreed to let me stay for so long.

I started saving for our tickets, and opened a special account, but within a couple of weeks I was made redundant, and we had to postpone the trip. I was unemployed for nearly seven months, and then I heard that the factory was recalling all those who had been made redundant. When I wasn't contacted, I wondered whether the incident with the supervisor had ruined my chances. Deepak spoke to the manager, and I was reinstated.

Tommy was going to India, and he bought me an open ticket so I could go with him, and return when I liked. Billoo praji and his family were also going to be there at the same time as us. As the time for the trip approached I went shopping in Southall with Sulekha, a friend I had met through Pummi, buying dress material for all our relatives. I returned with three black sacks stuffed with textiles. Mamma wanted us to take a television for her brother, and said we couldn't go unless we agreed to it. There were a lot of quarrels. Deepak said the TV was too heavy, and would take up his entire luggage allowance. Mamma wanted us to leave all our things behind and take it instead. I was afraid that Deepak would agree. He asked her to reimburse him £1,200, the cost of his shopping, if she wanted him to leave it all behind. Of course she refused.

A few days before we went to India, Daddy phoned us and broke down. I knew it must be something serious because Deepak kept saying, 'Daddy, talk, say something. Why aren't you talking?' He had just heard from the hospital that he had a brain tumour, and didn't have long to live. When Deepak put the phone down he burst into tears.

The day before our departure, Surinder tried to phone from Canada to wish me a good trip, but Deepak had changed our telephone number without telling me, so that I could not receive calls from my family in his absence. Surinder phoned my mother-in-law, saying she could not get through to me. Mamma knew why but didn't explain, and said she would pass on the message. She rang Deepak and gave it to him. I was furious that our number had been changed without my knowledge, and also that Mamma wouldn't even give my sister's message directly to me. I asked Deepak why he was trying to break my links with my family. He was drinking a cup of hot tea, and he threw it at my leg. It broke against my shin and I started bleeding. Deepak tied a bandage around it and said he would tear my mouth apart if I didn't stop crying.

When we went to say goodbye to Deepak's family, I was boiling inside so much that I didn't even wish them goodbye properly. Daddy was ill in bed, and I was particularly upset at not having said goodbye to him when I suspected it might be the last time I saw him. I didn't wish Mamma goodbye at all. She said, 'There's no need for you to stay longer. You're going with him, you'd better come back quietly with him.'

We spent the night at Dev's, because it was closer to Heathrow. When Tommy arrived I showed him my leg and told him what had happened. I asked him not to raise it with Deepak, because I was going to get him sorted out in India. We had all been brought up in the belief that it was the responsibility of our older brothers to sort out our problems. If Tommy, as a man, felt he could do nothing without their permission, then perhaps my powerlessness as a woman can be understood by comparison.

We had a lot of luggage, and had to pay nearly £300 for excess baggage. Tommy persuaded Deepak to drink whisky on the plane, and for the first time, reluctantly, he drank alcohol. I joined him. I was really excited. We are a very close family, and I was looking forward to seeing all my nieces and nephews. When Tommy went to the loo I said to Deepak, 'Now it's my turn to show you.' He replied that he wouldn't have come if he'd known that was my intention, and I said coolly, 'Why don't you ask the pilot to turn around and take you back?' I had become a lioness. Now Deepak would understand what helplessness felt like.

When we got to Delhi, Bindhi praji took us to the Gurdwara (Sikh temple) straight from the airport, and we were given *prasad*, food that has been blessed. The next day we flew to Ahmedabad. At the airport there was a huge welcome committee, at least fifty members of my extensive family, garlands of flowers and a fleet of jeeps, cars, scooters and motorbikes. Deepak was astonished.

All my relatives were very impressed by Deepak's good looks. When they told me, 'You've found a hero,' I kept quiet. I wasn't about to tell them that he was as cruel as he was handsome. As the son-in-law of the family he was indulged by everyone. Deepak was amazed by the wealth – the large bungalows, the servants, the cars and scooters. He asked me why I hadn't told him about all this.

One evening my eighteen-year-old nephew was going off on his motorbike to pay a bill, and he asked me to accompany him. That was enough to set Deepak off. He refused to let me go. I was really upset. I thought, 'He has such a dirty mind. This is my nephew who I rocked in my lap as a baby. What's his problem?' My nephew's face fell. He understood.

I was roaming from one relative's house to another, free as a bird. Deepak wanted me to seek his permission, even in India. I didn't care, I was in my element. My older sister Narinder remonstrated with him once for fighting with me over small things. Deepak had no concept of respect for his elders, and I was embarrassed when he answered back and she started crying. He was beginning to show his true self. I would silence my relatives if they started talking about him. They soon realised that I was petrified of my husband. Tommy had also told my other brothers about the way he treated me.

One day I broke down in front of my brothers and pleaded with them to liberate me from Deepak before he killed me. I told them I had come to India to find a solution. Kuki praji said that in a fortnight, after the wedding of Raghvir praji's daughter Baboo, my niece, he would catch hold of Deepak and sort him out. I said even two weeks would be a long time, with Deepak monitoring every move I made.

The next day my five brothers and Deepak were seated at the table. Kuki praji said to Deepak, 'You know, you will have to appear in our court too. We have to make a decision about you.' Deepak lost his temper. 'What decision are you talking about? Let's sort it out right now.' He threw his full plate of food into the kitchen. 'I shall go back to London,' he said. Kuki praji said, 'You came of your own free will, you will return at our will. We won't let you return until we've sorted this thing out.' Bindhi praji didn't know what was going on. I showed them my leg and said, 'He beats me at every opportunity. He has beaten me from the first day of our marriage.' The whole family had congregated by now.

When Bindhi praji saw my leg he completely lost his temper and lunged at Deepak, saying, 'Bastard, you dare to lift a hand against my sister?' Billoo praji intervened to separate them, and Bindhi's slap landed on his face. Billoo praji said that the family should not interfere in quarrels between husband and wife. Kuki praji was very angry. Here was Deepak admitting that he beat me, yet Billoo praji didn't think they should take any action. Bindhi praji whipped out the usual armoury of Punjabi swear-words, 'Mother and sisterfucker', and Deepak told him to leave his mother out of it. Bindhi praji said, 'What is Poochi to us, if not mother and sister?' Deepak said I was his wife. Kuki praji said, 'If you have the courage, if you have more rights over her than us, call her by her name even once in front of us.'

Deepak said he had good reason for behaving the way he did. 'You don't know what she has done to me. Even an enemy wouldn't do that.' I sat there wondering what he was going to say, but he said he was too embarrassed to elaborate. My brothers pressed him, wanting to know what low-down thing their sister had done, what he was going to say in his defence. He said, 'She killed my baby.' I felt my legs turn to water. I explained that I didn't want his children when I was so unhappy.

Bindhi praji said to Deepak, 'That is not a good enough excuse. She didn't want it, she got rid of it. We thought you were going to tell us something earth-shattering.' I seized my chance and said I wanted a divorce.

The food was going cold. Billoo praji and Deepak were both crying. Deepak was so shamefaced he told Baboo to go up to her room so that she didn't get put off the idea of marriage. She retorted that not all men were like him. A little nephew of seven said, 'Bastard, we'll kill you if you beat our aunty.' My sisters-in-law said that they had never been beaten by their husbands. All my family loved me. I was their favourite. They would lay down their lives for me, but my husband's love was not written in my destiny.

No one slept that night. Deepak stayed up talking to Kuki praji all night, enacting some heartbreaking drama, no doubt. The next morning when I came downstairs Kuki praji took me by the arm to Deepak and said, 'Give him another chance. He has promised not to hit you again. There are still two weeks until the wedding. Why don't you go to Delhi with Deepak and have a holiday? He would be foolish to break his word. We will go to any part of the world and beat Deepak up so badly that no one will even find his bones.' He said I should call them every day, reversing the charges if necessary, to report on Deepak's behaviour.

In Delhi, Deepak's relatives asked if he had given up his old habits now that he had found such a wonderful wife. They remembered when he had visited them when he was sixteen and had behaved very badly. When we returned to Ahmedabad Deepak didn't say a word. The whole family was shocked by his nonchalance, despite being publicly humiliated. When it was time for Deepak to return to England I accompanied him to the airport. In my heart I still wanted to leave him. I told him not to wait for me. My brothers didn't really support me. They never said, 'If you want to leave him that's fine, we'll stand by you.' I didn't believe that Deepak would keep his promise to mend his ways. I think my brothers had decided that if I got divorced it would be impossible to marry me off again. They didn't want the burden of an unmarried sister on their hands.

When Deepak reached London he telephoned to say that I could stay in India as long as I liked. He phoned again after a few weeks to say that I should return as Daddy was very ill. I didn't take this seriously, because Daddy had always been ill. Sometimes his eyes would suddenly roll upwards and he would say, 'O Pummi, O Deepak, O Kiran.' The first time I saw this happen, about a month after I got married, I was alone with him and was very frightened.

Every two or three days Deepak would ring and ask me to come back. He had painted the living room, he had bought a washing machine, he had bought a video. During one call, he started abusing me. I pulled the phone out of the socket, and fifteen minutes later when I plugged it in again he was still at the other end. When I went to spend three weeks at Narinder's house, near Poona, I told my brothers not to give Deepak the number. I refused to return. Tommy, who was back in England, rang to say that Daddy really was ill, and that I should go back. My brothers said I must believe Tommy even if I didn't believe Deepak. I decided that they were right. In March I bought presents and sweetmeats for Deepak's family and went to Delhi to catch the flight.

While I was in Delhi, Deepak rang to tell me that Daddy had died. It was too late to cancel my flight, but anyway Deepak said they were not going to proceed with the funeral until I arrived. For two or three days I could not eat. The one person I loved and respected in that family was gone. He was only forty-four years old.

I was really worried about Deepak's treatment of me when I got back, especially now that Daddy had died. On the return flight I phoned him from Dubai to make sure that he was going to meet me at the airport, as I had a lot of luggage. I ended the call with the words 'I love you.' I said this to indicate that I had no hard feelings towards him, and that he should bear no grudges for what had happened in India.

When I arrived at Heathrow it was raining heavily and the sky was overcast. I looked up and thought, 'I have returned to hell.' I had left the warm sunshine, the warmth of my family, my free-as-a-bird lifestyle, to walk into the arms of a monster.

When I got to Crawley there were lots of shoes in the corridor. I had not realised that the house would be overflowing, because relatives come to sit with the bereaved until the funeral takes place. Mamma was sitting and crying. I joined her, also crying. I think she was pained by the fact that I was unsuitably dressed for the occasion in my black jacket and jeans, and wanted me to go upstairs and change into a *salwar kameez*. In my immaturity, I had not realised that as the eldest daughter-in-law I should have boarded the plane suitably dressed. When I went upstairs to get changed I heard Deepak shouting about something and I said aloud, 'For six months I've been free of this, and now, the moment I am back, I have stepped into a world of rows.'

Daddy's funeral was held on the second or third day after I arrived. I never saw his face. I feel great regret about that. There were priests saying prayers around the clock in the house. On the thirteenth day after Daddy's death, in a ritual which emphasises the role of women as chattels of men, a widow went up to Mamma, smashed all her glass bangles (a sign of marriage), wiped the *bindi* (also a sign of marriage) off her forehead and pushed a white sari into her hands in a dramatic gesture of reducing her to widowhood. I had never seen this before, and I was horrified. Mamma was crying unstoppably. I too started crying.

I belonged to a society that had no respect for a woman's feelings. Having lost her husband, Mamma was now to be robbed of all other pleasures in life. After Daddy's death, I started feeling great pity for her. She used to cry uncontrollably, and lost a lot of weight. She'd say to her sons that they troubled her because Daddy was no longer there to protect her. Not that she needed his protection when he was alive.

ELEVEN

Beginnings and Endings

ONE DAY IN 1983 Tommy phoned from Newcastle. I told him how unhappy I was with Deepak and that I desperately wanted to leave him. Tommy was coming to London for a short holiday the next day, and suggested Deepak and I meet him at Dev's. I agreed, but when I mentioned it to Deepak he was furious that I should take a decision without consulting him. He refused to take leave from work, saying, 'Every woman asks her husband before she decides to do anything. You just ignore me. You and your brothers and sisters are so caught up in each other, you never think of others. Ask that dog to come to us.'

The first thing he asked when he got home after his night shift was whether I had rung Tommy. He started pushing me around, saying that Tommy and I must have enjoyed criticising him. I said I didn't want any quarrels as I had to go to work. I had started a new job, dispensing drinks and snacks at a restaurant at Gatwick airport. Deepak's mother was working there too, so he felt comfortable because she could keep an eye on me.

My employers used to provide a taxi to drop and fetch me, but Deepak sent the taxi away. He hit me. I started crying. He didn't sleep that day, although he had worked all night. He just sat in the living room, watching TV, to make sure that I didn't run away. I stayed up in the bedroom for hours. I felt like a trapped animal. In the afternoon I reached out for a bottle of Paracetamol. There must have been about twenty pills in it. I swallowed them all, then went down to the kitchen and started writing goodbye letters to all my family. I had to last out until

I had written to each of my nine brothers and sisters individually – no small task.

There was a knock on the door. It was Tommy, accompanied by Sukhjit and Dev's children. Deepak ignored them, and Tommy came into the kitchen and said, 'Come on, let's go. I've come to fetch you.'

I said, 'It's too late.'

'Too late for what?' he laughed.

I told him that I didn't want to live any more, that I'd taken too many pills, that I was going to die. 'Read these letters if you don't believe me.' Tommy tried to take me to hospital, but I didn't want to go. He rang for a taxi. Deepak offered to drive me. I started vomiting. They were both very scared by now. I was taken to the emergency section, where they pumped out my stomach. It is the worst thing that can happen to you. There was an Indian woman doctor there, and I told her the whole story. Despite that, I was not referred to social services or a women's centre.

[Kiranjit told the duty psychiatrist who saw her in hospital that her husband beat her. After hearing both her story and Deepak's, the psychiatrist concluded: '. . . it appears to be purely a family problem. She may have an immature personality and find it difficult to fit in with her husband and his family and seems happy with her family members.']

They kept me in hospital overnight for observation, and Tommy went back with Deepak to his mother's house. He was full of anger. He said to Deepak, 'Let's see what kind of a man tries to frighten women. Come on, show me. Fight with me.' Manju stopped them.

Mamma and Manju came to visit me in hospital. Instead of showing any sympathy, Mamma started abusing me. 'Bastard, you've shown us up, haven't you? Dragged our name through the mud.' Could she not see that her son was to blame? Does anyone attempt suicide when they are happy? To add insult to injury, she was swearing at me. I was so angry that, between gritted teeth, I threw all her insults back at her. 'You are the bastard, the prostitute, coming here to abuse me.' That was the first time I had ever fought back.

When I was discharged I went with Tommy by bus to Dev's. I did not want to sit in Deepak's car. I looked awful. Tommy spent his holiday listening to a catalogue of complaints from both his sisters. I stayed with Dev for a couple of days. Her advice was basically to go back and try harder. Who would keep me otherwise? She herself was living with her husband's family, and Tommy was having problems at home.

I went back because I wanted to keep my job at Gatwick. But when I got to work, they were surprised to see me. Deepak had phoned and said I didn't want the job any more. The manageress, a fat, kindly woman, called me into the office. She said I could have my job back, and gave me the phone number of the Social Services department when I told her my story. I pleaded with her not to tell my mother-in-law, whom she knew. She said, 'Your husband is a bully.' I didn't know the meaning of the word until I asked Deepak a few days later. Surprisingly, he kept quiet when I told him how I had heard it.

My friend Sulekha used to give me refuge. On one occasion when Deepak came looking for me, I hid behind her settee. As he sat there complaining about me, I could feel my bladder getting desperately full. I had a nervous reaction to his temper – I would either start vomiting or wanting to pee. When he finally left, I dashed to the toilet.

I felt stronger after my visit to India. My brothers had given me permission to go to a solicitor or the police for my protection. I decided I needed a solicitor. Sulekha, who had recently left her husband, recommended a local firm. I went to see the solicitor. He couldn't speak Punjabi, but he could understand it. I explained everything: how Deepak beat me, how Deepak blamed

Hanuman for making him angry with women. He advised a divorce. I explained that my family wouldn't allow it. Was there not a way of stopping Deepak's violence? He told me that he could get an injunction to prevent Deepak from molesting me, and asked me to write down my entire story, with what little English I had. I used to keep my notes on top of the bedroom cupboard so that Deepak wouldn't come across them.

On the day that I was due to take my statement to the solicitor, Deepak and I had a fight. He pushed me roughly up the stairs. I put my arm out to stop myself from falling and broke my little finger. I couldn't work because my hand was swollen, so the manageress let me go home early, which gave me time to go to the solicitor. I showed him what had happened, and he made me go to the hospital to have my hand properly bandaged while he got the paperwork ready. When I got back he drove me to court. I showed my hand to the judge and got an early date for the hearing.

When the papers were served on Deepak, his anger lit a fire in him. He went straight to his mother, and they came to our house. Deepak said, 'Bastard, the court belongs to your father, does it? When did you have the time to go?' My solicitor had told me not to be provoked, so I kept quiet. The old woman was marvelling at my new-found courage. Deepak wanted to hit me, but she stayed his hand.

Deepak dragged everybody in to dissuade me from going to court, but I said I would not be swayed from my decision, and that I would start proceedings for a divorce. Deepak wanted me to discuss it with my family, but nothing would change my mind; they didn't have to live with him, and the decision would be taken in court. I can be very stubborn. I can tolerate things for a long while, but when I reach my breaking point, that's it. They wanted to take me to Dev's, and I agreed, saying that I would not change my mind in any case. When I refused to sit in Deepak's car, Paul said he would make sure no harm came to me.

When we arrived I complained to Dev that Deepak and his mother had been harassing me for a dowry. Dev asked Mamma what dowry they had given their own daughter, and why they had initially told us that they wanted nothing. Mamma denied that she had harassed me. Deepak glared at me, saying that he would hit me if I talked too much. I dared him to do it in my sister's house.

Sukhjit jijaji asked Deepak what he wanted them to do. Deepak said he would write a letter through his solicitors promising never to raise a hand against me if I dropped the court action. Sukhjit jijaji reminded him that he had made promises before, and asked what my faults were to deserve his beatings. Deepak had no answer. Sukhjit jijaji said that I should drop the action, but that if Deepak were to beat me again I was free to pursue any option I wished. I respected Sukhjit jijaji, and told him that I would do this for him.

We returned to Crawley, and the night before we were due to appear in court, Deepak forced me to have sex with him. He promised to be careful, but I knew instinctively that I had become pregnant. He also extracted an assurance that I would not pursue the case, and the next day I told the solicitor that my family had pressurised me to drop the matter. He said I was making a big mistake. Deepak had to pay a solicitor to get the letter written and this was registered in court.

After the solicitor's intervention, Deepak rowed with Sulekha for putting me up to it, and said that he would make her pay. She told him to get out of her house, and threatened to call the police if he came again. Deepak went to Sulekha's husband and started criticising Sulekha which, although they were divorced, he did not appreciate at all. He rang Sulekha and advised her not to let Deepak into the house. Sulekha told me that although she enjoyed our friendship and was not intimidated by Deepak's threats, it would be best if we did not continue to see each other. I was deeply upset, but I did manage to visit her secretly a couple of times.

For a few weeks Deepak did not beat me. I told him I didn't want to go to court again, but that having done it once, there was nothing to stop me doing it again. I said he could lose his temper with me, but only if it was within limits, otherwise it would have no impact on me.

My Gatwick job lasted only three months or so, and while I was unemployed I offered to look after my friend Chandrika's children for half an hour every day after school. I had met Chandrika at Bale & Church. Once, when I was getting my wisdom teeth and my mouth was aching, she cooked a special meal for me. I looked after her children free of charge, saving her £10 or £15 which she had been paying to a childminder. This led to another row, as Deepak thought I was lying about the money. He pushed me to the floor so hard that my wedding ring got squashed into my flesh and I had to go to the hospital to have it removed. My fingers were badly swollen.

I went to stay with Deepak's mother for a few days. He phoned her and said that if I returned he would beat me within an inch of my life. I returned after a week despite my mother-in-law's advice. I told her I would go to the police if he dared to touch me. 'From today, I have no fear of *izzat* or of Deepak's volence.' I had no keys because I had left the house in such a hurry, but when I got to our house I found that Deepak had had the locks changed. He stood at the door and said I couldn't come in because it was his house. He let me in only when I threatened to call the police.

At this time I started being sick and craving cold sweet lassi, but Deepak made me salty lassi, which I couldn't touch. He thought I couldn't possibly be pregnant, but the doctor confirmed it. Deepak was thrilled. He rang his mother and Pummi to boast, as if he had accomplished some great feat.

I wasn't very well in the early part of my pregnancy, and couldn't even look at peas or eggs without vomiting. I was told to take complete bedrest, and I went and stayed with Pummi for a fortnight. Deepak had been looking after me very well, making me whatever I fancied, but something about his behaviour made me feel for the first time that he was having affairs with white women. He hardly visited me when I was at Pummi's, and when he did he would only stay for a very short time. On one occasion when he didn't turn up as promised, I rang him, and the phone appeared to be off the hook. Pummi was very anxious that Deepak might have fainted. She told me that he had fainted before in Kenya, which I hadn't known about. I later discovered that he suffered from epilepsy. We went to see if he was all right, but when we arrived Deepak wouldn't look me or Pummi in the eye. I suspected that either there had been a woman in the house, or that he had spent the night out, but I hid my feelings.

Deepak seemed to be working longer hours and more nights, but his pay packet never reflected this. On Saturdays he would tell me that he was on duty for five hours, from six to eleven at night, but I later discovered that there was no such shift. Knowing what I do today, I believe my suspicions were correct. On three separate occasions I had a very strong inkling that he was having an affair with a white woman. The man who would not leave my side for one minute had suddenly become happy for me to go anywhere I wished, and I was left on my own a lot during my pregnancy. When he came back late, I couldn't tell if he had been out drinking. He would sit and watch TV before coming up to bed, by which time I was fast asleep. But a wife can always tell when a third person occupies the intimate space between a couple.

Deepak went shopping with me for the baby and took me for walks. He asked Pummi's mother-in-law to knit something for our baby, because he complained his own mother was useless and wouldn't. She had planned to begin knitting only in the seventh month, because it was a bad omen to start earlier. Deepak didn't understand this, of course. But my mother-in-law took no special interest in me because of my pregnancy. She was annoyed that I went to see Pummi so often. Manju would cook for me and look after me when I went to Mamma's house. I would also visit Chandrika frequently, and she would cook all the delicacies I craved at odd hours.

Towards the end of the pregnancy, when Deepak and I were at the Gurdwara, I went to the loo and found that I had a discharge. I asked Deepak to take me home, but he wanted to go to his mother's house. I burst into tears. My labour pains had started, and all this man could think of was having a good time. I was too shy to start my labour in my mother-in-law's house. As it was, I was nervous about being naked in front of the doctor. I begged Deepak to take me home, and all the way he moaned at me for my stubbornness. Tears were the only thing written into my destiny. The child which I would shortly bring into this world was an unlucky child.

I went up to my bedroom and wept. After two or three hours Deepak came up and forced me to come down for a cup of tea. My pain increased, and Deepak phoned the hospital and was told to bring me in when the contractions were fifteen minutes apart. When we got to the hospital, I was shocked to find Deepak's mother in the delivery room. I asked her to leave, saying I was too shy to deliver my child in front of a circus, so she went. At 7.30 on the morning of 4 June 1984 I gave birth to a son. His face had been squashed by the forceps during delivery, and he was covered in afterbirth and looked really ugly. Deepak phoned his mother. She bought chocolates and announced the arrival of her grandson to everyone at work.

When I woke up at 4 p.m. I struggled with myself about whether I should see the baby, because I had been so disappointed by his ugliness. But by this time he looked much better. He had dark hair and fair skin, and he was so beautiful that I covered him with kisses. That evening everyone came to visit me. The moment my mother-in-law arrived she went to the nurse and asked her to ensure that I breast-fed my son, because I had announced my intention to bottle-feed him. The nurse said they couldn't do anything if that was what I wished.

On the sixth day I left hospital and went to stay with Mamma for forty days, as is the custom. She took sick leave, and she has never worked since. She had knitted lots of things, mainly in blue. I had said I would have nothing for the baby if it was a girl, so she knitted something in pink and lots of white frocks. Since Daddy's death this was the first joyful event in her life. She would not leave the baby, who we named Sandeep at her insistence, alone. He was her toy. She must have made a thousand *laddoos* (sweetmeats made from boiled lentils) and distributed them.

The day after I went back home she rang up to speak to Sandeep and started weeping on the phone because she missed him. Manju and Suresh would visit frequently to take him out. I was happy. For the first time I felt we were coming together as a family, and it was all because of Sandeep. Manju would buy lovely clothes for him, and she opened an account for him in the bank where she worked. She would take pictures of him eating, bathing, playing with his toys. All my brothers-in-law have changed his nappy, something none of my brothers in India would have contemplated.

When Sandeep was three months old I wanted to take a job packing shelves on Saturdays and three evenings a week in Sainsbury's, which was a five-minute walk from our house. Deepak agreed. I was paid £40 for seventeen hours' work. I was thrilled, because I wanted to save up and buy a house. The job meant that we needed someone to look after Sandeep for an hour in the evening between Deepak leaving for work and my coming home. I asked Chandrika if she would help out, and she agreed. Sandeep was popular with her husband and children, and she would keep him in the kitchen while she cooked.

A few months later, Manju became friendly with a woman called Rashmi whose first husband had died in an accident and who was now married to a white taxi-driver. She had an eleven-year-old daughter from her first marriage. She was a modern, educated woman who had been brought up in England and would talk freely to men and women. Deepak became attracted to her. He would sit with other women, playing the hero and laughing and joking, but would completely ignore me. He was showing off his ivory set – people couldn't see that he had a different set of teeth for eating. Only I had seen the molars in action.

Deepak would be playful with Rashmi, pushing her, pinching her, tickling her, finding excuses to touch her. Wherever she sat, he would follow and sit as close as possible. When she visited us, he wouldn't let her go home. He would do this with my other friends too, but I could not even talk to Paul without arousing Deepak's suspicions. I could not joke and relax. I couldn't leave Deepak now that I had a child, as a non-virginal woman is of no use in our society. Men, of course, can play around at any age. Before I became pregnant Deepak's mother used to tell him to hurry up and have kids, so I couldn't talk about leaving him. 'Take her to the doctor,' she would advise him. 'Go to the doctor yourself, bastard,' he would say through gritted teeth, 'She doesn't want my children.'

'What do you put inside her? Sponge?' she would reply. 'What kind of a man do you call yourself? All this sitting around in courts and issuing of threats by lawyers will all stop once you make a mother out of her.'

I used to be so embarrassed by this kind of crude conversation, but she was right that I would have fewer chances of remarriage with a child. I had no confidence, in any case. I didn't think I could survive on my own. I couldn't even go out alone in the evenings.

I didn't want to become pregnant again too soon after Sandeep's birth, so without telling Deepak I had a coil put in. I told Pummi about it, and she told Mamma, and they both kept nagging me about the dangers of a coil and told me that I was bleeding and losing weight because of it. I said I was losing weight because I was working hard and not eating very much, and Sandeep was still frequently waking up at night. I also had to trek miles to the doctor because Deepak wouldn't allow me to transfer to a nearby practice when we moved. Even our letters had to be picked up from his mother's because he wouldn't inform people about our change of address.

When I went to see the doctor I was feeling so weak that I burst into tears. I said I was constantly tired because Sandeep was so unsettled at night. On top of all that, Kuki praji and his daughter from India were staying with us, and so was Billoo praji from Canada. I was exhausted. The doctor told Deepak to take care of me, which he did. He would look after Sandeep at night, do the shopping, wash his nappies and so on.

Mamma told Deepak that I had had a coil put in, and persuaded him that it was damaging my health. Deepak kept nagging me after that. My weight had gone down from eight stone to six and a half and I went to see the doctor, who said that my excessive bleeding was due to the coil. He removed it and prescribed the pill, but Deepak never got them for me because he thought I would become sterile. He promised to use condoms, but of course he didn't use them all the time.

I became pregnant again when Sandeep was only nine months old. In the beginning I didn't have morning sickness, so I didn't even know. It was only when I started getting hot and cold flushes that I went to see the doctor. I described my symptoms, he asked me my age and then said I was pregnant. I couldn't understand how he could work that out from my age. I had mixed feelings – I wanted another child, and yet that would mean sinking irretrievably into an unhappy marriage.

The pregnancy went well at first, but after the third month I started being sick. When I told Pummi and Mamma that I was pregnant again Pummi thought I would have a girl. But I just knew that I would have a boy, as I had known when I was pregnant with Sandeep.

During this pregnancy there were a lot of rows, mostly over Deepak's cousin Gurjeet, who had started living with us.

Gurjeet's father had lived in Britain for over twenty years, but because he was having a relationship with a Filipino woman, he didn't want his wife and family to join him. They were living in poverty in India, and Gurjeet asked Mamma to organise a visa for him to come to England, otherwise he would commit suicide. When Gurjeet's father died, he came on a visitor's visa to attend the funeral. He stayed with Mamma, but he was ill-treated by Deepak's family, who begrudged him food, didn't like the times at which he ate, and generally ignored him. Indians brought up in Britain often look down on those who have recently come to the country because they can't speak English – Gurjeet and I had both faced this prejudice.

Gurjeet started visiting us and looking after Sandeep, and Deepak promised to help him get permanent residence. He came to live with us when Sandeep was nine months old. He would help out in the house with cooking, cleaning and hoovering, and he was good company for me. We would watch videos together and I would listen to his sorrows and his worries about his mother.

Within four weeks of Gurjeet moving in, Deepak started shouting at him and pushing him around, holding him by the throat and fighting with him. Deepak had lost all interest in the house. He did none of the household chores now, he hardly talked to me and he seemed to be at work all the time. I didn't have the courage to broach the subject with him. When I went to the doctor's for a check-up I went on my own. He had no interest in this pregnancy. I had my suspicions of him. We didn't sleep together sometimes for two months at a stretch, while he had hardly left me alone throughout my first pregnancy. It wasn't a happy time. However, if I could see it through for the remaining five months, then I would be finished with nappies and babies in one go.

One day Mamma and I had gone to visit Gurdayal uncle, the husband of Deepak's paternal aunt. He told us that Deepak had started drinking at work and that he kept a bottle in his locker.

It was Gurdayal uncle who had recommended Deepak for his current job, at the Post Office, and he didn't want to be held responsible if he got the sack. When Mamma took this up with Deepak he was furious with Gurdayal, saying that he would break his legs for daring to gossip about others when he himself went about with white women. I told Deepak to be careful. We couldn't afford for him to lose his job now. I asked him to drink at home, if he must drink, and said I would make him all the snacks he wanted. Drink only aggravated his bad temper. He had already been suspended from his railway job once because he had hit a man.

[Ranjit Ahluwalia described Deepak's volatile temper in his statement for the trial, although he was not called to give evidence.

'Deepak was a person who used to change his moods. At times he could be very pleasant and nice to everybody around him, but at other times he could become aggressive and short-tempered. He would treat Karen very rudely and roughly in front of people . . .

'Over the years Deepak's attitude has got worse and worse. More recently his temper became worse because he developed a heavy drinking habit . . . I understood that he was even involved in a fight at work with somebody else whilst he was employed by British Rail. I have even seen him be rude to his mother and shout at her and break things in her house . . .

'Throughout their marriage it would be fair to say that I had never seen Karen do anything wrong. I had never seen her behave in an unruly and improper manner in front of me. However, the way Deepak treated her became worse and worse and I am not surprised the way things have turned out – I was expecting something to happen a long time ago . . .

'On one occasion in 1983 [Deepak] had an argument with my wife and during the course of the argument he grabbed her by the throat. There was no point in trying to do anything about it because this was the usual behaviour from Deepak and when he

calmed down he would always say sorry, but sooner or later he would lose his temper again.']

Deepak hardly ever ate at home now. It felt as if he would always start a row just as we were sitting down to a meal, and then he would walk out. Because I asked him to vacuum the living-room carpet, which got dirty quickly, he moved the TV into the kitchen so that no one would sit in the living room and he wouldn't have to vacuum the carpet. He would complain to his mother that I made him work while I sat around doing nothing. She said, 'Don't treat my son like a servant while you're the lady of leisure.' I said I would continue to ask him to vacuum and do the shopping regardless.

On one occasion members of my family came to stay at our house when they were attending Tommy's second wedding. Surinder was visiting from Canada, and all the women were sitting upstairs singing songs and chatting. Tommy was already in bed, as the wedding was to take place early the next day. Deepak came in and insisted that we go to bed. Dev said he could go to bed if he wanted to, but when we said we wanted to carry on for a bit longer he grabbed the lightbulb hanging from the ceiling and threw it against the wall, plunging the room into darkness. The bulb shattered into tiny pieces, and must have burned Deepak's hand. We all sat there stunned. Deepak started shouting and arguing. Eventually he went out and sat at the top of the stairs.

When I was eight months pregnant I had to attend a distant niece's wedding in Hounslow. Deepak and Gurjeet were drunk and dancing away. I was following after him with my heavily pregnant stomach, saying, 'Sandeep is crying, can you warm up his milk, please?' I could hardly walk. Deepak pushed me away. I was angry that he would rather dance than warm up his son's milk. Tommy found me weeping in the corridor and warmed up the milk for me.

About a week before I was due to give birth, Mamma came

over. We were discussing how congested the kitchen was because Deepak didn't want to vacuum the living-room carpet. Deepak started shouting at me, and slapped me hard across the face. I was so angry I just lashed out and scratched his face. For nine months he had given me a hard time, and never helped me. He pushed and shoved me up the stairs towards the bedroom. When I got there I curled up to protect my stomach and prevent any injury to the child. Deepak was hitting me on my back and head, pulling my hair and calling me 'Bastard, bitch.' Suddenly he let go of me, saying, 'If you weren't pregnant, I'd've finished you off today.'

I didn't eat anything all that day, although I was feeling hungry and sick by turns. When Deepak went to work in the evening Mamma cooked for me, saying, 'You're mad. If you want to starve and die that's fine, but the baby inside you doesn't deserve to starve.' So I ate. I wept a lot that night – because of my weaknesses, because I had been foolish enough to have children by Deepak. At 4 a.m. I started feeling the labour pains. When Deepak returned from his night shift – or wherever he had been – he stayed downstairs and watched TV. I wept all day, but I was determined not to ask him to take me to hospital when it was time.

I couldn't sit or stand, I was so uncomfortable. At 6.30 that evening Mamma called to find out if I had eaten. She asked me to come and eat at her place. I declined, but I didn't tell her I was in labour. As I put the phone down my pains became sharper, and I rang for the ambulance. Deepak was lying upstairs in bed. He came down and asked me why I had called an ambulance when he was in the house. I said I didn't even want to talk to him. He tried to get me to cancel the ambulance. When it arrived he insisted on coming with me. At the hospital he started complaining that he had worked all night, and now he would have to be up all this coming night, as had happened with Sandeep. While he was moaning, he was also putting a cold compress on my forehead because I was sweating so much.

The midwife burst my waters, and in an hour our second son, Rajeev, was born, on 6 January 1986. When Deepak rang his mother to inform her she couldn't believe it, because she had spoken to me only a couple of hours before.

TWELVE

Lies, Ties and Suicide

DEEPAK WANTED ME to stay with his mother for the first forty days after Rajeev's birth, as I did after Sandeep's, but she refused. I realised that cooking for four extra people would put a lot of strain on her. Deepak, of course, wanted the run of the house for his other activities. I put my foot down, saying that I wanted to go to my own home with my child.

My mother-in-law would turn up early in the morning and stay till late. I now had to look after both the children and wait on her hand and foot. Once when I asked her to hold Rajeev for a little while she refused, saying her arms ached. I got annoyed and asked her why she bothered to come. 'If you can't help me out, then don't increase my workload by coming here.' She cut down on her visits after that. Deepak didn't help at all. The kids would keep me up at night, and both were in nappies and on bottles. I used to get so tired.

Manju's wedding was approaching. She had accepted a Sikh suitor, Santosh, from Hong Kong. I found that Rashmi had become central to the proceedings. No decision could be taken without consulting her: how much cutlery was required, what the menu would be, what sort of jewellery and clothes were needed for Manju. Deepak was transfixed by Rashmi, and would accompany the women on shopping trips although his mother did not want him to. I felt completely left out. Sandeep was teething, being sick and had a runny tummy.

I had no clothes for Manju's wedding, so Deepak gave me his week's wages and told me to go shopping while he looked after the kids. I went to Southall with Rashmi and Manju, and afterwards we went to Rashmi's brother's house, from where I rang Deepak. Hardly had I said hello than he asked to speak to Rashmi. He spent a long time talking to her. These things hurt.

Deepak and I had been discussing what we should give Manju for her wedding. I had suggested that the four brothers contribute £250 each and give it to Mamma so that she could make all the necessary arrangements for the marriage. The others agreed, apart from one who couldn't afford it as he wasn't working at the time.

One day Deepak announced that he was going to visit Rashmi because a friend of hers had a council flat in an area where we wanted to live. When I said I wanted to come along he wouldn't let me, and promised to return shortly. He returned after three hours. I began to wonder if he was having an affair with her.

During the women's sangeet for Manju's wedding, Deepak sat on the arm of the sofa next to Rashmi, and put his hand on her lap. I looked at him and Rashmi pushed his hand away. I was embarrassed that this was going on in front of all the family. I was also jealous and angry – angry because he had such double standards when it came to my behaviour.

When the dancing began, Deepak was all Rashmi, Rashmi. Mamma had requested that the music be turned down because there had been a death in the family. When nobody listened to her she got up and reduced the volume. Rashmi didn't like this, saying that they were in the mood for *bhangra* (Punjabi folk dancing), and she picked up her coat to leave. Deepak screamed abuse at his mother. He took Rashmi's coat off forcibly, saying that he would turn up the volume and that his mother just loved rows.

Deepak, Rashmi and Manju went upstairs to Manju's room. After fifteen minutes or so I went up to find them. Deepak was showing off the £250 I had put in his pocket for him to give his mother. He told me to get out of the room, and said he would come down shortly. Rashmi wanted to go, however, and

Deepak swore that if she went, he would kill himself. He went to his mother's medicine cabinet and swallowed all her tablets – she had drugs for arthritis, headaches, fever, you name it. And he had been drinking. He staggered downstairs with a great show of bravado and said, 'There, I'm dying, just to show you that I could do it.' He wrote a note saying that he was committing suicide, and added that his family had no hand in it, in case they got into trouble with the police afterwards. What was the issue? Music. And the solution? Suicide! Deepak was crying and ranting, and swaying from the hip as if he was in a trance. Everybody was watching him, stunned. Mamma was very angry. He pushed away anyone who tried to interfere.

An ambulance was called, but Deepak wouldn't go to the hospital. He fought off the ambulance driver and assistant, saying it was his sister's wedding, and he wanted to attend it. He was completely out of control. Finally, with the help of family members, he was pushed into the ambulance. I felt helpless. And so humiliated. My husband had dragged me through the mud with him. My youngest son was just thirty-nine days old.

Deepak was forcibly admitted to hospital, where his stomach was pumped. The doctors wanted him to stay on so they could monitor the effects of the medicines he had swallowed, but he discharged himself next morning, claiming he was perfectly all right.

The women were bathing the bride and putting bangles on her wrist when Deepak turned up. I was looking after the kids and, as the eldest daughter-in-law, doing the innumerable jobs that need doing in a bride's household. Kaushaliya said to Mamma that she should go and look after Deepak, as the after-effects of his overdose were making him sway and fall all over the place with weakness. But Mamma was boiling with rage. 'I wish the bastard would die right away and take the load off my shoulders. The groom and his family are going to be here any time now. How many places can I be in at once? If he'd stayed in hospital, at least I could have done my work in peace.' I sympathised with her. It was not the time for Deepak's dramas.

Daddy's brothers attended the wedding because they felt they had an obligation to do so in his absence, and they went to the hall with Suresh and Raju to make all the arrangements. After the ceremony we went to the hall for lunch. Deepak was sitting at the entrance like a gatekeeper, in his three-piece suit, weeping. As the guests trooped in, they could not help but notice him. There were at least three or four hundred people there. And, of course, they were curious. As many rumours as there were mouths floated throughout the hall that day. I tried to drag him away from such a visible spot but he refused, saying he wanted to die, and crying as if he was heartbroken. I felt like slapping his face. If I hadn't had two kids, I would have left him there and then.

He was looking around for Rashmi, and as soon as he caught sight of her he followed her around everywhere, falling over himself, drunk and weak from his last tantrum. She pleaded with me to keep him in check, but I told her I had no influence over him at all. My tongue had been cut out a long time ago. I was trying to hide my tears, and I pitied Rashmi.

During the wedding ceremony the immediate family stands by the bride and groom. Deepak was there, swaying and weeping. Poor Manju, to have her wedding spoiled by her eldest brother. Rashmi was sitting near Manju, and Deepak dragged her bemused husband into the family circle although he had no right to be there. The priest said it was a bad omen for someone to roam around in front of and behind the couple as Deepak was doing, and asked if someone would take him to one side. Deepak didn't miss a single trick in humiliating his entire family. Years later, when we were preparing for my trial, Deepak's uncle kept saying that I should produce the video of that day in court so that the judge could see what kind of man I had been married to.

Manju's new husband wanted to wash and dry his hair before the reception, and he asked Rashmi if he could do it at her house because it wasn't convenient to go anywhere else. And who should want to accompany them? They tried to put Deepak off, saying that they would be back shortly, but he insisted. While he was there, he spilt tea all over Rashmi's kitchen. She was furious. When they returned, once again Rashmi turned to me. 'Please keep your homemaker on a leash. I've only come because of Manju, otherwise I wouldn't have tolerated such humiliation.'

After Manju and her husband had departed, a number of guests returned to Mamma's house for the rest of the rituals, while some of the family stayed behind to clear up the hall. After all the ceremonies had been completed at Mamma's house, Rashmi and her husband left to go home. As her husband started the car, Deepak went and lay in front of it. It was winter, and a few inches of snow had settled on the ground. They couldn't move. With great difficulty, Sukhjit jijaji picked Deepak up and dragged him into the house. Rashmi's husband said, 'Deepak is not well. He needs treatment.' Rashmi came in and said to Mamma in front of everyone, 'I hope you don't mind me saying so, but your son is a real bastard. He has managed to humiliate me in front of everyone. People must think we are having an affair. His behaviour today has washed away all my efforts to ensure that Manju's wedding went well.'

As soon as Sukhjit jijaji let go of Deepak, he ran off in the direction of Rashmi's house. He was running blind, into the road, without stopping for traffic. Behind him ran Sukhjit jijaji, and behind him, Gurjeet. Finally, Sukhjit jijaji lost his temper and slapped him. They took him back to the hospital.

[The hospital notes say that Deepak claimed to have slept that afternoon. The notes say that he was 'drowsy and unco-operative. Sleeping deeply – little response until awake and then confused and aggressive.' When he saw the psychiatrist, Deepak said his problems were: 'wife getting at him – now head of family – organising sister's wedding – loves another woman'. He admitted to

'explosive outbursts of anger' and sudden 'changes of mood'. He was anxious about having a brain tumour because his father died from one, and he was referred for a brain scan. The psychiatrist concluded that Deepak was 'not suicidal' but 'failed to cope with stress'. When Kiranjit was seen by a psychiatrist after her own earlier suicide attempt, Deepak had been asked for his version of their marital problems. After Deepak's attempt, Kiranjit was not asked to give her version.]

Instead of getting stronger with age and experience, I was becoming weaker. There were voices rising in my soul: 'Let me show the world that I can live without this monster and bring up my own children. I can survive.' But my tongue would not support these voices. My anger against myself came out in tears.

The next morning Deepak returned home. He was very quiet, and I knew he was embarrassed and perhaps regretted his actions. I didn't offer him anything, not even tea. He lay in bed all day. In the evening he demanded his dinner. 'I haven't cooked you any,' I said. 'The kitchen lies in that direction, it's up to you.' I was full of hatred. Why should I always have to do my duty to him? Was I not a human being? Was I not allowed to get angry? To show my feelings? He rang his mother to complain, and she turned up to support him.

'Calm her down,' Deepak said to his mother. 'She wants me to leave.' Why should a grown man who knew how to fight and cause trouble need his mother every time I said I wanted him to leave? Could we not have discussed the matter between us?

His mother said, 'I don't want you back.'

I said, 'I don't either. I have two kids who need looking after. I can't look after him as well.'

'If my son is starving, he has a right to expect his wife to cook for him,' Mamma said, before launching into her own marriage and how, despite her husband's shortcomings, she had always fulfilled a wife's duties.

'She wants me to do all the shopping and the hoovering on top of my job,' Deepak complained.

'Mamma,' I said, 'you trained your children to wash their own dishes and clothes and do their own ironing. I expect that of him too.'

Deepak said, 'If you don't want to do it, you'd better leave. I don't want you around anyway.'

Under pressure, Deepak agreed to do the household chores. After Mamma left, I cooked for him. I didn't have a job at that time and I was intimidated by the thought of having to bring my children up on my own. Deepak and I carried on living together, two strangers under one roof.

Chachaji rang, cautioning me to be careful if I was contacted by the police about Deepak's suicide attempt. That really frightened me. I rang Rashmi and broke down, asking her to tell me the whole truth, now that this might become a police case. She swore that there was nothing between them, that Deepak was just a lowdown scoundrel. Fortunately, I didn't hear from the police.

Deepak was working the night shift in the Post Office, and I slept in another room with the children. He would fight with Puppi, as we called Gurjeet, saying that he would turn out to be like his father and go out with white women, that Puppi and I gossiped about him when he was at work – the usual nonsense. One weekend he wanted us all to go to Mamma's house. I wasn't very keen because I knew it would mean more rows. When we got there, a conversation between mother and son that had started as a joke turned into a fight, and they both turned on Puppi. I went mad. 'What's the matter with you, Deepak? If it isn't me, it's Puppi.' Later, I was drinking tea in the living room when Deepak threw a door open so roughly that the chair on which I was sitting was knocked sideways and the cup of tea and I went flying. He said, 'Bastard, I will kill you,' pushed me against the wall and put a knife to my throat. His mother tried to intervene but he said, 'That's it, I'm going to kill her. I'm fed up with her, she has made my life a nightmare.'

I said I would go to my lawyer there and then. I wriggled free and ran to the bus stop, where I bumped into Rashmi, who was going to Mamma's house. Deepak jumped into his car and drove it fast towards me as if he were going to run me over. Rashmi pushed me out of the way. 'Do you want to kill her?' she shouted. Deepak told her not to interfere. 'I'm not going to let her off today. Let's see how she goes to her lawyer.' Rashmi managed to drag Deepak into the house and I went to the solicitor.

[Rashmi provided a statement confirming the above version of events for the trial, but she did not testify in court. About the incident in which Deepak attempted to drive into Kiranjit, she says: 'The only way I can describe him on that occasion is that he was literally a madman. He drove the car onto the pavement towards her but he could not do anything because I was there and I stopped him. Deepak was very violent towards her, dragged her across the pavement, and he was literally tearing her apart. I saw the bruises on her.

'At the wedding . . . Deepak had been drinking. He had taken some pills as well, and his whole family wanted to ignore him. My husband and I ended up having to take him to the hospital because none of his family seemed to want to help him. My husband and I took him to Crawley Hospital and Deepak was using the foulest language and acting like a madman. I can only describe him as having a foul temper.

'It is not fair how that girl has been treated and I would describe her treatment as being used like a bag of rubbish. He was like a nightmare and she was a good and patient person.

'Although I cannot be specific, I saw bruises on her several times and I know she wanted to divorce him. He wouldn't let her do it and then he would apologise and be all right for a few days and then he would go mad again. There were so many incidents it's *almost impossible to refer to them, but Deepak's mother would always be on his side, and I heard her use bad language to Kiran.']*

I told the solicitor what had happened, and he advised me yet again to leave Deepak. I said my family would not approve. He suggested I get an injunction to stop Deepak harassing me. When Deepak got the summons, which fixed the hearing for ten days' time, he said he would only go to court if he could get a divorce from me. 'That's fine by me,' I said, 'but I'm going to carry on living in this house with both children.' Deepak said he would say this and this in court, that he didn't have a knife in his hands, and so on. I said I didn't want to hear his defence, he could save it for the court.

Pummi and her husband, Deepak's mother, Dev, Sukhjit jijaji and Tommy all tried to dissuade me from getting the injunction. But I was determined. The knife had been pointed at *my* throat, it was *my* hair that got pulled, *my* head that was bashed against the walls and battered with the heels of his shoes. I wasn't going to listen to them.

None of his family came to court. They said they didn't want to interfere in our fights. I had come to the end of the road. Deepak had turned an educated woman into an illiterate, useless person, a failed wife, a failed woman in every respect. I had him to thank for the complete lack of confidence I now had in myself. I had done everything according to my family's advice: taken a job, got a house, had children. When I had shown them how unhappy I was – quietly, not screaming and ranting in public like Deepak – they hadn't listened. Now I would go to court.

At the court Deepak cried like a baby in front of me, touched my feet and begged to be forgiven. When he was asked about the knife, he said vehemently that I was lying. Did he go into the kitchen and open a drawer? 'Yes.' Why did he open the drawer if he wasn't going for the knife? Deepak had no reply. He said something about always carrying a knife in his car because he had done an electronics course and he used it for repairing things. Finally, Deepak admitted that he had gone for the knife, that he had done it before, three years ago, that there were misunderstandings between us. He admitted every single thing. He said he would give a written undertaking not to touch me, that if he did he should be taken straight to prison. He apologised unreservedly. Deepak had boasted that he would show me how to construct a defence. He had woven all these stories in his mind, but they had got jumbled. I said in my broken English that he had tried to kill me before, that I didn't want to live with him any more, that I wanted a divorce.

Deepak said he had a new job with the Post Office which he didn't want to endanger, and that as there was no room for him in his mother's house because he had a large family, would the court please give him permission to carry on living in the same house as his wife? The judge agreed, but issued a protection order which would be valid for two years from April 1986.

Deepak and I continued living under the same roof. We had little sexual contact after Rajeev's birth. I thought that maybe the birth of children kills off sexual desire in men, or perhaps his attention was wandering outside, and the overtime he claimed to be doing was really sexual overtime.

I used to feel desperately tired in those days, looking after two young children. I would go out of my way to cook a hot meal for Deepak, but he would often leave his food untouched. He had no appreciation of my tiredness. The drudgery was also getting me down. I bumped into a friend of mine called Meena, and she was shocked by the way I looked. She suggested that I start working again, that once I got out and about and made new friends I would feel different. 'I'll get you a sitting-down job where I work,' she said, 'packing cutlery for aeroplane meals. The hours are great, from ten to six. I know the supervisor.' Deepak worked at night, so between us we could look after the children. I was quite excited by the prospect.

When I asked Deepak if I could take the job I put my arms around him and called him darling and sweetheart. If he had only given me a chance, I would have shown the fool heaven on earth. He agreed. The following day I had to go to Meena's to pick up the forms, so I woke Deepak and told him that he would have to keep an eye on Rajeev for half an hour in case he woke up. Sandeep was at his grandmother's. While I was at Meena's, Deepak rang his mother and started complaining that I was out having fun with my friends, that he had returned from night shift and his sleep was being disturbed, that despite being the mother of two kids all I was interested in was money and a job. When I returned, he created havoc, even though I had discussed the job with him and he had agreed. I was fed up with being cooped up. We didn't even go out for our evening walks any more. Deepak was at work for twelve hours a day, seven days a week. I finally convinced him that we could have a nice house if I brought in some extra money.

I would leave for work at 9.35 a.m. and get back at 6.30. Deepak had to start work at six, so we needed someone to look after the children for an hour in the evenings. Chandrika stepped in, and later I found a Gujarati neighbour, Shantaben, who would take Rajeev for an hour on the evenings when I was at work. Sometimes Puppi would do it, and sometimes Deepak would take them to his mother's house. One day Mamma said she couldn't manage with Sandeep on a daily basis. I tried to leave him with Shantaben, but she couldn't manage him. Suresh talked his mother into continuing with Sandeep.

I would stay up with the children till midnight, so that next morning Deepak would get a few hours' sleep before Rajeev woke up at ten. Or I would wake them up at 6 a.m. when I got up and keep them awake until I left at 9.30, to give Deepak even longer in bed. I wondered how he did so well with so little sleep. Sometimes at the weekends I would suggest that he take a nap, but he would say he didn't need one. By now I was sure that very often he was not working at all, but sleeping with some white woman somewhere. It was a bedshift, not a letter-sorting shift.

For my first week in the new job, along with a tax rebate I received £149. I was so thrilled I phoned Deepak at work. I blew the entire sum on him: I bought him a watch for £65, a Walkman for £35, and the rest I spent on a shirt. I wanted to thank him for looking after the children and giving me the freedom to work. It never occurred to me that they were his children too, and that there was no need to reward him for looking after them. He was overwhelmed. He said he would return the watch, as it was too expensive and he was scared of losing it.

Deepak was keen to move out of our council house and buy our own property, but I liked our house in Broadfields. It was very nice, with a small garden and fitted kitchen, and I had made a few friends in the locality. Margaret Thatcher had passed a law allowing council tenants to buy their houses and flats, giving them large discounts based on the number of years they had lived there and the amount of rent they had paid. All my friends were buying up their homes: Chandrika bought hers for £17,000. I was keen too, and kept trying to persuade Deepak to buy our house. But some of his family tried to dissuade him from buying a council house – they were made of cardboard; you couldn't even fix a toilet-roll holder to the wall. In the end he agreed with them, much to my disappointment. I knew that the market value of these houses was £65,000, while we would have to pay only £17,000. Deepak felt that council houses had no resale value.

The fragile peace that had been established by both of us being at work, with very little contact with each other, was torn apart by quarrels about which house we would buy. I said Deepak could move to wherever he wanted, and I would continue living in Broadfields. He said he wouldn't get the full tax relief if we bought two houses.

He won. We looked at a few houses through estate agents.

Langley Green was not considered a very good area, but we saw a house there which we liked at a price we could afford. It was well decorated, with a nice new carpet, a double garage and a very large garden. The house cost £56,000, and we needed a mortgage of £45,000 and an £11,000 deposit. We had saved £6,000 between us, and Deepak persuaded his mother to lend us the extra £5,000 until his two insurance policies matured, one in 1987 and the other in 1989. I didn't like this arrangement. If we had no money, why put on a show for the world?

In August 1986, when Rajeev was eight months old, we moved to our new house. Raju helped us move. When we had cleaned the old house and checked it twice over to make sure we had left nothing behind and turned the key in the lock, Deepak and I got into the car. We had not been together like that in ages. He held my hand and asked if I was happy. 'See,' he said, 'I have made you a landlady today.' I was thrilled. I had always dreamed of owning my own house. I remember handing over my entire week's wages, £130, to the driver who moved our furniture. The new house had beautiful wall-to-wall carpeting which would have cost us a bomb, but we paid the owner a little extra to leave it behind. I asked Deepak to promise me that there would be no fights in our new house, where we would live happily with our two beautiful children. He said, 'I promise.' My eyes filled with tears. I had hungered for his affection for ages. I so wanted a life of laughter and kindness.

When we entered our new twenty-foot-long living room, Deepak held me, gave me a kiss and asked if I was happy. We were standing on the very spot where, three years later, he would be sitting on my chest, beating me unconscious. Even as I said yes, an alarm bell started ringing in my head. I was filled with dread and the certainty that something terrible would happen in this house. I felt somebody was going to die there.

THIRTEEN

Teaspoons to Double Glazing

ON THE VERY FIRST evening in our new house, Deepak went out.

After much persuasion he had agreed to lay the carpet in the children's room, which we had brought from our other house, and to fix Rajeev's cot. He was cursing and swearing because he had cut the carpet wrong, so the join was visible across the centre of the room. He was also shouting because he wanted to have an excuse to go to the pub. I had wanted us to eat together as a family in our new house, but for Deepak the attractions were greater outside.

I was very tired with all the work that moving entails, and I fell asleep. I have no idea when Deepak returned that night. If his overtime included a stint at the pub, he may have slept on the living-room sofa. I felt I couldn't voice my suspicions to anyone.

I wanted to do up my new house, and became obsessed by the desire to create the ideal home. Once that worm has entered your brain, it is very hard to get rid of it. I wanted to save up for new red velvet curtains, which would be really expensive, as we had large windows in the front and patio doors at the back.

Having known how Indian men are with household chores, before my marriage I hadn't expected Deepak to even lift a glass of water if he was thirsty. But to my surprise, because of his mother he was wonderfully house-trained. He even cooked at first. Having got used to all the help he used to provide, I now found it hard to get used to the new Deepak, who muttered and complained endlessly about doing the smallest chore.

I used to get so exhausted. Deepak didn't care. Never once did he ask me why I was fading away. Never once did he suggest taking me out as he used to in the early days. Not a friend could we visit together. My only outing was shopping. I was working partly to get out of the house and partly to take the pressure off Deepak so that he could take days off and be with us. When he did have time off, however, he would go out. I used to think I should help him out with the household expenses, although all he was paying for was the mortgage and some of the bills. I met the rest of the expenditure. On top of that I would give him £25 or £35 a week as my contribution, which he happily accepted. I bought a vacuum flask so that he could take hot cooked meals to work with him. Not once did he buy me a gift or say to me that I should buy myself something.

One day I burst into tears over this. I said that I had come from a family where there were no shortages, and although Deepak gave me everything I asked for, he never gave me anything without being asked. I was not hungry for things, but for the gesture. Deepak didn't say a word. He knew it was true.

I started doing a lot of overtime, even working on my two days off each week. Puppi was doing night shift and giving me a hand with the children. I also found a neighbour who agreed to babysit. When her sister came over from Zambia, it was even better. She was in Britain for nearly two years, and because she could not work officially she used to do the childminding, and was very flexible about time and money. Rajeev got so fond of her that he would hardly come to us.

Within two months of moving house, I was made redundant. That was a great shock, especially as we now had mortgage payments of about £500 a month. However, my boss had said that they would recall me at the very first opportunity, which came up within two weeks.

In this new job I packed the meal trays for aeroplane passengers. The hours were even better than before, 6 a.m. to 2 p.m. Although this meant waking up a bit early, it gave me half the day for housework. I was also doing about fifteen hours' overtime each week. I would put Rajeev to bed late and Deepak would give him breakfast and take him to the childminder's by 10 a.m. Sandeep stayed mostly with his grandmother, although from time to time she would get fed up and refuse to look after him. Then, after a few days, she would start missing him and would take him back. I said angrily to Deepak that his mother was treating looking after Sandeep as a joke, and upsetting my routine. The childminder would get used to more money, and would feel peeved when it was reduced again. Deepak shouted at Mamma. It also upset me that Mamma showed so little interest in Rajeev.

As soon as I got home, I would go straight into the kitchen and cook Deepak's dinner, although I had been on my feet all day. It really hurt me when Deepak didn't even eat what I had made him. If I didn't cook, he would scream and shout and complain to his mother. If I quoted the number of times he didn't eat his meals, she would say that it was my duty as a wife to cook for him, never mind whether he touched his food or not. But what about his duties as a husband? Who picked him up when he failed in those?

In the last few months I had gained a lot. I had passed my driving test, I had made new friends, and because of my job I could spend more freely. But I had also lost a lot. The distance between Deepak and me was growing by the day. He didn't want to know what I was doing, and he never told me what he was up to. He constantly complained that I was obsessed by money and that I was losing sight of home and children because of this. It's true that my material desires were expanding. Having bought a house, I now wanted double glazing, a fitted kitchen, a new bathroom and an extension.

At work there were a lot of Gujarati girls who would discuss their husbands, joke and laugh about sex, and talk about the visitors who came to their houses. I would sit there like a stone. Deepak had no friends, so we never had guests. And how could I tell them that he and I hardly talked, let alone had sex? I was probably the most educated of them all, I came from a good family, and yet I had the most miserable life. If I did laugh at their jokes I would fall silent abruptly because that laughter rang hollow in my ears.

I used to get so tired in those days, with two young kids and a job. Mamma would ask what I did all day to make me tired. She never remembered the fifty or sixty hours a week I spent at work, the lavish meals I cooked when she visited and the high standard of cleanliness in our house. She never noticed that the children were well fed and always in clean clothes. Did that happen on its own? She thought Deepak did it all – changing nappies, doing the weekly shopping and making tea for me, the maharani. He always showed off in front of visitors, laying the table, making the tea. When we left her house we didn't even have a teaspoon to our name. Now we had a fully equipped house. I didn't get there by putting my feet up.

Mamma would say to Deepak that he had spoilt me, raised me above my station by letting me sit on his head, that if he had left me in her control, my tongue wouldn't be working overtime as it was now.

After Rajeev I didn't want any more children, so I made an appointment at the hospital to get sterilised. Deepak said he would have the operation instead, because it was easier for men and all his friends had had it done. I thought I couldn't put him to so much trouble. As it was he had to have a hernia operation because he carried very heavy mailbags at work. I wondered why he had volunteered, and whether it had anything to do with his other affairs. His mother had told me that just before he came to see me in Canada, a white woman claimed he had got her pregnant. He had said that the woman was harassing him with false claims. His jackets used to be muddy and covered in grass, adding to her suspicions that he was having sex with women in the fields.

When I went to see the doctor, he advised me that my husband should have a vasectomy, as sterilisation was a more complicated operation for women. Deepak had the operation.

At about this time we found that we had misplaced Puppi's passport. Deepak had been keeping it because he didn't trust Puppi not to run away with another woman as his father had done and neglect his mother and sisters. Puppi and I were terrified that I might have thrown it out by mistake with some old clothes. For two nights we searched everywhere, not daring to tell Deepak. On the third day we told him. Deepak threw a fit. He accused me of being a spoilt little rich girl who threw clothes out at my whim and fancy, and who would throw him out as well one day. It turned out that Deepak had it all the time. I hadn't looked through his papers for fear of angering him. If I listened to any of his cassettes and put them back in the wrong place, or left them standing at an angle, he would shout at me. He memorised the position of all his things, and if he suspected anyone of touching them he would be furious. As soon as Puppi had started his aviation catering job, he bought a TV and a video so that he wouldn't have to touch Deepak's things and annoy him. He also paid me rent of £40 a week. If Deepak invited him to watch a video, that was all right, but if we went and got a video out without his permission, he would row. Deepak needed to harass us as a way of dominating us.

Puppi's passport was crucial because he had been deported from Britain in 1985 when he came for his father's funeral on a visitor's visa. 'British Overseas Citizen' was stamped on his passport, which meant that he could only settle in Britain on a voucher quota system. He had already applied under that system, and was still waiting at the time of his father's death. Once he was in Britain he tried to extend his stay, but he was told that he would have to return to India and wait for his voucher. Because the stamp on his passport made him nominally a British citizen, the Indian authorities would not let him in without a visa, and sent him back by the next flight. Deepak kept saying that he wouldn't be allowed entry, but no one listened to him. Puppi was overjoyed. When he reached Gatwick he rang Deepak and asked him to fetch him. Deepak said, 'Bastard, why did you ring? It is their responsibility to get you home. You tell them to bring you back. I'm not coming.'

When he was sent back to India, Puppi returned empty-handed. He didn't have a penny to buy presents for his family. Nobody helped him out. With my week's wages and some money from Deepak I bought presents costing £50 so that he would have something to give his family.

Puppi had been pestering me to arrange a marriage for him, as no one else would do it. He was a responsible, domesticated type who had known poverty and was caring towards his mother and sisters. He had no bad habits and was very good-natured. I suggested my niece Jyoti, the elder of Raghvir praji's two daughters, who was educated and also good-natured. Puppi liked her photographs, and decided to go to India as soon as possible to meet her. He asked me to go with him. I wanted a holiday as well, so I asked Deepak for his permission. Surprisingly, he agreed, and said he would come too.

On the night before we were due to leave, in January 1988, Deepak said he was going to work. I did all the packing and got the children ready for bed. We had to take gifts for all the family, and had so much luggage that we had to go to the airport in two cars. I didn't believe that Deepak had really gone to work the night before. If he had, he would have slept all the way in the plane. He didn't even sit with the rest of us. Jyoti and her family, and Puppi's family, came to Delhi to meet us at the airport. We went to a relative's house, and Puppi and Jyoti got an opportunity to talk to each other. They liked what they saw, as did the respective families. The wedding was held within ten days of our arrival.

There was no conversation between Deepak and me while we were in India. When I bathed the children, he would dress them, that's all. But my brothers held a huge party for my birthday, and Deepak decorated the room with balloons and streamers. It was a façade we were maintaining for the family.

Deepak and I decided to buy some land in Ahmedabad for 130,000 rupees (about £2,000). Although I was happy with the idea, I realised that Deepak had an ulterior motive. He wanted me to settle down in India with the kids so that he could be free to pursue his affairs in Britain. I played into his hands, because I wanted to put the children in the best boarding schools in India, build a house and have them visit us either in India or in England for school holidays. My brother was working in the construction industry, so building a house would be cheaper and easier than usual. I contributed towards the purchase, and Deepak bought the land in my name and said proudly to everyone that he had made me a landlady. After we returned to England, whenever we had a fight he would say, 'Go and live in India.'

On this holiday I could do what I wanted, and Deepak didn't interfere. The only time he really lost his temper was when I fell ill because I ate *pani-puris* from a roadside stall. He was screaming at me while I was vomiting, and insisted on accompanying me to the doctor. He shouted at me all the way there in the car. When my brother Kuki's son, who was driving, asked him to stop yelling at me, Deepak started on him. He forced him to stop the car, jumped out and banged the door.

After Puppi and Jyoti's wedding, Deepak wanted to go to Delhi to stay with an uncle. I made some excuse about my clothes being with the tailor, and said I would join him a week later. Meanwhile, Puppi's mother had died, and Deepak felt he had the right to dictate how the funeral would be organised.

Deepak had a huge row with Puppi's cousin over this. They nearly came to blows. He also insulted Puppi in front of Jyoti by shouting at him and holding him by the neck. Even before Jyoti came to England she was nervous of Deepak.

When we returned to England, the routine of work started the weekend we got back. Deepak and I were as cold and distant as ever. I would cook, then eat with Puppi and the kids. Deepak would say he wasn't hungry, and would wait till we were finished before eating. I would ask how his appetite could revive in such a short while.

Deepak still complained that I was too caught up in making money. I asked what would be the point of me sitting at home. And anyway, overtime was compulsory in my job. Anyone who wouldn't do it would be shifted to another department, where the work was not that easy.

I began to fall ill frequently. My shoulders used to ache all the time because we had to carry heavy trays at work. Every night I went to bed with Panadol. Deepak refused to take me to the doctor, and I had lost so much confidence that I didn't dare go on my own. All I had to say was that I had a pain in the shoulder, but I was afraid I wouldn't even be able to string that number of words together. My body, my mind, my thoughts were completely under Deepak's control.

Sandeep was staying with Mamma three or four days a week. On our days off we would bring him home. He didn't like leaving Mamma, and she would often have to accompany him back to our house. When he was at home I would indulge him – take him and Rajeev to the park, into town, to Chandrika's house, play with them, put on music and dance with them, buy them chocolates. One day when we visited Mamma she said she couldn't look after Sandeep any more. Sandeep screamed and refused to come home. He had been present during our fights, and didn't want to leave his grandmother and the relative calm of her place. I felt my son was drifting away from me.

When Sandeep and Rajeev fought, Sandeep would see everything in his grandmother's house as his and everything in our house as Rajeev's. I would try to explain to Sandeep that Mamma was also Rajeev's grandmother because they were brothers. That day Deepak wrenched him violently from Mamma, shouting, 'Little bastard, son of a pig. We'll see how you don't come home.' Mamma said, 'Leave it, there's no point. I'll keep him.' There ensued a tug-of-war with a frightened little child in between. Of course, might won the day. Deepak slapped Sandeep across the face and threw him roughly into the car. He shouted, 'Stop crying unless you want another slap.' Sandeep froze – such was the child's fear.

Deepak started to receive telephone calls at around midday. When the phone rang he would say it was for him, and that I shouldn't answer it. If I picked up the phone it would go dead. If Deepak answered it he would say, 'Hi, love,' and chat and laugh away for fifteen or twenty minutes at a time. I felt angry and jealous. Deepak sat with a long face at home and then came alive when he was talking to outsiders. When I asked who it was he said it was a woman from work who was suffering from cancer, and he was helping her out. I said I didn't like her ringing, and could he ask her to reduce the number of calls she was making. If my family ever called when Deepak was at home, I would tell him it had been a wrong number. He didn't like them calling me, which was why he changed the number so many times without telling me.

One night early in 1989 I received a call. A heavy male voice asked to speak to Mrs Deepak Ahluwalia, then said, 'Your husband is having an affair.' When I asked who was calling, the line went dead. Despite my suspicions, I couldn't bring myself to believe him. Maybe, I thought, it was a mischievous call – Deepak found it easy to make enemies. When he came home he would lift the curtain gently and look out at the street, saying, 'I think someone is following me.' 'Don't be silly, who would want to follow you?' I would say. When a man is up to no good, the fear of discovery frightens him even more than the activity.

All these things were strengthening the suspicions which were building up inside me but which I had not yet voiced. When I told Deepak about the call, he didn't say a word. He quietly changed our telephone number again without telling me. I mentioned the call to Mamma, and we decided to visit Gurdayal uncle, who was working with Deepak, to see if he could throw any light on the matter. He told us that Deepak was having an affair with a white woman.

At about this time Deepak had a car accident when he was taking this woman home. When I went to pick up Rajeev, the childminder's husband told me that the car had been involved in an accident. Deepak's driving was awful. Every year it seemed he had an accident, every year he got himself a new car, and every year his insurance got more unaffordable. No wonder he had accidents if he was drinking and driving.

I can't remember how many times Deepak changed the telephone number after that. He never told me the new number, although I usually managed to find it out somehow. Once I found it in his diary. Another time I overheard him give it to his mother. Even after he changed the number, though, the man's calls continued. I spoke to him three times, and sometimes the phone would ring and no one would answer when I picked it up.

Meanwhile, another bone of contention was building up between us. My brother Tommy, who had gone into the hotel business in Northern Ireland shortly after we returned from India, had asked us to pay the gas and electricity bills for his house in England while he was away. Deepak agreed. The bills were small as the house was empty. Deepak and Puppi visited Tommy in Northern Ireland, found property was cheap, and decided to move there and go into the hotel business together.

I thought it would be good for us to start a business, so I contributed £4,500 of my own money and £1,500 of the money I had saved in the names of the children. Puppi put in £7,000, and Deepak £1,000. However, Tommy had recently been divorced, and because of his marital difficulties Billoo praji asked him to come to Canada. Deepak was furious. He said that it was because of Tommy that we were going to emigrate to Ireland, and threatened to tear up Tommy's passport. Tommy promised to return as soon as his domestic situation improved. It was humiliating to have my brother insulted by Deepak. If Billoo praji hadn't called Tommy then he might have committed suicide, he was feeling so low. Tommy had left a cheque for £425, for his bills and repairs to his car.

Deepak's anger at Tommy's sudden departure was expressed by a new line of attack: that Tommy had borrowed £500 from him and he wanted me to return it. But Tommy's bills had only come to £150 or so. I told Deepak that if he showed me proof of this 'loan' I would get his money back, but he never did – because there wasn't any. In three weeks the figure Deepak was demanding went from £500 to £700, then £1,000, then £1,200, then £3,000, and finally £7,000. I thought I understood the game he was playing. His second insurance policy was about to mature, and he would have to return the £3,000 his mother had loaned us for the deposit on the house. But I later discovered that he also wanted to buy a car to show off to his girlfriend. He thought he could do both by concocting an imaginary loan. He could also use this demand to harass and intimidate me. The reason he raised the figure to £7,000 was that I told him I would offset Tommy's 'loan' against the £7,000 I had given him. Deepak didn't want to return that money to me, so he raised the figure to match it.

He refused to talk to me unless I got Tommy to return this money. As Deepak was the youngest son-in-law of the house, there is no way that my brothers would have borrowed money from him. In our tradition, hospitality must flow in the opposite direction. Even the clothes I was wearing had been given to me by my family.

A nephew, Jyoti's elder brother, was getting married in Canada in July, and I was very keen to go. Of course we had just come back from India, and I knew we didn't have much money, but Deepak agreed – in fact he put pressure on me when I started having second thoughts about the extravagance. He said I should go even if he had to borrow my fare. That made me suspicious. He was very eager to get rid of me. He wanted his path rid of this stone – me. Mamma was very angry at my extravagance in taking two holidays in one year, but Deepak told her that Surinder had sent me the ticket, which silenced her.

I wanted to take Sandeep because he was now old enough to remember a holiday. Rajeev was still too young. Mamma refused to look after Rajeev, and Deepak didn't want any encumbrances. In the end Mamma said she would look after Sandeep, and Rajeev went with me. I took a great risk by taking three weeks off as sick leave. I could have lost my job.

While I was in Canada, Deepak rang a couple of times. His branch of the Post Office was closing down and he was being moved to Crawley, which was less than a five-minute drive away for us. His work times would also change. Night shifts had ended and he would be working from 2 p.m. to 2 a.m.

For some reason, one night as I was getting undressed for bed in Canada, a vision of Deepak having sex with a white woman flashed across my mind. I felt convinced that it was happening at that very moment, and that I had known about it through some kind of telepathic insight. On one of his calls to me Deepak had said 'I love you.' I could hear noises in the background, and I suspected that he was lying in bed with another woman and saying the words to her, but letting me hear them. I was his toy – he was playing with my feelings.

When I returned from Canada, I expected Deepak to show some signs of excitement. He didn't even say hello. The flight had been delayed by six hours, and I was starving and exhausted. Deepak hadn't cooked, there was no food in the house, not even bread. It was 10.30 at night. I asked him to get me something from Kentucky Fried Chicken. He refused, saying he had to go to work. I put Rajeev to bed and fried myself some chips before falling into bed. Once again, I was making the journey into hell. After all the parties and all that love from my family, I had come back to this chilling atmosphere. I don't think Deepak was really going to work. He was using it as a pretext to go and stay with his girlfriend. When he did return later that night he slept on the settee downstairs.

That routine continued for a long time. Deepak always made sure he was home before 5 a.m., when I got up for work. He said he slept downstairs because he liked to watch television after coming back from work. That really upset me. I used to stay up till midnight with the children so that they would wake up late and give Deepak a chance to catch up on his sleep, and he was wasting that time by watching TV. Mental torture is worse than physical pain. Everything became a source of friction.

Once when I came home from work I saw two cups in the kitchen, one of them with lipstick on it. When I asked Deepak who the woman was, he said it was the insurance agent. He must have had a sex change since we last met him. I am positive his girlfriend used to visit when I was out.

Even in money matters, Deepak had changed so much. In the early days he would put his entire wage packet into my hand, or he would ring me and ask if he could take £2 for his expenses. I used to feel embarrassed that he asked me such questions when it was his money after all. He wanted me to give up my job because he didn't want to look after the children. When I asked if his wages would cover all the household expenses, he would fall silent. I stopped doing overtime to try and minimise our quarrels. In the summer, when there were lots of flights, overtime was compulsory, but in the autumn the rules were relaxed. I applied for a transfer to a part-time job.

I was saving up for a special gold ring for Deepak's birthday, which fell on New Year's Eve, so for Christmas I could only afford to give him a cheap shirt, which he sneered at. The ring cost £129, and I bought a card from myself and one from the children. I left them in the kitchen because I knew Deepak would go in there for a glass of water when he came home from work.

The next morning there was no reaction. After ten minutes, Deepak said, 'Thank you for your present.' He liked it, and I was really thrilled. Despite all our quarrels, I was mad enough to make this gesture. I was behaving as if I wanted an award for being the good wife.

Puppi's wife Jyoti was due to join him in the new year. Shortly before her arrival I asked Puppi to help me with some shopping. He burst out that I would teach his wife all my bad habits, and that he was not going to pamper her as I was pampered. I was hurt and angry. This was Deepak talking. I told Puppi to leave my house and find a room. Things had become complicated by the fact that we were related from both sides now that my niece was married to him. Of all his family I was the only one to have helped him out, and this was what I was reaping. Puppi's presence in the house also made it difficult for me to a have a heart-to-heart with Deepak.

The idea of setting up a business in Northern Ireland had died a death, and Puppi wanted to buy a house now that he was married. But when he tried to withdraw his money from our joint account Deepak wouldn't let him, because then he would have to return my money to me. Deepak ranted at Puppi, pushed him around and held him by the neck to stop him getting out of the deal.

Deepak was manufacturing excuses to keep things boiling between us. The telephone bill was next. I refused to pay it because I hardly ever used the phone. The line was disconnected, but in a few days it was restored. Deepak couldn't get up to all his mischief without a telephone. I personally didn't need the phone at all.

Deepak wouldn't let me accompany him and Puppi to Heathrow to fetch Jyoti. They took her to Dev's house on the way back, and Deepak spent the whole time humiliating Dev by complaining about how Tommy had ripped him off.

On the one hand I was thrilled by Jyoti's arrival. Despite the age gap, our interests were the same. But on the other hand I felt that it would be even more difficult for Deepak and me to sort out our marital problems while they were living with us. That part of me wanted them to find their own accommodation as soon as possible.

Deepak had become a supervisor at the Post Office, and he used that as an excuse for leaving the house at 10 a.m. for a job that started at 2 p.m. and was barely five minutes' drive away. He said he had to do more hours and extra training for his new job. He brought out a bunch of keys and, holding out a small key, said he now had the office keys. I'm not that stupid. I know that offices have stronger locks than that. It was the key to that woman's house, and he could now come and go as he liked. He said he needed to get a good suit, as he was a supervisor. I went shopping and spent £200 on new clothes for him. When he wore the suit I felt proud because he looked so handsome. At one point I got so carried away that I tried to give him a peck on the cheek to wish him good luck. He pushed me away. I was so hurt. Not even an iota of feeling left for me.

The day before my birthday, Deepak went into town with Puppi and bought two gold bracelets, one for £60 and the other for £49. I was sitting in the living room the following day, chatting to Puppi and Jyoti, not expecting anything from anyone. Deepak was not talking to me, although he would laugh and chat with Jyoti and ask her to cook for him, which used to upset me. He had bought me a birthday card which he never gave me, but which I found in the cupboard later. It had yellow flowers on it and it said 'To my loving wife'. Deepak went upstairs, and sent Sandeep down with my present. Sandeep wished me happy birthday and kissed me, but Deepak stayed upstairs. When I saw the bracelet I was over the moon. I showed it to Puppi, who asked where the other one was. I laughed at him, saying that people don't wear two bracelets. He insisted there were two, because he had been with Deepak when he bought them. I went upstairs and asked Deepak. He turned yellow. He said he had returned the other bracelet because he didn't like it. The shop would not give cash, he said, but the refund would show up in the next monthly statement. On top of everything, I'd got the cheaper bracelet.

The next bank statement showed meals bought in restaurants, clothes from C&A, and more jewellery, none of which had ever entered my house. Mamma knew about the other woman, but she wouldn't let the water touch her feet. She wouldn't accept it until she saw the next bank statement. I felt betrayed, but decided to wait. A thief always gets caught out eventually, and Deepak was not having an easy time of it. Apart from family pressure, his girlfriend's ex-lover was threatening him. One day when he was bringing Jyoti back from Mamma's he drove really fast because he was afraid he was being followed. Jyoti was petrified.

I couldn't even talk to my male relatives without Deepak getting suspicious. Yet he had gone out and done it all, flouting his responsibilities as a father and husband. I hated the double standards of our society. I had been crying out for someone to save our marriage, but nobody had come forward. I couldn't talk to Puppi. He was younger than me, and older people are meant to resolve younger people's problems, not the other way around.

Deepak found Jyoti a part-time job at the Post Office two evenings a week. He would leave work to fetch her and drop her off. When Mamma saw him laughing and chatting with Jyoti she said to me, 'Have a quiet word with Jyoti and ask her to find another job. You know what Deepak is like, he can't leave a skirt alone.'

When Jyoti moved to a full-time catering job I asked her and Puppi to move house, because I needed time on my own to discuss things with Deepak. They arranged to move into a bedsit in a house around the corner let by a widow who lived on her own. A couple of days before they were to move out, Billoo praji's wife Devinder came to England to attend her father's funeral in Newcastle. She spent a night with us on the way. As soon as she arrived, Deepak started on Tommy. He told her that he had decided to leave me because our marriage was not happy. He lay down in the bed that had been made up for Devinder bhabiji and asked her to sleep with me, so that he wouldn't have to share my bed. She later told me that she didn't like the intimate way in which he touched her. When Devinder and I were alone, I told her how unhappy I was.

The next morning, as I was saying goodbye to Devinder, Deepak pushed me against the wall, banged my head against it and picked me up by the neck. I was standing on my toes so that the weight of my body pulling against his hand wouldn't tighten the constriction around my neck even more and make it impossible for me to breathe. He kept lifting me higher and I kept stretching my feet. He was slapping me and shouting, 'Talk, talk now, because we are going to make a decision today.' Devinder, Puppi and Jyoti were stunned. It was such a sudden transformation, like a hungry lion leaping onto some unsuspecting animal. When he let go of me I just walked out of the house, tears running down my face.

[Of this incident, Devinder's statement for the trial says: 'It was at this time that Deepak mentioned that he had another woman and he was leaving her, Kiran, and that his other woman was better than her in bed. Kiran said she would get a divorce. Deepak hit her on the head with a lot of force. I ran down the stairs and tried to grab Deepak's arm and he hit me and pushed me away.

I still tried to get between them, managing to pull him off. He turned around and looked at Kiran who was bleeding . . . he said if she tries to leave I will kill her. Kiran put on her coat and again Deepak hit her and it was awful.']

FOURTEEN

The Storm Clouds Gather

IN MARCH, shortly after Puppi and Jyoti moved out, both Deepak and I had the Saturday off. Since January I had been pleading with him to talk to me for five minutes. Without that outlet, you must understand how it was all building up inside me, a pressure cooker waiting to explode – fear, anger, hatred, confusion. I resolved to talk to him that day, to bring out all the things that had been bubbling away inside me for months, but after we got up and I made tea, Deepak saw Puppi through the window. He seized his chance, ran out and invited Puppi in. He stayed for nearly the whole day. I was seething. Puppi knew I had warned Jyoti that I was planning to have my talk with Deepak that day. I had wanted to talk about our future, our children, about Deepak's girlfriend, about the telephone bill, about Tommy – and I had lost a golden opportunity.

Deepak's comings and goings were now so unpredictable that I never knew how to organise childcare and whether I would be able to go to work in the morning. I lived in perpetual fear of being sacked because of the number of days I had to miss when I had no one to look after the children or when I didn't want to parade my bruises. Mamma would sometimes stay, but she would complain that she couldn't sleep, that she was ill, or that she couldn't watch Deepak's butchery.

One night I had another telephone call from the man who claimed that Deepak was having an affair. My English was so poor that I couldn't say anything beyond 'What?' I phoned Deepak at work to ask him if it was true. He said he couldn't talk there, and put the phone down. I then rang his mother. She pleaded ignorance and helplessness, but promised to talk to him.

Less than ten minutes later, Deepak came charging in and pulled me out of bed. Mamma was in the passage. He had told her that he would break my limbs today. From her serious expression and her pale face, I knew he must have uttered some vile threat. He started yelling, 'Tell me, which lover of yours rang tonight?' I said the man didn't give his name. He started slapping me, then picked me up and threw me to the floor. He sat on my chest and hit me wherever he could. I was trying to protect my face but it got covered in bruises. I was bleeding and screaming to Mamma for help. She tried to get Deepak off my chest. I became unconscious. When I came to, Mamma was sprinkling water on me. She asked me why I was crying when I should have known better than to provoke Deepak, and asked to be taken home. After dropping her, Deepak went off to his girlfriend. I didn't go to work for three or four days.

The children lived in fear, although Rajeev was too young to understand what was going on. But Sandeep knew that Daddy was beating Mummy. He remembers a lot, and it has had an effect on him. He even tells me things I have forgotten. He once reminded me of the day when Deepak was hitting me with his shoe and he shouted, 'Don't hit my Mummy,' and Deepak turned on him. He ran upstairs and hid under his bed to escape a beating.

At work, my eyes would keep brimming over. If I couldn't control myself I would sob in the little storeroom or the toilet until it passed. My boss noticed that I was wasting away, and asked if someone in my family had died. I wanted to say, 'No one has died in my family, but I have been turned into a living corpse,' but I didn't have enough English or the openness to share my innermost feelings.

I had to do overtime over Easter, and I asked Deepak to stay at home with the children. Again he punched me with his fists till I had blue patches all over my face, and again I could not go to work. Whenever I begged Deepak to talk so that I could know what my future would be, he would end up beating me. I rang my boss and said I had fallen in the street and that my leg was hurting so much I couldn't go to work. He warned me that my sickness record was poor and I was in danger of getting the sack. I told Mamma and she came over. I was sitting with a towel covering my swollen lips and bruised face. Deepak rang Puppi, wanting him to settle matters between us. When Puppi said he couldn't come because he was on overtime, Deepak said, 'My family life is collapsing around my ears and all you can think about is your damn overtime. Get a cab and come here right away.'

The next day, lying in bed with my face all swollen up, I took to alcohol. I could not stand the pain any more. The mental torture and my aching body had driven the sleep from my eyes. At first I would drink on the sly, at night. I would take a small sherry glass, fill it to the brim with anything that was lying about – gin, whisky, rum, sherry – and knock it back. Before, I had only drunk sherry occasionally. What did I know of mixing drinks? Did whisky go with water? Or Coke? Or lemonade? I would suck on a cardamom to hide the smell.

In our society, a woman who drinks is seen as immoral and without character. I used drink to help me sleep, but in a couple of hours the scenes of torture would crowd my brain and I would wake up sobbing. Then I would go downstairs and knock back another couple of drinks. I went to bed in the clothes I had gone to work in. In the morning I would get up, sprinkle some water on my face, brush my teeth and go to work, still in the same clothes. I had no interest in food. Soon I started drinking in the daytime. Somehow, throughout those drink-filled days I managed to see to the children, bathe them, clothe them and feed them. But I couldn't play with them. I stopped taking them to the park or to the shops. All I could do was cry. Sometimes I would see them sitting around helplessly and I would hold them close to me. Through my tears I would ask them to forgive me for being so consumed by grief that I couldn't pay them any attention.

Once Deepak unexpectedly returned home in the daytime and saw me lying on the floor of the living room. He didn't know that I had been drinking. He said, 'Go and look at yourself in the mirror and see the state of you.' I went to the doctor and told him my problems, how I couldn't sleep at night, how I was afraid of going home, how Deepak beat me. The doctor gave me some sleeping tablets, but they had no effect. I went back and asked him to prescribe some stronger medicine. That didn't have any effect either. I suppose mental pain can't be chased away as easily as that. Two or three weeks later I sat in the surgery sobbing, and told the doctor that I didn't want to go home. I said the children were scared because Deepak beat them too. The doctor said he would refer me to a social worker. I said I had come to him secretly and didn't want a social worker in case Deepak got to know. I think the doctor did take some action, because his report was submitted to court at my trial.

Deepak's mother wanted me to complain to the Postmaster General about Deepak's white girlfriend. I wanted to go and show my bruised face to her to let her know what was in store for her, but I didn't want to be beaten up, I feared for my safety. I tried to persuade Mamma to go and see the woman because she wouldn't incur Deepak's wrath in the same way. Sometimes she would say, 'I pray to God that someone will beat him up the way he beats others up.'

At about this time Deepak took a week's holiday. One day I was in bed crying as usual, and the children were playing downstairs. They broke a glass in the kitchen. Deepak forced me to come down and clear the mess up. He said I was mad to be crying for no reason. He caught hold of my hair and shoved me into the kitchen, then rang his mother and started complaining that I was crying so much that I was ignoring my duties as a mother.

On the third day of his holiday, Deepak was sunning himself in the conservatory when I asked him if he would do some shopping for the children. We were right out of cereal, biscuits and chocolates. He refused point blank. He told me to go shopping myself, but he would not lend me the car. I said, 'Fine, I don't need the car, but will you keep an eye on the kids?' He refused. He wanted me to take them with me to the shops, carry Rajeev and the shopping, hold on to Sandeep's hand to cross the road. I started crying, and asked him why he was taking his hatred for me out on the children.

Soon afterwards, his mother turned up. 'Has he beaten you up again?' she asked.

'No. He won't go shopping and he won't let me go shopping. Because he is lusting after a white woman, he has forgotten his children and their needs. What has happened to him?'

Mamma taunted and lectured Deepak, but he would not be moved. Then Suresh turned up, and for the first time I wept in front of him and told him what had happened. But what could he do? Deepak wasn't going to listen to anybody. Besides, his brothers would often say to Mamma that we were older than them and should be able to sort out our own problems.

One morning in March Deepak announced that he was leaving home. I knelt down and touched his feet, pleading with him not to go. I said I would do anything, I wouldn't talk to him at all if that was what he wanted. He picked me up by the arm, twisted it and shoved me aside, then started packing his suitcase. I was crying. The phone rang, and I answered it. A woman asked for Deepak. He took the phone from me and said, 'I'm coming shortly. I'm not going to live here any more.' When I asked him who it was, he said it was his solicitor.

I told him I couldn't manage the children on my own, and he said, 'Don't worry. I'll ask the social services to take them into care.' He knew that I would die before I let that happen.

Deepak took his suitcase to his mother's, so as to keep up the pretence that there was no other woman and that he was only leaving home because he was so unhappy. That day I wept and wept. I had sacrificed my life for him, and he had used me and then dumped me. I wrote to him, drinking alcohol and weeping:

Deepak please read this letter for me if you don't want to talk. First time in my life I reliese that how much I love you. I was so selfish or proud my self that I never bother about anything. But you teach me very good lesson. Deepak I don't think I can live without you in this house. This is your house please come back. Alright don't talk with me. You know I'm not greedy about this house but you and Sandeep Rajeev is first for me.

Deepak if you come back I promise you
  I won't touch black coffee again
  I won't go to town every week
  I won't eat green chilly
  I ready to leave Chanrika and all my friends
  I won't go to Dev Guddi Mohan's house again even I'm not
  going to attend Bully's wedding
  I eat to much or all the time so I can get fat
  I won't laugh if you don't like
  I won't dye my hair even I don't go to my neighbour's
  house
  I won't ask you for any help

Deepak life is dull without you. I don't feel like doing anything. If I was cleaning cooking or working before, I thought I was doing for you, because my husband was here with me. I can't cook or eat now. Honestly Deepak I spend 10 years with you. Please for this 10 years sake give me 10 minutes so I can explain you why all this happen. Please come alone after you finish work. Then if you still don't want to live with me I don't mind. I know I hurt your feeling very badly but still I have right to ask apologise from you.

Deepak Sandeep Rajeev they need father and Mother together. Sandeep understand everything. Please take care Rajeev he is very small. Deepak I said so many things to you please forgive me.

Deepak keep this letter with you if you don't trust me. I'll wait for you tomorrow evening. I promise I won't take long time. This is my last request to you by this letter. Otherwise life is still going on.

Poochi Please for god sake don't tell anybody about this letter. It's not only my insult you too involve in it.

I admitted that everything was my fault. If I could have stopped breathing, I would have promised to breathe only so many times in five minutes if it would please him. At my trial, my barrister read this letter out in court as evidence that I was leading the life of a slave.

The next day Deepak came to the house with Mamma. He was in the habit of checking that everything was in the right place when he returned home, and he would also go through my pockets. He found the letter and said, 'Here you are, Mamma, read this letter. She has admitted all her faults.' He was laughing at my pain. Fortunately he did not read the letter out loud to Mamma. I would have been so embarrassed. Thank goodness I had shied away from writing one of the things I had wanted to say: 'If you want my body every day, I will let you.' If I was then what I have become today, perhaps I would have written that line and added, 'To hell with family honour.'

Although he said he had left home, Deepak would keep coming back unpredictably for short periods to keep an eye on me. He was like a grasshopper. He never did anything with patience, never sat and played with his children. If he had nothing to do, he would just drive around aimlessly in his car. He wouldn't leave me or live with me. I was hanging in limbo.

I was managing childcare between Puppi, Jyoti, Mamma, Suresh and Raju and the childminder.

One of my nieces, Bully, was going to get married in Hounslow in April. I wanted to go, but Deepak said he didn't, and wouldn't let me either. He was upset that his mother hadn't been invited. I said I was earning, I was independent, and if I felt like going I would. When the day dawned he insisted on taking me. He said he wouldn't give me the chance to show my family what a bad husband I had.

I was very upset that day. There was alcohol at the wedding, and Deepak was dancing and having fun. I started drinking secretly, and I got drunk. When we got to my cousin's house I was sick. I went to the toilet and ran the tap on full to cover the sound of my retching. Then I lay down, saying that I was tired after having worked all night. Manju's husband came to talk to me, and when I told him that Deepak was having an affair with a white woman he said he had known for ages that Deepak couldn't even leave a dog alone.

While we were there, Sukhjit's older brother said to me, 'You must learn karate.' Everybody except Deepak and me burst into laughter. I didn't dare laugh because Deepak would have thumped me afterwards. On the way home I wanted to sit in the front of the car because I was still feeling sick. Deepak didn't want to be seen with me at his side. He complained to his mother that my family were putting me up to all kinds of things because they thought I was the innocent party. 'You go around making a fool of yourself, I'm not surprised they say things like that. No wonder I don't get invited when you are my ambassador.'

After the wedding Deepak started living at home again, on the condition that we slept separately. His mother had told him that if I lost my job because of having to look after the children it would be worse for him, and that he shouldn't be playing with his children's lives. He made his bed in the boxroom, and I slept with the children.

I was very confused in those days. Deepak hadn't left the smallest chink through which I could find a way out. I felt guilty about my drinking, but I couldn't give it up. Part of me wanted to commit suicide. If I died, Deepak would find out how difficult it was to look after children *and* go to work. I went to the chemist and bought £6 worth of Paracetamol and Anadin. I ground the pills into a fine powder and put it in a bag, waiting for an opportune time to take it with alcohol. All my problems would be solved.

I rang Mamma. 'I'm fed up,' I said. 'I can't see a way out. I'm going to kill myself. I have £800 in my account. Use that for my funeral expenses but for God's sake make sure that Deepak doesn't come to my funeral. When the boys get married, give their wives one gold jewellery set each. You know, the two sets I was given when I got married. I'm going to make you a signatory on the boys' accounts where I have been putting the child benefit. Please, please bring them up in such a way that they don't turn out like their dad.'

She started laughing. 'Are you mad? I know my son, he won't lament your departure. He'll bring in a stepmother to look after the kids, probably one of his white girlfriends. She'll enjoy the house which you have decorated and furnished with your sweat. No other woman will look after your children the way you do.'

I thought she was right. Why should I give up my life and let Deepak go on enjoying his? My children would suffer with another woman as their mother. Maybe I should run away instead. On Mamma's advice I got a safe-deposit box at the bank and put my jewellery there to keep it away from Deepak. I also put the children's and my passports in there in case I decided to take them away to live in India or Canada. When Deepak made threats against me, I said he could only carry them out if I was still here. He got suspicious and asked for all our passports. He forced me to give him the children's, but I refused to part with mine. He said he would find me and kill me whichever part of the world I might settle in. He wanted me to accept a situation in which he would have affairs while I lived with him and looked after his children. If I showed the faintest sign of independence, he would harass me because he wanted me completely under his thumb. If he really wanted us to part, surely he would have agreed to talk to me about the future. He knew his relationships with white women wouldn't last. They wouldn't be interested in bearing his children.

In mid-April there were *Baisakhi* (Punjabi new year) celebrations in a local hall. Jyoti and Chandrika asked me to join them, and I asked Deepak to come along. He said he was going out with his friends, and told me to go by cab. I knew which friend he meant, so I said I wouldn't go, but he was so keen for me to go out that he agreed to drop me. I got dressed with great care, hoping Deepak might be stirred by my beauty again and return to the fold. I did a twirl and asked him for his opinion. He gave a half smile and turned away abruptly. I nearly asked if she was more beautiful than me but I bit my tongue in time.

When I got to the hall, people were congratulating me. I asked why, and they said, 'Your husband has been promoted.' Once upon a time I would have been proud of Deepak's advancement, but today I had no pleasure in it. *She* had reaped all the benefits, not me. I told my father-in-law's eldest brother, tayaji, how unhappy I was, how much Deepak was beating me. He asked if my brothers knew. I said they couldn't do anything because Deepak sat with a knife on the table saying, 'Let's see how they get past Gatwick.' Tayaji's advice was that my brothers should beat Deepak to a pulp, and then he would never lay a finger on me. I felt I had wasted my time. I was a problem only for my brothers and sisters. I found tayaji's wife and I wept in front of her. Hansapur aunty, another family friend who supported me tirelessly later on, was sitting nearby. She was listening to me carefully, but not a muscle moved on her face.

At about this time I had the idea of running away for a few

days so that Deepak would know what it was like balancing the demands of home and work. I wrote a note in English saying, 'We cannot live under the same roof. Look after the children. Bye for now.' I took the children to Jyoti's, and told her that I had to go out, and if I didn't come back in time Puppi should drop them off at Mamma's or hand them over to Deepak. I didn't tell Jyoti where I was going, because Deepak would have beaten it out of her. I then went to stay with Chandrika.

When Deepak got home and read the letter, he went to Jyoti's and dragged her to his mother's house, where he and his mother shouted at her. He then called Chandrika, who said she didn't know where I was. Mamma rang Dev and started abusing me: 'She's dragging our name through the mud. I've done so much to help her out and she didn't even tell me that she was planning to do this. She's betrayed my trust. I won't be able to marry my other sons off if this gets out.'

That night Chandrika confessed to me that she had known about Deepak's affair since January. Her cousin who worked at the Post Office had told her. Chandrika had seen Deepak with the woman when she had gone to a party and left her children with me for babysitting. She had wept for me. Although I had suspected Deepak of having an affair, this was the first time I had actual proof. I told Chandrika that the next time he hit me, I would hit him back. I was full of anger. He had betrayed me. I drank and cried a lot that night. I had intended to go to work the next day, but I couldn't get up in time for my bus at 5.30 a.m. I was so confused and so mad and so determined to get to work that I phoned Deepak to ask him for a lift. I didn't know what I was doing. I knew he would come to my workplace in search of me anyway.

When Deepak found out that I was at Chandrika's he was furious that she had lied to him. I kept saying I didn't have much money, that I had to go to work and could we talk after that, and I would agree to any conditions laid down by him. After much persuasion, he agreed. When I got into the car, he slapped me and started shouting. The first thing he wanted to know was why I had given our next-door neighbour our telephone number, which he had recently changed. I didn't even know it myself, so how could I have done that? His real anger was about my leaving home, but he started at a tangent. He had received another anonymous call from his girlfriend's ex-lover. He slapped my thigh.

'Let me get out,' I said. 'I want to get out here. I'll make my own way if you're going to hit me and shout at me.'

He said, 'What made you think that I was going to take you to work? You think I'm going to drop you off here? Today you will go where I want you to go.'

I started pleading with him to take me to work because I would get sacked. 'This job is for my children, for you. Don't mess around with it.'

He said he would take me to his mother's, and that he would beat me so much that I would remember my parents. 'How dare you leave home, you prostitute, you *vaishya*, woman without character!' He was banging on the steering wheel and shouting.

I didn't want to go to Mamma's house under any circumstances, and begged him to take me home. When we slowed down at a mini-roundabout I tried to open the door and jump out of the car. Deepak pulled up, came round to my side and pushed me into the back seat (it was a two-door car), saying that if I tried any more tricks like that he would drive over me and make chutney out of me. He was using me like a punching bag. Clumps of hair were coming away in his hands. I lifted the collar of my jacket to protect my face, but somehow he managed to chip my front tooth with the gold ring on his finger when he punched me. When I started crying loudly, he let go of me and drove off in the direction of his mother's. I reached out from the back seat and caught hold of the steering wheel, trying to turn the car in the opposite direction. He grabbed my hand and twisted it so hard that, as a reflex action, I sank my teeth into his right earlobe, which started bleeding. The blood was dripping down his shirt. I was petrified. I knew I would pay for his bleeding ear. I screamed that I wouldn't let go until he agreed to drive to the police station. We were both locked helplessly in each other's grip. He couldn't drive because he was holding my wrist with one hand, and I was holding on to his ear.

He swore by his dead father that he would take me to the police if I let go of his ear. I let go, but I held on to his shoulders to make sure he didn't turn the wheel in the wrong direction. He was driving fast. Suddenly he stood on the brakes. I was flung back.

He took his seatbelt off and started beating me around the head and body, even harder than before, if that was possible. He was screaming, 'I'll send you straight to hell, you bitch. I want blood for blood.' He took a long screwdriver and a spray-can out of the glove compartment. He was kneeling on the driver's seat, facing me in the back seat. He held the screwdriver barely an inch away from my eyes and screamed, 'I'll dig your eyes out of your sockets and spray your blinded sockets with this. You have five minutes left. In five minutes you are going to lose your sight and your life. Pray, bitch, pray, you bastard, pray to your God, to your mother and to your dead father.' I brought my hands together and started praying feverishly, the top half of my body rocking backwards and forwards. If I stopped praying, he would bring the screwdriver closer. Then he straightened up and drove to his mother's. I thought I was going to die any minute.

When we got to Mamma's it was a quarter to seven. Normally it would have taken only ten minutes to drive there from Chandrika's. It had taken us an hour. I had been beaten for an hour. I wouldn't get out of the car, and he dragged me out by the arm. When his mother asked what had happened to his ear he said, 'Ask your wonderful daughter-in-law. People think she is an innocent little darling. Now you know her real character.' He pushed me so violently that I went flying to the far side of the living room and banged my forehead so hard against the wall that it came up in a lump.

Deepak's mother could only see her son's bleeding, swollen ear, and started yelling at me. When he started hitting me, she cried out to Raju for help. Raju came downstairs in his pyjamas and pulled Deepak off me, shouting, 'Stay away from her. Take her home and beat her there, if you must, but don't come here with your quarrels, don't destroy our peace.' Mamma pointed out Deepak's bleeding ear. Raju said, 'Is Deepak's ear blinding you to his cruelty towards Kiranjit?' Even in court, Raju told the truth.

I stayed on at Mamma's, while Deepak went to his girlfriend's. I know this from her statement to the police in which she referred to dressing his wounded ear and washing his blood-stained clothes. I will never forget the scene of the screwdriver for as long as I live. Deepak went to Puppi's that evening to show off his ear and to boast that he had pounded me to a pulp and chipped my tooth in return.

I didn't phone my workplace that day. I didn't go to work the next day either. I was covered in bruises, and every part of my body was aching. That beating had strengthened my resolve to give Deepak as good as I got. At the most he would kill me. That was better than this life filled with tears.

FIFTEEN

A Circle of Light

WHEN DEEPAK FOUND ME at home he said, 'How do you have the courage to return? With what face are you coming back?' He started lashing out at me. I hid my face behind the red velvet curtains. He put a kitchen knife against my throat: 'Blood for blood, what do you say?' I kept completely still and quiet. If I had uttered one word, I think he would have driven that knife through.

He said, 'Call your brothers in India and Canada. I want a decision on our marriage now.' When I agreed, he said he would cut their legs off if they put one foot outside Gatwick. Then, suddenly, he made tea for both of us. I refused to drink mine. This was the first time in ten years of marriage that I had refused – tea had always been our peace offering. 'What is all this about?' I asked. 'Why aren't you considering the children in all this? How long will this go on? I'm tired.' Deepak didn't answer.

That month's bank statement arrived. Still there was no refund for the bracelet, although once again there were things on it which had never entered my house. I took the statement to Mamma, but she said she wanted to see the next month's before making up her mind. She also said a very hurtful thing: 'If you aren't getting on, I'll look after the children. You go where you want.' Didn't she know how important the children were to me? Because I had no one else to talk to, and there was no one else who might have some influence over Deepak, I carried on talking to her. Besides, I was too embarrassed to raise the matter outside the family. I felt so hurt that no one cared for me and my pain, they were interested only in the children. I was being flicked aside like a fly from a glass of milk. I was the outsider, the irritation. Everything would return to normal if I went away. I said to her, 'Did you leave your children when you were suffering with your husband? I'm like a wounded lioness, my anger knows no bounds when my cubs are threatened. You know I can't abandon them.'

Mamma was to repeat my comment about the wounded lioness in her statement to the police, but she could not remember it in court when she was asked to repeat it. Out of a sense of self-preservation, I lied in my statement and said this conversation never took place. When Deepak's younger brother Anil came home and asked what was going on between Deepak and me, Mamma said she didn't know. I said, 'Why don't you admit the truth, that Deepak is having fun with white women and then coming home and beating me and the kids?' They both fell silent.

In March, Deepak had received £3,000 from his insurance policy. Instead of giving it to his mother as he had promised, he bought a sports car, an XR-3, to show off to his girlfriend. He also needed £500 for the insurance on the car. His premiums kept rising because he had accidents every year. He wasn't doing any overtime, and he had to pay the mortgage and the rates. He couldn't afford the £500, so he drove the car without insurance. This really worried me because he used the car to ferry the children around. I rang the police anonymously and informed on him. That shows how much I was boiling over. I have been describing Deepak's evilness, but I could be wicked too. The police picked him up in Pound Hill after he dropped the kids off at school. When he got home that day he was looking depressed. I asked if everything was okay. He told me what had happened: 'If I find out who squealed on me, I'll break every bone in their body.' He then rang the insurance company and spun them a long story, asking for his policy number and blaming their inefficiency for his paperwork being incomplete. For some reason the company accepted it was their fault and issued him with a policy. This saved him from the police, and was to stand him in good stead for what was to come.

One day I came home from work and, having left the keys behind, knocked at the door. There was no answer. I noticed Deepak's car parked in front of the garage, and wondered why he wasn't letting me in. I went to the childminder's and rang Mamma. She said, 'Deepak and the children are here. Haven't you noticed the car? Someone has damaged it. The tyres have been slashed. Don't touch anything because the police are coming for fingerprints.'

I went back to have a look at the car. The paint had bubbled up and there was a whitish liquid on the roof. I felt it was the handiwork of the man who had been making the threatening phone calls. Deepak claimed, without once looking me in the eye, that it had been done by a jealous colleague at work who wanted to bring him down now that he had been made supervisor.

The night before, Deepak had gone to his girlfriend's. Her ex-boyfriend had seen his car parked there and had damaged it. Deepak used to drink and drive, and I think he drove home without noticing that his tyres were flat. She didn't live far away.

Secretly, I was thrilled. His prized possession had been damaged. He looked at his car more often than he looked at his own face in the mirror. Now he would have to walk to work, and he couldn't drive his mistress around. I had been so jealous at the thought that she was riding about in his car. I wished that man would beat Deepak up or maim him in some way so that he could understand what pain is. Such thoughts were taking up regular residence in my brain now. Deepak's constant cruelty towards me was like stoking embers into a raging fire again. This anger had no outlet. I wished I was a woman who frequented pubs and clubs and could have found a man friend to beat Deepak up.

No one would sort out my problems. No one suggested that I should leave him. Although they knew that I could have got social security and survived on my own, that there was free schooling and health care, they were still thinking according to the centuries-old tradition. I myself didn't know that financial help was available from the state. I only knew about unemployment benefit and child benefit.

Strange thoughts began to enter my head. Next time he threatened to blind me, I would throw chilli powder in his eyes. I wanted to give him pain, too. I resolved to buy some caustic soda to blind him temporarily. I remembered how much it hurt when I had got a grain of it lodged in my eyes at work many years ago. My pain was strengthening my resolve to stand up to Deepak.

I went to my friend Vimla, who used to work at Bale & Church, and said I wanted three tins of caustic soda because I wanted to clean out my saucepans and kill my weeds. When I got home I realised it was the wrong kind. It was a liquid. I took it back. I had to wait till the next staff shopping day to get the right kind. It was cheaper to buy from the factory.

I actually did want to clean my pans, and I scrubbed some of them and filled a particularly bad one with caustic soda solution. Before I went to work I put it on the top shelf of a cupboard at the top of the stairs, out of reach of the children. Deepak noticed it, and said to Raju and Puppi, 'Do you know she's planning to kill me?' He showed them the pan of caustic soda. When they asked me about it I said, 'Don't be silly. Do you think caustic soda can kill you?'

Once again Deepak started demanding the money he claimed Tommy owed him. I gave him my stock answer, that I wanted to see the receipts. He asked for Surinder's phone number in Canada, but I deliberately gave him the wrong one, saying it was the only number I remembered. He shouted that he would ring my brothers. 'See, you bitch, let's see whether fire shoots out of their backsides when they hear their sister weeping down the phone because I've beaten her.' Billoo praji and Tommy were not in when he rang them. Devinder asked if everything was all right, and Deepak said, 'I want you to pass on my message to those bastards about how I ill-treat their sister because they haven't returned my loan. Come, Poochi, talk to your sister-in-law.' He dragged me roughly by the arm and shoved me up to the telephone. As I said 'Hello,' quaking at the thought of what would happen next, Deepak beat me on the head with his knuckles and the receiver, screaming, 'Tell those bastards how you heard Poochi scream. They've eaten up my money. They will remember their dead mother when they see what I've reduced their sister to. I'm going to kill her.' Devinder was crying and shouting, 'Don't hit her, Deepak.' I was being beaten up in England and my sister-in-law in Canada was listening helplessly to my cries.

Deepak was enjoying listening to us both weep. He told Devinder that he was going to beat me some more, and put the phone down. That same day my brother posted a cheque for £500. Deepak rang his mother and boasted how he had made Devinder hear my screams. 'Listen,' he said. 'You too can listen to this weeping bitch.' I was so weak I could hardly stand, let alone take the punches that were flying at me. How cruel can a human being be? His knuckles had turned blue, he had been hitting me so hard. In between my sobs I was screaming, 'Mamma, Mamma, help me.' His mother couldn't bear to listen. 'Bastard, let go of her,' she shouted, and said she was coming round. When she arrived she tried to talk to Deepak about his responsibilities as a father, and to persuade him to give up his mistress.

That night I phoned Dev and wept on the phone. The following day Sukhjit jijaji and Mamma came. I needed to talk about the future. I wanted a divorce, and we had to talk about the children, my job and so on. Deepak just stood there mutely.

Sukhjit asked us to go with him to his house, where we could discuss things in peace. Deepak said he would come later. Although he wouldn't admit it, he wanted me out of the way so he could go to his girlfriend's. There was no point in me going alone, so finally Sukhjit and Mamma left. As soon as they had gone Deepak went out.

Two or three days later my bruises had cleared up a bit, and I felt ready to face work again. When I got up at 5 a.m., there was no Deepak. I went to Puppi and Jyoti's house, and stood on the pavement and shouted to wake them up so they could babysit. I rang Mamma from work and told her that Deepak hadn't turned up. Her advice was to hold on in there, that men eventually come home after straying. I couldn't endure it any longer. I had held out for so long in a relationship that was unhappy and unstable. If this was the lifestyle Deepak wanted, why did he persuade me to have his children? For the first time I told Mamma about my abortion of her first grandchild. She was shocked.

In that last fortnight, although we were not sleeping in the same room, Deepak would demand sex every other night, then roll over and go to sleep. If I tried to talk to him he would ignore me. Sex was the last thing I wanted. I didn't want another woman's dirt inside me. But I thought it might bring him back to the fold. Besides, if I'd refused him, I'd have been beaten up. I felt dirty and hurt. I was his plaything. I put a knife under the mattress, thinking, 'The next time he tries anything, I will cut his thing off. I will teach him a lesson for playing around with women, for satisfying his lust as and when he wants.' The knife lay under the mattress for three nights, but I couldn't bring myself to use it. I was afraid that Deepak might discover it and use it on me, or become convinced that I was trying to kill him, so I put it back in the kitchen. And anyway, I couldn't bear to see him in pain. After I had bitten his ear I had asked him endlessly to forgive me. I never knew I had it in me to draw blood.

I was so confused. I wanted to go to the solicitor's to get a divorce, I wanted Deepak to come back so we could live together normally again, I wanted to kill myself, I wanted to run away, I wanted to inflict pain on him, I wanted my family to bring about a reconciliation. I didn't know what I wanted.

Puppi and Jyoti were moving from their bedsitting room to their own house, and they came over to fetch some belongings they had left with us. Deepak was trying unsuccessfully to fit their things into the two cars, and was getting increasingly aggressive. Puppi and Jyoti were petrified. To divert their attention, I asked Puppi to help me pour some petrol into the tank of my car, as I found it hard to unscrew the cap. There was a little petrol in a cider bottle in the boot.

Finally we drove to Puppi and Jyoti's new house. While Deepak helped with the unloading, I remained in the car. I had no present for them, and it would be wrong to go in without one. Puppi pleaded with me, and I got out of the car and stood on the pavement. Deepak was getting angry, and told me I had better go in. As he had not been talking to me, I refused to talk to him. He pushed me very hard into the back of the car and started to assault me, shouting and hitting me, mainly around my thighs. Sandeep and Rajeev were terrified. I remained silent, because I didn't want the thing to escalate and ruin Puppi and Jyoti's first day in their new house.

Deepak wanted me to drive the car away. He tore the tax disc up and said he would call the police the minute I drove off and tell them I was driving around without road tax. He started pounding the car door with his fists, saying he wanted me to drive while he sat in the back and bit my ear off, as I had done to him. I started crying. The children looked on helplessly. I began to drive, but Deepak ordered me to stop, demanded that Puppi drive him into town, made Jyoti sit in the car with me and told us to go to Mamma's house. Mamma was furious when she heard what had happened, and asked Anil to talk to Deepak. He refused, because Deepak would not listen to him, and he didn't want to waste his time when his exams were imminent.

The next day, when Mamma was present, we started talking about the threatening phone calls Deepak had been receiving. The last time the man had left a message saying that he would 'knock him down' if Deepak didn't leave his woman alone. I asked what 'knock him down' meant. Deepak didn't reply. I was scared for the children's and my safety. Mamma said she wasn't surprised by the phone calls when Deepak was defiling other people's homes. Deepak said there was no truth in the man's claim. She said there can be no smoke without fire, and told him to desist from his old *goondagiri* (ruffianly behaviour) in Kenya when he used to jump into girls' bedrooms through the window.

I asked him why he wouldn't let go of this woman who was causing so much trouble in the house. He took his shoes off and started hitting me around the head and shoulders with them. Mamma intervened. 'This is why I don't like coming to your house. I am fed up with your problems. Don't ask me to help.' The children were there, and looked frightened. Whenever Deepak threatened me or hit me, they would go very quiet and watch from the other side of the room.

That night Deepak went out and didn't return. Mamma phoned the neighbours to see if I was all right, as our line had been disconnected. I told her I had no childcare for the next morning. She said she would send Raju round, but as he had no car, I had to go and fetch him. I couldn't sleep all night again. Deepak and I had entered a new phase of our relationship. In the past, when he hit me or shouted at me, he would apologise afterwards and he would listen to me. Now he just played with me and my feelings as if I was his toy. He was endlessly and relentlessly cruel. I kept hoping that he would be all right in three or four months, that he would return to his family. But the problems were getting bigger. Deepak was inventing new excuses for rows, and I had no hopes for the future. On Sunday night he came back from work at around 10 p.m. I had just put the children to bed and had got into bed myself. 'Has your brother sent my money?' he demanded. I didn't reply. 'I want that money here tomorrow. I know you're not asleep.' He pulled the bed covers back. I said, 'Mamma and Raju have told me not to give it to you. When it arrives I will give it to Mamma for safekeeping so that you can't get it out of me by force.' He was furious. He caught hold of my ankles and twisted them in such a way that my whole body had to follow and he rolled me from left to right, yelling, 'I'll break your legs. We'll see how you don't pay up.' I screamed with the pain, wondering what kind of new torture he was dreaming up for me.

The next day was Monday 8 May 1989. I was not going to work until Thursday. Deepak said he was doing overtime and had to get up early. He asked me to wake him up at 7.30. When I did, he said he would get up when he received a phone call he was expecting. As I went downstairs, I remembered that the telephone had been disconnected. I got Deepak up with a cup of tea. In the post was a letter from Canada addressed to Deepak in Tommy praji's handwriting. I took it up to him. The letter said we should try and live together in peace. A cheque made out to me for £500 was enclosed. Deepak started shouting, 'The bastard doesn't trust me, so he sends a cheque in his sister's name. Did he borrow money from you or from me?' I said it was no big deal, I would simply transfer the money to his account, but he started lashing out at me. I screamed and ran into the toilet. He carried on hitting me on the back and shoulders. Rajeev woke up and saw what was going on. As my crying got louder, Deepak let go of me. He went into the front room and started tinkering with a video recorder.

He told me a friend was coming to pick him up and take him to work. At midday I asked if he wanted lunch. He said he only wanted some toast. As we sat down to eat, he asked me to deposit the cheque in his account. While I was eating he suddenly demanded to be dropped off at work. I left my food half-finished.

On the way to the post office I asked Deepak to set that evening aside to discuss our future. I planned to make *pakore* (vegetable fritters), his favourite snack. He was offhand, saying he might have do to overtime. 'Make sure you have £200 ready to hand over to me tonight, because I want to pay the telephone bill early tomorrow morning. I urgently need the phone reconnected. If you don't, I'll skin you alive.'

After dropping him I went straight to the bank and withdrew £500 from my account for him. Then I went to Mamma's with Rajeev and Sandeep and told her how Deepak was beating me. My whole body was juddering with sobs. 'He beat me last night, he beat me this morning. He's got his money. Now what excuse does he have? He's set up a new one of wanting money for the telephone. I don't know how I'll escape a beating tonight.' In front of my children, I was crying like a child. I showed her the letter from my brother to prove that he had paid off his so-called debt, so Deepak couldn't pretend he had never received the money. I was not going to give him the extra money he wanted. I had already contributed £150 for the previous telephone bill. I couldn't bring myself to go home. I stayed and watched television until 6 p.m. I asked Mamma to come with us, as protection for me. She said she couldn't watch that monster beating me up, and that she had to go to Tesco's. I pleaded with her to come. I knew he was going to beat me again. My body was aching with the pain of all his beatings.

Sandeep wanted to go to the shop with Mamma to get some chocolates. Rajeev was a little under the weather, so I thought I would take him home with me. As I sat in the car, the road ahead was filled with pain. My mind was going round and round on one point – he had wanted the money, he had got it, now why was he torturing me? When I got home I cleaned the kitchen, made the *pakore*, fed Rajeev and sat down with a cup of tea. The TV was on and I was staring blankly at it. My thoughts were stuck in the same groove: how would I save myself? I had to make plans to defend myself. I thought, 'If he beats me tonight, I will throw caustic soda at him. That will blind him. But only temporarily. He'll wash his eyes out with cold water and then he'll come chasing after me again. He'll have pain for a few minutes and then he'll be all right. This will be physical pain, not mental pain. No, it isn't good enough. If he beats me, I will beat him back. I'll do something to his feet when he is asleep so that he gets a scar for life, so that he can't run after me.'

I had some petrol in the lean-to next to the conservatory. The petrol cap on my brother's car was very tight and I couldn't get it open, so I kept a container of petrol so that Puppi could fill up the car for me whenever I needed it. I had a half-formed idea of setting Deepak's feet on fire. It was like looking at life through a microscope. There was a circle of light falling only on his feet. My mind was focused on that, the rest was in darkness. I wanted him to know the meaning of pain. I thought I would set his feet on fire while he was asleep. He would wake up and put the fire out but because of the burns he would not be able to run after me. I was not to know that the room I had decorated so lovingly only two months ago would also go up in flames, that my expensive curtains would be damaged, that the new lampshade would catch in a sudden flare. The rest of the picture had been shrouded in darkness.

I fed Rajeev, all the while looking at the clock. It was 9.30 p.m. I thought I would drop Rajeev off at the babysitter's and fetch Deepak from work. Because of his offhand manner that morning, I wasn't sure whether he was expecting me. I left a note for Deepak in the kitchen that I was going to McDonald's.

On the way to the post office I thought, 'He has always denied having relations with a white woman. Today I will catch him red-handed.' I would follow them if I saw them together. In all my life, I had never thought I would stoop so low. I waited outside the post office till 10.15, but Deepak didn't emerge.

Perhaps he was doing overtime. I picked Rajeev up from the babysitter's and went home. As I inserted the key in the front door, Deepak opened it. I was surprised, as I hadn't seen him come out of the post office. He asked me where I'd been, and I said, 'Didn't you see my note?' He went upstairs, and I asked if he wanted tea and *pakore*. He said yes. I put Rajeev to bed.

When I called Deepak down for tea, he wanted it brought upstairs where he was repairing the video recorder. He wouldn't talk, so I went back downstairs and switched on the TV. There was a film showing a ship on fire. The flames from that fire were licking the flames of anger in my heart. I wondered whether I should try and force Deepak to talk, or whether I should leave him alone. A little before midnight, I switched off the television and went to bed.

I tried talking to Deepak before I went to bed. I asked if he had liked the *pakore*. 'Okay,' he said, not paying much attention. Within ten minutes of my lying down, he came into the bedroom.

'Where is the money?'

I didn't reply. He said he knew I wasn't asleep, and kept repeating that he wanted the money right away. He pulled the quilt off my face. I sat up, wondering what he was going to do. He went into the passageway where he was ironing his clothes and started talking very loudly, abusing me, my brothers, anyone he could think of. I told him to lower his voice because the next-door neighbour had complained that he made a lot of noise and because Rajeev was asleep. That made him even more angry. 'I wish you would come back to us, Deepak,' I said, 'for the sake of our children. I don't mind you having an affair even.' I promised to stop doing all the things that irritated him.

He refused to talk unless I gave him the money. I knew it was only because he was wining and dining his white women instead of doing overtime that money had become tight. He caught me by the hair and threatened to rip my mouth apart if I kept talking about his white women. He was waving the hot iron about in his other hand, and the tip of it burnt my right eye. I started screaming. I didn't want my face scarred. I had always covered it up when he beat me. As I started crying, he pushed me aside. He was threatening to kill every member of my family. I was frightened by the intensity of his hatred for me. I ran into my bedroom, but as there was no lock on the door, that was hardly any protection.

I had done everything today to make him happy, and in return I was beaten. My whole being was on fire. Deepak finished ironing and started watching TV in his room, as if he didn't have a worry in the world. I thought I'd put the caustic soda in a saucepan and throw it in his eyes and ask him how he could watch television, how he could sleep in peace, when I was burning up inside. I went downstairs and knocked back a couple of sherry glasses filled with whisky or vodka, I can't remember which. I found a saucepan without a handle and mixed a couple of tablespoons of caustic soda in it. The pan became so hot I had to use an oven glove to carry it upstairs.

I hadn't eaten all day, and the drink made me feel dizzy as I climbed the stairs. I was too frightened to use the caustic soda in case Deepak snatched it from my hands and ran after me, so I left the pan on the bathroom floor. I fell on my bed, tired and drunk. My head was spinning and I couldn't sleep. I was filled with self-hate. I had not had the guts to use the caustic soda. As I lay there, the last ten years flashed through my head. Why did he persuade me to have the children when I didn't want any? Why did he waste my life? As the scenes of violence rolled by, one after another, I fell asleep.

When I woke again, it must have been about 2.30 a.m. I was woken by the sound of Deepak's television, the crackling of a blank screen. Deepak was snoring. I went into his room and tried to wake him up. 'Deepak, Deepak,' I said. I wanted to shout, 'Talk to me. I can't eat, I can't sleep. How long will we

carry on fighting?' He just rolled over. I switched the light on
and off, and then on again. I switched the TV off, thinking he
would wake up in anger, but he kept on sleeping.

I went back to my room for a second. I was filled with anger
that he could sleep so peacefully. I wanted to disturb him. I
went downstairs, opened the drinks cabinet and gulped down
two more glasses of alcohol. I went into the lean-to and got the
can of petrol. I wasn't going to use all of it. I only wanted a
glass and a half for his feet. I wanted him to know what pain
was. No one can sleep when they are in pain. I picked up the
nappy bucket and put a small amount of petrol in it. I lit a
candle. Nearby there was a cloth tied to a stick which I used
for cleaning the tops of cupboards. I took that too. The candle
was so close to the petrol as I climbed the stairs. It was a huge
fire risk, but I was oblivious to everything.

I stood outside Deepak's room. Next to the door was his
double bed. His feet were at the end furthest from me. To the
left of the bed was the television. Against the left-hand wall was
the wardrobe. I put the bucket down. I stood the candle in a
plastic beaker, Rajeev's drinking cup, on the ironing board in the
boxroom, which was within reach from where I was standing. I
went to the bathroom and brought back an empty tin which
we used as a tumbler for bathing. I dipped it in the bucket,
filled it with petrol and aimed it at Deepak's feet. It didn't quite
reach him. I threw another half-tin, going closer and closer to
his bed. As I bent down to throw a third lot, he woke up. I ran
for dear life.

*[In his statement, Deepak said: 'She was rushing around and I
was dazed. I have never seen her rush so much at that hour.']*

He got up and shut the door. I soaked the cloth duster in
petrol and lit it with the candle. I opened the door. Deepak was
standing with his back against the wall. His head was turned
towards me and he was staring at me. That is the last time my

eyes met his. I threw the burning stick into the room. I don't
know where it fell.

I shut the door, and suddenly felt an immense anxiety for
Rajeev. I rushed into his room, woke him up and ran down
the stairs with him, through the living room and the extension,
and out behind the garage. There was a narrow space between
the garage and the garden shed, and I stood there shivering
with Rajeev. We both had bare feet. I don't know how long I
stood there. I was wondering when Deepak would come running
after me when I heard the voices of my neighbours, then the
sirens. Perhaps a fire engine. Perhaps the police. There were
sirens ringing in my head. I didn't realise my house was on fire.

Deepak's room was at the front of the house, and I was in
the back garden. People were shouting, 'Come out!' I thought
that as a crowd had gathered, I would be safe from Deepak. If
he tried to hit me, someone would save me. I went into the
extension, sat Rajeev on the settee, and put his shoes and socks
on. Then I walked into the hall and got his coat. The neighbours
were banging on the windows and the door. There were two
or three men standing there saying something which I could
not understand and could not hear properly because the
windows were double glazed. I was so cool. I opened the window
and asked, 'Where is my husband?' I wanted to be sure that he
wasn't within hitting distance.

[In the police interview, Kiranjit's behaviour was interpreted as
calmness and calculation. She tried to explain that she hadn't
realised the gravity of the situation by saying, 'I didn't put too
much fire.' The policeman commented, 'That shows me that what
you did was calculated.']

The men were shouting, 'Come outside, your house is on fire!'
Then there was the sound of a huge explosion upstairs. I got
scared, but even then I didn't realise the extent of the fire. I went
and got Rajeev and passed him through the window. They were

shouting for me to get out too. I went calmly into the hall again, and put on my shoes and my bomber jacket. I could have just walked out of the front door, but instead I went all the way back to the living room and climbed out of the window.

When I got out, I started looking for Deepak. There were fifteen or twenty people out there, and two fire engines. I couldn't see Rajeev either. I looked up, and saw flames coming out of the window. Had I done that? I had only imagined his feet on fire. I just stood there, dazed. Someone came up to me and told me not to worry, that my son was in a neighbour's house. As I was on my way there, my eyes fell on the open doorway of the house opposite ours. Deepak was sitting there covered in a blanket, speaking on the telephone.

[One of the neighbours, Joan Jessop, said in her statement to the police that Deepak came running towards her house screaming, 'I'm burning, I'm burning.' Her husband put Deepak's hands into the kitchen sink filled with water, but he ran out of the house and lay on the lawn, rubbing his arms on the grass and screaming, 'I'm burning.' She put a coat around him, but he threw it off, ran to the front and spat on the grass. He went grey and said he felt sick. She brought him a bowl, into which he retched a small amount of black substance. According to Joan, Kiranjit had 'a glazed expression' when she told her that Deepak was in their house. Asked if she wanted to see him, Kiran said, 'No, no.'

A number of neighbours commented on the fact that neither Kiranjit nor Rajeev was in their night clothes. This was interpreted by the prosecution as a sign of premeditation. One neighbour, John Upton, banged on the window and asked Kiran to come out. She said she was waiting for her husband and closed the window. John said that Deepak was continuously screaming, 'I'll kill you! I'll kill you!']

Deepak was obviously calling his mother and brothers. 'Oh, God, they will kill me,' was the thought that went through my mind. He seemed fine, as if nothing had happened to him. I dodged into the crowd so he wouldn't see me. I looked in on Rajeev twice. I asked for a glass of water, which a neighbour brought for me. As I was drinking it, a policeman came up and asked if I knew what had happened. I said, 'I don't know.' My house was on fire, I was worried about my son, I wasn't going to talk to any policeman. He asked if my husband smoked. I said, 'I don't know.' And I didn't, really.

Maybe the neighbours thought it strange that I didn't go up to Deepak to ask if he was all right. But I was told later that some of them had offered to give evidence that they had often heard him shouting at me over the past three years, while I had been a model neighbour, quiet and pleasant.

While I was standing there watching the fire engulf my dream house I started scratching my left arm, and felt something come away under my fingernails. I looked down and saw that my entire arm was burnt. I couldn't work it out. I am right-handed. How did my left arm get burnt? And when? The arm was covered in blisters, and my nails were burnt. As the skin came away, I felt searing pain. I went to a neighbour and asked for some cream.

An ambulance arrived and I saw Deepak get into it. That was the last time I ever saw him. As he was standing in the light of the ambulance I thought, somewhat irrelevantly, what a handsome man he was, pity about his mental state. I couldn't see any burns on him. In fact there appeared to be a healthy pink glow on his face which accentuated his good looks.

[Statements from firemen who attended the house that night testified to the difficulty of putting the fire out. Every time it was doused, it kept igniting again. They threw the bed, which was the seat of the fire, out of the window. The mattress and pillows reeked of petrol. One of the fire officers found the oven glove under the duvet in Kiran's bedroom, and the bucket with some petrol in it.

The fire investigation officer said in his statement: 'It was *realised at this stage that a serious crime may have been committed and all personnel who were not directly involved in firefighting and fire investigation were ordered to leave the building. An urgent request was made to the police for the attendance of a scenes of crime officer.' Various fire officers describe the saucepan in the hand basin in the bathroom with a 'light-coloured frothy substance' at the bottom. Kiranjit remembers putting the pan on the floor just behind the bathroom door. She believes that Deepak may have used the pan to pour water over himself, in which case it would have had no trace of caustic soda in it.*

When they got to the hospital, the ambulance driver asked Deepak what had happened. Deepak said, 'My wife is mental. I was in bed. She set fire to the house and threw caustic soda over me. I went to the bathroom and put water over myself. She came in and threw more caustic soda over me … My wife's brother had done me out of eleven grand.' The driver described Deepak as totally coherent although in a great deal of pain.]

A second ambulance arrived for me. Thank goodness I didn't have to travel with Deepak. He would have got me by the throat. I took Rajeev with me. I was in a lot of pain. I felt as if I was getting constant electric shocks all over my arm. The ambulance man kept sprinkling cold water on my arm, which reduced the sensation of burning. The water ran into a bucket.

[The ambulance men who took Kiran to hospital said they smelt petrol on her clothes. They got no reply to anything they said to her, and said that 'The child sat next to his mother who did not acknowledge him.' Some of the neighbours also mentioned that Kiran did not seem concerned about Rajeev.]

In the hospital's emergency ward I sat in a room with Rajeev. A nurse dressed my arm, put a clear polythene bag over it and secured it at the elbow with a rubber band, then gave me a couple of tablets for the pain.

I kept kissing and cuddling Rajeev and asking if he was all right. I could hear Deepak talking in a loud voice to a doctor in another cubicle, telling him that it was my fault. There seemed to be no pain in his voice. I thought he had escaped unscathed, and started to worry that he might find me. The doctor came in, looked at me briefly and went away. The nurse asked me to sit discreetly behind a curtain. When I asked why, she said they were taking my husband to another room, and that if he saw me there might be trouble.

The burning sensation had stopped. Liquid was dripping from my arm. Rajeev was looking at me – I was in a state. My hair and eyelashes had been singed, and there was a burn mark caused by the iron under my eye.

In a little while my mother-in-law turned up. My life ebbed from every pore when I saw her. I was preparing myself for any punishment they would mete out to me. I sat there with my head bowed, my arms falling limply in front of me, unable to look her in the eye. If I had not been feeling guilty, I would have looked directly at her and said, 'Look, look at your son's handiwork.' She stood there and stroked my hair, saying, 'He is my blood. I knew this is what this bastard would end up doing. Don't worry, I am with you. I will see you through all this.' I didn't know that both my brothers-in-law were sitting outside with Sandeep. I sat in silence while she kept up a monologue of complaints against Deepak. I switched off after a while.

The police arrived and said that I had to accompany them to the station to give a statement. I stood up and, without any fuss, said goodbye to Mamma. I took my engagement ring from my pocket and gave it to her. Maybe I was symbolically ending my marriage at that point. When I saw Sandeep, I kissed him and told him to be good and to look after his little brother, and that Mummy would soon come home. I told Mamma that I would give her money to look after the children. I expected to be away for a couple of weeks while my arm was healing.

[The hospital notes and the statements of various doctors and nurses who were involved in Deepak's care build up a picture of an indomitable will in the face of severe injuries. Deepak's burns were initially washed with saline solution, and then he was showered for two hours. He felt faint at one point, but did not lose consciousness. He kept repeating essentially the same story he had given the ambulance driver as the nurses peeled off what clothing they could but left the pieces of cloth sticking to his burns in place. One nurse, Yasmin Hassam, said that Deepak was vomiting blood as he was talking. In her statement, she gives a detailed account of her conversation with Deepak and the conversation between Deepak and his mother:

'I said, "If you've got anything to say I'd say it now because you'll get very ill. I'll write it down for you." He replied, "At three o'clock in the morning I was fast asleep, my wife threw caustic soda over me and while my mouth was open I swallowed some of the soda. All my bedclothes were stuck to me. I ran out of the room and got in the bath. I realised that my wife was up to something else, she was trying to lock the bathroom door from the outside. I didn't stay there long. I rushed out of the house and the next thing I knew the house was on fire." I said, "Why did she do it?" He replied, "I asked her for a divorce." I said, "Were you having an affair?" He replied, "No." I said again, "Why did she do it then?" He replied, "Her brother took £11,500 from me and her family wanted more." . . . He went on to say, "My wife's a witch, she's an evil woman, she wants me to die." I said, "Has she done anything to you before or have you ever touched her?" He replied, "If I told you my story you would have tears in your eyes."

'By that time, as he'd had an injection, he started to pass out from time to time, and it was apparent that he was in a great deal of pain . . . Shortly after this his mother came to see him with his small son. Deepak and his mother had a conversation in Punjabi, and although I cannot hold a conversation in that language myself I do understand it perfectly. His mother said to him,

*"What happened?" He replied, "She threw caustic soda at me."
His mother said, "But she said that before she'd thrown the caustic
soda at you, you burnt her hand with the iron." He replied, "I
swear on my dad's grave, I didn't touch her." His mother said,
"How did the row start?" He replied, "When I came home from
work, I asked her to make me some dinner and she told me to go
to hell, so I went to sleep on an empty stomach. At three o'clock
she came in the room and threw the soda at me." . . . His mother
said, "I've been told that you have got a white girlfriend." He
replied, "I've got nobody, it's lies." . . .*

  *'By then it was time to place him in an ambulance to go to
Roehampton, and whilst placing him in the ambulance his mother
shouted to him again in Punjabi, "Where does your girlfriend
live?" Deepak replied, "Somewhere in Ilfield." His mother said,
"What's the telephone number?" But by then Deepak was going
into a deep sleep due to the drugs he had been given.']*

I was locked up in a police cell. They gave me a stinking
blanket and pillow. I felt the walls were crying with me. I had
come out of one hell and gone into another. I fell asleep for a
little while. When I woke up the police asked me the name of
my solicitors. They said they would ask them to come down
to the station first thing in the morning. They brought me a
toothbrush and a cup of tea.

  At 9.30 a.m. my solicitor turned up. When he asked me
what had happened, I could hardly string two words of English
together. He said, 'I told you, Mrs Ahluwalia, to get a divorce
from this man. If you had listened to me, you wouldn't have
ended up in this situation.' I gave him a summary of the last
few months: Deepak's violence, his threats of giving the children
away to a social worker. I admitted to everything I had done.
I wasn't even thinking about the law and how words can be
twisted and given an interpretation that could be damaging. I
was just talking as the thoughts came to me.

  My solicitor said I would be sent to Holloway, where I would have my arm treated while I waited for bail. When he left, I was locked up again. In half an hour the police came for me again, and took my statement in the presence of my solicitor. Before they switched on the tape recorder, I asked the policemen why they were taking a statement. One of them said that they wanted to know what I had done, and that as I had tried to kill my husband they were charging me with attempted murder.

They asked me if I wanted an interpreter, but I refused. The very first question that was put to me when the interview began was, 'Mrs Ahluwalia, do you know why you are here?' I repeated what he had just said to me: 'Because I tried to kill my husband.' At my trial, the prosecution had a field day with this 'confession'. It was repeated again and again. But these were not my words. I had merely repeated what the police officer had said to me.

Whatever question they asked me, I would end up talking about Deepak's violence and how he had threatened to blind me with the screwdriver, then burst into tears. But the police were not interested in the history. They kept bringing me back to the previous night. As I was talking I thought I noticed my solicitor gesturing to me to be discreet, so I didn't go into further detail. That interview went on for about forty minutes.

I was in a real state when I got back to the cell. I felt unclean, the place smelled, and I knew I had done something terrible. I later found out that, in the words of one psychiatrist's report, I was in a serious depression from which it would take me years to recover.

In the afternoon the police interviewed me again. I can't remember if my solicitor was there or not. They said they had been to see my husband in hospital, and asked if I had put anything else on him as well as petrol. I said no. 'Did you mix any vegetable oils or chemicals with the petrol?' I said no. 'But the doctor's report says that there was something else apart from petrol.'

[During the interrogation the police explained that the doctors reported that the substance thrown on Deepak had an effect like napalm, which sticks to whatever it touches and keeps burning.]

Deepak had said in his statement that I had thrown caustic soda on him. He hadn't mentioned the petrol. One of the police officers banged his fist on the table and said roughly, 'Tell us the truth. We know what you have done.'

I got angry. I said between gritted teeth and tears, 'I am telling you the truth. I hate you. You are scaring me.' I thought he would beat me up. I knew that the Indian police regularly beat up prisoners. They questioned me for a couple of hours.

[This was the third time Kiranjit was interviewed that day. The transcript runs:

Police Interviewer: *You said something earlier. I'll quote your words. 'I didn't put too much fire . . .'*
Kiranjit: *Yes.*
PI: *You said that about giving yourself time to get out of the house. 'I didn't put too much fire . . .'*
K: *I didn't.*
PI: *That, that shows to me –*
K: *No, no, no –*
PI: *– that what you did was calculated.*

The police questioned her relentlessly about her apparent calmness after the fire.

PI: *Everybody who spoke to you this morning [unclear] interviewed has commented about your calmness.*
K: *Yeah, I was [inaudible].*
PI: *Your calmness. Do you understand what I mean when I say calm?*
K: *Yes.*

PI: *Now it appears to me that if you can act in a calm and collected manner, which you obviously have, by going down the stairs, taking the time to put your child's shoes and socks on in the front room, knowing that the room is on fire upstairs –*

K: *Yeah.*

PI: *This is all calm, cool and collected.*

K: *At first I wanted to run and get out from the garden side.*

PI: *But everybody said how calm you were.*

K: *Yeah, I was shatter I was so [inaudible] I couldn't deny what this, what was going on.*

PI: *No, you're, you're mistaking my words. Do you understand what I mean by calm? Calm is not nervous –*

K: *[Inaudible]*

PI: *Calm is not shattered. Do you understand what I mean by the word calm?*

K: *I couldn't. I couldn't cry that time I couldn't, I just wasn't, watching my husband and my son and my house. I couldn't do anything that time.*

PI: *You were calm because what you did was deliberate, wasn't it?*

K: *No, no, I wasn't calm.*

PI: *Well, people have told us that you were calm.*

K: *I was quiet with shock. I was watching my husband, [inaudible] crying, was watching my house [inaudible], I done a lot of work in this house, last year I done [inaudible] and painting, over £2,000, done overtime, my house [inaudible], I was very shock . . .]*

I told them that I had bought caustic soda to clean some pans. I didn't admit to mixing it that night. They asked if I had gone to the bathroom. I said no, not after I had lit the fire. They said that there was water and caustic soda solution all over the floor. I realised that while I was hiding in the back garden, Deepak must have run the bath and got into it to douse the fire. He must have picked up the saucepan and used it as a tumbler, pouring caustic soda all over himself. In the tub they found the towelling nappies which had been hanging up to dry. Maybe Deepak pulled them down to dab his burns. Right to the end I was blamed for the caustic soda, although the forensic department found no traces of it on me or on my clothes.

The next day I was taken to the pathologist in Crawley Hospital, wearing a baggy white paper jumpsuit that made me look like the man on the moon. I was so embarrassed. My wounds were dressed and photographs were taken of my injuries. When I got back to the police cell, Suresh and Sukhjit jijaji visited me. There were tears in Suresh's eyes as he patted me on the leg and said, 'Do you know what you have done? Deepak is suffering from 40 per cent burns.' When he said Deepak might not pull through, I didn't believe him.

That evening I was driven to Holloway.

[The morning after the fire, Deepak was transferred from Crawley Hospital to the burns unit at Queen Mary Hospital, Roehampton. The consultant's statement describes his condition. Some burns were deep, covering his face, neck, chest, shoulders, arms and thighs. There was grey discoloration and the skin had a leathery texture. There was 'absence of sensation to pin prick'. Deepak was monitored every fifteen minutes for the next three days. He had difficulty breathing, and his eyes were painfully sensitive to light. His hands were placed in plastic bags and elevated on supports and pillows to prevent swelling. He was given a full blood transfusion, and his condition was described as 'stable but critical'. He was progressing well until 12 May, when he developed a high temperature and a serious blood infection – septicaemia.

Although Deepak was in no fit condition to make a deposition, a statement was taken from him on 12 May. Present were Kiranjit's solicitor, two policemen, two nurses, a justice of the peace and a clerk. The interview lasted forty-five minutes. Deepak asked for water frequently and used his oxygen mask occasionally. His ver-

sion of events was more or less similar to what he told the nurse, although there were some exceptions:

'I was virtually a prisoner in my own home. My wife said I couldn't go out. I have never refused her to go out ... When she threw it [caustic soda] at me, it caused fire straight away. It causes fire if it is in solid form. At the same time the room she slept in smelt of paraffin, this was week in and week out. I kept asking about it and she wouldn't tell me.

'After she threw the stuff I went straight to the bath tub. I laid in, open [sic] the taps. I was already on fire. When I got under the taps the fire went out ... When I was in the bathroom she rushed in and poured some more stuff on me. She rushed out again. I don't know what she threw at me. I was smothered in water. The stuff she threw then was liquid in a bucket. She said, "I have a present for you."'

After he had finished the statement it was read back to him. He added, 'I wish to add that I didn't burn her and I didn't burn her arm.'

Deepak's septicaemia responded well to antibiotics until 14 May, when his breathing became laboured and his kidney functions deteriorated. He suffered a fatal cardiac arrest at 4.20 a.m. on Monday 15 May.]

SIXTEEN

Another Life Sentence

MY TRIAL WAS HELD at Lewes Crown Court in December 1989, seven months after the incident. As the day drew closer I became ever more restless, and asked the prison doctor for sleeping pills to help me calm down. The other girls would ask for the pills rudely, as if they had a right to them. If they were turned down they would shout at the doctor or even try to attack her. The doctor, who was Indian and understood our culture, kept asking me why I hadn't left Deepak, especially as I was an educated woman. I tried to explain the constraints, how every attempt to leave him had failed or been overridden by my family.

At Holloway the traffic of women coming and going was unending. When prisoners were released I would think how lucky they were, but often they would return within a few weeks. I couldn't understand why they came back. They told me I was lucky to have a family who cared about what happened to me, that their only family was the network of prisoners and officers who had befriended them. They were fed and clothed in prison, and didn't have to worry about bills and housing. They had got used to prison life.

Most of the women in Holloway felt deep hatred for men. Most of them had been beaten and abused by men, and were simply more comfortable in the company of other women. Many of them felt they didn't need men, who only wanted to own them and their children. For the first time I saw lesbians making love, cuddling and kissing in corridors, just out of sight of the officers.

I came across women who had committed many different kinds of crimes – credit card fraud, drug offences, murder, women who belonged to the IRA. I got support from all these women, and from the prison officers. No inmate ever called me a killer. They didn't believe that I could do a thing like that, and were convinced that my husband must have been such a bastard that he pushed me to it.

I felt safe in Holloway, although there was quite a bit of violence. The F word was common. Women would fight with each other and with the officers. Most of the fights were caused by sexual jealousy. At times like that I would cover my eyes and be plunged back into those days when Deepak would stand towering over me. The inmates taught me how important it was to fight for your rights. They didn't give in to rules and regulations. They were not afraid of punishment. I compared myself to them and felt weak and hopeless and ignorant.

At this time Ranjit chachaji, who had volunteered to give evidence on my behalf, told me something that came as a huge shock. When he heard about our marriage, chachaji was surprised that Deepak had managed to trap some innocent, since he had a history of mental problems and had been admitted to Manthari Mental Hospital in Kenya in 1976. After we were married, Deepak had mentioned this, but so briefly that I never really understood why he had gone into hospital in the first place. He described how he had been kept there against his will, chained to a bed, and how he had tried to jump out of the window. Other visitors, like Hansapur aunty, told me that Deepak had thought himself possessed by the god Hanuman.

Shortly before my trial, Pragna told me she was going to India on holiday. I felt let down and upset – she had made all these claims about how SBS would help me, and here she was going off to have a good time. She brought Hannana Siddiqui with her, and said that Hannana would support me through the trial and help in any way she could. When I saw her, I thought, she is shorter than I am, what can she do for me? But Lal Bahadur Shastri was one of India's best prime ministers, and he wasn't very tall. Pragna asked me what I wanted from India, and I asked for a pair of silver earrings.

I was worried about being cross-examined in court. I had changed solicitors again, and when I asked my new solicitor about this, she advised me to be consistent. The other side would try everything to break down, twist and distort my story. I was given the tapes of my police interviews to remind myself of what I had said. I listened to them on a borrowed Walkman and wept as I heard myself recounting my own life story. The police told me that they had found an oven glove on my bed, and asked what I had used it for. I couldn't remember. Only after a lot of thought did I remember that the saucepan had become very hot when I was making up the caustic soda solution, and because it had no handle I used the oven glove to carry it. The reason it was on my bed was that I had gone and lain down after bringing the saucepan upstairs.

Because I had changed my story to my solicitor's clerk, I used to wonder how much she trusted me, what parts of my story she believed and what she didn't. At first I told her that I had been angry with Deepak and had taken the petrol to him and said, 'Go on, then. If you want to kill me, kill me.' When he picked up the petrol I thought he was going to pour it on me, so I pushed him and in the confusion the petrol splashed on him, he was set alight and I ran away. I told her I was angry because Deepak had been trying to force me to have sex, and because I couldn't bring myself to say this to the police I gave them a different version. As I was talking in English, I couldn't make things very clear, and this went against me at my trial. Later, I was shocked by some of the things I had said because of my poor English.

[The report of the prison psychiatrist, Professor Roderick Evans, refers to Kiranjit's two versions of how the fire started:

'*The first account is consistent with that given in her statement to the police. More recently she has maintained that the fire was started by her husband after she had dared him to carry out his threat to burn her. She alleges that he came into her room demanding sex, she felt frightened and resisted. In her desperation she went downstairs, collected some petrol and took it upstairs, handing it to her husband. In the confusion some was spilt, and she maintains that he ignited it.*'

This second version did not allow the psychiatrist to explore the possibility of diminished responsibility – that Kiran was suffering from deep depression and may have committed the act at a time when she was not in control of all her senses. Professor Evans's report, written two months before Kiran's trial, was not helped by the fact that she gave him a different version of events from that she gave the police:

'*She showed no disturbance of thinking or comprehension, and no abnormality of perception. Her affect was totally appropriate to her situation and reacted accordingly.*

'*There is no indication that at the material time her state of consciousness was altered nor any evidence to suggest that her reason was distorted by any psychotic process ... She does not suffer from any form of mental disorder, and can be regarded as being sane in the legal sense. As assessed by the usual criteria she is fit to plead.*'

Kiranjit gave the correct version of events to Dr Sumners, who provided a psychiatric report at the request of her family, primarily to support her application for bail. He concluded: '*This lady does not represent a risk either to others or herself and [I] would hope that this would be taken into consideration both in terms of bail and ultimately of disposal.*'

When Kiranjit met him on 29 June 1989, Dr Sumners reported that she still had a painful left arm, left hand and left ankle from the beatings she had received from Deepak on that night. '*He [Deepak] eventually burnt her on the face with a clothes iron. During the interview she showed me a red area on the left side of* her face ... Mrs Ahluwalia told me that she had not planned to set fire to her husband, and that what happened was an impulsive action. She said she had done it because she was so terrified of what he would do to her the next day ... It appears that what she did was the culmination of a ten-year period of physical and emotional abuse by her husband and was not premeditated. Mrs Ahluwalia states that she wished to do to him what he had done to her and there seems to be no particular reason to believe that she wished to kill him ... She is fit to plead.'

On 17 November 1989 Kiranjit was seen by Dr Weller, a psychiatrist appointed by her solicitors, to whom she gave the 'accident' version of events. Of the last few months of her marriage, he notes:

'Mrs Ahluwalia became exceedingly depressed on having her worst fears [about Deepak's girlfriend] confirmed, lost her appetite and about a stone and a half in weight. She had difficulty getting to sleep and was waking early in the morning. Everything seemed a great effort, although she struggled to perform her household duties. She had never had any great interest in sexual relations because of her husband's behaviour, but she now lost her libido completely ... This pattern of symptoms is called endogenous depression, which denotes a depressive condition of particular severity, going beyond any understandable reaction to stress.'

Dr Weller refers to the statements provided by neighbours about the night of the fire to support his assessment that Kiranjit was in an 'abnormal state of mind':

'Mrs Jessop gives an apt description of a disturbed emotional state of disassociation, a state induced by momentous emotional events that is consistent with automatism, where the mind does not go with the body ... These statements show that Mrs Ahluwalia had no insight into the gravity of the situation, and indicate her abnormal mental state which seemed to move from one of intense emotional turmoil to a dissociated calm, quite inappropriate to the horrendous circumstances.'

Of the two different accounts, Dr Weller puts forward Kiranjit's

*own justification of why the version she gave the police was untrue
without comment. He concludes:*

'*I do not believe that Mrs Ahluwalia represents a danger to
others, her young children need her, and she them. She impresses
me as an obedient, reticent, rather charming lady, who is very
unhappy and cried frequently during the interview. She has been
treated unconscionably for the ten years of her brutally unhappy
marriage by an unfeeling, uncaring and unfaithful man, of
capricious, unstable moods and a violent disposition. His behaviour
was so extreme, with attacks on colleagues at work and other
members of his family, as well as threatening his wife with a
knife and repeated physical attacks on her and his children,
that it is highly suggestive of a pathological condition, episodic
dyscontrol.*'

Dr Weller's report was not used at the trial.]

Preparing for the trial was like my college exams. I would
walk up and down the exercise yard, completely oblivious to
the other women, making lengthy defences for myself. I got so
worked up that on the Saturday before the court case I fell ill.
I had a high temperature, my ears were blocked up, and I
constantly felt the urge to go to the toilet, where I would pass
blood.

When I was being taken to the court on the Monday, I felt
as if a fog had filled my ears. I had Babaji's *gudka* (holy book)
with me for luck. I used to pray to Babaji every day, although
I no longer had any faith in him, as he had allowed me to be
reduced to this. But I hoped to have some peace in my soul as
a result. I prayed in the van all the way to the court.

When we arrived, the barrister came to visit me in the cell.
I asked her what I was supposed to say. She said I would not
be called to give evidence that day. The prosecution would
present their case first. I would be called last. All I would have
to say on the first day was 'I am guilty of manslaughter but not
guilty of murder.' I couldn't remember those words for the life

of me. They were too big for me, and I was nervous. She wrote them down on a piece of paper.

The court was small and informal, and I was close enough to the public seats for Hannana to reach out and touch me. Ranjit chacha came up and greeted me with 'Sat shree Akal' – Mamma later asked me whether I was some close relative of his. Southall Black Sisters had packed out the galleries with women supporters. That felt comforting and good.

When I was asked to plead, somehow or other I managed to say those few words, and then I collapsed in my chair. A huge weight had rolled off my shoulders. My ears went red as if all the heat from my body was escaping though them. I hate the word murder. After that, the prosecution started their case – one allegation after another. On 9 May 1989 Mrs Ahluwalia poured caustic soda on her sleeping husband. She was so calm and cool, she bought petrol and she murdered him in cold blood. The nine men and three women of the jury were listening carefully. I was shocked by their appearance; they looked as if they had been dragged off the streets. A couple of the men looked really awful.

I thought, yes, he was sleeping, but I tried to rouse him twice, and he just rolled over and went back to sleep. I had forgotten to tell my solicitor that Deepak had got out of bed and shut the door and that I had opened it again. This information came to the surface only when Pragna dug it out of me when she was preparing my appeal. I had blanked out so many vital details. I felt helpless in that court. I had to listen to everything in silence. I wept whenever I understood the allegations that were being made against me. The police gave evidence, the pathologists, and many others.

[Statements were given to the police by fifty-five witnesses, including a large number of police, firemen, ambulance men, hospital staff and neighbours. Ten witnesses gave evidence in court, and the statements of twenty-five others were read out. From the family

Raju, Deepak's mother and Gurjeet (Puppi) were called to give evidence.]

What legal arguments went on in court I cannot tell, because I didn't understand them. All I could see was that their mouths were moving, my QC was getting up and asking questions, witnesses were leaving the stand. Behind me were seated members of Deepak's family. I couldn't turn around and look at them, but when I was taken in and out of court I would see them, as well as my own family and women from SBS. Every day at lunchtime I would be given pizza and chips.

The prosecution made much of a letter I had written to Mamma shortly after I went to Holloway. They regarded it as my 'confession':

Mum I'm fine here, but the day I talk with you on telephone I'm really very much worried and disappointed. How is your leg now. Mum you have to look after yourself now. I know its to much pressure on you, but be brave. Things between me and Deepak are gone so far I knew we can't stay under one roof. Mum since last four month you knew how much I suffered with him. Whenever he came and goes always hit me and arguing with me. Mum he always kept telling me I want divorce I don't want to do nothing for the kids. Either you take the kids or give them me. Mum he ruined my life. If he divorce me five year before I wouldn't do anything like this. I try my best to save this marriage not for myself but for Sandeep and Rajeev sake.

I'm here now in prison's hospital. Yesterday they cut whole my blisters with scissor. Mum, before I give pain to Deepak I burnt my arm first, because I wanted to share his pain with me. Mum I don't want to kill him. I know my children need father, course I knew what life without father or mother is. You know how much I used to love daddy. Mum if I wanted to kill him I wouldn't let him go out from his room. And I swear I didn't use any caustic soda on him or his car. Mum you have to believe me. In these four month I used to come everyday in your house and told you every single thing. You was the only person with whom I shared my all pains and difficulties.

Mum I know everybody hates me now. But please think about my past. Its your son who made me like this. Mum all the time Sandeep Rajeev and you come in front of my eyes I couldn't sleep or eat. I miss you a lot special my Rajeev. Please mum look after yourself with them too. Mum this time argument was for his girlfriend, there wasn't any condition or complaint between us. She ruined my house my kids life. Mum when Deepak was on holiday I followed him in taxi. She was sitting with him in his new car.

Mum I know I'm not your blood. Certainly you got more sympathy or feeling for your son. But please tell the truth everybody don't take single person side. Everybody will come and see you. Please tell Suresh to arrange babysitter for Sandeep Rajeev. If he can't then I'll talk with my solicitor. Mum you are already sick I don't know how you manage with Sandeep Rajeev all the cooking cleaning you have to do on your own. Mum how Sandeep Rajeev go to school without car. Tell somebody to take that car back and showed the brakes.

Billoo Tommy they all rang me from Canada. I think Bhindi is coming too from India. Mum its just waste of money and time. Nobody can't do nothing. It all finish. We lost each own trust and faith. We don't have any feeling. Mum I bet in hospital Deepak won't think about Sandeep Rajeev or house. He must be kept dreaming about his girlfriend how they spent 5, 6 month together in Croydon, Horley, Horsham or Ilfield.

Mum on Tuesday when he came home 10.15. I made Bhajia and two cup of tea for him and took it upstair and try to talk when he doesn't reply my questions I go back downstair finish my tea watch t.v. for half an hour come to bed. Then he come to my room and ask for telephone money. The argu start he threats me again for burn my face with hot iron. That night I couldn't sleep. I got up at 2.30 and I did what you see. Mum everybody know he's a very big liar. He made the big story in front of Policemen as well. Mum before he lie why not he think for Sandeep Rajeev as well. Mum please take that money and put on Sandeep Rajeev's separate new account with your name not Deepak's name. Please mum that's my money for my sons. I don't mind if you spend but don't don't give it to Deepak its my heartly request to you.

Mum I think I have to spent another 6, 7 weeks here in prison. There is another 3 girls with me in this room. Same like hospital. They give us all facilities but I miss Sandeep Rajeev a lot. Mum they are the parts of my body. I can't stay or live without them. I'm their mother Mum please try to understand my feeling. Tell me could you live without your children. So how can I. Mum when I comes out I'll find any flat or room for myself and kid. Don't worry I won't stay with you or Langley Green. Deepak done so many paap [sin] so I give him agni-ishnaan [firebath] to wash his paap. I done jail yatra [pilgrimage] to wash my paap. I am paapi [sinner] now.

Mum when you go to hospital or saw him anywhere just tell him never touch or hit women again. That is the biggest lesson I taught him. Mum in 10 year he give me very hard time but this time he cheated with money with overtime with his work, car, pub, his affair, lie about insurance, lie about Tommy's money insurance for kid and special for my kid's shoping. I will never forget that day when I beg him for my children shoping. Mum I love Sandeep Rajeev a lot.

Mum read my letter 3–4 time. I'll ring you on Monday afternoon.

Once again Mum forgive me if you forgive I don't care about the world.

When my mother-in-law was called to give evidence, she did it through an interpreter. I had an interpreter sitting next to me, and he asked if I understood the proceedings. I didn't want him to talk and disturb me so I said yes, and tried to work out what was going on. Mamma denied that Deepak had ever been violent towards me, and said she had no idea that he had a girlfriend. The prosecution's barrister asked her what I had said to her two days before the incident, and read out an extract from her statement in which I had said that I was a hungry lioness, out for Deepak's blood. Fortunately Mamma had forgotten this conversation when she was cross-examined. The prosecution tried very hard to get her to remember these words, but my QC objected that the witness was being led, and the judge sustained the objection. I remembered the conversation, but in my statements I denied it had ever taken place. I hope I will not be judged too harshly for that lie. I wanted to get out of prison.

In the middle of Mamma's testimony the case was adjourned until the following day. Mamma's behaviour at this point is worth recounting. When the judge told her that she would have to return the next day, she entered into a long argument with him. 'I can't come tomorrow,' she said. 'I don't want to come tomorrow.' When the judge asked why, she said she had to look after her grandsons because she loved them. The judge said he was sure she could make other arrangements, but she kept arguing. The judge said she could bring them to the court and that they would be looked after outside. She still refused. In the end he ordered her to come the following day. All the papers carried this story.

[In her statement Deepak's mother, Krishana Ahluwalia, said: 'Deepak was in Canada for only one week, and it was during this time that he first met and then married Kiranjit. I know that Kiranjit had gone to Canada from India and that her time there was running out. She did not have a permit to come to England.' According to her, the marriage was happy for the first four or five years. Kiran did not like her mother-in-law because she never

226

offered her tea. Kiran used bad language and did not uphold traditional values. She had no interest in the children. Sandeep was with Krishana almost all the time since he was born, as was Rajeev since 1988. Kiran did not help Krishana when Deepak's father was ill and she was working nights.

In the last five years of Deepak and Kiran's marriage, the troubles began. Kiran wanted a divorce and took court action. Krishana said she did not try to dissuade her from this because she was told about it only after the event. Krishana never saw any injuries on Kiran but she saw scratches and other marks on Deepak three times – in 1982, 1986 and 1989.

Krishana attributed the problems in the last three years of the marriage to the money owed to Deepak by Kiran's brother and to Kiran's resentment of Deepak's new car. Deepak had been frightened that Kiran was going to poison him. He left her in March and stayed with his mother for a fortnight, returning only when Kiran rang and promised not to hit him or provoke him. On the day of the fire Kiran was with her mother-in-law from 3 to 7 p.m. She had said: 'I am not going to stay with him. Either he will die or I will die. You know what a wounded lion does. The three of us will die.' Krishana did not know what Kiran had meant. Kiran had two sides to her personality: polite to most people, but difficult with Deepak and his immediate family.

In the witness stand, according to the notes made by Hannana Siddiqui of Southall Black Sisters, who attended court every day, Krishana's testimony followed a similar line. She had never been present during Deepak and Kiran's rows. On the day of the fire, when Kiran was going home after visiting her house, Krishana asked if she could go with her, but Kiran refused. After Kiran's letter to Deepak begging him to return was read out in court, Krishana commented, 'Yes, I knew about these things. She used to drink black coffee, Deepak detested it.'

Krishana said that Deepak had gone to a psychiatrist because Kiran had wanted him to: 'I understood he told him that Kiran was mad, not him. He went on the advice of Kiran's relations as well to clarify there was nothing wrong with him.' Under cross-examination, Krishana said that Deepak had frequently changed the telephone number because he did not like receiving calls from Kiran's relatives. It had nothing to do with his white girlfriend. Kiran would somehow find out the number and her relatives would start ringing again. When she was re-examined, Krishana said that Deepak changed the number to protect Kiran when he was working at night. He never kept the number from her, but gave it to her himself. Asked about using the word 'agni-ishnaan' in conversation with Kiranjit, she denied it.]

After Mamma, it was Puppi's turn to give evidence. He said he had never seen Deepak hit me, although Deepak had a very hot temper and was constantly losing it with him, that he would take him by the throat, would not let him meet his friends, would treat him like a woman, would break crockery and furniture. My QC asked Puppi to tell the court how Deepak's family had threatened and beaten him to prevent him from giving evidence that might help me, and how he had got an injunction against Suresh.

[In his statement, Gurjeet said of Deepak and Kiran's marriage: 'The arguments used to take place every two days or so, and although they were quite serious rows they would always make it up. For example they would argue for an hour, but after two more hours everything would be all right between them. They both used to push and shove each other when they argued but I never saw either of them physically hit each other. Deepak used to shout and bang furniture. I saw him break cups and throw plates around the house when they argued whereas Kiranjit didn't break or throw things but would shout and scream loudly at Deepak.

'In my opinion they were both as bad as each other in their fights, with neither being more to blame than the other. The fights were always about silly things around the house, for example cooking meals or doing housework or looking after the children . . .

'Because of all the arguments I tried to stay away from Deepak and Kiranjit, but it came to my notice that Deepak had a girlfriend in Crawley and was going to leave Kiranjit ... I have heard Kiranjit say to Deepak: "You keep the children," and he has said the same to her.'

Gurjeet went on to relate the story of how he and Rajesh had tried to persuade Deepak not to leave Kiran for his girlfriend a few days before the fire. In an additional statement a week later he gave an account of the financial issues between Deepak and himself: 'When my father died in 1985 he left some money in his will. This money consisted of an insurance policy which in 1986 matured and I got a cheque for about £3,000. This money I gave to my auntie, Mrs Krishana Devi Ahluwalia, mother of Deepak Ahluwalia, for safekeeping and her to mind for me. In June 1986 Krishana Ahluwalia loaned the money to Deepak in order for him to purchase a house. Although at the time I did not know about the loan it was acceptable to me as I trust the family to pay the money back. I asked Deepak for the money back on several occasions, however he told me that he didn't have the money. Eventually Deepak told me that he would pay me my money with an insurance policy he owned. When he got the money he bought a car, an XR3i Ford Escort. I asked him for my money and then he told me that he had used the money he was to give me to pay the debts of his wife's brother Tommy ... I believe that Deepak gave Tommy £4,000 which is why he was unable to pay me.'

In the witness box, Gurjeet testified to Deepak's possessiveness. When Gurjeet's friends rang him, Deepak would get upset, so Gurjeet told them not to ring any more. Under cross-examination, he described how Deepak held Kiran by the neck when Devinder was visiting from Canada, and the time when Deepak had held a knife to her neck when she was pregnant with Rajeev.]

Raju was the next to give evidence. He told the court that my married life was not happy, that he had saved me from getting beaten by Deepak on a number of occasions, that Deepak had a girlfriend. The prosecution had called him to give evidence about the caustic soda, because Deepak had shown it to him a few days before the fire. At first Raju denied that Deepak had ever threatened me. Then my QC asked him why he had slept the night at my place if it was not to protect me from further violence. At that point, Raju admitted that he had seen Deepak beat me once. He said that I had been violent towards Deepak too, and referred to the time I had bitten his ear. My QC asked him why he could only talk of the bleeding ear, an incident which I had always admitted. Surely, he said, if Deepak could beat me in front of Raju, then we could only wonder what he might have done in the car to provoke me to bite his ear. I was pretty satisfied by Raju's evidence.

[Rajesh's statement referred to the £4,000 that was a bone of contention between Deepak and Kiranjit. He accepted that Deepak had a girlfriend. He described the ear-biting scene and how he separated Deepak and Kiran when Deepak grabbed Kiran by the hair and slapped her about the face. He told how he and Gurjeet had gone to talk to Deepak about his marital problems on the Sunday before the fire: 'During the conversation he [Deepak] said to me, "Kiran is trying to do me." When I asked him what he meant by that he said, "She is trying to kill me." . . . He then told me about a pan of caustic soda which he said Kiranjit had put in the bathroom. As I was going up the stairs he came out of the bathroom with a large aluminium saucepan. The pan was empty but it did have a funny unpleasant smell.'

Despite the fact that only traces of petrol, and not caustic soda, were found on Kiranjit, the prosecution made much of the caustic soda. Under cross-examination the official pathologist, Dr Iain West, testified that it was not possible to distinguish between a chemical burn and a flame burn, although blistering on Deepak's inner right thigh was consistent with contact with corrosive chemicals. However, Dr Heath, the forensic pathologist appointed by Kiranjit's solicitors, believed that there was 'no evidence of chemical burns'. *His report was based on photographs of Deepak's body, which he did not have an opportunity to examine. There was no discoloration, no 'brown ulcerated areas' of the kind caused by caustic soda. It was his contention that there could not have been caustic soda on the bathroom floor as there were no burn marks on Deepak's feet.*

In his summing up, the judge quoted scientific evidence that traces of caustic soda were found on the bathroom floor ten days after the incident. However, no such traces were found in the bath. The judge concluded that a caustic soda solution must have been poured on the floor, because it had spread over a large area. He explained the fact that Deepak's feet were free of caustic soda burns by agreeing with the official pathologist that Deepak would have needed to soak his feet in a concentrated solution for a prolonged period before suffering burns. The fire investigator, Mr Jenkins, said that the bathroom floor was wet with a viscous liquid on the night of the fire, although he hadn't made a note of it at the time, and no other officers had noticed anything but an ordinary wet floor, consistent with someone having had a bath.

'After the fire,' the judge said, 'the fire detective Inspector Coates arranged for the house to be sealed, you may think for obvious sound reasons, but for some reason that is not explained, the family of the dead man were given a key and allowed to go to the house. This was described as being early after the fire, therefore presumably that would mean between the first and second visits by Mr Jenkins. The implication is clearly made that the family would have the opportunity to put caustic soda on the bathroom floor, and the suggestion is that this is how the film which gave rise to the high Ph reading could have got there.']

Now it was my turn to give evidence, but before I was called my QC played a tape of my interview with the police to the court. As I heard myself crying while I recounted my life story, I started sobbing. That was the first time I had shown my feelings openly in court. All my family members were crying along with me at this point. My QC attempted to read from the letter I had written to Deepak to demonstrate the degree to which I was willing to enslave myself for the sake of keeping the family together. 'Despite the fact that he has beaten her from the very first week of their ten-year marriage,' he said, 'she had wanted to try and please him.'

My mother-in-law's testimony, and my fears about the jury, completely undermined the ground I stood on. I could not bring myself to give evidence. All my confidence slipped away. I felt as if I had been ensnared in a web, by people who had heard my tale of suffering, night and day. Sandeep and Rajeev had already lost their father, now they would lose their mother too. I was also loath to testify about the intimate details of my life with Deepak in front of the entire family from both sides. I decided that I would not speak, but would exercise my right to silence, and refuse to go into the witness box. When I told my solicitor that I would not give evidence she tried hard to persuade me otherwise, but I was determined. The court had all the evidence in front of it – doctors' reports, injunctions, work manager's report. The doctor's report described the bruises he had seen, the prescriptions for sleeping pills and the referral he had made to social services when I had told him about my husband's violence. My manager said in his statement that a previously good worker had slipped into days off and extended periods of illness, that he had often seen tears in my eyes but had never got an explanation for my depression, that I was losing weight rapidly and used to shake a great deal while working.

Chandrika and Devinder were called to testify to the violence against me. My lawyers felt that as Chandrika was outside the immediate family, and as she had seen my bruises, her evidence would be powerful. Devinder recounted the telephone incident, and acted out incidents when Deepak hit me in front of her.

[From the judge's summing up of the defence case, it appears that the primary defence was a lack of intent to kill, and the secondary

justification was provocation. The logical flaw in this two-pronged approach was that 'provocation' was inevitably diluted if the defence were also denying intent. Furthermore, the primary defence dictated that the evidence should focus on the incident leading to Deepak's death, whereas provocation could only be developed through the history of violence. According to Kiran's appeal solicitor, Rohit Sanghvi, 'That shift in emphasis, from the history to the moment, probably, in our view, robbed the defence prong of provocation of its sharpness.']

The trial did not quite finish in one week, and on the weekend that intervened my brothers Billoo and Bindhi, and Sukhjit jijaji, came to visit me in Holloway. They were upset with me for not stepping into the witness box, and felt that I might have been able to sway the jury if I had told them directly how much I had suffered. My tears could have had a very real impact on them.

On Wednesday 6 December, the judge started his summing up.

[Mr Justice Leonard's summing up directed the jury to the conclusion that there was an intent on Kiranjit's part to cause serious bodily harm which resulted in death, and therefore amounted to murder: 'If you are satisfied she poured or threw petrol over the deceased man and then ignited it with a naked flame, members of the jury, you ask yourselves what else she could have intended to do, other than to cause really serious injury.'

Despite the evidence of Deepak's violence provided by the defence, the judge described the marriage merely as 'unhappy'. He quoted from Kiran's letter, which the defence had described as a 'charter for slavery': 'Deepak, life is dull without you,' and commented: 'I suppose you could say life without violence and unhappiness could be dull, but she is actually saying "life without you is dull".' He went through the evidence of domestic violence provided by the defence and concluded: 'You will remember all

this material was relevant to the marriage breaking up, and erupt-
ing into violence from time to time, unhappily for the defendant.
Deepak would, unfortunately, violently inflict injuries on her from
time to time, though fortunately it would appear none of that was
of the highest severity.'

The judge asked the jury to come back with a unanimous
decision: 'It is only after a considerable period of time, and after
I have given you further directions the law requires of me, I can
accept a majority verdict.']

The jury retired at midday on Thursday. The judge called
them twice, but both times they said they could not reach a
decision. On the third occasion, at around 5.30 p.m., the judge
said he would arrange overnight accommodation for them. At
that point the foreman asked for another five minutes. The jury
came out, and announced that they had found me guilty, by a
majority of ten to two.

My head was spinning – I couldn't believe it. My QC protested about the jury taking all day and failing to come to a
decision, then making up their minds in five minutes. The judge
said he could not interfere with the jury's decision.

All the law could see was a woman who had committed a
horrific crime in cold blood. The majority of the jury were men.
The judge, the law-makers, were all men. The law was made
for the protection of men. They could sympathise with a man
for the loss of his life, but not with the woman who had suffered
while that man was alive. If there had been any Asian women
on the jury, they might have understood the pressures in my
life. Men's responsibilities end with giving sperm, women's responsibilities begin at that point, and they kill themselves in the
process. My faith in British justice died on that day.

I was asked to stand up. I stood in a daze. The judge asked
me if I had anything to say. I remained silent. He then sentenced
me to imprisonment for life. As I heard the sentence, my head
fell forward, but I didn't cry. What did that mean, life? Would

I ever see my children again? There was a hushed silence in court, and a collective sigh was let loose by my supporters.

When my family came to visit me outside my cell below the courtroom, my sister started crying loudly. I was too stunned to cry. There was an ocean building up inside me. My legal team were all disappointed by the verdict, but my QC said they would let me know whether there were any grounds for appeal.

Although I had committed such a terrible crime, the real criminal was Deepak. My sister-in-law Devinder said to the *Crawley News* that she had lost faith in British justice: 'I've learned something about British justice, which has saddened me. I know now that if you tell the truth and are honest, you pay the price.' Mamma told the *Crawley Observer*: 'He was a devoted father and he loved Kiranjit . . . What Kiranjit did was very, very bad. I can never forgive her for doing that.' In the Gurdwara, she gave everybody *prasad* at the good news that I had been given a life sentence. It was only when the thought that my children had become orphans entered my mind a few days later that tears broke through the overwhelming numbness of my pain.

SEVENTEEN

Campaign and Be Damned!

WHEN I RETURNED to Holloway, I ate as if I hadn't eaten for ages – double bacon and eggs. The first thing the officers did after strip-searching me was to take my fingerprints and my photograph, in profile and full frontal. That photograph room felt like a hanging room. There was a round wooden podium in the centre of it. I had to sit on an old wooden chair with a very straight back, small seat and a raised block in the centre which I had to sit astride with my legs apart. This was to make sure prisoners didn't slump when their photo was being taken.

As a convicted prisoner, I now qualified for an extra set of clothes – four instead of three. I had been promoted. But I could now only do my private shopping monthly, instead of weekly. And my spending limit was £10, whereas on remand it was unlimited, depending on the amount of money you were sent by your relatives and friends.

When you become a lifer, you spend the first week in the hospital wing in case you need treatment for depression. I ended up in the same cell I had been in when I was on remand. The woman who had abused her daughter was still in that cell for her own protection from the other prisoners. When she heard that I had got life, she sobbed. I was surprised at her emotion, when I myself felt hard as a stone.

Within a couple of days, I got fed up with the C1 routine. There was no education or work there, and I asked the nurse for a transfer. 'I want to keep busy. I don't want to think about my life or my past.' She sent me to the kitchens to help out.

As soon as there was a vacancy I was sent to the reception wing, where I had to spend three nights on my own.

I could not concentrate on anything. There is a five-line mantra that we are taught as Sikhs to repeat to ourselves to ward off fear:

> *Ek un kar, satnaam karta Purakh,*
> *Nirbhau, Nirvaie, Akal Murat,*
> *Ajuni Saibhang, Guru prashad jup.*
> *Ad such, jagat such*
> *Hai bhi such, Nanak ho si bhi such.*

> (There is one God, He is the truth, the creator,
> Without fear, without enemies, He never dies,
> He is beyond birth and death, self-enlightening.
> He was the Truth in the beginning, He was the Truth
>   through the ages,
> He is the Truth now, Nanak says, He will be the Truth in
>   the future too.)

I was so frightened in that cell that I kept repeating those lines. It was a filthy room with cobwebs, dirty walls and dirty bedding. I thought that life imprisonment really meant life. I didn't think I would get out for at least twenty-five years. I didn't dare calculate how old Sandeep and Rajeev would be by then. I felt that Deepak was all around me, laughing at my condition. As I ranted at the bare walls, I felt there was no God in this world – God was only an excuse to drive people mad. 'From today,' I said, 'I will not believe in God. Everything is dead for me. This law, family, husband – I don't respect anything. If there was a God, he would not have brought me to this. This God is blind, just like British justice.' I had read the whole *Granth Sahib* by the age of sixteen, all 1,420 pages of it, and this was my reward!

I looked through the tiny slit of a window. It was dark. This was now my life. I could see a friend in another part of the prison, and thought how lucky she was to be able to share her cell with other women. I could not sleep. I was waiting for the nurse to bring me my sleeping pills (it is standard practice in prison to prescribe pills for those who have just been arrested or convicted). At 11.30 that night I got them. The next morning I had no desire to get up or brush my teeth. I had tea. When anyone who knew me saw me, they would say they were sorry about my sentence. They were disbelieving and angry. 'This fucking law' was a common sentiment, and was even echoed by prison officers in the same language.

Billoo praji brought me press cuttings of the trial. I was shocked to see the headlines in the Crawley papers: 'MURDER: Wife Gets LIFE for Fireball Killing', said the *Crawley News*. Daily reports of my trial were carried under the strap 'Fireball Murder Case'. Although some headlines appeared to be sympathetic (' "Wife Treated Like Slave" Claim'), the articles carried Deepak's deathbed denials and quotes from Suresh like: 'I can never forgive Kiran not just for killing my brother but for the way she tried to damage his name.' They also included sections on 'Gran's Custody Bid'. Photos of our house appeared with captions like 'House of human torch terror'. The *Crawley Observer* of 6 December 1989 headlined its report 'Human Torch: Spurned Wife Tells how she Doused Romeo Hubby in Petrol and Flamed it'. A week later the headline was 'I've Got a Present for You', a reference to Deepak's claim that I uttered those words as I set fire to the room.

After four days I was transferred to B4 wing, which was for LTIs, long-term inmates: murderers, drug smugglers, IRA members. When Judith Ward, who had been wrongly convicted for blowing up a coach as an IRA activist, came down to Holloway from the top-security prison at Durham, she was put in the cell next to mine. I asked her how long she had done, and when she told me seventeen years the life drained away from my body – surely I would do thirty years. It was not until nine long months after the trial that I was told what my tariff would be – twelve years. My children would be eighteen and sixteen when I next saw the light of day.

I had asked Sukhjit jijaji to buy me a Walkman with £50 that Billoo praji had given me, and Pragna got me cassettes of bhangra music I had asked for. I would also listen regularly to a radio programme in the evening which played Indian music.

I tried to convince Billoo to return to Canada. He had spent enough money staying in England all this time. He should go back to his job and home. I pleaded with him to make sure that Dev got custody of the children. I had lost everything. It was important that I didn't lose the children as well.

Every day I waited for my solicitor. I became really anxious. We had to lodge the appeal within twenty-eight days of sentencing. The night before she came, in the third week, there was a huge commotion in the prison. It was a pitch-black wintry evening, and I could hear women shrieking and howling. I was sharing a cell with four other women, and we looked out of the window and saw police and prison officers searching the grounds with torches. A rumour went round that a bomb had been planted. I was in such a state that I was convinced someone was trying to kill me, and I asked to be moved to another prison. When I was asked why I thought somebody was trying to kill me I couldn't give a sensible answer, and I finally realised how worked up I was getting.

My solicitor said they had read my case over and over again, and she was very sorry, but they could not find any grounds for appeal. I was stunned. That day my tears were unstoppable. I was flapping my arms and legs about to keep afloat.

I wrote to Southall Black Sisters. That was the only straw I had left. Pragna was on holiday in India. When she got back, she and Hannana came to visit me. Pragna had brought me some silver jewellery, and although I couldn't take it from her as it was against prison regulations, I could admire it. She said that they would do their best. They would find a solicitor, they would run a campaign (she explained the meaning of the word). She said they had no money to pay for solicitors. I couldn't offer her any. I had only £500 which I had kept aside for my funeral. Nor could I ask my family for money. They had done enough. And until leave to appeal was granted, I would get no legal aid. Pragna said that an appeal could take ages, and at the end of the road there was no certainty of victory.

I gave Pragna my statement and other legal papers. She explained that she would deal with my case, and Hannana would sort out the children's custody and property matters. Hannana advised me to lodge an appeal in any case, as she felt I shouldn't miss the deadline in any circumstances. My family and my solicitors were advising me to make a submission to the Home Office to reduce my tariff instead. Pragna wanted a photo of me for the campaign. I said my sister had one. It was really old, taken in 1977 to send around to prospective suitors before I met Deepak.

When Pragna brought copies of the leaflet SBS had had printed, and told me that they were going to distribute it widely, I was shocked. The leaflet described my life with Deepak and my trial, explained my legal position and gave an update on the campaign:

> The campaign wants Kiranjit out of jail. Domestic violence is the real crime! Kiranjit has suffered for her action and it will continue to haunt her. But for her years of horror no one who knew her was prepared to help her live in peace. We cannot abandon her now!

Supporters were asked to join the campaign, to distribute the leaflet, sign petitions, write to the Home Secretary, to MPs and to me, and to send donations. I said I didn't want so much publicity. I felt that everybody in the community was already mocking me, and now the whole world would know. Pragna asked what those people had done for me, those people who I held in awe and high esteem. If they had helped me out before, I would never have ended up in this situation. She said, 'Forget about *izzat*. Fight for your life and children.' She argued for hours with me, trying to convince me that I was not a sinner and a murderer. Would I have done what I did if Deepak had not been cruel to me? The truth of her words carried weight with me.

When I got back to my cell that day, I was very restless. Would my family feel that I was dragging their name through mud by agreeing to such a campaign? Had I not given them enough grief? Then suddenly I thought, to hell with all this *izzat*. My reputation can't sink any lower. I won that battle with myself, and gave Pragna the go-ahead.

Pragna would visit me twice a week, for a whole day at a time. Because we shared a common language, I found I could communicate my deepest feelings to her. She explained everything at great length, and for the first time in my life I felt I was making informed decisions. She asked me to tell her my entire life history. I started my story in Chak, and she took detailed notes. It seemed frustratingly slow – I thought my life sentence would be completed before my life story.

[Pragna visited Kiranjit seventy times. Kiranjit's statement ran to 350 pages.]

And what use would it be? I would get headaches, I would cry and get worked up unnecessarily, thinking nothing would come of this, that it was a waste of time. Sometimes I suspected that Pragna was actually writing a book under the pretext of preparing a legal case. As we got closer, this became a standing joke between us. I became dependent on Pragna and Hannana's visits, and felt a sense of dread at the thought of them coming to an end. They filled in the vacuum caused by the reduction in the number of family visits permitted after conviction. The prison officers were surprised by the number of legal visits I was receiving. I would also pass messages to my family through Pragna. I asked her for her phone number, and when she gave it to me I was shocked that she trusted me enough to do so.

One day Pragna told me that at an SBS meeting they had decided that if I agreed, a television film should be made of my case, because the publicity would be really useful. It was to be made by Gita Sahgal, one of the SBS women, for the *Dispatches* series on Channel 4. She also told me that they had found a solicitor, Rohit Sanghvi, who would act for me. I had read about him – he had recently represented an Asian servant woman who had been ill-treated by a Kuwaiti princess and won unprecedented damages for her.

I will never forget Rohit's first visit. I was very impressed by him, just as I had been with Pragna. He chain-smoked furiously, and told me that he would do everything in his power to find some grounds for appeal, although there was very little hope. He said that if he could find even one chink he would double it in size. He asked me to recreate that day, scene by scene. He took out a piece of paper and drew a layout of the house, asking me detailed questions about where the furniture was and how big each room was. He wanted the history of each and every implement I had used to light the fire. Then he asked me to stand up and recreate that scene, to explain how I went upstairs, what I was carrying in each hand. 'Close your eyes and forget where you are. Go back to that day.' It was only then that I remembered that I had attempted to wake Deepak – and other things that I had not put in my statement, when my mind had gone blank. Rohit asked me to make a diary of the week preceding the fire for his next visit. He was showing such interest, even without legal aid, that I felt there was a ray of hope at last.

The campaign for an appeal was to be launched at a public meeting in Crawley in June 1990. Pragna asked me to write a speech which could be read out to the audience, so that people

would understand what I had lived through in my own words.
I told her I would have it ready for her next visit. I went back
to my cell and poured all my feelings into the speech, which I
wrote in Hindi:

Dear Ladies and Gentlemen,

First of all I want to thank you from my heart for taking
some of your precious time in order to come to this meeting.
Although I cannot be present with you, your loving sympathy
gives me courage in enduring this sentence. I will always be
obliged to you for having understood my pain and helplessness.

My heart is full of things to say, but it is difficult to decide
how and where to start telling my story. My culture is like my
blood – coursing through every vein of my body. It is the
culture into which I was born and where I grew up which sees
the woman as the honour of the house. In order to uphold
this false 'honour' and glory, she is taught to endure many
kinds of oppression and pain, in silence. In addition, religion
also teaches her that her husband is her God and fulfilling his
every desire is her religious duty. A woman who does not
follow this path in our society has no respect or place in it.
She suffers from all kinds of attacks and much hurt entirely
alone. She is responsible not only for her husband but also his
entire family's happiness.

For ten years, I tried wholeheartedly to fulfil the duties
endorsed by religion. I don't wish to compliment myself, but
I was a very good daughter-in-law, wife and mother. I tried
to make my husband and my in-laws happy in every way
possible. I put up with everything. But I also tried several times
to escape from the trap of my anguished married life. But each
time, my husband and family put pressure on me, in the name
of upholding their *izzat*. Keeping up appearances also stopped
me leaving. The result – at my age I am undergoing imprisonment in jail far from my children. Were they at fault, that they
should have their mother's love snatched from them? Not only

243

have they lost their father's love but their mother's as well.

I didn't even want to become a mother because I was so unhappy in my marriage. For five years I managed to avoid it. I didn't want my children to have to suffer as well as me. But my mother-in-law's insults and my husband's beatings made me a mother twice over. In my culture, if a woman doesn't have a baby soon after marriage then she has to endure constant taunts. Today, writing all this down, I realise that first marriage was forced on me, then a denial of divorce was forced on me, and then motherhood was forced on me. What combination of force and helplessness was it that kept me in a ten-year sentence and now sentences me legally to punish me for who knows how long?

After my marriage I forgot how to laugh. I could not eat or drink when I wanted to; I could not make friends with whoever I wanted to; I could not see my family and other relatives too often – I didn't have permission to. Small things were always flaring up into big fights. It wasn't only me but my small children who suffered as well. They were always scared and cowed down. But even though I tried to compromise as much as I could, I was made use of in every way possible. I could not make either my in-laws or my husband happy.

Today, I have come out of my husband's jail and entered the jail of the law. But I have found a new life in this legal jail. It's in this cage that I have found a kind of freedom. I have been given love by the officers: love which I never found outside. Meeting others, I had the freedom to talk to them which, when I was free, I never had. I have met many different kinds of people, experienced their environment and learnt many things. But I am sad that I am not getting a proper education here. This is a world apart from my world. My world was just my home and my children. That's all.

My greatest sorrow, the punishment inflicted on me, is that I have been separated from my children. I think about them all the time. I cannot eat properly or sleep properly. They need me and I need them. They are still very little, so I cannot explain things to them. Every time they come here they say, 'Mummy, come home.' How can I tell them where Mummy is? Or where home is? I have lost everything. I never thought in my wildest dreams that my mistake would have this result. That night I had lost the strength to reason or think. I never thought that I would be wounded for life. A wound that will never heal.

For ten years I lived a life of beatings and degradation, and no one noticed. Now the law has decreed that I should serve a sentence of life. Why?

No one asked why all this had happened. Though I had two little children, I worked without rest for fifty or sixty hours a week in order to build up my home. Why would I set fire to that house? Why did everyone use me as they chose? Though I was the mother of two children, I couldn't take any decision on my own. I could not even name my children as I chose. This is the essence of my culture, society, religion, where a woman is a toy, a plaything – she can be stuck together at will, broken at will. Everybody did what they wanted with me. No one ever bothered to find out what kind of life I was leading after I was married: one of physical and mental torture.

Now, at least, I am grateful that everyone has tried to understand my pain, to share in it and to continue doing that. From all sides, my friends and relatives are helping me. Even if this meeting does not result in any specific help for me I will not be disappointed. I would never want any sister or friend to ever undergo such suffering. There are countless women who have been subjected to such oppression – there is only one thing that prevents them from challenging or being freed from this kind of married life. This is my society, religion and culture. I will never let this religion and culture influence my children. I will never let them be stifled by the bondage of arranged marriages. I will give them the right to live their own lives.

In jail, I have seen women fight for their rights. I have seen them making their own decisions. I too must become strong to make decisions on my own for my future. Being in jail has opened up new possibilities which I never had before. Before I end, I want to express my heartfelt thanks to Crawley Women's Aid, Southall Black Sisters, the National Union of Students [who had written letters of support and organised a petition], social workers and Crawley probation officers [they helped organise visits from my children and advised my family on a wide range of matters] who have helped me in so many different ways.

If my words have caused any offence, if I have forgotten anything, I ask your forgiveness.

Thank you.

When I handed Pragna the speech, she asked me to read it out to her because she couldn't read Hindi. My emotions and anger poured out at the thought of how a society reduces a woman to nothingness, no matter how strong she is. Pragna had tears in her eyes. She couldn't believe that I could write so well. She made me read it again, and told me, 'Don't waste your life, Kiranjit. Write a book one day, write plays and stories. You have a talent for writing.' I thought, here is a woman who has understood my pain, which other women, like my mother-in-law, could not. I felt close to her. She was not just a worker, but a friend.

Pragna told me they were expecting two or three hundred women at the meeting. A coachload was going down to Crawley from Southall. Sukhjit was going to give a speech, and so was SBS.

On the day after the meeting I phoned my sister. She told me that I had become a superstar. There were so many women there, and they all supported me. Women were crying – one was so upset she had to be carried out of the hall. SBS's arrangements had been flawless. Meena, another SBS worker, had worked very hard for the campaign. I tried to arrange to meet her, but it never quite happened. Posters had been plastered all over town, even on dustbins. Ranjit chachaji told me that he had stuck posters back up when they were torn down. He had asked the gurdwara and the church to put up posters, and went around trying to convince people to support me.

My fear of publicity had been ill-founded. Instead of disapproval, I got love and support and adulation. For many of my family members it had become a *tamasha*, but there were others, like Hansapur aunty, who had come to support me. Deepak's eldest uncle and aunt also went to the meeting, supporting me openly for the first time. The only national newspaper to cover the meeting was the *Independent*, which quoted from my speech. The local press carried news of it, but to them I was still the 'hubby-killer'. The *Crawley News* headline was typical: 'Free the Fireball Killer: Human Torch Murder was Self-Defence'.

Although I was a lifer, I was getting some special privileges. I would beg to use the phone to call my children because they were only allowed to visit twice a month. There was one probation officer who was always so busy that he could seldom spare me the time to call my children, but when I showed him my campaign leaflet and a press cutting his whole attitude changed, and he would let me use the phone every Thursday. He would go into the next office to give me privacy, and I often phoned not only my children but also other family and friends. When a person becomes famous, they can get by in so many ways. I could hardly believe it. He was letting a convicted murderer sit in his office and use his phone for forty-five minutes to an hour every week. Two or three visits a week from SBS and fortnightly visits from my family made such a difference to my imprisonment. Other inmates were jealous about the special privileges I was getting, and I was careful not to tell them too much. I hadn't shown any of them the leaflets for my campaign as yet.

One day at breakfast time while I was drinking tea, a six-foot tall officer beckoned to me. I wondered what she wanted. She pointed to the front page of the *Ealing Gazette*, on which there was my picture and one of an SBS worker. Almost the whole page and the middle spread were taken up by the article, which was headlined 'When Home is your Prison, who will Dare Try to Escape? How Family Honour can Become a Killer'. It opened with the lines: 'For most Western women, "*izzat*" has little or no meaning. But for many Asian women it means many years of humiliating beatings, sexual abuse, emotional and physical pain.' The article went on to tell my story, and carried quotes from Pragna and Sukhjit. The officer wanted to check that it really was me, because my photograph was so old. She was shocked when she read about Deepak's cruelty. I asked if the circulation of the paper in the prison could be stopped, because other women might feel envious of me. I even went to the senior officer, but she said it was too late as the papers had all been sent out.

I had got used to Holloway, and had made friends with other lifers. There was Gloria, who had been sentenced to life one week before me. And there was fifty-year-old Mary, who had got two life sentences for setting her boyfriend alight with petrol. His friend who was with him also died. She maintains to this day that she was innocent of the crime. I became very close to her, and called her Mumsy.

I shared a cell with Lizzy, who was serving twelve months for petty crime. She used to weep a lot for her daughter, who had been given away to foster parents who didn't allow Lizzy to visit. There was also an Indian girl who was in for cheque fraud. She had a young baby and was kept in the mother and baby wing. The baby was chubby and cute, and was very popular. This girl kept in contact when she left, and still sends me cards. I used to make Indian-style tea for all of us on a small gas cooker, and we would sit in the cell and drink tea and chat.

All the inmates got together and talked about sex, drugs and rock 'n' roll. Once when they were talking about oral sex I brought up my food. After that they would bring up the subject whenever they wanted me out of the cell.

We also had to work, at least for the first six months of our sentence. I was sent to the sewing department. I can't sew to save my life, but I got on well with the woman who ran the section, Mrs G. She liked me and let me get away with a lot. She reminded me of my mother – her age, her smile, her forehead, her height – and I used to give her lots of affectionate hugs. She was sympathetic to my situation. She would cut the other girls' money when they didn't turn up for work, but although I had so many legal visits, and also had to go for physiotherapy because my shoulder gave me a lot of trouble, she never cut mine. She would just say indulgently that I had a very good excuse. Mumsy once jokingly complained to her that I was now swearing a lot, so I said, 'That's not fucking true. You fucking know that I don't fucking like to swear.' Mrs G put her hands on her ears. 'No, no, Karen, this language doesn't suit you at all.'

My first job was making aprons. I told Mrs G I couldn't work the machines, and asked if I could cut the material instead. She let me. There was a production line of five or six women. When I was in the mood, I would do piles of material. For some reason, I was quite popular with the women. I took care to dress neatly and to keep up appearances. I didn't talk about my problems except to my personal officer and a couple of the women I became friendly with. I never shouted or screamed at anyone, and I tried to be as pleasant as possible. Some of the lesbians approached me and told me that I was very beautiful, that I had lovely hair, that they had dreams about me and so on.

My children were constantly asking me about the scars on my hand where I had burnt it. Because they were too young to be told the truth, I thought I would get a wristband made to cover the marks for their visits. Red was my favourite colour, so I picked up some red cloth and black netting from the sewing section and asked a friend to sew me a wristband. In Holloway, however, there is a thing called 'the red band rule'. Some of the inmates are allowed to leave the prison or go anywhere inside it for duties like shopping or gardening, and they wear a red wristband to which their photograph is attached. When my children came to visit I wore my red band, which as far as I was concerned didn't look like the authority band. A prison officer asked me about it, and despite my explanations she put me on report. She thought I might have been wearing it in an attempt to escape, although she apologised to me when she heard my explanation, saying, 'But rules are rules.' Being on report meant that you had to appear before the governor and justify your actions. If you failed to satisfy him you would be put in solitary, and a note would be put in your file, which would be a blot on your record, and could affect your parole. The officer gave me the form on which I was supposed to give my side of the story. I was terrified. I didn't sleep all night. I didn't want to be put into solitary. You're not allowed out even for exercise or meals. Even the toilet is inside your cell.

I asked Lizzy to write my version on the form. Next morning at 6 a.m. I was locked in the solitary block. I wept and wept, and couldn't concentrate on anything. At 10 o'clock the doctor came to visit. She was astonished to see me there, and wondered what I could possibly have done wrong. Then I was taken to the hearing, presided over by the prison governor with officers sitting on either side of him (in case I took it into my head to attack the governor) and two more by the door.

One of the officers had my file. She read out the record of my behaviour in prison, and that I had never been on report before. I was asked to talk in my defence. I was weeping profusely. The governor got up and checked my scars to verify my story. He let me off with a warning not to do it again. Although I had been friendly with the officer who reported me, I was so angry with her that I didn't talk to her for two months. Lifers have to be very careful how they tread in prison. I wanted to go out on the first parole. I was also embarrassed by the whole incident. I became a joke in the prison, and some of the officers and inmates started calling me 'red band'. Others asked how I could be so silly as to have chosen red.

Despite all this, in prison I felt I had not a care in the world. I had hardly any work to do, and I was making friends and having a better time than I had ever had with Deepak. I felt guilty about the sentence that had been imposed on my family and their grief, and about my children's orphanhood. My brother-in-law Sukhjit had a tough time bringing them to see me every fortnight. The children were living with their grand-mother, and it was a very long journey: he would have to go from Hounslow to Crawley to fetch them, and then to Holloway. They would get carsick and throw up all over his car. I used to tell them to help Dev masi when they stayed with her, because I was conscious of the burden on her. It saddened me that although they were so little, they had to grow up faster than other children.

By the time I had spent fifteen months in Holloway, I had become quite settled. I liked the regime there. But as a lifer, I was only allowed to serve my first stage in Holloway. I had to move after that. I was scared of going to another prison, where I would be locked up for longer, in case the isolation drove me crazy. I was told that I was going to be moved to Bullwood Hall in Essex, which I had heard bad things about: it was a strict regime, intended to strip you of your humanity. Pragna tried very hard on my behalf to keep me at Holloway. There was another option – to go to Durham. Although this would put me a long way away from my children and SBS, I had heard that the regime there was relaxed, and that you were allowed out of your cell from eight in the morning until eight in the evening. I was told that if I went to Durham I would be allowed to come to Holloway for five weeks every four months to receive visits. Then I thought I could have all the visits with my children that I had accumulated in that time.

Despite my representations to the Home Office to be transferred to Durham, I was sent to Bullwood Hall. The only consolation was that some of the women I had befriended at Holloway – women like Mumsy, Maria and Barbara – had also been sent there. I would not be completely alone.

EIGHTEEN
==

My Faith Returns

I ARRIVED AT Bullwood Hall – or 'Bullshit Hell', as it was known among the inmates – at lunchtime. The reality was worse than the rumours. My cell was the size of a boxroom, the floor was filthy, and so were the mattress and blankets. When I saw this hell, I realised I had been living in a five-star hotel until then. We were locked up from 4.45 in the afternoon until eight the following morning. There was a bucket in the cell, but I would always try to hold out till the next morning. It's a very long time to wait with a full bladder. If the officer on duty was nice she might take you to the toilet, otherwise they would plead understaffing.

I had brought along with me two or three Hindi novels from the library at Holloway. The library at Bullwood Hall was just a small room, and I read some of those books four times before my order for more books finally came through. Later one of my supporters, to whom I had written saying I found it hard to read English books, sent me some Hindi novels. She went to Southall and chose them by their covers.

I couldn't tune in to the Asian radio programmes on my Walkman in Bullwood, so when Tommy was due to visit me from Canada I wrote asking him to buy me an AM/FM radio. The guards let me have the radio, but not its aerial, in case I committed suicide with it. In January 1991 I wrote to the Home Office pleading to be allowed to have the aerial. My request was granted over a year later.

The man who was in charge of work – making Christmas

crackers and flower arrangements for Mothers' Day – was often quite hard on the women. He would put them on report or cut their money without blinking an eye, but for some reason he gave me a lot of support. There was another man, Mr M, who was very kind. He would even buy chocolates for us with his own money.

Every lifer is assigned a personal officer to whom she can tell her personal and legal problems in strict confidence. This officer also writes the report which is submitted to the parole board, so it is very important to keep on the right side of your personal officer. Mine was Mrs Bott. I showed her all my press cuttings, hoping that her attitude to me would be different if she realised the kind of campaign that was being fought outside for me. I became very close to her, and she gave me lot of courage and support.

Although I was pleasant to everyone, some of the women played a trick on me when I first arrived. While I was out of my cell they poured a jug of water into my bed, then covered it up with a bedcover so that nothing was visible. When I got into bed at 9 o'clock, I thought I had wet my bed. Although this was only a childish prank it made me worried, because some of the inmates were dangerous. The trick was carried out by a woman who had a mental problem. She was doing life for killing her sister's lover. She couldn't tolerate him ill-treating her sister, so she strangled him. She was on drugs twenty-four hours a day. I complained that I didn't feel safe, and wanted to go back to Holloway.

We were not allowed medicine or razor blades in our cells, nor were we allowed to keep sanitary towels, tampons, soap or toilet rolls, all of which were kept in a small storeroom. Every month we were given a big box of tissues. Every Thursday we got two clean sheets, two towels and two pillowcases. Clean blankets and bedspreads were handed out every six weeks. Our personal monthly spending on toiletries, batteries, stamps, tele- phone cards, snacks, sweets and soft drinks could not exceed

£30. For our work we received £3 per week, which went up after a while to £3.30. If I had worked in the kitchen I would have got £6, but I thought it would be more useful to pick up skills for the future. I learned to make flower baskets, and went on various courses. I also went to the gym and played badminton to keep fit.

Meanwhile Hannana was beavering away at the child custody case. She gathered statements from members of the family, social workers, teachers and others. I was desperate for Sandeep and Rajeev to live with Dev and Sukhjit, rather than with Deepak's mother. Hansapur aunty and Ranjit chacha played a central role. They wrote to the social services and the probation service, and encouraged other friends and relatives to write as well.

Hannana wrote a long report on the care of children in our culture, which had an impact on the case. The court welfare officer's report was informed by the SBS report, and was favourable to care and control of the children being transferred to Dev and Sukhjit, whose accommodation, education and relative youth were taken into account. They had other children, and the family environment was happy and stable. The SBS report said that Dev and Sukhjit encouraged contact between my children and myself, whereas their grandmother's negative comments about me would distort their relationship with me. Mamma also did something that adversely affected her case. She was caught shoplifting, and the story appeared in the local press under headlines like 'Murder Gran Cops Clothes Pinch Rap' and 'Tragic Gran in Court'. She pleaded the death of her son as mitigation, and was fined £25. Cuttings were sent as evidence that she would not be setting a good example for the children.

Despite the fact that it involved uprooting the children from their grandmother's home, with which they were familiar, to one which they didn't know well, Dev and Sukhjit won custody of the children. It was at this point that my faith in God was restored. It was also at this point, when they had achieved a near-miracle, that I unreservedly placed my life in the hands of SBS. At the same time, I felt worried about the extra strain on Dev, whose life was already full to the brim with work.

[At about this time the local Crawley paper the Evening Argus *carried an article on Rohit, entitled 'Solicitor's Fight to Free a Jailed Wife'. It said: 'Lawyer Rohit Sanghvi has waived costs amounting to tens of thousands of pounds to take on Kiranjit Ahluwalia's appeal case. He said, "I am acting from a sense of justice. She has no right to be in prison." ']*

The *Dispatches* programme was due to be broadcast any day. Two dates in November were cancelled because of the Gulf War and Margaret Thatcher's resignation, but it was eventually shown on 30 January 1991 at 9 p.m., by which time we were locked away.

When I saw Miss Newton, the senior prison officer, the next day, I asked her what she had thought of the programme. She said it was so sad that she had been unable to contain her emotions when she saw it. She was convinced that I would be too upset by it, so she would not allow me to see it until Mrs Bott came back from holiday. Waiting those two weeks for her return seemed interminably long.

I found instant stardom. Every officer who passed me would call me 'superstar', or make some reference to the programme. One of them even asked why I had waited so long to do what I did, and wasted my entire life. She said she would have done it in the second week of the marriage, and by now she would have served her ten years and been freed. Mr M told me that his wife had watched the programme in hospital, and told everyone there that I worked for her husband. He wanted me to sign the case of his video for him.

When Mrs Bott returned, Amelia Rossiter, who was also in

the programme, and I watched a video of the programme with her. When I saw the pictures of my wedding day, pictures of Deepak and my brothers, I cried a lot. Every scene of my life came flooding back. Mrs Bott kept wanting to switch it off, but I wouldn't let her. She held my hand when it got particularly difficult. That ocean which could no longer be contained came bursting out through every chink. I wanted to see the programme again properly because I had cried all through the first viewing.

The programme was called 'The Provoked Wife', and set out to answer the question 'Why is the law unable to recognise the provoked wife?' It focused mainly on my case, but also looked at Amelia, Sara Thornton and Joan Calladine. I felt particularly sorry for Amelia, who was ill with asthma and over sixty-five years old. There were interviews with Rohit, Pragna, Sukhjit, Dev and the police officer who interrogated me. There were also shots of the Crawley meeting, so for the first time I could see with my own eyes how my speech was received and who had turned up to support me. An actress narrated my story.

Pragna had asked me several times to get in touch with Sara Thornton, who was in Durham, and the day after I saw the *Dispatches* programme I wrote to her. By chance, she had decided to write to me at the same time, and our letters crossed. Sara said she was coming to Bullwood Hall in April.

I was in the exercise yard when she turned up, and we embraced like long-lost friends. Rohit was also representing her, and our campaigns were being run more or less in tandem (Justice for Women was organising her campaign), so we had a lot of things in common. She was a short, thin but very active woman, and a fiery character, whose answers were ready even before you had time to frame the question. She had tremendous courage – by comparison with her, I was pathetic. She had vowed to carry on fighting till the end of her life, whether she won or lost. I too wanted to fight against prison conditions, but at the same time I didn't want to blemish my record so that I wouldn't get out as early as possible. I wanted to be a goody-goody.

Sara said that the staff and governor at Durham were relieved to see her go because she was such a troublemaker. She believed that rules were meant for breaking, and she made her presence felt on her very first day at Bullwood Hall. When she arrived, the prison officer said she could not take her CD player into the cell with her. Sara said that if Durham, which was a top security prison, could allow women to have their hi-fis, she couldn't understand why she wasn't allowed to do so here. She refused to budge. She went to see the governor, who turned her request down. She then demanded to see the senior governor. Eventually she was allowed to have the CD player, on condition that she left it outside her cell so that the other women could share it.

That was her first victory. Her second was enabling prisoners to receive flowers. When her visitors brought her flowers she fought for the right to keep them, as they gave the prisoners so much pleasure and beauty. As a result of her struggle, flowers are permitted at Bullwood Hall. On another occasion, Sara refused to work in the factory because the light was so poor. She was ordered to go to the solitary block, but when the officers came to fetch her she barricaded herself in her cell by pushing her bed against the door. Within seconds fifteen officers had gathered. They had to unscrew the door to get her out.

Sara wrote to Judge Tumim to complain about the conditions at Bullwood, and asked him to visit. When he came, each cell was 'improved' with a potted plant. Despite his visit, Bullwood was often understaffed, so the prisoners' two-hour 'association' time would be cut. Over bank holidays we would sometimes be locked up for fifteen hours at a time.

Sara was preparing her case for appeal, and had a great deal of knowledge about legal matters. She would write letters on behalf of the other women and advise them on how to conduct their cases. She told me to push my solicitor and SBS to find grounds for appeal, because she thought they weren't doing enough. Unfortunately, some of the other inmates became jealous of Sara. Some of the lifers were resentful because they claimed not to have committed the crimes for which they had been sentenced, and felt that they were in a far worse position than Sara, who had, as she acknowledged, committed a crime. I was always very careful to do things discreetly, and tried to advise Sara to do the same. Once another inmate told an officer that they were going to beat up Sara because she was getting on their nerves. When the officer warned Sara, she was in shock. She couldn't work out who could hate her so much. It was a pity that she became unpopular because she had a very big heart, and would give away anything you asked her for. The others would use her. I tried to tell her to be generous after she was released.

Sara and I used to fantasise about our husbands. We would imagine them sitting on a bench in the exercise yard which we could see from a window in the prison corridor. Sara would make me laugh by saying that Deepak and Malcolm had become friends on the other side, and spent their time discussing their respective wives.

One day I wore a pair of earrings that had been given to me by the children's social worker. It was against the rules to wear drop earrings at Bullwood Hall, and an officer put me on report. I was sent to the solitary block, where prisoners are locked up all day, including mealtimes, with no exercise. I begged to be given some other punishment and the governor let me off, saying that I would not be allowed any private spending for one week.

I was put on report another time when my room was searched and they found a razor blade. I was too shy to admit to the officers that I used a blade to shave my legs, and that I had asked Sara to lend hers to me. Prisoners are not allowed to keep things like razor blades in their cells in case they commit suicide. I thought that this time I would not get off lightly. I said in my defence that I was too shy to ask for a blade. I was vomiting, as I always do when I am nervous. The governor cut my private spending for a month. All the women thought this was excessive, especially since it was nearly Christmas. Sara typed out a petition to the governor and got all twenty-eight women in the prison to sign it, asking for clemency to enable me to buy presents for my children. The governor said she would talk to me if I wrote to her directly. I said that I would agree to my canteen spending being cut, but that it was really important for me to send cards to my supporters and to buy presents for Rajeev and Sandeep. She agreed. This was another victory for Sara.

After the *Dispatches* programme I started receiving a lot of mail, twenty or thirty letters a week. Most were from women asking me to remain strong and confiding in me that they were often a hair's breadth away from the situation into which I had fallen. I had to reply to all these letters, if only to thank the writers. It gave me something to do. Letters are a great way of lifting a prisoner's spirit. Stamps were a bit of a problem, but my visitors would smuggle them in. Because my English still wasn't very good, Mumsy would draft the replies for me and I would copy them out in my hand.

Shortly after my arrival at Bullwood a woman called Joan, who has remained a solid support to this day, started writing to me. After our initial exchange of letters, I decided to write to her on my own, without Mumsy's help. I couldn't even understand my own letter. I would apologise to Joan for my poor English, saying that I couldn't explain the things I wanted to tell her. Joan rebuilt my confidence by insisting that she understood my letters perfectly. I would tell her all about prison life, and about the campaign being run by SBS. I urged her to go along to their office, which she did.

Joan wanted to learn Punjabi, so I would end a lot of my letters with a lesson. She wrote to many MPs drawing attention to my case, and to the courts, asking for clemency.

[From the MPs Joan asked for understanding because Kiranjit was 'born into a restrictive culture which is totally alien to our Western society . . . where women are treated as equals'. In prison, she said, Kiran risked coming 'under the influence of perverted sex and drug barons'. She wrote to all the women Members of Parliament, the Prime Minister and other MPs. Some pleaded pressure of work, or gave the standard excuse that the matter should be dealt with by the Member representing the constituency Joan lived in. But Alice Mahon made representations to the Home Secretary, David Waddington: 'The effects of years of domestic violence must be considered and their effects weighed. Fear and desperation resulting from such violence is not always displayed in immediate and passionate violence.' Diane Abbott wrote to Angela Rumbold, and Clare Short pointed out that she had already made representations. Rosie Barnes wrote to the Home Secretary: 'From what I know of this case it does not seem that this is a woman of murderous nature. The circumstances which led to her conviction were particular and terrible.' Most of the replies referred to the freedom of the courts and the Home Secretary's inability to intervene unless there was some new evidence that cast doubt on the safety of the conviction.]

I got letters of support from some MPs, including Jo Richardson, Labour Member for Barking. I didn't know who MPs were at first, but when I found out, I was really proud to receive those letters. And Dave Nellist, the Labour MP for Coventry South-East, visited Sara and me at Bullwood Hall.

[Joan wrote an open letter to Lord Justice Beldam which started: 'While I deeply respect your knowledge of the law, I have no respect of your knowledge of women . . . You, and all fellow judges, need instruction on the intricacy of a woman's mind, if you are to continue giving judgement on such as Sara Thornton. Being married does not prepare you for such a complex subject, unless you remarry maybe a dozen times!' To the Home Secretary she wrote: 'Please would you kindly take some time to think carefully, as I

did, about the situation of the woman I am appealing to you about and then, perhaps, take the enclosed literature home and ask your wife to read and give her views.']

Joan even wrote to Prince Rama Verma of Trivandrum in India, asking him to pray for me at the time of my appeal: 'She is well worth all the time and effort spent on trying to get her released from prison.'

When I first told Joan my story, she asked me whether I had had my period around the time of the fire, because one of the grounds for an appeal could be pre-menstrual tension. She wrote to me three or four times a week. We became very close through our letters, and closer still when she started visiting. I had to start all my letters with my prison number, 'TP3808', and Joan said that the number became stamped on her brain – she even tapped it into her cash dispenser once. I told her about the Colombian prisoner who was done for smuggling drugs. She was caught at Heathrow dressed as a nun and carrying cocaine in a hollowed-out Bible, but had forgotten that nuns don't wear make-up or nail polish. I would complain to Joan about my neighbour on the right-hand side, who cursed and swore and moaned all the time and should have been in a mental hospital. She was a black woman of about seventy who had tried to smuggle drugs hidden in a dead baby's body. The air hostess became suspicious when she didn't feed or change the baby, and it didn't cry or move on such a long journey. I told Joan that I wanted to write a book about my experiences. She replied, 'Of course the book has to be written ... not by an Indian author but by an English person who has studied at great length the customs, possibly lived for many years in India.'

Sex was a very regular topic of conversation in prison, and I would write to Joan with all the choice bits I picked up. When I heard that 'doing it' on the spin dryer made it much more fun, she wrote back that 'his dick would fall off with the vibrations'. There were pictures of naked men everywhere. I told

Joan that one guy's penis was as big as Rajeev's leg. When police officers visited the prison the women would curse them, using language the like of which I had never heard before: 'Fuck off, your penis is small and useless. We're feeling sorry for your wives and girlfriends.' Joan said my letters had her in stitches every time.

We wrote about all kinds of things:

Joan I laugh when I read in your letter that you're totally against the poll tax. Me too. But I don't have to pay any tax. I got rid of everything – mortgage, tax, poll tax etc. I got long-time holidays. Only thing I don't understand this govt. On one side they wasting billions pounds on us special prisoners. Gave them long life sentence. I mean I'm 34 years old and doing nothing felt like such waste of life. On the other they ask people for poll tax. Special poor ones.

Little by little I discovered that Joan worked for a funeral director. I found out that she was particularly busy in the winter, when she had to deal with eight to twelve old people a day, compared to five a day in the summer.

I became very worried that I was losing too much weight, and I wrote to Joan: 'In prison everyone pray for freedom. Only I myself pray for freedom and a little bit more fat. Greedy person.' One of my supporters kept sending me Bibles of all shapes and sizes, which I donated to the prison chapel. I had so much correspondence to answer that I wrote to Joan:

I was thinking as well I need secretary to write to all my kind supporters. And for a minute I thought let me write to Mamma first if she could arrange for me. As she always saying to everyone about me, QUEEN ordered her all the time . . . In Punjabi she calls me MAHARANI. Its more superior word to queen . . . Well sister Maharani can't cook anymore as she got professional trained chef here and officers are my waiters who serve me my dinner with always bloody cabbage and potatoes and three times ham in a week.

Joan wrote back: 'You must be mad wanting to come out of prison ... You never have to get wet to post letters or get the shopping. You've got servants to do it all for you.'

SBS and the Home Office were receiving a lot of letters (Mr M wrote to the Home Office to ask for my release, and lobbied all his friends to do the same). I started getting letters from men and women in other prisons. I don't know how they heard about me, whether they saw the programme or whether it was word of mouth. One of the prisoners who wrote to me was Harbajan Singh Dhillon, who was in Long Lartin, a top-security prison where the men were serving from twenty to thirty years up. He wrote in Punjabi and sent me a prayer from the *Granth Sahib*. I was very impressed by his letters. When SBS organised a petition requesting my release, I sent forms to him, and almost all the inmates of Long Lartin signed it. I got nearly eighty-five signatures from there, a prison which held many men who had killed their wives or girlfriends.

Another man, who was in prison for drugs offences, wrote to me. He talked about our culture and how it made men feel safe to beat their wives, and confessed to having beaten his own wife. Now that his family were so far away he missed his wife desperately, and had resolved never to beat her again.

[*The man sent a petition to SBS along with a covering letter:*

My reasons for writing this petition are given below. But first, very briefly, the background as to how I got involved.

After reading an article in the Independent *newspaper (2/7/ 90) with the heading 'Campaign seeks the release of Asian woman jailed for murder'. To say that I was astonished would be the understatement of the decade, I just could not believe the judgement passed on this poor woman (to whom I subsequently wrote as any Asian brother would to his sister in her hour of need).*

I am 31½ years of age ... My elder sister was married (through an arranged marriage) to her cousin in 1975. She came to the UK with her son to live with her husband in 1977. The next ten years of her life and her two sons' lives would be hell. While the sons watched on helplessly, their mother was subjected to inhuman beatings, without mercy, which subsequently resulted in hospitalisation for treatment.

On one such day, I was awakened by my cousin early in the morning who informed me that my brother-in-law came to my place and looked worried and that he left as soon as he found out that I was home. On hearing this I quickly got dressed and rushed to my elder sister's flat. The sight that greeted me on my arrival nearly drove me insane. I still, to this day, have nightmares. When the doctor at Whipps Cross Hospital saw my sister, he said, 'Are you an animal?' He thought it was me who had done it as he saw that my white dinner jacket had blood on it all over. My sister's head, forehead and above the right eye was all cut. The wounds were deep. She had blood clots and marks on all of her body. She had been beaten with TV stand and TV aerial wire at 3 a.m.

Before I had a chance to tell the doctor what actually happened, my sister told me in Punjabi, told me is the wrong word. She pleaded with me not to tell the doctor. She made me say that she fell off the stairs.

It was obvious that the doctor did not believe me and all because of 'Family IZZAT'. I can go on and on ...

I am not saying that I have been an angel! I have treated my beloved wife rough as well. I have knocked her senseless on many an occasion! But!! I have repented. I saw the light. And I have come out of the darkness, by the grace of God. I pray that may the Almighty God forgive me for the pain I caused unknowingly to my beloved wife.

We men from the Indian sub-continent are brought up wrong. And it is about time someone did something about it.

Kiranjit Ahluwalia is just one woman whose life has come to light. There are thousands of Asian women suffering. Kiranjit *should be released unconditionally, reunited with her children, and praised!!!*

I am not praising her for the murder for 'NO HUMAN HAS THE RIGHT TO TAKE ANOTHER HUMAN LIFE, EXCEPT!!! IN SELF-DEFENCE.'

And this is exactly what she did. This is not and cannot be called 'Pre-meditated murder'. This so called 'WESTERN CIVILISED SOCIETY' and Justice, seems to me, for their own only.

How can one judge put one woman in prison for LIFE and yet! another judge puts another woman on probation for 2 years. She also killed her husband because of the beatings she got. Could it be that this woman was WHITE!!!

Justice has not been done. Justice is crying out, and screaming out to all of us. The so called guardians of the free society. FREE KIRANJIT AHLUWALIA!!!! FREE KIRANJIT AHLUWALIA!!!!

Let us show this daughter, this mother, this woman, this sister but above all this human being that her sacrifice for ten years in the name of this false man made family 'izzat' have not been a waste.

Let us, the so called 'guardians of the free society' unite Kiranjit Ahluwalia with her 2 children. And let us pray that she finds happiness. Insha'allah (God willing).]

Pragna was so impressed by this letter's critique of our culture that she wanted to meet its author and ask for permission to print it in one of our campaigns. Instead, by mistake, she ended up meeting Harbhajan Singh Dhillon.

[Stress and long hours at work led Pragna to confuse the two names. She thought it was Dhillon who had written the letter, especially since he and his probation officer had started phoning and writing to SBS begging them to start a campaign for him. By a shocking irony, the Dhillon case had been a major campaign in SBS's early days – he had burnt his wife and three daughters alive in their house. The community had failed to condemn the violence

of Asian men against their families, which it saw as unimportant compared to the larger struggle against the National Front in Southall.]

When Pragna found out who he was, and that he now wanted SBS to fight a campaign for his release, she asked how I could possibly communicate with him. But I had not known what his crime was. I could only accept his support at face value, and maybe he had genuinely repented his crime. Anyway, what harm was there in writing to the man? After all, he was paying for his sins. He had served eleven years already. He would tell me about his prison routine and I would tell him about mine.

Eventually Dhillon did tell me about his crime. It was a long letter. He said his wife used to nag him. He had bought the house for her sake, but nothing ever made her happy. She wanted to go to work, while he wanted her to look after their children. She wanted to send the youngest daughter to India so that she could go to work. Dhillon and a white friend drank a bottle of whisky and set the house alight. The letter sent a shiver down my spine. After reading it three or four times, I tore it up as Dhillon had asked me to do.

Another man who wrote to me, Satpal Ram, is serving life for defending himself against a group of white racists. His brother is campaigning for his release. Other inmates promised to carry on campaigning for me when they were released. One young woman, Julie Baker, gave me a lot of support. She would get my petition signed in pubs and clubs, and even got policemen to sign it.

At Christmas time I got lots of flowers. Joan sent me wrapping paper for my children's presents. I got flowers on Christmas Day, a call from Surinder, Tommy, Billoo and Devinder in Canada, and seventy or eighty cards.

Once when the kids had come on a visit and were playing in the children's section, Rajeev had a nosebleed. I wanted to cuddle him, but we were not allowed to move from our chairs.

I could not touch my own son. There were individual officers who would break the rules for the sake of humanity. Once, when the children hadn't eaten the chocolates I had bought for them, the officer wouldn't let me take them back to the cell. I pleaded with her because I would just have to throw the chocolates away. I saw that she was going to stand her ground, so I shrugged my shoulders and said, 'It's up to you. You don't love me any more, do you?' When I got back to the cell she slipped the chocolates into my hand, saying, 'I never gave you any chocolates, did I?' Some of the officers would smuggle stamps in for me.

In February it was my birthday. As I was putting on my trousers early in the morning, officers came to my cell door and sang 'Happy Birthday to You'. At home, no one had ever celebrated my birthday except Surinder, who shares the same birth date. I wondered how the officers found out. All the women in the wing sang 'Happy Birthday' as well, and presented me with a huge card made by them. I got forty cards, and flowers from SBS, Joan and Justice for Women. I distributed my flowers to the other women to bring beauty into their cells. Sara gave me a big potted orchid with yellow flowers, and I got a mystery Valentine card. When Sandeep and Rajeev came to visit, Rajeev told the officer at the gate 'It's my Mummy's birthday.' I went to church, and wept because I was missing everyone, and phoned Surinder in Canada. I also got some rather strange letters from men who were attracted to my picture, and Valentine's Day cards, which I had never received in my life before. One of the men was called John. He never sent me his address. Maybe he didn't feel safe. I thought that was funny, a man who didn't feel safe.

I got a number of diplomas at Bullwood Hall: two in English, one in typing – something I never managed to achieve when I was with Deepak – and I also learnt hairstyling and flower arranging and attended a fashion design course. I couldn't concentrate on the computer courses. I thought I might work as a designer for my brother Billoo, who had opened a clothes factory in Canada, when I came out.

Sara Thornton's appeal was coming up, and her papers would lie spread out across her cell. Rohit had advised her to plead diminished responsibility, but she wanted to plead provocation. Although on a matter of principle she was quite right to insist on this, it was not going to help her case. The only way the justice system can accommodate women who say 'enough is enough' is if they can be shown to be not in full control of themselves when they did it, if they can be seen as mad, so as not to upset the social order.

Sara had hyped herself up for victory, and she promised to campaign for me on her release. When I asked her what she would do if she lost her appeal, she said she would go on hunger strike.

The day of her appeal arrived. When she returned to Bullwood Hall from the High Court I was impatient to hear the outcome, but there was no decision that day. Sara said she had gone to court without any knickers on, as a symbol of her defiance, and she made sure that she broadcast the fact. The case lasted three days, and on 29 July 1991 I heard from the wing cleaner that Sara had lost. I was shocked. If Sara couldn't win, then I had absolutely no chance. I wept for days. When I saw Sara and hugged her, I was the one who was crying. Sara was so brave. She never showed her disappointment. She said to me, 'Don't cry. The fight isn't over yet. I will win.'

When Pragna next came to visit, I felt hopeless. I had taken a tissue with me because I usually ended up crying on these visits. I was too upset to speak, so I took a pen from Pragna and wrote on the tissue, 'Hard luck Kiranjit Ahluwalia. Live in hell for life. Nobody like me, even Patel.' I felt I would leave that prison only in an urn of ashes. British law is invincible. There is no mercy. Once somebody has been ensnared in its web, it doesn't let them go until they die. So many women had

269

committed suicide in prison. Some go mad, some die of illness. During our meeting, I could feel Pragna's impatience with me. She had travelled a long way, and she could not drag me up from the bottom of the ocean to which I had sunk. As she was leaving, she asked what I had been scribbling. I gave her the tissue.

For a whole week I didn't bother to turn on my cell light. One morning I was unable to get up. All I wanted to do was sit in my cell and cry. The prison officer was surprised, as I was always ready bright and early. I wept in unstoppable waves of sorrow, thinking about how old my children would be when I was released – that is, if I didn't die in prison. Would they want to know me? Would they recognise me? What had I done for them as a mother? Would they call me a sinner and a murderer? I asked the prison officer to make sure that my body was sent to India for the funeral. 'I hate England,' I said. 'I don't want to put even a foot on this land.'

I said to Mrs Bott, 'I don't want any more legal visits. They are just a waste of time, because I am not going to get out. Why should I repeat my history again and again when I am going to die in prison?' Mrs Bott booked an appointment with the doctor, and I was prescribed sleeping pills. For the second time in my life, suicide seemed an attractive option. I started to save up my nightly sleeping pills, pretending to swallow them and stockpiling them in my cell. But after three days the pills were stopped, and as I was unable to sleep without them I took them over the next few days.

George Delf, who was spearheading Sara's campaign, gave her a press cutting about a man, Joseph McGrail, who had walked free two days after she had lost her appeal. This man had killed his alcoholic wife. We were very upset by the news. Sara said, 'That's it,' and went on hunger strike. I couldn't bear it. I would save my fruit and biscuits from mealtimes and buy her chocolates and hide them in her room and plead with her to eat them secretly to keep her strength up, but she would not. I told her I was not strong enough to watch her die.

Pragna (who had also been visiting and advising Sara) and Rohit tried to persuade her to stop her hunger strike. The prison authorities sent her to Holloway, where the facilities were better. I told Pragna that I wanted to go on hunger strike to support Sara. Another lifer said she would do the same. My only weakness was my family. If they got to know they would come running from Canada and India. Pragna and I discussed the implications. She felt that I should be careful, as a hunger strike could affect my appeal and prejudice the judges against me. I said to her, 'Give me the word and all the other women are ready to go on hunger strike.' We were angry that men got out while we were not considered even after the way we had suffered in violent relationships. But Pragna's note of caution made me think that perhaps I should go on hunger strike for just two days, as a symbolic gesture. I had even prepared a press statement, which I handed to Pragna. Word spread around the prison somehow, and the women who resented Sara complained to the governor that I was encouraging people to go on hunger strike to support her. I admitted to the governor that I intended to go on hunger strike as a gesture of support for Sara, but told her that I hadn't asked any of the others to join me. She said she might have to send me to Durham, where I wouldn't be able to see my children. In the end, thoughts of my children and my family's stress got the better of me, but I really regretted not going ahead. If all of us had done it together it could have had a tremendous impact on the country; it might have changed the course of history. We wanted to say that Sara was not mad, and that she was not alone in her anger.

The failure of Sara's appeal, and her hunger strike, got a lot of publicity, and I too got coverage as a result. That gave an impetus to both our campaigns. A month later Sara came back to Bullwood. Her sister and daughter had come to visit her all the way from California. She could not resist her daughter's pleas to give up the hunger strike, which lasted twenty days, ending on 22 August 1991, and created an uproar throughout the country.

It was announced that Teresa Gorman, the Conservative MP for Billericay, was going to visit Sara and me personally. All the other lifers made representations to the governor that they too should be visited, so the governor made sure that she spoke to them too. I was really nervous that I wouldn't be able to talk to Teresa Gorman, and I asked Gloria, a prisoner I was friendly with, to come with me and talk for me. Teresa Gorman wanted to know if I had made any attempts to leave my husband, and I explained how my family had put pressure on me to stay in the marriage. She asked when the violence had started, and wanted an update on the campaign. I told her about SBS and the support I was receiving from many quarters, including members of Deepak's family.

In the House of Commons the Labour MP for Stoke-on-Trent South, Jack Ashley, introduced a Ten-Minute Bill aimed at changing the law on provocation, and there were demonstrations in front of the Home Office organised by SBS and Justice for Women. Many women all over the country were angry that Sara had to go on hunger strike to draw attention to the injustice of her situation.

There was a lot of publicity, but no progress on the legal side. I was getting fed up. My sister Dev was also putting pressure on me. Her workload had doubled with all the publicity and endless visits from family friends. It was all right for me in my idleness in prison, but the housework was killing her. Raghvir, my eldest brother, was visiting from India, and he said I should get the publicity toned down, because it was affecting the family.

Sara said that SBS must have made a lot of money from the awareness that had been raised by her hunger strike, and wanted to know what they were doing with it. She advised me to write to Rohit to stop my campaign until the appeal had been granted. I said I would need help to draft the letter, and Sara agreed to do it for me.

When Pragna and Rohit next came to visit, Pragna had come prepared to give me hell over that letter. She flung it down in front of me, banged on the table and said, 'What is the meaning of this? What do you think of yourself? How can you accuse us of making money from your campaign? You haven't written this letter. This must have been written by Sara.' I tried in vain to cover up for her, but the language in the letter was too sophisticated for me to have written it. Pragna said, 'Tell me in writing that you don't want us to run the campaign.' I said, 'If you want to shout, go away. You came, decided from home, that you were not going to do any work with me, that you were going to fight with me.' Rohit was with Sara while all this was going on. I refused to be treated like a child. But when the row finished, the atmosphere returned to normal, and I agreed that SBS should continue with the campaign. I had become very close to Pragna. I could tell her things that I couldn't tell other people. If she didn't come for a couple of weeks because she was on holiday, I would feel distraught.

One evening in October Rohit rang and asked to speak to me. We were locked up, so the prison officer told him that she would pass on the message. Rohit said it was good news, and that he wanted to convey it to me himself. The officer asked him to ring again at ten the next morning. When the officer told me that Rohit was going to call with good news, I started pacing up and down.

My appeal had been granted on 12 September 1991, but Rohit was only advised of this in writing a month later. He said the door was now open again, but the outcome was not at all certain. Apparently the judge had specifically said in his letter that I shouldn't hope for too much. 'Don't worry,' I said to Rohit. 'I learnt my lesson from Sara Thornton.' He said it would be like making an elephant pass through the eye of a needle, but if he gained one point, he would try and multiply that to five, five to ten. At least I wouldn't have far to fall, as the prospects were bleak from the beginning.

I wrote to everybody with the good news – all my relatives, Joan, Dhillon, everyone. Someone had pricked a tiny hole in the black paper bag that had descended on me, and my eyes were being blinded by that pinprick of light. I tried to keep their hopes in tight rein, just as Rohit had put the dampeners on me – there was only a 2 per cent chance of success. Given the weak grounds that I was standing on, this would be halved to 1 per cent, at the most.

Joan tried to build up my courage to go into the witness box, sending me model questions and answers. She wanted me to sort out housing, and suggested jokingly that I apply for a mortgage giving my address as 'Bullwood Hall', which sounded posh enough to bamboozle any building society. Sara was convinced that I was going to be successful. But then, she had been optimistic about her own chances.

After I heard about my appeal, I could not remain involved in prison life. Despite everything, there was something telling me that I might come out next year. I told Raghvir that I would come out in 1992, and if not then it would be 1998, as my sentence could be shortened to eight years with good behaviour. Behind my certainty lay the prediction of an astrologer I had visited in India in 1982. She told me that a great disaster would befall me, but that it would be resolved in 1992, 1998 or 2002.

Rohit sent me the grounds for appeal. I was confused by them. There seemed nothing that would stand up. I took those papers out a hundred times. I sat with a dictionary, trying to understand each word, but they just swam in front of me, refusing to surrender their meaning. I felt that the judge would send us on our way within a few minutes of the start of the appeal case. When Pragna came she tried to explain the grounds to me in detail.

One great consequence of getting leave to appeal was that I was given legal aid. Poor Rohit had laboured so hard on my account, without reward. I felt a great relief. I hoped that we would win, just so that Pragna and Rohit's labour could bear fruit.

[There were two grounds of appeal:

1) *The trial judge, Kiran's new lawyers said, had misdirected the jury on the questions they had to consider in relation to her defence of provocation. The legal definition of provocation given by the judge was accurate: 'Provocation consists of acts, of a series of acts done or words spoken which would cause a reasonable person in the defendant's position to lose her self-control suddenly and temporarily . . .' However, the appeal lawyers took issue with the fact that the judge asked the jury to take account only of certain characteristics when considering whether a reasonable person in Kiranjit's position would have been provoked into doing what she did: 'The only characteristics of the defendant about which you know specifically that might be relevant are that she is an Asian woman, married, incidentally, to an Asian man, the deceased, living in this country. You may think she is an educated woman. She has a university degree.' On the evidence before the jury, they could have found that Deepak had been frequently violent and abusive towards Kiranjit. But the judge provided a closed list and did not direct the jury to include 'battering' as a relevant characteristic which affected the gravity of the provocation to her. On this basis, the appeal claimed that the conviction was unsafe and unsatisfactory.*

2) *There was also more detailed evidence from Kiran herself given to Pragna in seventy-odd interviews. Prior to her trial, Kiran had still been suffering from the trauma of the events surrounding Deepak's death, and had not been able to provide a full picture of the degradation she had undergone at his hands. This assertion was supported by Dr Weller, who had seen her before her trial, and who said that the depression from which she was suffering was shot through with humiliation, shame and sexual abuse, inhibiting her from giving a full and frank account of her suffering. On this basis, the appeal lawyers were asking the court to admit Kiran's full statement as fresh evidence.*

Andrew Nicol, the new counsel, used one event from Kiran's new statement to show how it put a different complexion on the events touched upon in her limited statement to the police. She referred to the screwdriver episode in the police interviews, and told them that she had bitten Deepak's ear in order to protect herself. If her new evidence was admitted, she would add that she had tried to run away but had been forced by circumstances to seek Deepak's help; that he had twisted her arm so badly that a year later she still needed physiotherapy and that he was trying to twist the injured arm again when she bit his ear; that she wanted him to take her to a police station but he would not; that he had threatened to blind her with a spray can and to gouge out her eyes with a foot-long screwdriver. The grounds of appeal noted that Mr Justice Leonard would have had to acknowledge the severity of the violence had all this evidence been placed before him. The document explained that Kiran was unable to give evidence at her trial because she could not face the prospect of being examined about her intimate life with Deepak and that she had only come to terms with her marriage and Deepak's death since her trial.

Leave to appeal was granted on the misdirection ground but not on the fresh evidence ground.]

Now I co-operated with Pragna in drawing up my statement with renewed vigour. Although I had admitted to everything, there were a few things that I had not been able to bring myself to be honest about. One was the fact that on the night of the incident, I had gone out not to McDonald's but to see if I could follow Deepak with his woman in the car. That was such a lowdown thing to do that I just could not bring myself to admit to it. Mad, really, when you consider what else I had done and confessed to. Pragna and Rohit kept prodding me for the truth, which I finally told them. Because I had hidden a few things like this, they did not trust me entirely. Pragna and I would have terrible rows. Even when I was telling the truth she would wound me deeply by not believing me. She would try to convince me that it was crucial for them to know every detail, so that they could make an accurate assessment of my mental state at the time of the incident.

The caustic soda was another issue that kept coming back to haunt me. I did finally admit to having mixed it that night, but I didn't use it because I was afraid that it might only incapacitate Deepak temporarily, and enrage him so much that he would beat the hell out of me. I also confessed to Pragna that I had taken to drinking in the last few months.

Rohit had become my psychiatrist. He would take me back, day by day, to the months before Deepak's death. I remembered a lot of things that I had forgotten. 'Would you have killed Deepak if he didn't beat you?' Rohit asked. 'Of course not,' I replied. 'I didn't want to kill him. I didn't want him to be free of the pain of living. He has been liberated yet again while I end my days in prison, while my children and my family have been sentenced to misery. I wanted him to have a scar that he would remember for life.'

Pragna told me that I would be visited by psychiatrists from both the defence and the prosecution. She told me to let her know when they were coming, so she could be present to monitor the proceedings and interpret for me. She had got permission to be present. I was far more relaxed than before the first trial. I could show anger, grief and even laughter, wherever the story took us, unlike the previous time, when I was afraid to show my tears in case it made it easier for them to take my children away from me.

[Rohit instructed Dr Mackeith, a psychiatrist, to comment on whether it was understandable that Kiran had refused to testify at trial. He felt that that line of argument was weak, but suggested that Dr Weller's reference to endogenous depression in his report could be pursued and used to support diminished responsibility as a ground for reducing the charge of murder to manslaughter. Rohit

instructed Dr Reeves to advise on provocation and diminished responsibility. Dr Reeves kindly agreed to provide a report without charging a fee, and he saw Kiran in autumn 1991. His report kept away from the 'dangerous ground' of provocation, but gave a view on diminished responsibility:

'If she is telling the truth, and that is for the Court and not for me, I have absolutely no hesitation in saying that should the Court find she had an intention to kill or do serious harm, then at the material time she had an abnormality of mind as would substantially impair her responsibility. This was a mixture of serious depressive illness and complete exhaustion. Both highly disinhibiting factors. Obviously the whisky may have played some part, but having heard her story, the abnormality of mind far outweighs the alcohol ... I think myself, his [Deepak's] inability to discuss her future was the actual trigger, even though she had it in her mind to harm him. What she did, of course, was to cross the Rubicon. Again, I have seen this before. The woman finally does something which is very dangerous and then realises she is probably going to be killed. So at that moment the fear of imminent death overcomes all other inhibitions and they act with serious and extreme violence, as happened in this case.'

After looking at Dr Reeves' report, Rohit asked Dr Weller to provide a second report based on the true sequence of events rather than the 'accident' version. Dr Weller commented, strengthening the diminished responsibility ground. Rohit sent these three reports to Andrew Nicol. Legal aid was then obtained for Geoffrey Robertson, QC to act for Kiran. On his advice, Rohit wrote to Dr Gillian Mezey, who had done a lot of work on the 'battered women's syndrome'. Her report gave a full description of the syndrome and applied it to Kiranjit's case, although she did not interview Kiran prior to the preparation of her report:

'Victims of domestic violence experience a range of symptoms including battered women's syndrome, depression, generalised anxiety, stress-related symptoms, suicidal ideation and suicidal attempts ... The features of battered women's syndrome include *a sense of hopelessness, helplessness and despair . . . and an inability to act . . . Women may remain in abusive and violent relationships because they perceive no escape routes, the experience of battering undermines the woman's self-esteem, she is likely to attribute the violence to her own failure to please her husband, and to a failure in her role as wife, mother and home-maker.*

'Battering relationships characteristically isolate the individual from contact with the outside world and external reality. This isolation from normal social contact has the effect of depriving the woman of the knowledge that what is happening to her is abnormal and unacceptable, that it doesn't happen in all relationships, while at the same time increasing her emotional dependence on her partner . . .

'Men who batter are typically very contrite immediately afterwards, they express remorse and guilt, promise never to repeat the abuse and request forgiveness. The apparent distress of her partner evokes feelings of sympathy and protection in the woman, whose instincts are to want to preserve the marriage and to believe these promises to reform. The majority of women, therefore, do not attempt to leave a relationship after the first few battering events, arguing that it is their responsibility to stay and make the marriage work and hoping for change . . .

'Follow-up studies of women who have left battering partners consistently report inadequate housing, a fall in the standard of living, unemployment, difficulties in obtaining child care, lack of social and family support, loneliness and isolation. These difficulties are so daunting that a substantial number of women return to their violent partners through an inability to survive without their support and "preferring" an existence that is familiar to them to the uncertainty of the outside world.

'Women develop various behavioural strategies to enable them to survive from one battering incident to the next. Most often the tactic of "lying low", of acquiescing and submitting, appears to be the most effective means of self-protection, particularly early on in the relationship. As the violence escalates, which is the most usual

pattern, appeasing strategies which may have been effective earlier become less effective, the violence becomes more unpredictable and occurs without obvious warning. The woman becomes less able to interpret "danger" signs or anticipate a violent assault and, therefore, is less able to avoid or protect herself against that violence.

'In my view the depression resulting from her [Kiranjit's] chronic victimisation will have altered her capacity to make rational judgements or to perceive the situation in an objective or dispassionate way. Prior to the index offence she alleges she was assaulted with a hot iron and this will have acted as a catalyst to the expression of pent-up rage, despair and anger against her husband. Her apparent lack of concern and "dazed" affect immediately after the fire-setting is similarly consistent with a dissociated state that one would expect in response to the shock of what she had done, as is her apparently irrational behaviour in the immediate aftermath. Her confused account of events is further suggestive of someone who had undergone a severe and devastating trauma rather than a woman who is fully in control of her thoughts and feelings and behaviour.'

Dr Glatt, who gave expert evidence on behalf of Sara Thornton, drew similar conclusions.

Pragna then discovered Dr John Merrill, who had done a lot of work on 'psychological disturbance in Asians living in Britain'. Dr Merrill supported the two-pronged appeal based on provocation and diminished responsibility. He concluded that Kiran was 'likely to be suffering from a severe depressive condition preceding the death of her husband . . . her dissociated reaction after causing the fire further supports the diagnosis of depression . . . Occurring in the context of Asian culture, prolonged experience of violence, and a depressed, over-controlled state, I consider the provocation sufficient to cause a reasonable woman to react as Kiranjit Ahluwalia did.' Dr Merrill's report, submitted at Rohit's request, and also free of charge, examined the role of women in Asian, specifically Punjabi, communities. It concluded that Kiranjit was provoked:

'Self-immolation is a common method of suicide by Asian women whether living in India or Britain . . . Seven of the fifteen female Asian suicides I studied in Birmingham were a result of burning although burning is almost unheard of among white suicides . . . A further cause of death by fire is the so-called "dowry-burning" where brides are murdered if their families fail to provide the dowry demanded from them.'

These reports were forwarded to Andrew and Geoffrey. On the basis of them, the grounds of appeal were amended to include diminished responsibility as a new ground.

Pragna also felt that while the judge, in listing the characteristics that the jury should consider in relation to Kiran, had mentioned her Asian origin in passing, a largely male, all-white jury would not be in a position to give full weight to the relevance of Asian culture to Kiran's case. She prepared an expert report on the experience of Asian women facing violence. It highlighted the reasons why women found it difficult to leave violent relationships: traditional family structures which become more oppressive in emigration; the uprooting of children from familiar surroundings; and the descent into poverty and life on state benefits. All of these factors are compounded by language problems and the ignorance of rights. The report examined the position of women in Asian communities, their expectations and the expectations of them, the practice of dowry and arranged marriages, the stigma of divorce, and the overarching concept of izzat, or family honour, which defined and subordinated the role of women. The report was submitted along with the other papers.]

Another lifer, Carol Peters, came to Bullwood Hall at this time. Now the three of us 'hubby-killers' were together. We had lost Amelia Rossiter, whose appeal had been successful in April 1992. I was very happy for her. She was so ill, immobilised by arthritis and asthma, that she couldn't even comb her own hair. How could she be a danger to the public? She had been in prison too long – three years.

NINETEEN

Through the Eye of a Needle

MY APPEAL WAS FIXED for early July, and then changed to 20 July, the day before my fourteenth wedding anniversary – I had gone from being bride to convict. I was very superstitious about numbers, and I asked Pragna to get the date changed. It was bound to bring me bad luck, and I was sure to lose my appeal. I used to think that the number nineteen was unlucky – every time I got a room at Holloway, it was number nineteen; our council flat was number nineteen; the house that we bought was number nineteen. I also hated the number seven. I came to England on 7 July, and on 7 December I was sentenced to life imprisonment. Pragna of course refused, saying that I was being far too superstitious, and that the date would not affect the outcome.

Pragna told me which barrister, which QC, which psychiatrists had been appointed, their backgrounds and why they would be good for my case. Joan wrote to tell me that the publicity leaflets had had to be reprinted because of the change in the date of my appeal, and thousands of envelopes had to be unstuck and resealed so that the right information went out to all my supporters. She had gone out flyposting my leaflets and posters late at night with other women from SBS. They had been caught by the police, and one officer had stuck his finger in Pragna's face and said that if he caught them again, 'I'll nick the lot of you.' After that, police cars followed them everywhere. Joan was acting as lookout while the others flyposted, and she was accosted by an Indian man who thought she was 'on the game'.

Joan felt in her bones that my appeal would be successful on the grounds of diminished responsibility, because no psychiatric report had been presented at my original trial. She had studied three other cases in which the judge had directed the jury to acquit the defendant on the basis of such reports. She wrote: 'You and I are both heading towards happiness. I feel fate is weaving its web towards the grand finale.' I promised to cook her lots of Indian meals when I was released.

Pragna kept me informed about the campaign, the meetings that had been organised, the press coverage that had been gained and so on. The news that my leave for appeal had been granted was reported in all the national papers.

[In July 1992 a number of newspapers ran articles on the legal issues raised by Kiranjit's appeal. A report on domestic violence published by the Victims' Support Scheme and launched by Princess Anne also helped to keep the issue alive in the public mind. On 18 July the Guardian *ran a half-page article on the abuse and brutality Kiranjit had suffered, under the headline 'Battered Wife who Killed Brings Provocation Test Case'.]*

When Geoffrey Robertson, my QC, came to visit me in Bullwood Hall, I felt intimidated by his towering personality. I had asked Pragna to ask him what sort of clothes I should wear to court. He suggested that I wear clothes that fell half-way between gaudy and shabby. He must have been thinking of Punjabi women dripping with gold and colourful *salwar kameez*.

[Meanwhile SBS was collecting statements from members of Kiranjit's and Deepak's families. A central figure, Kiranjit's brother-in-law Sukhjit Walia, had not previously given a statement. He now gave a detailed account of Kiranjit's marriage right from the beginning.

Kiranjit started to tell us that she wanted a divorce because Deepak was abusive, irrational and violent to her. During this period [1982–83], I saw injuries after Kiranjit was subjected to a severe beating from Deepak. I saw bruises and cuts on nose and eyes. I was told that Deepak had hit Kiranjit with a belt with buckles which was twisted around his fist and punched her with it several times . . .

[After Kiranjit's suicide attempt] Tommy brought Kiranjit to London to our house – she stayed with us for more than two weeks. After this period, Kiranjit's mother-in-law rang me and said she wanted Kiranjit to return because if the marriage breaks down, it would bring the family into disrepute and the marriage prospects of the other children would be ruined.

About the family gathering organised to bring about a reconciliation between Deepak and Kiran, Sukhjit said:

We felt that it was better for the marriage to work because we were worried about the reputation of the family. Also we were worried that she would have a hard time as a divorced woman, she would not have support.

At the family meeting, Kiranjit's mother-in-law said that because she was the eldest daughter-in-law, then she was carrying the banner for the whole family – she had to make the marriage work, or her family would be dishonoured. I insisted that there should be a legal binding – that in the presence of a solicitor, Deepak should give an undertaking not to attack Kiranjit in any manner . . .

Deepak did give an undertaking, and for a short while, it had a restraining effect on him. Soon after this, Kiranjit gave birth to Sandeep. During the family meeting, Kiranjit's mother-in-law had complained that Kiranjit had had no children – that this was against the idea of a stable home and that married women should start a family . . . Six–seven months after giving birth, Kiranjit again started to suffer violence . . .

I witnessed an argument between Kiranjit and Deepak in my own house. Deepak started to shout at Kiranjit for no reason and threatened to kill her. This frightened me as I had never seen him in such a terrible temper – Kiranjit was expecting her second child. I hid Kiranjit in a bedroom and Deepak was going up and down the stairs all night, looking for her. He could not get into the bedroom because the door was locked. Deepak was swearing and shouting loudly, threatening to kill Kiranjit.

Towards the end, Kiranjit's mother-in-law would ring me about the arguments. She told me that Deepak did not like Kiranjit helping her brother and 'robbing' him ... I visited Kiranjit's mother-in-law who said [Deepak's girlfriend's ex-lover] was trying to kill Deepak and had thrown acid on the car. I then went with Deepak and his mother to see Kiranjit. When I saw Kiranjit, I was horrified – she was covered with bruises and cuts, her eyes were swollen, cut lips, bandages on her hands. Deepak was in a temper and I attempted to persuade Kiranjit to come and stay with me. Kiranjit expressed a fear that if she left, she would not be able to return to her own house and the children would be taken away from her. I said nothing like that would happen and I felt she had no proper sense of judgement as a result of months of violence. Kiranjit refused to leave. Kiranjit's mother-in-law did not want her to leave, saying that all wives have to go through such treatment and she had had the same treatment ... Deepak wanted Kiranjit to leave – I thought this was because he wanted free access to the house for his girlfriend – to get Kiranjit out of the way, with the children with his mother and they then could spend time together at the house. Kiranjit expressed the same fear and therefore refused to leave ...

[After Deepak's death] the grandmother takes the children to the house where the fire took place and has told them that their mother has killed their father. She has done this in a very hostile manner which was aimed at alienating the children from the mother.

The children, although they continue to have a very good

relationship with their mother and ourselves [Sukhjit and Dev had won custody of Sandeep and Rajeev], they have been disturbed. They have drawn pictures of a house on fire and a man on fire and they have questioned us and Kiranjit on why she killed her husband. They have suffered from nightmares and have shown disturbed behaviour, especially Sandeep. The grandmother has access to the children and still fails to work towards their rehabilitation or building a more constructive relationship with us or the children's mother.

Rohit telephoned Deepak's mother in a search for further leads. This is what she said about Kiranjit:

Kiran had come from a wealthy family in India, was used to having servants, and treated Deepak like a servant ... Deepak was an excellent man, a good son ... only Deepak took care of the children, Kiran never did. She would not even change their nappies. Deepak did so. Deepak even had to cook for himself.

When Rohit asked if she could find it in her heart to forgive Kiran, she said: 'I'm not God, am I? Forgiveness is in the hands of God.']

I wrote to my brother Billoo in Canada and Bindhi praji in India and told them not to come over for my appeal because they had spent enough money on me as it was. I said they should come only when I was released.

Pragna was meanwhile preparing me to give evidence in case a retrial was ordered. I was quite nervous about this, but I was determined not to repeat the mistake I had made at the first trial in not going into the witness box.

I told Pragna that I would ask to be transferred to Holloway, as Sara had done when her appeal was imminent. That would make it much easier for my solicitors and all the other experts who would need to visit me. Permission had to be granted by the Home Office because I was a lifer, but Mrs Bott got it arranged very quickly, and ten days prior to the appeal I was transferred to Holloway. I said tearful goodbyes to all my friends in Bullwood Hall. They made a lovely card for me which was signed by all. I compared my card to the one they had given Sara when she had gone for her appeal. Both were very appropriate. Sara's card had three judges on it who were snoozing, bored to tears, as Sara droned on and on about her case from an endless scroll of paper. The prison officer was saying, 'I want to go home,' and looking at her watch. Mine had a gate drawn on it and I was walking slowly to my freedom. The day before I left Bullwood, a Sikh priest read special prayers and brought lots of Indian food.

On the day of my departure, I couldn't eat with excitement. All my belongings had already been sent off to Holloway. As I left Bullwood Hall I resolved not to look back, because we have a superstition that if you look back, you will go back.

After two years of being banged up, the sheep in the fields and even the motorways seemed strange and fascinating. I felt like a newborn baby, the world held so much fascination for me. I wanted to fill myself with all these sensations and store them up for the long years ahead when I might still be in prison. I was shaking with fear and anticipation. I had been sedated to calm me down, but the officers commented on my obvious nerves. On the way the driver of the van became hungry, so they stopped at a McDonald's. The officers debated whether I should be handcuffed, but decided that I was safe and wouldn't need restraining. They asked if I wanted anything. I was hungry, and Big Macs and milkshakes used to be my favourites, but I couldn't bring myself to say yes. They bought me a bag of chips anyway. I ate them slowly, relishing each one. Compared to the chips in prison, these were excruciatingly delicious. They just melted in my mouth.

At Holloway I had to face the same lengthy entry procedure that I had had to endure over two years ago. I was supposed to have only four sets of clothes, but I had brought along two other smart sets, sent from Canada by Surinder, to wear in court. Eventually I was allowed to keep them.

Before coming to Holloway I had written to Janet Gardner, whose campaign was being run by Justice for Women. I offered her support, as we were in the same boat, and she wrote to me from Holloway. When I arrived in Wing 4 I asked the officers to point Janet out to me. I hardly knew anyone there. Most of the women from my time had either gone home or been moved on to other prisons. I was standing looking out through the window when a woman emerged pushing a trolley. I looked at her, and she was looking back at me. I went up to her and asked her if she was Janet. We embraced. I had found a friend in Holloway too.

I was getting a lot of mail and media coverage. On Thursday evenings I used to listen to a Radio 5 programme called *Eastern Beat*, which was presented by Danny Choranji and Parminder Kathkar. A couple of times they mentioned my name, and passed on birthday greetings or messages to cheer me up from my family. One Thursday, while I was writing to a supporter and listening to the programme, Danny announced that I was going to be the topic of discussion that evening. My favourite presenter and my favourite programme were going to talk about me. Then I heard Sukhjit jijaji's voice. He talked about the campaign, my marriage, the bruises, how I went to him for help, the forthcoming appeal, his hopes for my release so that I could look after my children. There was a phone-in, and all the calls were sympathetic. I was amazed by the level of publicity.

I was interviewed by journalists from the *Guardian* and the *Independent*. I thought how really lucky I was to have all this support. If I had received a fraction of this help before, I would not have been in that situation.

The day of the appeal dawned. Predictably I hadn't slept the night before, although I was on medication. I had the runs, but thankfully I wasn't ill. I didn't have a temperature and my ears didn't feel dead. I had my period, and I stuffed my jacket pockets full of tampons. Due to some error in the prison computer that morning, my name did not appear on the screen, which meant that the prison officers did not realise I was due to go to court. No one came to collect me. The court was waiting for me, and I had been sitting in my cell and waiting since 6 a.m. At ten an officer came up and said, 'Aren't you supposed to be in court today?' 'Yes,' I said, panicking. 'I've been waiting.'

They took me to the High Court by taxi. I was wearing a silk trouser suit sent by Surinder, and Pragna said I looked so good in it that I should wear it the following day too. She wished me luck, and said she expected a box of *ladoos* when this was all over. 'Now you're talking like a Guju,' I said. 'A Punjabi would have asked for a crate of whisky.' The officer told me that hundreds of supporters were chanting slogans for me outside the court. The court was full of my family, Deepak's family and my supporters. Their presence made the atmosphere of the appeal completely different to the previous trial. I felt emboldened by them.

The prosecution read out their case against me, including the allegation about the caustic soda. I cried tears of frustration that nobody believed me on this count. Legal arguments raged all day, but I couldn't understand them. I was tired just sitting in court, and I wondered how Geoffrey could carry on talking so long. My ears were anticipating the words used by Sara's judge, 'Appeal dismissed,' and were not listening for anything else.

[Geoffrey Robertson, QC, put Kiranjit's case eloquently. He argued both provocation and diminished responsibility, and summarised the history of Kiranjit's brutal marriage. The letter that had been written by Kiran to Deepak, promising him that 'I won't laugh', played a pivotal role in Robertson's depiction of the extent to which Kiran had been pushed:

The most eloquent evidence of Kiranjit's characteristic of a beaten and battered wife came from a letter she wrote to Deepak after he left her – temporarily – a short time before the fire. Described by her counsel as 'a charter for slavery', it was in fact the most abject and desperate plea by a wife for human contact and dialogue from her husband it is possible to imagine.

Geoffrey read out the letter in full, and quoted that part of the judge's summing-up at her trial which dealt with it:

It is respectfully submitted that the learned judge failed (consistently with his direction on 'characteristics') to direct the jury as to the significance of this letter as evidence of the defendant's character and, at the time of the offence, as evidence of a wife who has reached the nadir of self-abasement to save her family, and who has no resource left when confronted, at the very end, with her husband's last act of violence coupled with his determination to desert her. The judge takes the unimportant phrase 'life is dull without you' out of its context (it is an appeal to Deepak's ego, and any sentiment he may retain about their ten years together, in order to beg ten minutes of his time to discuss their situation) and it is used as the basis for an unjustified comment that this wretched woman might actually find violence and unhappiness palatable. He fails to note that this letter (produced by Deepak's mother at a later stage) corroborates Kiranjit's most important statements to the police.

Justice Taylor, in his judgement, gave the letter the weight it merited by quoting the passage which makes eleven promises to lure Deepak back to the family home. He said of the letter:

The state of humiliation and loss of self-esteem to which the deceased's behaviour over the ten years of the marriage had reduced her, is evidenced by a letter she wrote him after he left her for three days about April 1989. It is a letter on which Mr Robertson strongly relies. In the course of begging him to come back to her and to grant her ten minutes to talk it over, she made a number of self-denying promises of the most abject kind.]

When the day was over and before I was taken back to Holloway, Pragna came to see me. Neither she nor Rohit would tell me how they thought the case was proceeding. Pragna often hid things from me because she didn't want to raise my hopes. She preferred to frighten me with her pessimism. I told her I was feeling great because of the level of support I had. I asked her to get a black jacket for me from Devinder because I was feeling cold despite the stuffiness in the courtroom. One of the prison officers who was accompanying me started doing her make-up, because she wanted to look good on TV.

When I was driven to the court with a few other women the following morning, the flashlights of the waiting posse of photographers momentarily lit up the dark interior of the van. One of the officers quickly covered my face, which I didn't appreciate. The other women were astonished, and asked if I always got that kind of publicity.

At the end of the next day, the judge said he would give his decision ten days later. Time has never moved so slowly. Every second loomed in front of me like a mountain that was so high that I would never reach its summit. I was relieved that I hadn't got a judgement on the twenty-first, my wedding anniversary, as I was convinced that it would not have been in my favour. My family were also restless. Billoo praji and his wife, who had come from Canada, were stunned by the support that had been drummed up for me by SBS. When they had gone to the SBS offices to give an interview, passers-by thought they must be film stars, and asked for their autographs. Although I had written to them about the campaign, they didn't really understand the extent of it until they saw it for themselves.

On Friday 31 July 1992, Lord Chief Justice Taylor delivered the court's decision.

[*In his judgement, the Lord Chief Justice, Lord Taylor, considered each of the grounds of appeal in turn. The grounds had been developed further since the original application for leave to appeal was granted. He rejected the defence argument that the trial judge's direction to the jury, relying on the classic definition of provocation as 'a sudden and temporary loss of self-control', would have prevented the jury from considering any act of provocation which did not occur immediately before the defendant's act. Lord Taylor felt it was open to the jury to consider the interval of time in each individual case and to decide whether in the interval the defendant had regained self-control or not. In the course of considering provocation, he extended the definition to include cumulative provocation by saying: 'We accept that the subjective element in the defence of provocation would not as a matter of law be negatived simply because of the delayed reaction in such cases, provided that there was at the time of the killing a "sudden and temporary loss of self-control".' For the first time, a superior court had stated explicitly that a delay would not in itself negate the defence of provocation. This was recognition that the provocation did not have to be followed immediately by a loss of self-control; a delay need not deprive the defendant of the opportunity to argue provocation. This was the experience of most women who killed after suffering violence at the hands of their partners over a period of time. The significance of this was lost in most of the media coverage of the case, which dwelled on the fact that that the campaign to release Kiranjit had failed on its own terms: to have her conviction quashed on grounds of provocation. Lord Taylor said: 'Mr Robertson's argument in support of this ground of appeal amounted in reality to an invitation to this court to change the law ... Where a particular principle of law has been re-affirmed so many times and applied so generally over such a long period, it must be a matter for Parliament to consider any change.'*

Lord Taylor rejected the argument that the trial judge's direction to the jury on another aspect of provocation was flawed, i.e. that he gave the jury a closed list of characteristics to consider when deciding whether a reasonable person would have behaved as Kir-anjit did. The defence had argued that the judge did not include the 'battered women's syndrome' which could have materially altered the jury's decision. Lord Taylor felt that whilst the history of ill treatment had been laid out, there was no medical or other evidence before the trial judge to show that Kiran was 'marked off or distinguished from the ordinary [woman] of the community' to enable him to include it in his list of characteristics: 'We consider that Mr Robertson's criticisms of the learned judge's direction are unfounded.'

On the third ground of appeal, diminished responsibility, Lord Taylor felt the defence was on stronger ground. Referring to Dr Weller's report, he said: 'The present case is most unusual ... It is unclear how this potentially important material came to be overlooked or was not further pursued at the time of the trial. We have been told, we assume correctly, that the appellant herself was not consulted about this report or about the possibility of investigating it further.'

The original solicitors were invited to comment, and this is what they said: 'We wrote to Mr Sanghvi and confirmed that the report of Dr Weller was handed to Mrs Ahluwalia although this was not specifically recorded in the attendance note. How would you like us to clarify that further? As you appear to be relying on the information you received from Mrs Ahluwalia we are now confirming to you that we categorically recall, without any shadow of a doubt and so that you do not misunderstand us, we are stating clearly that the report of Dr Weller was handed to Mrs Ahluwalia; the report of Dr Weller was gone through in detail with Mrs Ahluwalia and we confirm that we had specific instruction not to seek further medical evidence and specific instructions not to call Dr Weller. Can we make this any clearer? The fact that this is not in the attendance note does not detract from the memory of the writer and again we confirm that Mrs Ahluwalia, if she is stating that she did not see or read Dr Weller's report and did not have it explained to her, is wrong.'

The junior counsel writes: 'The decision NOT to reply on the medical report of Dr Weller was Mrs Ahluwalia's. It was made on express instructions to her solicitor in my presence and in the presence of Leading Counsel. Given the importance of the decision, an entire morning's conference at Holloway Prison was allocated to this specific issue. A full note of Mrs Ahluwalia's decision was taken at this time.'

The leading counsel writes: 'It [Dr Weller's report] did not support diminished responsibility, though that is what he would have been asked to consider. It offered at best the glimmer of a possibility that further work might, and I emphasise the word might, take the position forward to an unknown degree. For experienced defence barristers, it was of little use as it stood ... Thus it was that consensus was arrived at. That we would not take Dr Weller any further as things stood. Kiranjit was fully in agreement, indeed this was a course that she preferred because of her worries about the children. When we speak of express instructions, we do not mean that there is a box to be ticked and signed like on a hire-purchase form. Merely that the lay client agrees with a decision made.'

Lord Taylor cautioned that his decision to declare the verdict unsafe and unsatisfactory must not be seen as a carte blanche for people running two defences, one at trial and another at appeal. The court ordered a retrial on the grounds that the Crown had not obtained its own medical reports, and ought not to be deprived of that opportunity.]

I sat with my head in my hands. I could hear people clapping, so I knew it must be good news, but I don't remember looking around to see the reaction in court. The judge had quashed my conviction and ordered a retrial. Someone said, 'About time, too.' I was thrilled, although the good news was somewhat dampened by the knowledge that I would have to sit through a lengthy retrial before I would know the final outcome. I would no longer be branded a murderer. I could feel the public anger at the suffering I had been put through. Billoo praji and Devinder started crying with happiness. He had hoped that I would be released while they were in England so that he could settle me down before he went back to Canada. He had been house-hunting for me. Rajeev and Sandeep were also hopeful that they would see me that day. But I was not granted bail, which I thought was really unjust. There were no sensible grounds for refusing it. I was not a threat to society, and there were young kids who were desperate to be with their mother.

In the cell below the courtroom, my lawyers and Pragna came to see me. Geoffrey Robertson said I now had another chance to present my case. When Pragna hugged me I said, 'I told you 1992 would be mine.' Pragna asked me what I wanted her to say to the waiting press hordes. I told them that I wanted to thank my supporters, and that I was happy that the charges had been dropped and that I had been granted a retrial, and another chance to prove myself. This was a victory for Rohit and for SBS.

My supporters were really angry that I hadn't been released on bail. When I was taken by prison officers to a waiting taxi, Fawzia from Brent Women's Refuge was standing there shouting, 'Let her go!' If the driver hadn't braked, she would have been injured. He was having difficulty negotiating his way through the crowd. When he reversed, they would advance on him and prevent him from moving forward. My ears were ringing with cries of 'Kiranjit zindabad! Free her now!' He eventually pulled clear. As the crowd faded into the distance, their cries were relayed again on the radio news in the taxi.

When I got to Holloway the officers said, 'Congratulations. You'll be going home soon.' Some new women in reception were watching the news on television. They asked me, 'Wow, what did you do?' I said, 'Killed my husband,' almost brazenly. What a difference from that first time in reception. Today I was speaking with confidence. This was not me talking. This was the voice of my supporters. The officer at reception handed me a letter addressed simply to 'The girl who was on the news today, Holloway Prison'.

[There was extensive media coverage of the day's events. On the Channel 4 News at 7 p.m., the reporter said: 'There were vocal protests when, despite the fact that her conviction had been quashed, she was not granted bail.' Julie Bindel of Justice for Women was interviewed by BBC News: 'In one way, it's good that they're recognising that Kiranjit needs a retrial, that it's unfair; but it's absolutely disgusting that they won't give her bail. She's absolutely no danger to the public, and she has children to look after.'

The legal implications were analysed, and experts were trotted out to comment on various aspects of the decision. On Newsnight, Sandra Horley, the director of Refuge, debated with Sir Ian Perceval, the Solicitor General, the issues raised by 'battered women's syndrome'. Sir Ian responded: 'I'm horrified at the suggestion implicit in what Ms Horley says that anybody in full possession of their senses could stick a knife in somebody and kill them or set them alight with petrol without being guilty of murder.'

Most of the coverage did not seem to understand why it had been such a landmark decision. Although Rohit and Helena Kennedy, a barrister who has represented a numbered of battered women who killed, were quoted on this, the bulk of the reporting implied that there was no progress on the legal issues because Lord Taylor had refused to allow Kiranjit's appeal on the grounds of provocation, and allowed a retrial instead on the basis of new medical evidence which showed that she was suffering from severe depression at the time she killed her husband. Helena Kennedy said that Lord Taylor's ruling made the defence of provocation far more accessible to battered women.]

Because of that one word 'retrial' uttered by Lord Taylor, I was now to be admitted to Wing 3, not 4. I was a remand prisoner again, and I had all my privileges restored, although I had to return the flask of hot water which is given to long-term prisoners so they can make themselves tea or coffee at night. I could now have visitors every day. I had forgotten about that. I could also do my private shopping every week, and receive parcels from my family. Other prisoners would get their families to send cigarettes for them to me, and I would also shop for them. I went to the governor and asked whether she would allow us to watch Hindi films, as there were a number of Indian women who would like to see them. It was approved. Dev would send three or four videos through Joan every week. They were popular with everyone, not just Indian prisoners.

One morning when I was in the exercise yard, four black women approached me, menacingly I thought. One of them said, 'Are you Kiranjit Ahluwalia, whose picture was in all the papers for killing your husband?' When I said yes rather nervously, they said, 'Well done. The bastard must have deserved it.' One of them lowered her jumper and showed me her scars, saying that her bastard of a husband had thrown acid on her and had tried to kill her with a knife. They said that I should count them among my supporters.

I still felt trapped by the demands of preparing for the retrial. I was fed up with all this crying and digging into my past again and again, but I couldn't refuse to co-operate. The prosecution and defence psychiatrists came on the same day, and I spent at least six hours weeping and telling my story. I told Pragna, 'Please, please, let me rest for at least one week.' My head was splitting apart with pain. I asked for sleeping pills, but the prison doctor said there was no doubt that I was going to be released, and that I should relax in that knowledge alone.

I was also feeling the pressure of publicity. A TV crew was waiting outside, and they wanted a statement in my own voice. I gave them a tape-recorded message that I had lit the fire that day because I had no other way out, that it was an act of ultimate frustration:

It all became too much that night. He had made me a physical and mental wreck. I saw him sleeping and I thought, how can he sleep when he has done this to me? I lost it. I never meant to kill him. I just wanted to cause him pain, like he caused me. I thought if I hurt his feet, he wouldn't be able to come after me again. I never thought he would die.

My message to other women was, don't suffer in silence, ask for help, and don't do what I did. This was broadcast on the television news that night.

Although the widespread support had given me confidence, I felt I couldn't physically cope with the queues of visitors, the growing mailbag and so on. I had to make sure that two or three visitors didn't turn up on the same day, otherwise some of them would have to go away disappointed.

One of my regular correspondents was Maria Dami. She was steeped in Indian culture and religion, and always had a folk tale that would be relevant to the advice or encouragement she was giving me on any occasion. She lived on her own except for a teddy bear called 'Kirry', who would send me a note and a drawing, addressing me as Auntie Kiran. Maria was a member of the Conservative Party, and during the general election she would describe the work she was doing for her local party. After my sentence was quashed, she wrote:

I feel that as soon as the police or social services become aware of a case the two partners should have to take counselling by law and the wife should go onto an 'at risk' register and be visited by social services. On a second offence, the husband should be arrested without the wife having to press charges. He should go to a psychiatric hospital for a few weeks' treatment. If after coming out he commits a third offence (that is if his wife will give him another chance) then he should lose all entitlement to the home and property and have a mandatory three years' imprisonment if he returns to the house again.

Also the court should have the right to automatically dissolve the marriage.

Maria advised me not to get embroiled with my family, and not to allow them to dictate my actions. Joan, who got on well with my family, disagreed with this, but there was some truth in what Maria was saying. The only thing Joan and Maria felt the same about was SBS: 'I agree with Maria that SBS can be overpowering, so you have to be on your guard otherwise you can be swamped by their enthusiasm.'

I will never forget the way my family helped out. Surinder used to send clothes, and the children got more love and presents showered on them now than both father and mother had ever been able to give them. Hansapur aunty was one of my greatest backers. She drummed up support for me in the community, persuading people to change their attitude to me and to understand the pressures that had driven me. She gave my family a great deal of moral support, and helped Dev win custody of the children. She felt it was very important that the children should not be separated from their mother. She would ask Deepak's family, especially Deepak's eldest uncle Tayaji, who was reluctant to support me openly, to let bygones be bygones.

[In his statement for Kiranjit's appeal, Tayaji regretted his previous inaction: 'I bitterly regret not intervening. Had I done so, this may never have happened. I believe the system in the Indian community failed Kiranjit. We failed as relatives, because we were weak, and because we did not want to upset her mother-in-law. From all we relatives knew about Deepak's violence, when we first heard that Deepak had got burned, we thought that Deepak had thrown petrol on Kiran and had got burned in the process himself. There was amazement that she should kill him, rather than the other way around. I attended the trial with other relatives of Deepak. The defence did not call us. They said we were hostile to Kiranjit. That is not so. We could not speak the truth for her because we *could not upset Deepak's mother. I wrote to the Home Secretary after her conviction. I felt that it was a failure of the Indian community and of the Indian system that produced the situation that she did what she did. The family, of which I am head, would like her set free.']*

The support I got from Sukhjit jijaji was absolutely tremendous. He ran around, speaking at campaign meetings, giving interviews to the media, bringing my children to visit. When I was in Bullwood Hall, he would start the journey at 8 a.m. so my children could visit me for an hour and a half. In Holloway we were allowed all-day visits by our children, from 9.30 a.m. to 3.30 p.m., once a month. Leslie from Crawley Women's Aid, Julie from Justice for Women and Joan helped to lighten my family's load by bringing Sandeep and Rajeev to see me a few times. They could swim and play and bring food from home so that we could eat together like a family. I had three all-day visits before I was released, and in the course of them I grew very close to my children. Sukhjit made donations to Crawley Women's Aid in gratitude for their help.

I felt very vulnerable about the children, and I turned to Joan for advice. I knew Dev was very busy, and couldn't give them enough attention, and being in prison I couldn't do much. So I was constantly worried about their lack of firm parental control. Once a teacher reported to Sukhjit that Sandeep had stolen something. Joan suggested that a police officer should be asked to talk to him, to give him a fright and stop him from stealing. She also thought that giving him pocket money would take away the need to steal. Sandeep would not obey anyone but Joan.

Joan and I would analyse the children's behaviour in our letters. Once Joan wrote: 'I've been thinking about Sandeep and the way he never refers to "Daddy". He says you killed "my grandmother's son" or "your husband" but never "my daddy". I should think he has forgotten him and doesn't relate to "your husband" at all.' Another time, Joan reported that 'Rajeev said "When they live together again, they won't fight any more, they will be nice to each other." I asked "Who are you talking about, Rajeev? Who is they?" He said "Deepak and Kiranjit Ahluwalia."' Rajeev told Mrs Bott, 'You know she killed her husband.' In another letter Joan wrote: 'I hope by the time your sons are old enough to marry, Western influences will have helped Asian women and that the women will be treated as equals, not inferior beings who have to serve the menfolk and have no life of their own.'

Before Sandeep and Rajeev's first visit, I had been dying for green chillies. My sister sent me chicken curry and chappatis, and I had a bag full of goodies for the children – Coke, crisps, chocolates and sandwiches. My kids were so understanding that they refused to eat the Indian food so that I could have it all. That day I talked and played with them to my heart's content. Joan brought so many toys. We had to carry the heavy bags with us as we moved from place to place. I made tea for them, and watched them draw and paint. I asked them about their daily routine, their schools, their friends, whether they liked living with Dev masi and so on. I even asked them if they thought that what had happened to Daddy was my fault. They said it was not all my fault – 'Daddy used to beat you.' They told me about incidents that I had forgotten, or that only they had experienced. Sandeep told me of a time when Deepak had chased him because he had said, 'Don't beat my mummy. I will tell Grandmum.' Sandeep had hidden under his bed, but he was caught and soundly beaten. Rajeev was funny. He talked about times when he wasn't even around. Perhaps he had heard someone else talk about them, or heard about them on the radio.

When Joan came to fetch them, Sandeep's face dropped but he accepted the inevitability of the situation. Rajeev screamed the place down. I found it very hard. His screams of 'Mummy, Mummy!' echoed in my ears and soured the happiness of the whole day. Joan extricated him from my arms with great difficulty. I felt she was dragging the life out of my body, so painful was that separation. There was no place for human feelings in this law. Joan's eyes filled with tears. When she left she sat with Rajeev in her car, hugging him and promising to bring him back again.

Joan wrote a letter to the Lord Chancellor, full of anger against the judicial system. She wished she could tell the judges how she had witnessed the inhumanity of children being dragged away from their mother, so that the system could be changed.

I asked her to bring towels and swimming trunks the next time because the children wanted to go swimming. She also brought me a takeaway meal from an Indian restaurant so that Dev didn't have extra cooking to do.

There were two more prosecution psychiatrists I had to meet. These visits used to turn me into an empty shell. One of them asked why I had wanted Deepak back, when the terms of that return would be so harsh that I would be giving up the basic things in life. I said that children need their father, and that I felt I was not strong enough to meet their needs alone. If Deepak had spent a few minutes talking about our future, maybe I wouldn't be in this situation today. When he talked about giving the children away to social workers, that was the limit. No mother would allow that. She would starve first.

[*The two Crown psychiatrists, Dr Pitcher and Dr Bowden, in reports dated August and September 1992, reveal a great deal more reluctance than the defence psychiatrists to conclude that Kiranjit was suffering from diminished responsibility. Dr Pitcher dwelled at length on the conflicting accounts given by Kiranjit and the opposing views of Dr Roderick Evans and Dr Weller:*

This is a very difficult case upon which to express a confident opinion at this stage . . . Taking into account all that has been said by other experts, and subject to the Court being satisfied that the relevant facts of the case do favour the defendant's account of what occurred and the background thereto, I can say that I am satisfied that at the material time she was the victim of a degree of stress such as alone must have rendered her desperate and impaired her judgement as compared with a person enjoying a state of normal mental well-being.

Paul Bowden for the CPS gave a more confident view:

I believe that the majority of evidence points to the fact that Mrs Ahluwalia was significantly disordered mentally at the material time. This mental disorder was a mixed-affective state (both anxiety and depression), moderate to severe in degree. It is also my view that this mental disorder would amount to an abnormality of mind (arising from disease) in terms of Section 2 Homicide Act 1957.

As with abnormality of mind, the issue of impairment of mental responsibility is also a matter for the Court. To the extent that it is a medical issue my view is that Mrs Ahluwalia's mental disorder affected all her mind's activities at the material time, and it follows that her mental responsibility for her acts leading to her husband's death was substantially impaired.]

TWENTY

High on Hope

IN THE WEEKS THAT followed, as the preparations for the retrial rumbled on, the euphoria I felt after Justice Taylor's judgement turned into anti-climax. One day I was feeling so low that I rang Joan and asked her to visit. While I was with her, an officer came and told me that my solicitor was waiting to see me. Joan got up to go, but I told her to let them wait. It would only be Pragna or Rohit, and they would just chew up my brains, make me cry and then go away again.

When Joan left I was still in no mood to see them, and I went to the visiting room reluctantly. Rohit and Pragna were waiting impatiently, and I was surprised to see my barrister there too. Pragna beamed at me and hugged me. All three of them were looking at each other, wondering who would start talking. Rohit said, 'Andrew, you go ahead.' What was this news, that neither Pragna nor Rohit were willing to go first?

Andrew Nicol said they had got very good news, but – what was this but? He said that the prosecution had rung his office to say that they would accept a plea of guilty of manslaughter. 'But manslaughter can carry a sentence of five to ten years,' Andrew said. 'The judge could give you seven years. As you have already done three years, you may have to do another couple.' My face fell. But at least it was not twelve years. I shouted with joy, and told Rohit and Pragna that it was their victory.

[The prosecution had concluded that they had no option but to concede that Kiran's plea of manslaughter was supported by the

psychiatric evidence, although her lawyers had also made it clear
that they would seek to reopen the issue of provocation before the
jury. In the event, the prosecution accepted the plea, but only on
the basis of diminished responsibility. With their duty to Kiran in
mind, her lawyers did not feel that they could reject the pros-
ecution's position and stand on principle with regard to the provo-
cation plank of Kiran's proposed defence.]

Pragna made me swear that I would not divulge the news to
anybody, not even to my family or Joan. The media were so
involved in my case that if the slightest hint of this leaked out,
it could adversely affect the outcome. Pragna had not even told
the other SBS women, even though they had worked day and
night with her on the campaign. I found it very difficult to sit
on news like this, although I realised that Pragna's concerns
were valid. Not all the public would be in favour of my release,
and any adverse campaign in the media could sway the judge's
decision.

Andrew told me that in a week's time, on 25 September,
I would have to attend court and enter a plea of 'Guilty of
manslaughter, not guilty of murder.' After he had left I asked
Pragna why I had to appear in court just to mumble those few
words. All I could think of were the practical problems of a day
in court. I would have to get up at 5 a.m., hang around in
reception for a couple of hours, be strip-searched at both ends
of the day, do my entire packing and lug all my things to court
and back. Couldn't Rohit or Andrew do it on my behalf? Pragna
pleaded with me that as I had come so far with them, I must
not get stubborn at this last, most crucial hurdle.

The next day, my restlessness could not be held in check. I
could not bear the weight of this big secret. My joy would
threaten to burst forth from me as I went about my daily
business in prison. At midday I phoned Joan, who didn't live
far from Holloway, and begged her to visit me. I couldn't tell
her that I was crying with joy.

When she arrived with her husband Ron, she said, 'I know what you want, you want two glasses of Coke.' The Coke in prison was always flat. I said I had a very big secret, and told her that I would be going to court on the twenty-fifth to enter my plea, and that she must attend even if the world turned upside down. She said she wasn't sure if she could get time off from work, but I promised I would never put her out again if she would only agree to come on that day. 'You have sacrficed so much for me. I'm asking for just one more.' I didn't tell her that my plea had already been accepted. All I said was that I had great hopes that it would be. Joan kept saying that it didn't seem important enough for her to be there on that day, and advised me not to ask the rest of my family to turn up. After she had gone, I wrote to her and asked if I could go to her flat to call my family in Canada and India if I was released on that day. I didn't want to give Sukhjit jijaji and Dev any more trouble.

The night before my appearance in court I couldn't sleep, flying high on hope as I was. Even if I got eight years, I would only have to spend another two or three years in prison. Surely I would get out at first parole. No officer could turn me down on grounds of conduct. I might have to do probation, but that was fine.

I must have ironed my black jacket and trousers four or five times. I even dyed my hair twice. I wasn't satisfied with the first colour. It was too dark, so I used auburn. I emptied my cupboards, and told my cellmates to keep their radio on because there would definitely be some news about me. The bird was waiting for the cage to open.

At 5 a.m. the prison officer came to wake me up. I was up anyway. I washed my hair in the basin and dried it with my fingers. I didn't change my clothes because I knew I would be strip-searched. I asked the officer if I could leave my clothes and papers and all my junk in the waiting room so I wouldn't have to lug them all the way to court and all the way back again. She said, 'Rules are rules. I'm sorry. I would have liked to help out. In any case, what makes you think you're coming back?'

In reception, a fellow prisoner brought me some tea and wished me good luck. I wanted to say that I was nervous, but because my English was poor I said, 'I'm so excited. I just want to get this day over with.' She cautioned me not to put my trust in British law – 'Remember Sara Thornton.' I kept running to the loo, to pass one drop at a time.

The officer who was accompanying me apologised for having to handcuff me. I was horrified. I had never had handcuffs on before. She said she had to do it because of the crowds and the media. I begged her: 'I won't let my supporters or my family down by doing anything silly. Please don't, it will be so embarrassing.' Handcuffs would be a truly visual symbol of the chains of law that had bound me. Finally she agreed.

As the van turned into the court there was a blinding flash of light. It was those cameramen again, lying in wait, jumping up with their cameras held outstretched, clicking at random. The driver accelerated away out of reach.

In the court building I asked the prison officer not to lock me up, but as she was on her own she couldn't agree to that. I sat in the cell with a hollowness in the pit of my stomach and a foul taste in my mouth. The prison officer came to inform me that my hearing had been adjourned from 9.30 until after lunch. That was the last straw. As I got closer to freedom, wanting to rub shoulders with her, she walked away, always that little bit out of reach. I had all my letters with me but I couldn't bring myself to read them, nor could I make myself listen to my Walkman. I started feeling sick. I went to the loo and brought up all the millions of cups of tea I had drunk that day. I felt as if the walls of my stomach were stuck together. I asked the officer for food, and she brought me pizza (warmed up in a microwave, yukk!), chips and peas and a small tub of ice cream. This was the same meal I had been given during my trial. I had been given a life sentence then. I would not eat it again – it would bring me bad luck. I ate the peas and chips, but not the pizza.

In half an hour I was told that a psychiatrist was waiting to see me. I groaned, but I had no choice. If I didn't go, Pragna and Rohit would jump on me from a very great height. Every step felt as if I was dragging a ton of weight with me. I couldn't work out why I had to see another psychiatrist at this late stage.

A young and beautiful woman was waiting for me, not one of the crusty old types I had got used to. She asked the same questions: When were you married? When did he start beating you? What happened that night?, and on and on and on. It took one and a half hours. The psychiatrist was surprised that I was so upset. 'I am fed up with repeating my history,' I told her. 'That is all I have done for the last three years. I want to forget it all.' I was locked up again. Neither Pragna nor Rohit had come to see me. I couldn't work it out.

When I was finally taken into the courtroom, it was packed out. At least at eye level; I didn't have the guts to look up at the public galleries, but I knew from the hum – even silence has a hum – that they were full. I was sitting close to the judge. When it was my time to speak, I stood up and stuttered, 'Guilty to murder, not guilty to . . .' Oh, my God, I had said it the wrong way around! I was shaking like a leaf, and the judge was glaring at me. I quickly mumbled it out in the right order, took a deep breath and collapsed into my chair. I had done my bit. A huge weight fell away from me – now I could sit and enjoy the rest of the proceedings. If those seven words seemed like insuperable obstacles, what kind of a witness would I have been? I remembered the last time I had had to utter them. Would it be any different this time? Surely all this campaigning and hard work would pay off.

Then the familiar catalogue of my sins was droned out by the prosecution – including the reference to the caustic soda. Why would nobody believe that I did not throw any caustic soda on Deepak? The judge said he had already decided. I thought all those tears in front of the psychiatrist had been a waste of time. As the judge carried on talking, his voice started to fade. I could not get my ears to maintain a grip on his voice. I could see his lips moving, but I felt as impenetrable as a rock. I could feel my impatience for the result cradled by the impatience of the waiting crowds – my supporters were also waiting for the climax.

Then, suddenly, I heard clapping. I felt as if I was emerging from a deep slumber. It must be good news. The clapping was followed by cheers – 'Hip, Hip, Hooray!' What was going on? I was thrilled, but I was so dazed that I didn't think of turning around to look at my supporters and smile at them. I sat in the chair for an everlasting minute, my eyes shut, before I stood up. I had been so broken by the system that even now I wanted permission from the judge: 'Can I feed my children? Can I play with them? Can I sleep with them now?' I looked at him thankfully.

The officer came up and congratulated me as I left the court-room. I joked with her, 'You've brought me good luck. You should have been here at my original trial. You can't lock me in that cell now. I am free.' She said, 'I never wanted to.' I had left £150 with the authorities. They had to do the accounts. I picked up my jewellery and money from the reception area downstairs. A probation officer approached me. I wanted to see Rohit and Pragna and my family. All this happiness inside was choking me and I needed to share it. But I had to go through all the bureaucratic motions of leaving prison – another long wait.

The legal team was waiting for me in the visiting room. Everyone asked me how I felt. All I could say was 'Great!' Rohit just kept laughing as he looked at me. How could I ever thank him and Pragna? I felt SBS had won rights to my soul after what they had done for me.

While we were hugging and kissing, the police officer in charge of the court cells waited patiently. He beckoned to Rohit and me and advised us that there was a large crowd of reporters and supporters outside. For my own safety, he wanted me to walk towards the cameras with a semi-circle of police officers around me – 'Only this time not because you're under arrest.' I was absolutely overwhelmed. I wanted to thank my supporters once before I left. After that, they could do anything they liked. Pragna said that a press conference had been organised in Conway Hall, near Holborn. She and Rohit asked me what I would say to the waiting press. I was so happy that no words would come to me. There was so much to say that I could say nothing. I felt intimidated. I wouldn't be able to speak in front of cameras and mikes. The barristers got together with Rohit to formulate a statement about the landmark decision. Geoffrey kept talking to me, and I nodded and said 'Yes,' but I didn't take anything in. It was too hard for me to communicate my emotions to the press. I invited my lawyers to the party which had been organised for that evening, saying, 'Please come. This time I will be there.' (After the successful appeal hearing there had been a party which I couldn't attend, thanks to the judge refusing bail.) As arranged, I told Pragna that I wanted to go to Joan's flat to call my family in India and Canada and let them hear the voice of my freedom. I also wanted to see Sandeep and Rajeev, who would be waiting at Joan's.

When I got outside, there was a cordon of about twenty policemen holding back the crowd. Hannana was on the other side of them, and they wouldn't let her through till I intervened. Pragna had disappeared, and Rohit went in search of her. I didn't want to emerge without her by my side. When she turned up we walked through the cordon and into the waiting crowd. My supporters started jumping up and down, reaching out to try and touch me. Some of them had the words 'Free Kiranjit Ahluwalia' painted on their faces. Those supporters whom I recognised, I acknowledged. I held Hannana and Pragna's hands. I wanted the world to know that this was SBS, that they were responsible for getting me out. Rohit was with us too. We walked, our hands held aloft, into the cheering crowds – the photograph was to be printed across the front pages of the world's newspapers and would stir the nation's conscience. Dev and Sukhjit jijaji were there, and I hugged them and asked them to stand back so that SBS and I could walk together. I had asked SBS to save one balloon with 'Free Kiranjit' printed on it for me to see. Someone passed it to me and I sent it soaring into the sky. All I could say through the loud-hailer which someone was holding up in front of me was thank you to all my supporters for all that they had done for me and that I now wanted to go and see my children. I even forgot to do what I had promised the inmates of Holloway – to wave to them in front of the cameras. Pragna and Rohit then addressed the crowd as well.

[Kiranjit's release was covered by every television and radio news bulletin that day. On the early evening ITN news, Kiran was shown saying as she was released from the court, 'Very pleased, very pleased. Please do not forget my friends, we need help.' Pragna and Rohit were on either side of her, with Hannana, Maniza (another supporter), Sukhjit and his daughter and Ranjit chachaji immediately behind as Kiran walked to freedom. Fawzia said: 'I think it is an important decision for other battered women serving life in prison.' Sara Thornton spoke from Bullwood Hall: 'It's got to give everybody hope and it's got to make people realise that women who live in an atmosphere of violence do react differently.' All the commentaries described the emotional scenes outside the Old Bailey as Kiran walked free.]

As the police had suggested that I should keep my time with my supporters brief, Rohit hailed a taxi and pushed me into it. All four of us hugged as the door shut.

When we reached the hall for the press conference, I had to give so many interviews to the press, radio and TV. Even the Indian media were there.

[Channel 4 News broadcast part of the press conference. Kiran said: 'It was a great shock for me. I wasn't expecting anything and I'm very pleased. Finally justice has been done for me . . . We [i.e. Kiran and the other prisoners] have already suffered enough. We deserve some happiness in our life. With us, our children, our families, they are suffering.' On the same bulletin, Sara Thornton said: 'I see my case alone. I don't really see my case as depending on others. Perhaps other cases depend on mine. I've got hope anyway.']

The cameras were flashing away and I was smiling widely. But nowhere could I see my children – those pieces of my soul were still far away. I had told my family not to tell Sandeep and Rajeev that there was any hope of my release, because they might be heartbroken yet again. Joan had picked them up early in the morning before she came to court, and left them with a neighbour who had a son of their age.

Pragna kept saying that I had to be on time for the party, and I was eager to leave. When I got to Joan's flat I asked if I could go into her kitchen and make Indian tea for myself. I had become so familiar with Joan through her letters and her visits that I didn't hesitate in the slightest before making this request. I made tea for everybody, then I called Surinder in Canada. We were both crying. Next I rang Tommy. He cried so much when he heard my voice that his wife got anxious, thinking the news must be bad. She rang Surinder after our call was finished, saying there was something wrong with Tommy. He just kept saying 'Poochi, Poochi,' and crying. There had been a lot of pressure on him. He had met the cost of the custody case and sent lots of things for the children. He also felt responsible for having provided Deepak with yet another excuse to harass me in the last months of our marriage, and blamed himself for my imprisonment. I called Billoo praji and Bindhi praji in India. Bindhi praji wanted me to come to Ahmedabad. His voice was also tremulous.

After the calls I went into the kitchen to make some more tea while Joan went to her neighbour's to get Sandeep and Rajeev. She didn't tell them that I had been released, but only that she had a big surprise for them in her flat. She told them to keep their eyes closed until she said they could open them. I was waiting at the top of the stairs.

I will never forget the look on their faces when she told them to open their eyes. Their eyes and mouths fell open, they yelled, 'Mummy!' and ran upstairs. 'You're not going back again, are you?' they asked. I said, 'No, I promise. I will never go back to jail. We will live together for the rest of our lives.' Joan took a photograph. It was an unforgettable moment. The children were asking endless questions, telephones were ringing, my family were all talking at once. Then I had to get ready for the party. Dev felt I should be behaving more circumspectly, like a widow. She felt I shouldn't go around giving interviews and attending parties. I might be happy to be free, but I must remember that Deepak's family had lost a son.

When we got to the party, which was held in a pub opposite the Old Bailey, everyone was there. I was introduced to them all. I don't remember who I met that evening and who I didn't. Up till that point I had only tasted the tea of freedom. The food so far had been prison fare. Now I saw piles of food – samosas, chicken legs, pakoras, chillies, onion salad, chutneys, everything I could dream of. I wanted to eat all of it. I picked up a green chilli, but put it back on the plate. I didn't have the courage to eat it. I had to tell myself, 'I am free now. I can eat without permission. I don't have to stand in a queue with a blue plastic plate and take only what the officer lets me have.' But the habit of the last three years was so ingrained that I had to wait for someone to invite me to eat. It was two hours before I started eating.

Sandeep and Rajeev were sitting with me, happily watching the proceedings while I tried to feed and water them. Everyone was dancing. I was very happy, but I could not bring myself to dance, although people were trying to pull me up on to the floor. After all, my husband had died because of me. Even now that I was free, I couldn't get up and dance. I finally agreed to have a glass of wine, and got up and clapped to the music. I saw Meena (from SBS), Pragna and Hannana dancing. I couldn't believe that these serious women could dance so well.

At 2 a.m. the party ended, and Sukhjit jijaji and Dev drove us home. We would stay with them until I found my own accommodation. After 1,200 days in prison, I was going to sleep in a room which would not be locked on the outside. I slept with my children, although Dev offered their double bed just for me. I could not sleep all night. The absent sound of jangling keys, to which I had become so accustomed, was echoing in my ears. Scenes from the courtroom, of my supporters, of the inmates from Holloway, kept appearing before my eyes.

I got up early and savoured the freedom of going to the kitchen and making myself a cup of tea. Dev and Sukhjit jijaji were looking through the morning papers. They laughed at the way I was savouring the little pleasures that freedom affords, and that we take for granted. I couldn't believe that I could bathe at my own time, that I could eat chappatis, and go anywhere I pleased.

Every newspaper carried the story of my release. I noticed the dramatic change in the headlines. Newspapers that had called me 'Fireball Mum' and 'Killer Wife' when I was convicted now had headlines reading 'Battered Woman Wins Campaign'.

[The article in the Independent quoted Geoffrey Robertson's words that Kiran had reached 'the nadir of self-abasement' in the months before Deepak's death: 'Chanting and singing women carrying balloons and flowers swamped Kiranjit Ahluwalia in a wave of emotion as she left the court.' The Guardian quoted Pragna: 'Kiranjit's experience is an indictment of our society, our families and our legal system.'

In the weeks and months that followed, papers and magazines

as diverse as the Malayalam-language Kakakumudi Weekly *from Kerala, India and the* Anarchist Black Cross Bulletin *(which commented that 'In the end it is all divide and rule, and violence against women or the threat of it is one of the foundations of authoritarian society') carried news and analysis of Kiranjit's case. Almost all the coverage was sympathetic, although there was the occasional sniping, like the article in the* Spectator *of 10 April 1993 when Kiranjit met the Princess of Wales at the relaunch of the Chiswick Refuge, which commented: 'The charity, a Chiswick refuge for battered wives, wanted me to be "received" by her [i.e. the Princess], meaning I had to stand in line with three other women: Maureen Lipman, Helena Kennedy and a murderess.'*

In an article entitled 'Trial by Fire' published in the Times of India *a month after her release, Kiran is quoted as saying: 'My release is not only my victory but a victory for women all over the world. Domestic violence is a crime, and women put in prison for defending themselves have suffered long enough. There are others serving life sentences for killing violent husbands, and I will now help them. I will join the campaigns to release them, and I will do volunteer work to raise funds and help them.'*

A number of articles, with titles like 'Sisters Under the Skin' and 'Freedom with Help from the Sisterhood', praised the role played by Southall Black Sisters in helping Kiran win her freedom.]

I got Sandeep and Rajeev ready for school. This was a moment I had thirsted for and had been deprived of – to see my children in their school uniforms. But if I had missed their very first day, I could at least take a photo of the first time I saw them in their uniforms – a moment I would preserve forever, as I had said at my press conference. I ironed their uniforms and watched them get dressed. I wanted to see what degree of independence they had achieved in all those years of living without me. Dev said that their head teacher had been very helpful. Their school reports had been sent to me in prison, and they had sent me birthday, Valentine's, Diwali and Christmas cards.

I took them to school, and their teacher came out especially to greet me. She sang the praises of my children. Everywhere I went I was recognised, I had received so much publicity. When Pragna phoned, I boasted about how I had taken Sandeep and Rajeev to school. She said I would have to go to the SBS offices in Southall, as they were receiving lots of calls from journalists wanting to interview me. I felt intimidated. I was afraid of getting about on my own.

They booked a cab for me, but I said I didn't want to spend money on cabs. Pragna said, 'Don't worry, we'll pay for it and one of us will drive you back.' The taxi driver was Asian, and he recognised me. He radioed his office and said, 'Guess who's sitting in my car?' I was worried about what his response to me would be. He told me that he had three sisters, and that if any man did anything remotely approaching what Deepak had done to me, he would react far worse than I did. He gave me his address, and said that I should consider him my brother and call on him for help any time I needed it. He said I had set an example for other women which would give them courage. It meant a great deal to me to get the support of an Asian male.

I was very keen to see the SBS offices, and I was amazed to find that they were like a shabby, simple two-bedroomed flat. I couldn't believe that a big nationwide campaign had been run from there. The SBS women advised me about what I should say to the media, and warned me that I shouldn't talk about the children because their custody was still at issue. One of the workers would sit with me during every interview and support me if I went wrong.

Dev and Sukhjit jijaji were on TV and in the papers too. All their customers would come into the shop and say they had seen them. Dev enjoyed all the attention. The customers would say, 'We never knew that you had so many pressures in your life. No wonder you looked so pale.' They would say to Sukhjit that he had been incredibly supportive of me – usually in our society, sons-in-law expect to be waited on hand and foot by their wives' families. He could have sat back and refused to help, as I had five brothers to fall back on.

There were endless visitors all day. Flowers, chocolates and Indian *mithai* (sweetmeats) were being delivered all the time. Relatives from India were calling. We were getting telegrams. On the fourth day Pragna accompanied me to GMTV to be interviewed live for breakfast television. I had lost my voice, I had done so much talking. My jaws were aching. I had a temperature and I hadn't been sleeping, because I was still in prison mode. Pragna said I would only have to talk for five minutes. After that the doctor told me to rest, and I put a stop to all interviews. Joan would take me to the park or the stables where she kept her pony to help me escape the media and the constant stream of people.

That weekend the children were due to go to their grandmother's for access. I told Mamma that that wouldn't be possible, as it was my first weekend with them, and as their mother I should have priority. She agreed – she didn't have much choice.

Surinder came to visit me from Canada three weeks after my release. She had said that she would not put a foot on English soil until I had been freed. SBS organised a party. My eldest brother Raghvir from India was also present, and a lot of my friends and relatives were invited. I met at least twenty women, mostly SBS clients, that night. They all came up and hugged me and shook my hands and told me of the courage that I had given them by my example. Little children would come up and touch me curiously and with pleasure, as if I was something special, and say, 'We saw you on television.' Everyone wanted their photo taken with me. I saw tears in many of the women's eyes. I knew that they had suffered, and my heart went out to them. They cursed their own weakness and praised my courage. 'You have opened the doors for *lakhs* [hundreds of thousands] of women. Men will learn their lesson.' They said they felt the weight slipping from their shoulders when they talked to me.

Even after separation and divorce, many of the women were facing continuing harassment from their ex-partners over children and property. They felt that I was truly free, while they were still trapped. They recounted experiences of how close they had come to suicide and to killing their husbands. They wanted me to continue being an example to women. 'Show the world how well you can survive. Be a mother and a father to your children, and show everyone that you can bring them up well.' We feel we are too weak to manage without our husbands, to educate our children on our own. We are not weak. It is society that weakens us, it is fear of our husbands. If this fear can be exorcised and the fear of social customs and ideals can be thrown overboard, then we will be truly free. We can do as much as, if not more than, men. We can work hard, we can study, have a career. Only confidence needs to be snatched back from men and society.

Crawley Women's Aid was there, and so was Justice for Women. To my amazement, so was Janet Gardner. No one had told me that she was coming. She was serving a five-year sentence for manslaughter, but was allowed home for two days every so often. When my appeal was coming up, she had said that she was going to be on home leave, and would join the picket. I was really anxious that if she did anything like that she might spoil her own prospects for parole and home leave. Two months after this party, Janet was free too.

Another prisoner from Bullwood Hall was also present. She had been framed by the police on a drugs charge and given a long sentence. A campaign had been run for her, and the police officer involved had finally been suspended. She was out on bail. Pragna said that all three of us would have to go up on the platform and talk.

I had applied for housing from prison after my appeal had been granted. Joan's eldest daughter, who is a housing officer for Hounslow Council, sent me forms to fill in. She said there was a five- to seven-year waiting list, so even if I wasn't released then, it would still be a useful thing to do. I was too embarrassed to fill in the forms – it felt wrong to be so optimistic. But my relatives, especially Ranjit chachaji, persuaded me to send them in, because they were convinced I would be coming out.

[*The standard reply from Richmond upon Thames's housing department to Kiranjit when she was in Bullwood Hall was: 'Your application will be assessed according to a Points Scheme which takes into account factors such as overcrowding and lack of basic amenities . . . The council does not normally take account of the poor physical condition of accommodation. If you are a private tenant and your home is in poor condition you should contact the council's Environmental Health Department.'*]

Maria Dami had also applied on my behalf to Aasra Housing Association, whose director she knew. The council offered me a two-bedroomed flat within two weeks of my release, but I turned it down. There was a Kentucky Fried Chicken place underneath, and it was a rather rough-and-tumble area. Given the publicity my case had received, I was not happy about the location. They offered another small flat close to Dev's, which I also turned down. I wanted a three-bedroomed house with a garden for the children.

Meena from SBS succeeded in finding somewhere suitable through the Ealing Family Housing Association. I didn't want to go as far as Ealing, but Pragna convinced me that it would be a safe place to live, and I got the house with a garden that I wanted. It was a very quiet area. I was over the moon. I had only been entitled to a flat, and here I was, moving into my very own dream house.

I could not move in without Sandeep and Rajeev, who were legally in Sukhjit and Dev's custody. In April 1993 I won custody of my children, but not without a time of nailbiting anxiety. The child psychologist had to recommend that they live with me, and my mother-in-law did not oppose my application.

All my aspirations were fulfilled – I had my freedom, my children, my family, a house. Joan drove me to Crawley so that I could pick up all the furniture that had not been damaged. She literally held my hand to give me the courage to walk through that house and into the room where I had lit the fire.

I decorated my new house in exactly the same style as my old place. I have the same wallpaper in the living room as I had before. I had never done any painting or wallpapering before, and it took me two months. I even picked up the carpet from the old place and fitted it. When I first moved in I didn't know how to switch on the heating or fix the dining table – all of which Joan helped me do. Meena helped me apply for income support and secure a grant for furniture. I got £900 to help me buy the essentials. Joan showed me how to open a bank account and drove around with me to help find a good school for the children.

When I first went back to Crawley, everyone was very curious to see me, as if my past and the experience of prison had turned me into a Martian. People would come and visit Chandrika and Puppi while I was staying with them. Hansapur aunty took me to the Gurdwara, and lent me her daughter's Punjabi suit. I was anxious about the reception I would get, but I was very warmly received. I told her that it was her voice that I was hearing from these people's mouths.

Ranjit chachaji, who used to come and visit me faithfully with Sukhjit jijaji, was at a loss as to what to do with his time after my release. Despite his heart problems he would get up at five in the morning once a fortnight, snow or storm, and visit me with the children. He knew how much I had come to rely on those visits.

The first time I went to fetch the children from their grandmother's, I was staying at Chandrika's and I walked across on my own, much to the dismay of my family. I was afraid, but I took the name of God and went. I rang the doorbell and went and stood on the pavement. Dev had phoned my mother-in-law and asked her to get the children ready. Mamma was shocked that I had come to fetch them on my own. After that, Leslie from Crawley Women's Aid would sometimes accompany me.

I wanted the kids to maintain their connection with their grandmother, and I will not do anything to disrupt those ties. The initial agreement was that the children would see her once a month, that I would fetch them and she would drop them off, and during the school holidays they would be with her for half the time.

After fifteen years, laughter had returned to my lips. I had snatched the confidence I needed back from society. I thought that people would hate me for what I had done, that they would stone me, call me a killer, that they would not let me live in peace. But instead I found I had won their support, respect and understanding.

I feel sad that my experience continues to be replicated elsewhere, that women continue to be battered and humiliated. The police should take domestic violence more seriously so that women can be protected, and the government should provide funds to establish more refuges. If men could be made to see the consequences of their actions and society could support other women, then there would be no more women and children suffering today. Men and women would be walking shoulder to shoulder towards a bright future.

EPILOGUE

The SBS Story

IN DECEMBER 1992, the civil rights organisation Liberty awarded Southall Black Sisters (SBS) the Martin Ennals Award for Civil Liberties. It was the ultimate recognition for our work in the campaign to free Kiranjit. At the reception afterwards we were all excited. High on the buzz. With a couple of drinks inside her, Pragna found herself in a corner with Kiranjit. 'Tell me, Kiran, did you tell me everything, the whole truth?' Kiran laughed. 'Do you really want to know?' she said. It was partly tease and partly warning.

Do we want to know? The fight to free Kiranjit had been a fight to establish the 'truth', and a fight for 'justice'. What did these words mean? Whose truth, and whose justice? Was the justice we were talking about to be delivered by the courts, or was it the justice thousands of women up and down the country had demanded? And whose truth were we serving? We had wanted to put Kiranjit's own story before the courts, for at the heart of the campaign was the desire to establish the truth by allowing her to tell her story. Yet Kiranjit walked free without ever having gone into the witness box.

These considerations were forgotten when she emerged from the Old Bailey, to be greeted by a crowd of drenched but exuberant women who had been standing in the rain for the last five hours. The news of her release had already filtered out, announced by Meena, who shouted, 'We did it! We did it!' over and over again. The hugs and kisses and tears had stopped. The picket was still, drawn up in tight formation, waving multi-

322

coloured balloons, the trademark of the campaign. We turned to face the exit from which Kiranjit would emerge, jostled by a phalanx of cameramen who had also been waiting, confident of their story. And finally there she was, a small figure, with Hannana and Pragna on one side, wearing their widest, most triumphant grins, and Rohit, Gurdev and Sukhjit on the other. Kiranjit was united at last with all those who had fought for her release. For that moment, our truth and their justice were fused. And our triumph was symbolised by the pictures of Kiranjit with her head held high and her arms in the air clasping Pragna and Rohit's hands. It was a brief, perfect moment. And then Kiranjit was surrounded by the reporters demanding their soundbites, and whisked off to a press conference, while Meena marshalled the footsoldiers to prepare for the party that would welcome Kiran back to the world.

But the euphoria was tempered with mutterings caused by Pragna's disclosure that she had known some time before what every journalist in London also seemed to know: that the prosecution was going to accept Kiranjit's plea, and she was almost certain to be released. Hannana and Meena were particularly upset not to have been told about this, because they had fought side by side every step of the way. SBS and the other women campaigners had remained in ignorance because Pragna had kept faith with the lawyers. She had been told as part of the defence team, but Andrew Nicol had stressed that any leak, even if it was inadvertent, might damage Kiran's chances. As SBS was fielding press enquiries every day, Pragna felt that she could not risk any mistakes being made. Absolute truth would have to be subordinated to the ultimate needs of justice.

In retrospect, Pragna's instructions that arrangements for a party should definitely be in place made sense. We had celebrated before, but those celebrations had been muted by Kiran's absence, and Meena was reluctant to organise a party when a wake might be more appropriate. SBS is of course a collective, but Pragna, as the longest-serving worker, was the first among equals. So the party was arranged.

Everyone was there: the three workers of Southall Black Sisters, Pragna, Hannana and Meena, who had nurtured the campaign from the beginning had recently been joined by a fourth, Sadhna; the volunteers – Jaswinder, who had made 'Free Kiranjit' T-shirts; Rajdeep and the management committee, Daksha, Muneeza; Shakila our banner-maker, who had worked on a film with Gita; Julie Bindel, Harriet and other friends from Justice for Women were also there, as were Fawzia and Shefali and other women from our sister organisation, the Brent Asian Women's Refuge. Rohit had been lured away from his files to savour his triumph. Andrew and Geoffrey came with their partners. For a while it seemed that Kiranjit might not attend at all, as there were rumours that some of her relatives thought she should adopt behaviour appropriate to a widow in mourning. But finally, having gone to see her sons, she arrived with them, and Gurdev and Sukhjit.

The singing, dancing and celebration which could have gone on and on lasted only that night. Over the weekend the workers had to prepare reports to submit to Ealing Council, the funding body, by Monday morning, to justify SBS's grant. On Monday evening the management committee met, but the talk was of accounts and future work plans. Normal life, that is working with women facing domestic violence, had reasserted itself. A celebratory bottle of champagne lay warm and unremarked on a filing cabinet.

Looking back now, in the course of writing this piece and pooling our thoughts on the campaign and the enormous education and transformation we all underwent, we realised that there were many areas that we had not discussed, issues and anecdotes which remained hanging in the air. This sense was to become, particularly for Pragna, an obsession, where the two demands – for 'truth' and 'justice' – fuelled each other, but were to lead to conflict too.

*　　*　　*

Pragna: 'It was an education, because we began with a vision that feminism was going to enter the law courts, and we were going to end up with a feminist interpretation of the law. We took it on precisely because here was a woman who, instead of being at the receiving end of violence to the point where she gets battered to death, which was our experience, commits the ultimate act of survival. That for me was the challenge. We took it up because here was a woman on the other side of the law, and we had to understand and deal with that experience. We've seen battered women kill themselves, we've seen them be killed. Now, here she is killing. If we are also talking about women as survivors, this must be the ultimate act of survival. In the end, though, it was also an education about the constraints in the law.'

Even within SBS, views differed about the exact meaning of things. For Pragna, Meena and Hannana, at any rate, this case was special from the start.

Hannana: 'There was a sense of destiny. When the case went to trial I was hoping that Kiran would be freed. I knew there wasn't much chance, but still I hoped the trial would be the end to it. But there was a sense of destiny that we would have to start a campaign, that we would have to go to appeal. We would have to raise issues that we hadn't raised before, it had to be done.'

Yet the involvement of SBS had very tentative beginnings. Pragna felt 'It was a stroke of luck that we were able to respond when Crawley Women's Aid rang and asked for help. They said, "There's an Asian woman in prison who's killed her husband. People say she had experienced violence. We don't really know what to do." I had several meetings with them and also introduced Hannana, as I was going on holiday to India just before the trial.

'When I first went to Holloway, I was overwhelmed by a sense of powerlessness. There's a huge automated structure which you have to pass through. It's far ahead of anything in any other prison I've visited since then. The doors open automatically, whereas all the other prisons are manually operated with a lot of keys clinking. The first time I met Kiranjit, it was in the main visiting room which has lots of little desks. Three of us (two women from Crawley Women's Aid and I) were directed to a desk, and we watched Kiranjit come in. I think I expected her to be more traditionally dressed, perhaps wearing a *salwar kameez* and looking very haggard and older, perhaps in her forties. Then she walked in and she was dressed in trousers and a shirt and she had short-cropped red hair, and she was very thin. In fact, I'd had my own stereotype. Maybe I expected her to look like Iqbal Begum, which was our only other knowledge of an Asian woman who had killed her husband.

'We skirted round the issue of what she wanted at first. We talked about SBS and what we did. How we knew lawyers and could help ... She said yes, yes ... She told us to talk to her family and that she trusted her lawyers because her family had found them. She'd already changed once. Later we found out that her family weren't allowing her to change lawyers, and she'd already had a very hard time getting legal aid transferred. We couldn't push it too much. We knew we had to show her that we wouldn't let her down, and at that stage it seemed that the best thing we could do was work with social services and the probation service to sort out her access to her children.

'I couldn't talk to her about the case, about what exactly had happened; I had to skirt around it, though I was dying to know. It was very difficult to know if we should take up her case or whether we should campaign when we didn't really know what had happened. Initially Kiranjit didn't trust us. She had already seen an Asian women's group. I don't know who they were. She didn't know who we were, she didn't know how voyeuristic we would be and she didn't know if we were going to deliver. It was really difficult. Then, just as she was about to go to trial, the only person she knew from SBS, me, went away on holiday. And I'd never really been able to put my questions to her. The first time she described what had happened was when Hannana came with me.'

Hannana didn't have such clear expectations as Pragna: 'I remember we met in an office and that she was quite weepy. She told us her story, or rather it was *a* story. Her husband was violent, they had had an argument that day, and she took a bucket upstairs. The thing I remember most is that she had picked up her son Rajeev and dashed out with him and hid in the garden shed. She was crying her eyes out and saying, "I don't know why I did that. I didn't know what was happening around me. I didn't realise there was a fire. I'd gone back into the house and they kept telling me to come out. I saw my husband sitting in the house opposite and I didn't realise he'd been burned." That was the first time we heard her story.

'When Pragna left I took over seeing Kiran. We wanted to do something to support her, but we couldn't have publicity or a picket or anything like that because we still knew so little about the case. We suggested that what we could do was to pack out the public gallery with women and children, so Kiran wouldn't feel isolated.

'We worked with Crawley Women's Aid on this, and they got a lot of local women over and women from elsewhere. There were some Asian women too. But many of the women we knew who were involved with SBS and the refuge, such as Meena, Muneeza and Fawzia, couldn't come because a case that they had spent years preparing for was being heard at the same time. They were supporting Laxmi Peria Swamy in a civil action against her former employers, who were members of the al Sabah family, the ruling family of Kuwait. And their attention was wholly concentrated on trying to bring the case to a successful conclusion and supporting Laxmi in the ordeal of having to go into a witness box and retell her story of ill-treatment and torture. Laxmi was awarded over £300,000. It was the first time a jury had awarded damages this high in a civil action for damages brought by a domestic worker against a former employer. For SBS and the Refuge it was the biggest case they had ever taken on or ever expected to take on.'

THE TRIAL

The next time Hannana saw Kiranjit was in court: 'It was a different kind of structure. You had the prisoner near the gallery and you could actually touch her. Whenever she was brought out we could touch her and hold her hand. She used to shake hands with people and chat with her family. It was good for her to have that kind of contact with people. The jury was sitting on the left-hand side and the witnesses on the right.

'I was basically in overall control of co-ordinating support for Kiranjit and I was trying to make sure that things were all right – that people were coming in and packing the gallery, speaking to the solicitors and the relatives. It was the first time I had met Kiranjit's family. I struck up a good relationship quite quickly with them – some of them had come from Canada. Sukhjit and Ranjit were there too. Most of them didn't understand court procedures and I told them what was going on.

'Even though we had attended other trials we still didn't completely understand what was going on. When the jury was being selected, the women in the gallery were getting annoyed because they were all white and mainly men. We tried to discuss the problem with the solicitors because we felt so frustrated. They told us you could only challenge members of a jury for a specific reason.'

Other elements of the trial were both bewildering and informative. Even Hannana heard about aspects of the case for the first time: 'The prosecution called in expert witnesses such as forensic scientists. There was a lot of evidence about caustic soda and petrol and whether Kiran had mixed the two or had thrown caustic soda after Deepak had come out of the bedroom and tried to go to the bathroom. I found it fascinating, because there seemed to be more to it. Why would they mention caustic soda? Why go into the details? They seemed to be trying to pick out the contradictions, because on the one hand they were saying that there were largely petrol burns and not many chemical burns. Did she throw the caustic soda? Other forensic evidence showed no evidence of chemical burns. Then there were other witnesses. Kiran's mother-in-law and Deepak's brother Rajesh gave evidence, as did the police.

'When Krishana Devi, the mother-in-law, gave evidence it was obvious that she needed an interpreter. She kept trying to speak in English and express herself. She was very emotional and shaky, you could tell she was nervous. When she was asked whether Deepak had gone to see a psychiatrist, she said yes. What was the result of that? She said her son was OK, but the psychiatrist said that Kiran was mentally ill. That's how she dismissed the whole thing. She got stroppy with the judge because she had to come in again to continue giving evidence. She said that she couldn't come the next day because she'd got the children, there was nobody else to look after them. She was addressing the judge directly. This is what often impressed Kiranjit's relatives. This woman was not afraid of taking on authority.

'Rajesh was asked whether Kiranjit had come around with Deepak once when they'd been fighting. Deepak had scratches on his face. Rajesh agreed that Deepak had hit Kiranjit in front of him, but said you could understand it because she had scratched his face. So he had a right to hit her. That's how he explained the violence.

'Then the defence came in. I was hoping they would bring in as many witnesses as possible – Gurdev, Sukhjit, the uncles, Ranjit and others who had witnessed the violence. Instead they'd called Devinder, Kiranjit's sister-in-law, married to her brother in Canada, to explain that Kiranjit had faced violence in her marriage. But she didn't live here and had not really witnessed it. Chandrika was a woman who Kiran worked with in the factory. She talked about violence, but they also brought her in to explain that people who worked at the factory sometimes took caustic soda home. Kiranjit had taken it for cleaning purposes, though she didn't work in the factory at the time of the incident. The defence was trying to repair the damage caused by the prosecution's suggestion that she had thrown caustic soda on Deepak as well as petrol. They were trying to show that she had innocent reasons for buying it.

'I was surprised when the calling in of witnesses suddenly stopped. It was hard to know how the defence were constructing their arguments. Kiranjit had pleaded guilty to manslaughter on the grounds of provocation, and not guilty to murder. It was the first time I had heard the definition of provocation, and that it reduced the charge of murder to manslaughter. I understood that provocation was a "sudden and temporary loss of self-control", but I didn't know enough about it to say whether they were building it up adequately or not. They talked about the violence and the "slave" letter, but that wasn't sufficient to understand not only the violence she had faced but the pressure of *izzat* which would keep her in her marriage.

'I asked the QC, the senior barrister defending Kiran, if she would give evidence. He said that she hadn't decided yet, but he might play the tapes of her interview with the police, which he felt were extremely moving and would have a good effect on the jury. We didn't know then that Kiran had changed her story, so it was really baffling to us that she wasn't speaking. They played the tapes, and it was very hard to make them out. The jury had police transcripts before them. When Rohit took on the case, he spent hours making an accurate version of the transcripts of what Kiranjit actually told the police.

'At the end the prosecution summed up. Their argument was that this man could not have been provoking Kiran if he was asleep. Yes, she had experienced violence, but they played it down, saying that Kiran had been "knocked about a bit". They read Deepak's declaration and said that he must have been in a delusionary state because he had said things that just didn't make sense. They tried to use the evidence selectively, but they also had to say that some of it didn't make sense.

'The next day the defence presented their case. I was in an anxious state, so Meena and I worked on a statement and that night I wrote up something – whatever came to mind – and took it with me on the train down to Lewes to give to the QC. But though I tried to hunt him down, I couldn't find him. I handed it to a junior barrister who gave it to him. He read it on the train, and said, "This is wonderful ... I like the way you write." It was my last-ditch attempt to get something across, though it was already too late. He then used my phrasing and arguments in the summing-up.

'Instead of the jury being introduced in the course of the trial to the idea of the pressure that women face to make their marriages work, and the particular forms that pressure takes for many Asian women, through evidence presented by witnesses for the defence (which SBS had offered to help with), it was coming out for the first time in the summing-up.

'The judge was Justice Leonard, who a few years before had given a higher sentence for burglary than for a very violent rape in the Ealing vicarage case. The QC had said to me earlier that he felt that the judge had made up his mind. You could only hope.'

The atmosphere was very tense during the judge's summing-up. The women in the gallery were getting restive, and they started to jeer. They were reprimanded by the lawyers.

Hannana: 'I was already very worried by the time the judge began to sum up. The way he handled the violence issue seemed to trivialise what Kiranjit had faced. He seemed to be almost flippant. It made me very angry. The jury was told to make a unanimous decision, and they were out for several hours. Then someone came and said that they couldn't decide, so they were told to make a majority decision. The jury came in again, and some people in it were crying when the verdict was announced. Kiranjit was found guilty of murder by a majority of ten to two.

'There was a total hush. Everybody was in a state of shock. Then they started shouting things – "Shame" and so on. I can't remember how Kiranjit was reacting. People began to cry. Kiranjit's QC said to the family, "I don't need to explain what I feel." I think the relatives were allowed to go and see Kiran at that point. Only Devinder spoke to the press, saying she had lost her faith in British justice.'

Kiranjit was convicted of murder because the prosecution persuaded the jury that this was not a case of provocation as known to the law. The mass of evidence showing that she had equipped herself with 'weapons' in the form of petrol and caustic soda made the crime seem not only premeditated, but peculiarly vicious. The cultural background to Kiranjit's actions was not explained to the jury. And academics such as Susan Edwardes have pointed out that men who plead provocation have often killed with their bare hands, by beating, strangling or kicking. Women are usually not physically strong enough to do this, and the act of picking up a knife (as in Sara Thornton's case) or gathering what could be interpreted as offensive weapons is taken to be evidence of premeditation. In addition, the defence could not show that Kiranjit had lost her self-control immediately when she was provoked. There had been a time-lag of several hours between the time of her last fight with Deepak and her throwing petrol on him. This gap was interpreted by the court as time for 'reason to gain control of the mind', a cooling-off period rather than one in which Kiranjit's passion boiled over.

Deepak's injuries, which the jury had seen photographs of, were horrific. Burning is a very uncommon form of homicide in Britain, whereas in India it is one of the commonest forms of both killing women and of suicide. It is also a common form of suicide among Asian women in Britain. This information was not given to the jury to try and put into context why

Kiranjit had thrown petrol on Deepak. Instead, the prosecution used the *agni-ishnaan* letter to build up a picture of a vindictive woman. At the time the letter was written Deepak was still alive, and Kiran had responded angrily to a phone call from her mother-in-law, who had suggested that she had given her son a firebath. The tone of the letter was, in fact, one of remorse and misgivings about both her own conduct and Deepak's, rather than of revenge, as suggested by the prosecution.

Kiran's failure to testify was also damaging, because it meant the jury did not hear her own account of her marriage and her actions. A history of the violence Kiranjit had faced was not systematically built up in court, although the arguments in the paper that Hannana had thrust into the defence counsel's hands in desperation at the last moment were used twice: first during the summing-up by the defence, and again by her QC when he read out a very emotional statement in mitigation of the tariff – the length of the sentence set by the judge. There was no serious attempt to address the question of why it had been difficult for Kiran to end her marriage.

The defence case was a mixture of provocation and no intent to kill or cause serious injury. The changes in Kiranjit's story had probably caused the defence to alter their strategy several times. For instance, she had told her lawyers at one point that the fire was an accident, caused during a struggle with Deepak, but she changed this story before the trial. Accident is an absolute defence, because it negates all intent, lawful or unlawful, whereas provocation admits unlawful intent but is designed to take into account the cause of the offence, and so reduces it from murder to manslaughter. The problem with Kiranjit arguing that the fire had been caused by accident was that there was no independent evidence to support it, whereas there was expert evidence for the prosecution theory that the fire in the bedroom had been started deliberately (though the fire on the ironing board was accidental). Kiranjit's defence team failed to impress on her at an early stage the hopelessness of this argument. Her instruction to her solicitors that the fire was an accident was contrary to her statement to the police immediately after the incident, when she said that she had intended to cause Deepak pain.

When the defence was changed to the two-pronged one of provocation and no intent to kill or cause serious injury, it was still full of contradictions. Since Kiran had admitted wanting to cause Deepak pain, was her defence arguing that she was provoked into inflicting a non-serious injury? If she had time to consider whether the injury was to be serious or not, could she be regarded as having been provoked? In any case, would the jury believe that the terrible injuries Deepak suffered could have occurred if there was in fact no intention of causing him serious harm?

In view of all the difficulties in preparing Kiran's defence, it was surprising that her lawyers asked for the date of the trial to be brought forward. Assuming that she would be found guilty of manslaughter, and would receive a prison sentence, they had not argued that she should spend the pre-trial period out on bail, and had felt that her period on remand would count as part of her final sentence. Yet other women, such as Sara Thornton and Janet Gardiner, were given bail although they were charged with murder. Kiranjit may have found it harder to get bail in any case because it appears that when women from minorities come before the courts other factors come into play. There may be a fear that the women will abscond abroad, even if they are rooted in Britain with children and property, as Kiranjit was.

Imprisoned and separated without warning from her children, Kiran had to cope with all the pressure of prison life, including advice from other inmates. Pragna later discovered that they had frightened Kiran so much by saying that arson was a serious offence that it had seemed to her to be by far the major problem that needed explanation.

THE CAMPAIGN AND LEGAL ISSUES

The trial had brought Hannana much closer to both Kiranjit and her family. She would try and spend lunchtimes with the family during the trial, and while some of them were suspicious of her, others like Devinder could see that she was being helpful. It was now possible to try to discuss what could be done. We did not know at that stage how difficult it would be to overturn Kiranjit's conviction.

There is no automatic right of appeal under English law. You cannot simply rerun the trial on different grounds, or argue that the defence was not sufficiently well-prepared. You must have new evidence or find a material irregularity in the conduct of the trial, or a misdirection in the judge's instructions to the jury on a point of law. Kiran's barrister had said he could find no grounds in the judge's summing-up on which he could base an appeal. At that point her legal aid ended, and any further work would have to be done free of charge. We had not only to find a new solicitor, but one who would be prepared to work without pay.

Hannana went to the famous but self-effacing criminal lawyer Gareth Peirce (who was later to be played by Emma Thompson in the film *In the Name of the Father*): 'She said, "I know this is a bit circular, but is there anything you can give me, any new evidence? Because I can't work on the case if there isn't." She was apologetic because she knew how difficult it would be to reopen the case without new evidence, and also that it would be extremely difficult to actually find the evidence without working on the case in the first place. But I had nothing to give her, and she was probably inundated with work as the Birmingham Six appeal was about to come up.'

We then considered whether we should go to Rohit Sanghvi, whom we had first met when he was a young solicitor working in a law firm in Southall. A workaholic with an infectious enthusiasm for the law, he had become a friend on whom we relied for free legal advice on a variety of problems. He brought the same meticulous attention to bear on a rent agreement as on a major criminal case. At the time of Kiranjit's trial, Rohit's five years of painstaking preparation were coming to a head in the civil action brought by Laxmi Peria Swamy against abuse by her employers, sisters of the Sheikh of Kuwait. As a lawyer we trusted him absolutely, and relied on his legal knowledge. There was one problem: Rohit was in no sense a feminist.

Hannana: 'Kiranjit's solicitors had advised that we couldn't go to appeal but should put in a petition to reduce the tariff. An appeal has to be lodged within twenty-eight days after the trial. At the last moment I decided we should lodge the appeal anyway, and rang Rohit for advice as to how to fill in the form. Since we had no grounds for appeal I asked him what I should put down. "Put 'Grounds will follow'," he said.' For the next three years we would be searching for the grounds of appeal.

Rohit was extremely sceptical at first: 'When Pragna tried to persuade me to take on the case in January 1990, I said, "You have a good principle to fight on, but this is the wrong case. It's a deliberate killing, premeditated." Pragna wouldn't leave me alone. She harassed me for four hours, piling on details. Finally I said to her, "Go to prison and get me her story." I explained how she should take a detailed statement.' It was the start of Pragna's, and by extension SBS's, legal education, and Rohit's feminist education.

Pragna described to Rohit the kinds of problems she had encountered in working with women in violent relationships. The workers at SBS had dealt with many women who took a long time to leave their husbands. They often needed extensive counselling before they came to a decision, and there were frequent cases of women who would leave for a brief period and then go back after their families had effected a reconciliation. It was not unusual for women to return even after they had gone to court to get an injunction against their husbands. These problems occurred even when they had the backing of a women's centre and had been fully informed about their rights to housing and social security. Kiranjit's experiences and her inability to leave were not hard to understand. But no one in SBS had any experience of women who have killed. On the whole, the paradigm we had was of a battered woman. How were we to fit Kiranjit's experiences into the law? Were we arguing that if she had killed as a conscious and deliberate act, she was justified in doing so? Were her actions the only logical course to follow if she was afraid for her life? Was it a reasonable act of survival? Had she killed then in self-defence? If, on the other hand, she had killed on the spur of the moment, because she had lost control of herself, or had suffered from an abnormality of mind, then we had to argue that she was not entirely innocent of a crime, that she was guilty of manslaughter. She had intended harm, but only momentarily. What she had done was understandable, and did not deserve a jail sentence, but she was not completely innocent. We felt that she had been provoked, but she had clearly not acted on the spur of the moment. We couldn't force Kiranjit's experiences into the narrow definition of provocation that was accepted by the courts. In order for the defence of provocation to succeed, three things had to be established: first, that Kiranjit herself was provoked; second, that a reasonable person with Kiranjit's characteristics would have been similarly provoked; and third, that the fatal attack followed the provocative event immediately. If there was a time lag of even a few minutes, then a 'reasonable person' could not remain provoked. The possibility of diminished responsibility we dismissed almost contemptuously. It would 'medicalise' Kiranjit's defence and force us to depend on the knowledge of experts from the 'psy' professions to interpret her experience. It would also have branded her 'mad' if she wasn't 'bad'. It was a defence which as feminists we considered almost unusable.

For a long time Rohit argued that running a two-pronged defence of provocation and diminished responsibility was logically inconsistent, and that to run both would reduce the potency of each argument. He warned us that we had to be logically consistent in trying to construct a defence. We could not pick and choose elements of Kiranjit's case and fit them randomly to the requirements of different defences in the law. We would have to construct a case based on the entire picture. This was very difficult to do. Pragna: 'One of the frustrations was that her case did not fit easily into any of the defences. We wanted to stretch the boundaries. But we had already seen Kiranjit constructed in a number of different ways.'

THE RECONSTRUCTION OF KIRANJIT

In the immediate aftermath of the trial we were depressed and angry. In court we had seen Kiranjit portrayed as a cold-blooded murderess. Some of the evidence was damning, but she looked very small and vulnerable; a broken woman. Naturally she had made a particularly strong impression on those who had met her and had attended the trial. We stood by our gut feelings over the case. When Hannana was subjected to sceptical questioning as to whether Kiranjit's story was believable and why she hadn't left home, Gita recalls her saying that, 'She's not a very strong woman. She should not be doing life for murder.' At this time she appeared to be passive, without any resolve. She was still heavily reliant on her family, who were urging her not to appeal. Even so, she was willing to go for it, but it would be a long process.

Although Kiran was still in shock, SBS was trying to see what could be done immediately. Kiran's concern was not her own future but what would happen to her children. She asked SBS to try and sort out the custody case.

At the same time Rohit had instructed Pragna to act as his

legal clerk and to record Kiranjit's story. His reasons were legal and forensic. We couldn't reopen the case without access to all the facts. Pragna's skills were those of a feminist activist. All the skills that she used as a worker at SBS, giving advice and counselling distressed women, came into play. But her role as inquisitor in recording Kiranjit's life history was much more intense than anything she had done before.

Pragna: 'We had to build her up again and give her some hope. That was very difficult. It began with having to take her story. That was very important too because she'd never had that kind of attention before. Most people want to be able to talk about themselves. To hear someone say, "Go back, tell me about your childhood, tell me about yourself and your parents." All that helped. Though I don't think when we started that she saw what it was all going to lead to.

'When we started she was so guilt-ridden that she was talking to a Sikh priest and asking for absolution. She did co-operate with us, but without really having the will to fight. The turning point came when Hannana won a victory over the custody of the children. We tried to egg Kiran on so that she would find the strength within herself.

'I had to get her to start thinking of herself as a fighter if she was going to have a chance of surviving a court case. Our early talks were very exploratory, trying to get her thinking of all her circumstances, thinking of all the pressures that might have been placed on her. What did she think of her religion, what did she think of her culture, what did she think of her mother-in-law, why did she get married? Get her to talk about all these things and to look at all those pressures so that she could begin to see that wrong was done to her as much as she had wronged.'

But the forensic processes required by the law were different from the needs of counselling. Pragna found herself holding back sometimes in her relationship with Kiran. 'I had to be very careful when I was questioning her not to put words into her mouth. She was very good at pre-empting, thinking through what she thought we wanted to hear. I was very careful not to give her literature about battered women until much later. Of course she had a copy of her own interview, and I gave her pamphlets and other campaign literature so that she was informed, but I was always very careful not to give her anything more.'

THE CRAWLEY MEETING

After a number of meetings in Crawley to discuss campaign strategies with the women from Crawley Women's Aid and Crawley Women's Centre who were keen to support Kiranjit, it was decided to hold a public meeting in Crawley to launch the Free Kiranjit Ahluwalia campaign formally. The leaflet had been finalised and was used to gather support. Hannana had already started interviewing family members for her report on the custody of Kiranjit's children. Now she was to ask for their public support at a local meeting run by feminists. Their response was unexpected; several said they would come. Most of us were amazed that members of Deepak's family would agree to support Kiranjit and our campaign in this way. Others, though sympathetic, preferred to work behind the scenes. In the only similar case we had heard of, Iqbal Begum, who had stabbed her husband to death, had not only been extremely isolated in the community before she killed her husband, but had suffered a lot of hostility after her release following a campaign by the group Birmingham Black Sisters (who have since folded). She had been condemned by an extremely conservative community from Mirpur (in Pakistan) for what she had done.

There were probably two major reasons for this. Although both Kiran and Iqbal Begum were subject to codes of *izzat* and strong notions of family honour, Kiran's community was more liberal. Though they didn't encourage her to leave home, family members were saddened and uncomfortable about justifying the violence against Kiran. Their guilt over their inaction showed in their dealings with Hannana. For example, Harjit, Deepak's uncle, gave Hannana his letter to the Home Secretary urging clemency for Kiranjit, but he did not wish to speak out publicly. In fact, though he had written the letter he could not bring himself to post it, and asked Hannana to do it for him.

It was fortunate for Kiranjit that Deepak was not only violent towards her but also to others in the family. This had not protected her when she lived with him, but it was a crucial element in mobilising people to support her. Kiran's supporters commanded respect within their community; nevertheless their willingness to put themselves on the line publicly was unprecedented in a campaign on domestic violence.

Most of the Crawley women had never been involved in a campaign like this. Though SBS had worked on campaigns where women had been killed by violent men or had committed suicide, such as the cases of Balwant Kaur and Krishna Sharma, our campaigning had always been much more localised. We had organised meetings and demonstrations in Southall and picketed courts where appropriate. When Balwant Kaur was killed by her husband we had regularly picketed all his court appearances and his trial, demanding that he be imprisoned for murder. When he was sentenced to life, with a recommendation that he serve a minimum of twenty-five years, we were overjoyed. Now we were trying to secure the release of a woman who had killed her husband. By the time of the meeting Kiran had served one year in prison.

We were planning our first major public meeting in a strange town far from the women who had supported us over the years. The logistics were frightening. Not only did we have to make sure that women's groups were informed and persuaded to come, we had to pay attention to little details such as encouraging Crawley women to serve food at the meeting. Women who had travelled up from London would not be able to find anywhere else to eat.

One night in the run-up to the meeting, Pragna had come

home triumphantly with a tape of a speech by Kiran. She also had the text of it, written in Hindi. Pragna had worked hard to persuade Kiran to write a message for the meeting, but even she was taken by surprise when she heard what Kiran had to say. Of all the statements and speeches made during the whole campaign, that speech was the most eloquent and moving. It became the testament which was central to the campaign, marking Kiranjit's passage from silence to speech, from being a victim to becoming a survivor.

As people began to arrive in the hall, the atmosphere was tense. There were rumours that Deepak's family had threatened to come and break up the meeting. But as women poured out of the coaches that had brought them down from London, we realised that if there were any troublemakers they would have a large audience to reckon with. Crawley Town Hall was full. The audience was overwhelmingly made up of women, including many connected with the refuge in Crawley and several Asian women's refuges in London. Desperate women with their own campaigns to fight were there too, such as a mother trying to find a child who had been kidnapped by the father. But key members of Kiranjit's family had also come. Deepak's uncle Ranjit sat in the front row. In addition there were cameras: Gita, a member of SBS, was trying to make a film about the case. The camera had to be set up carefully so that those women in the audience who wanted could have their anonymity preserved.

As people began to take their seats, they faced an enormous banner hanging on one side of the platform. It had a white background and showed a red figure dripping blood and towering threateningly over a small black figure. The slogan read: 'The real crime – Domestic violence. Self-defence is no offence.' The second part of the slogan had long been used by the anti-racist movement to justify people defending themselves against racist attacks. SBS had converted it into a feminist slogan, and used it in campaigns against domestic violence. Shakila had spray-painted the banner for the meeting by hanging the cloth against a wall in the SBS office, producing both a cloth banner and a wall painting. The painting remains there as a reminder of the campaign. The banner was to dominate all our subsequent meetings, and even the wall painting was to do duty as a backdrop for numerous interviews and photographs.

The meeting was chaired by Lesley Clarke from Crawley Women's Aid. On the platform were Gurdev and Sukhjit, the feminist writers and activists Bea Campbell and Liz Kelly, Hannana and Fawzia Ahmed from the Brent Asian Women's Refuge, who translated throughout the meeting.

Kiranjit's speech was played on a tape recorder over speakers, and was read out with great passion in English by Fawzia. Though her voice was indistinct, Kiranjit was listened to intently by the audience. It was the first time we had heard her voice, the first time she had chosen to tell her own story. By the end, it was difficult to hold back tears. Some of the men were particularly affected. Both Sukhjit and Ranjit were wiping their eyes. It made one wonder what their thoughts were. Was there a measure of guilt, a feeling of having failed Kiranjit? Were they surprised at her eloquence? Had she ever been able to articulate her feelings in her family?

Sukhjit gave a long and emotional account of Kiranjit's married life and how she had suffered. He also laid the blame for her plight squarely on the system that prevented her from leaving: 'It was an open secret, all the family from our side and the in-laws' side knew either Kiranjit would die from Deepak's hand or she would do something to herself.' He was still fighting for custody of Kiran's children, and was glad that he had managed to get them access to their mother, access which they had been denied for six long weeks after her conviction.

Liz Kelly from the Feminist Coalition Against Child Sexual Abuse described the movement for refuges and the support needed for battered women and their children. Her presence on the platform was the first in a long series of joint actions as the campaign developed.

Bea Campbell described a film on which she had worked called *I Shot My Husband and No One Asked Me Why*, about battered women who had killed in America. She described the existence of the battered women's defence in the USA, which put the woman's story at the centre of her defence: 'The important point of the campaign in the courts is to challenge the idea that the law of self-defence is only relevant in a high noon situation, where he's got a gun and you've got a gun. They're challenging the idea of a necessary equivalence between the assailant and the defendant. They are also challenging the idea that the only appropriate occasion for self-defence is that a woman feels that she is in imminent danger.' She compared Kiranjit to Francine Hughes, an American woman who had killed her husband by setting his bed alight. After a feminist defence was mounted Francine Hughes was acquitted. Bea Campbell's film had been watched by SBS when it was first transmitted. For many months it remained a sort of guiding light, providing the only clue as to how such a defence could perhaps be mounted for Kiranjit.

The film and our political slogans concentrated on self-defence, but we had already begun to be aware that the legal issues were less clear-cut. To demand justice was to mount a campaign based on self-defence for Kiranjit. Self-defence is the only complete defence to a charge of murder – that is, it's the only defence which claims that the killing is justified, and that the defendant is innocent. As Bea Campbell had pointed out, it is very difficult for women to use the defence because women tend to kill in very different circumstances from, say, men having a brawl in a pub.

Hannana spoke last, raising the legal issues. Like the American campaign SBS wanted to put the woman's story at the centre of her defence. Hannana argued that the idea of 'cumulative provocation' would have to be introduced into the law if women's experiences were to be reflected in it, so that the history of violence rather than just the immediate provocation could be included in the defence case. Already we were arguing the beginning of a legal strategy which was less than a complete defence, though we concentrated on the necessity of women's experience of domestic violence being recognised by the law, rather than the details of legal strategies.

Hannana explained the importance of the meeting for SBS after ten years of campaigning on domestic violence. This was the first meeting we had ever organised for both men and women, as we thought it was vitally important for all Kiranjit's supporters to be able to participate. Hannana talked about the importance of *izzat* in controlling women, and also about how, following the women's movement in India, we had been able to subvert traditional ideas of honour and shame. In 1984 we had demonstrated in front of the house of Krishna Sharma, who was found hanged after receiving no help from the police to escape from a violent marriage. We had hoped to shame the family who had driven a woman to her death, just as women demonstrating outside the houses of those who were killed for dowry in India wanted to dishonour the families in front of their neighbours and turn a private family matter into a public issue.

After Hannana's speech there was a break for refreshments. Normally this would be the signal for people to drift away, for with translations, the speeches had gone on for a very long time. Yet the atmosphere was so charged with pent-up emotions that women clamoured to speak. They talked about themselves and their own pain. For some it was the first time they had described the ordeals they had been through. They spoke in front of a large mixed audience, saying things they had been unable to say before, even to close friends.

Ranjit too spoke from the floor, and offered his support. The campaign had to build on the interest that had been generated in Crawley to get people to sign the petition urging the Home Secretary to give Kiranjit an early release.

Deconstructing the Story

The first big victory was the awarding of custody of the children to Gurdev and Sukhjit in October 1990. It gave Kiranjit a huge boost and helped her to feel that her case was not completely hopeless. It was a victory for SBS too. Hannana had worked hard on a report for the court welfare officer in which she argued that it would be in the children's interest as well as Kiranjit's to award custody to people in her family who were sympathetic to her, rather than to a hostile mother-in-law who might be obstructive of prison visits. This was the first sign that anyone in authority could sympathise with Kiranjit or respond to her needs, when she was a convicted murderer with a long sentence to serve.

While it was extremely important to establish a complete history of all the violence Kiranjit had suffered so that we could incorporate it into the appeal, it was also necessary to examine the events of the final night. Rohit pointed out that Kiran's first statement to her lawyers at trial was thirty-four pages long. Twenty pages dealt with the incident itself, and only about fourteen with her matrimonial history. Pragna's final statement from her was five hundred pages long; about fifty dealt with the incident itself. It was taken over a period of a year, at intense weekly and then bi-weekly meetings. In all, Pragna was to see Kiran seventy times and Rohit about fifteen times. For most of this period, neither of them was paid any legal fees.

After months of trying to establish Kiran's history, Pragna was able to broach the night's events. At the very least she had to put the prosecution's case to Kiran. What was her account of events, and of the different statements she'd made? What was true, and why had she concocted certain statements? If her appeal was to be based on the most feminist defence possible within the law, then we should try to understand exactly what her intentions and state of mind actually were and try to reflect the 'truth' in constructing her defence. But to do this Pragna had to simultaneously be both sympathetic and sceptical, perhaps even disbelieving of some of the things Kiran told her. Scepticism and disbelief are not normally weapons encouraged in the feminist armoury. For some feminists, to deploy them is tantamount to blasphemy. Yet trying to uncover the truth was to become almost an end in itself for Pragna, amounting to obsession.

She cited an example of her problems with Kiranjit: 'I spent a long time trying to uncover the facts. At one point in her earlier statement she talks about making various trips during the last day, the day of the incident. She was telling me of a different number of trips each time. I was forever amending her first statement, and that used to make me very angry. Sometimes when it got really difficult I just could not get through to her. I would have to bring Rohit in – he was more authoritative because he was a solicitor. She had a different relationship with him – calling him Rohit bhaiya [brother] and all that. She always listened to him. On this occasion, I had to bring him in because I was getting nowhere. She was giving me contradictory statements about her trips to McDonald's and the events around it. She said that she had gone to McDonald's, leaving her child with a neighbour. That always niggled me because I couldn't understand why she had done that. If you go to McDonald's you take your child with you. In any case, why go out when Deepak was expected back home? She was supposed to be waiting for him when he returned from work. She left a note for him. There were an awful lot of things there which didn't ring true. I was trying to uncover them. Then she said to me that she had gone to the gates of the factory where Deepak worked and come back and then gone to McDonald's. There were three or four trips in one night. The next week I would go and see her and she would go back to two trips, then the next time she would say something else. Rohit and I would prepare the questions we needed to ask in advance and discuss how we would deal with them.

'In this instance, Rohit started very gently to talk to her. He was really superb at explaining things and gently drawing people out. He treated her with the greatest respect and chivalry. So he sat there talking to her while I was feeling really angry. He drew all these diagrams about events, saying it was really important to pinpoint the exact time that they happened. It was an education to watch him. Kiran let slip that she had gone to the factory to spy on her husband. Rohit was in full flow, and he missed it. I said, "Hang on a minute," and brought him back. I said to Kiran, "You didn't go to McDonald's, you went to the factory to spy on your husband." She admitted it. What it was, you see, was that she didn't want us to see her as cunning. Possibly she didn't want to see herself that way either. I often used the word *chalak* when I was talking to her. I'd say, "We're not trying to find out whether you're *chalak* in that sense, cunning."

' "I don't want the world to think I'm a *chalak* woman," she said.

'I said, "You are an educated, bright woman. If that's what you were doing you should say so and explain why – earlier you told me that you were desperate. You didn't know where your future was any more so you wanted to go and find out if he was going to go off with his girlfriend. That's fine." But she was struggling with herself.'

Once while Kiran was in prison there happened to be a picture of Deepak's girlfriend in the local paper in Crawley. SBS decided to show the picture to Kiranjit. We felt that Hannana should be the one to do it, since Pragna felt she was running into brick walls with Kiranjit in trying to establish what exactly had happened. Hannana: 'So I went to the prison and showed her the picture, and she became very angry as she looked at it. She said, "If it wasn't for her, I wouldn't have tried to hurt him. She's made my life hell." '

Pragna later pursued the same point. She asked Kiranjit why

she had acted as she did, and Kiranjit responded simply, '*Badla.*'
Badla generally means retaliation.

We had accepted Kiranjit's explanation that she never
intended to kill Deepak, that she had taken a little petrol and
'sprinkled' it on him hoping to 'cause pain'. But if his death
was about *badla*, were we defending a retaliatory act, or a
revenge killing that was planned, as the police had implied, in
cold blood? Were we supporting an argument that, like men,
women were justified in taking retaliatory action for adultery?
We were fighting to remove double standards, and had started
with a vision of introducing feminist principles into the law.
Was this to be reduced to getting a version of 'equal rights': if
men had a 'licence to kill', should women also have access to
it? If this was all that we were arguing, we would have come
into conflict with women's groups who had been campaigning
to have men jailed for killing in a fit of jealousy, including our
sister group the Brent Asian Women's Refuge, in which many
of us were involved. We had jointly picketed the trial of Balwant
Kaur's husband, demanding a life sentence for the man who
had broken into the refuge and killed her in front of her three
young daughters. We felt very uncomfortable about the problem
of jealousy in a marriage. It didn't fit our own ideals of why a
battered woman would be driven to kill – out of fear for her
own life. If Deepak was threatening to leave Kiranjit, could she
have feared he would kill her?

By this time, in early 1991, Pragna had already had very extensive meetings with Kiran, and had got to know her more inti-
mately than any other woman she had ever dealt with at SBS.
She would sometimes feel guilty about the amount of time she
spent with her compared to the time she had left for all the
other women. The result of this intimacy was that she came to
know Kiranjit in all her contradictions. Through Pragna and
Hannana's work we were beginning to find out that there were
more than two ways to look at Kiranjit – she was neither a
cold-blooded murderess nor a passive victim of domestic

violence who had killed out of fear and despair. These were certainly present in her descriptions of her last day with Deepak, but they were not the only ones. Anger, too, was in part a basis for her actions. SBS had spent a lot of time presenting Kiranjit's case by emphasising the violence she had faced, and by stressing that women, particularly battered women, did not necessarily commit violence in the same way as men. We had been influenced by a number of American cases in which women committed homicide when the men were asleep or incapacitated. They seemed to fit Kiranjit's case. But now we had to fit another element into her story. What were we to make of the anger and the desire for *badla*? Could we confine *badla* to the narrow limits that Kiranjit had set: that she wanted Deepak to feel pain as she had, that it in no way encompassed an intention to kill him? Pragna said, 'She felt completely trapped in her marriage. She had tried to leave it and hadn't been able to. Now Deepak was threatening to leave her and she would be able to do nothing about it. He had threatened her similarly before but had come back, and she was afraid that if she left he would always come after her. It wasn't simply a matter of adultery, or leaving her, it was in the context of his continuing violence. I think she has been treated very harshly for what she did, and the bottom line is she should not have had a life sentence or gone to jail. That's what kept me going.'

But the question of *badla* raised a number of problems when we were looking at a possible defence. If Kiranjit had feared that she was in imminent danger of being killed by Deepak, and had retaliated as a reasonable act of survival rather than through loss of control, it might be possible to argue self-defence. But there were problems. The time-lag between Deepak's last act of violence and Kiranjit's retaliation was considerable. In giving her statement to Pragna, Kiranjit never claimed that her life was in immediate danger, or that Deepak was about to kill her. While we could argue self-defence politically, we could not pursue it in law.

Media

The Crawley meeting had resulted in our first national coverage, a sympathetic news report by Heather Mills in the *Independent*. The media paid little attention to the early stages of the campaign, although Gita had got *Dispatches*, the Channel 4 current affairs programme, interested in covering Kiran's case.

There had been no other representatives of women who had killed their partners at the Crawley meeting. We had to try to find them, so as to find out how widespread the problem was. The research for the *Dispatches* programme on battered women who kill fed into the campaign, while the legal and campaigning work became the basis for the programme. It was called 'The Provoked Wife', and was transmitted in January 1991.

Shakila started working as a researcher, tracking down other women who had committed homicide. She saw a letter to a paper written by Sara Thornton, complaining of police inaction against her violent husband: 'If the police had helped me he would have been alive.' Shakila wrote to Sara in Durham Prison and began a correspondence which resulted in Sara agreeing to take part in the film. We also found Amelia Rossiter, who agreed that her lawyer Mike Fisher should be interviewed about her case. Sara and Amelia, along with Kiranjit, were to become the public face of the campaign. We did not and still do not know how many battered women are doing time in British jails for killing their partners. But the names of these three were known to campaigners through the work done on the programme.

We needed as much detail as possible, so we tried to get hold of the transcripts of Kiran's trial. This was one of many small educations in the law. Theoretically a court trial is open to the public, and anyone may attend or have access to the proceedings. In practice, it costs a great deal of money – about £2,000 to order a full transcript. Eventually we managed to get a complete text of the judge's summing-up, but no other transcripts. We passed it on to Rohit, about nine months after he first took on the case. This provided a crucial piece of the puzzle. It was an essential step in finding the grounds for appeal.

THE SEARCH FOR GROUNDS FOR APPEAL

After Rohit had been given the judge's summing-up, we gathered together to discuss it. Initially, he thought it was a legally impeccable summing-up, and like Kiranjit's QC at trial he did not see any hope for an appeal on the grounds of misdirection. He could not share the sense of outrage of the women who had been present at the trial, who felt that the judge had not taken seriously the violence Kiranjit had faced. Instead, he began working his way backwards through the legal texts to acquaint himself with all the judgements on murder cases, and the case law on provocation.

Rohit: 'I'd read the judgement about twenty times, looking for an opening, looking for what the judge had failed to mention rather than what he had said. One night it occurred to me that he had failed to mention that Kiranjit was a battered woman.' Rohit reread the legal texts in the light of his find, and applied them brilliantly to Kirajit's case. In particular he analysed in depth a previous judgement of the House of Lords – DPP v. Camplin, 1978, AC 705 (House of Lords) – which had decided that the 'reasonable person' had to be invested with the same relevant characteristics as the defendant. This meant that in Kiranjit's case, the abstract category of a reasonable person was to be regarded by the jury as a person very similar to the defendant. When the judge had described her, he had said: 'The only characteristics of the defendant about which you know specifically that might be relevant are that she is an Asian woman married, incidentally, to an Asian man, the deceased, living in this country. You may think she is an educated woman. She has a university degree.' He had therefore given the jury a closed list of characteristics which they were to consider relevant. They were not able to consider any other characteristics which may have been present at trial. At no point in the list of characteristics had he described Kiran as a battered woman, and therefore, by inverted logic, she was content in her marriage. Such a reasonable woman would not have been provoked into doing what Kiran had done. This omission was something that we tried to build on. In doing so, we started on the route that Kiranjit's defence was to take: the beatings she had suffered were introduced as a *personal characteristic* of Kiranjit rather than as a social fact, a part of her environment. In the USA, there is a move to explain the effect that repeated battering can have on women by introducing sociological and statistical evidence. For instance, objective evidence can be introduced to show that women have very few alternatives to staying in violent marriages, and that provision for women's safety, such as refuges, is very inadequate. Statistical evidence can also be used to demonstrate that women may have a well-founded fear that they will be killed. Many women are killed not when they are living in a violent relationship, but when they are attempting to leave it or have left it. These facts can be used to show that a woman's subjective perceptions of the danger she is facing are backed up by objective reality. In such a defence, the main evidence presented would be the woman's experience backed by statistics and other factual evidence, not a medical interpretation of her state of mind which sought to explain or justify her subjective perceptions as though they had no grounding in reality.

In our case, if battering were to be regarded as a personal characteristic of a more or less permanent nature, its effect would have to be explained by medical experts. So we began, with a mixture of reluctance, distaste and fascination, to enter the world of forensic medicine and mental disorder.

We needed a psychiatrist to address the question of Kiranjit's long silence. If he said that her silence was reasonable, we could make an application for her testimony to be introduced as new evidence. It would have been the first time that the defendant's own evidence formed the basis for an appeal.

When Kiranjit had made a detailed enough statement we looked around for a psychiatrist to show it to. It was not the complete statement, but it was a very full account of her life and the events which led to Deepak's death. Pragna discussed it with her partner Raju Bhatt, a lawyer who had often represented prisoners and other people suffering severe stress as a result of harassment. He advised us to go to a forensic psychiatrist who had a very good reputation, particularly in looking at the effects of long-term confinement on people.

Pragna: 'We didn't have a clue who to go to, but as he'd been so highly recommended we went to him. I suppose I was a bit nervous, but I thought he would be sympathetic to the general issues we were trying to raise. I thought Kiran's case would move him. We met in Rohit's office for him to give us an opinion. He said Kiranjit's statement was completely self-justificatory, of course she did it and there was no reason for her to be treated any differently from any other murderer. It was devastating. Not only was he not able to make any positive recommendations regarding the desirability of keeping her in prison, he totally dismissed the case, saying, "Find a better case, don't waste your time on this one." '

The psychiatrist's reaction made us realise what we were up against. Presenting a history of violence was not sufficient to ensure a sympathetic response for Kiranjit. We had to show why Deepak's violence made her do what she did, and demonstrate the links between it and her actions.

Pragna: 'The one very important thing he did, and that was very good, was to look at the early psychiatrist's report that suggested that Kiran had been suffering from "endogenous depression" at the time of the incident, and suggest that we follow that up and ask why the report did not go on to state that Kiranjit was suffering from diminished responsibility.' This was to prove a very useful piece of advice indeed, one that changed the course of both the legal case and the campaign.

After Rohit had discovered the misdirection in what appeared to him to be an otherwise impeccable summing-up – the judge's failure to mention battering as a characteristic of Kiranjit – he set out to find another ground for appeal. Rohit: 'I approached Dr Weller, who had examined Kiran while she was on remand, to enquire whether it was understandable, and therefore reasonable, for Kiran to have kept silent and to have refused to testify at trial. If so, we would be able to put in the further ground that we now had, from Kiran herself, a new, amplified story, which ought to be admitted by the appeal court. This was the fresh evidence ground of appeal.'

When Dr Weller confirmed that Kiran's inability to speak at trial was understandable, Rohit instructed Andrew to draft the grounds of appeal. At this stage the papers would go before a single judge who would either grant or refuse leave to appeal. Kiran was some eighteen months out of time to apply for leave when the papers were lodged. Rohit was still not optimistic.

The legal team decided to use the absence of 'battering' as a characteristic of Kiranjit in the trial judge's summing-up in the first ground of appeal. The second was Kiran's amplified statement, taken by Pragna over the past eighteen months and more. This, they reasoned, presented fresh evidence. But never before had it been argued that the defendant's own evidence, her own story, could be new evidence, and the law required that any material alleged to be new should not be such as not to have been reasonably available at the original trial. If it was, or could have been, available, then the failure to adduce it should not entitle the defendant to enjoy a second opportunity at the court of appeal. How could Kiran's own story, even in its fullest form, not have been reasonably available at her trial? Rohit therefore supported the second ground with Dr Weller's opinion that it was not surprising that Kiran had been unable to testify at her trial, given her circumstances and the experiences she had been through. It had, after all, taken more than a year to obtain full instructions from Kiranjit, after much counselling and gentle, if persistent, questioning. For the campaigners it was vital that Kiran should have an opportunity to tell her story herself. It would have meant a breakthrough, bringing the phrase 'breaking the silence' into the courtroom.

Pragna was determined not to give up. Like other members of SBS she was experienced in debates on race and gender in academic and political circles, but had never been involved in medical discussion of these issues. So when an announcement for a conference on gender issues and psychiatry landed on her desk she decided that she must go. The price was a problem. It cost £40, and with SBS's very tight finances there was no money to pay for it. Pragna rang them up: 'I explained that I was from a women's group. They wouldn't give me a reduction but they did agree that I could attend the sessions if I did some work, so I served tea and coffee and carted these heavy glasses around during the breaks and rushed to catch the sessions after I finished clearing up. It was the sort of conference where the flower arrangements must have cost thousands, but the level of discussion was pretty abysmal. There was no mention of race issues at all. It seemed to be years behind the discussions we have, since the starting points were so conservative. But everyone was there, so it was quite useful to meet people. Helena Kennedy, who was always helpful, was there, as was Katherine O'Donovan, who gave us advice, and I met Dr Gillian Mezey for the first time. There was even a woman reading a paper at a workshop on Kiranjit. She looked quite embarrassed to see me, and suggested that I should be talking rather than her. But I was pleased to see that someone was raising the case.'

SBS decided to hold a seminar on battered women who kill, and to look at the defences available to them. We invited people from a wide range of disciplines – academics, lawyers and psychiatrists. We had a very mixed response. Rohit, of course, was there, as was Andrew Nicol, a barrister who had been instructed by him. He had represented Laxmi Peria Swamy in court and already knew some members of SBS. Like Rohit, he was working without pay as Kiranjit was still not receiving legal aid, and he had kindly agreed to come even though it was a Saturday. There were a few old campaigners like Liz Kelly, with whom we had always been in touch. But the rest were a very mixed bag indeed. The seminar had been quite complicated to organise, since the main work of SBS and Pragna's visits to Kiranjit had to continue without interruption; and it caused some surprise that an advice centre rather than an academic institute should be mounting such an ambitious event.

By now we were well acquainted with the relatively small amount of literature on the subject by criminologists and legal academics, but our ignorance of the factions among academics was still oceanic. We had no idea who was speaking to whom, who considered themselves pre-eminent in the field and so on. We must have unintentionally offended quite a number of people. Our most useful discovery was Katherine O'Donovan, who read a very good paper on gender biases in the law faced by battered woman defendants.

The biggest gap in our knowledge was the phenomenon called battered women's syndrome. This had been developed by an American psychologist called Leonore Walker as a branch of post-traumatic stress disorder, which was becoming recognised as a long-term condition suffered by people who had been involved in a traumatic event. This could range from a one-off incident such as a fire or an air disaster to imprisonment or torture. Walker had developed a checklist of symptoms which were used to determine whether a battered woman was suffering from the syndrome. The best-known of these were 'learned helplessness' and 'diminished perception of alternatives'. Both were used to explain why many women who are suffering at the hands of a partner are unable to leave violent situations. The first was based partly on animal research which showed that caged animals subjected to electric shocks do not attempt to leave their cages when the doors are opened. This apparently applies to prisoners kept in confinement, too, and explains the apparent passivity of many victims of violence as a tactic of survival in the face of overwhelming odds. 'Diminished perception of alternatives' suggests that the battered woman cannot see any way out of her situation. In her perception, and this was crucial, there was no way that she could run and hide from the violence.

Many people were opposed to the theory. They felt that it medicalised the problem of the defendant, reducing her knowledge of her partner to the status of her perception. In fact, researchers have shown that many battered women make repeated attempts to leave their partners or to seek help for their plight, and that they are in grave danger if they attempt to leave, often being hunted down. They are failed by a lack of safe alternatives, by the refusal of society to recognise domestic violence as a crime, and by the priority put on codes of honour and romantic love, in which violence is an acceptable part of the relationship.

BWS also created a typical battered woman who kills. What defence, we worried, would be available to a woman who did not fit the picture, who did not conform to the checklist of symptoms? A woman, for instance, who was perfectly competent in running her life, who knew what the alternatives to remaining with her partner were, and who appeared to kill from anger and rage rather than despair.

We were very hazy about the answers to these questions. And though battered women's syndrome had become widely talked about as an essential part of the 'battered women's defence' in the USA, we had no idea how it worked. We shared the scepticism we had heard voiced by British feminists like Liz Kelly, but we were very anxious to have the case for battered women's syndrome put by an advocate for it. The only ones we knew of were in America, and since we were organising the conference on a shoestring we couldn't afford to fly anyone over. This didn't deter Pragna from trying to suggest to some American lawyers that they might like to attend our conference anyway. Sadly, even she was unable to persuade them to come. Nor could she get any British psychiatrists to attend.

The only psychiatrist present was an Indian gentleman who had abandoned psychiatry for film criticism, and who told us with impeccable feminist logic that it would be dangerous as well as intellectually inconsistent to trawl through different disorders, picking and choosing at random, particularly when we were all keen not to medicalise the issue. But this whiff of pure idealism was too strong to be taken neat, and so had to be ignored altogether. For the underlying purpose of the seminar was to find a defence for Kiranjit. Once we would have been pleased to discover that we were well informed about the law, but now we realised that no 'expert' could hand us a ready-made, off-the-shelf defence. General principles could be established, but each case was unique, and especially in trying to reopen a case, we would have to construct our arguments from scratch.

SARA THORNTON'S APPEAL

We first came across George Delf, Sara Thornton's friend and adviser, during the making of the *Dispatches* programme. He had come down to London for our seminar, and made contact with Rohit. He was looking for someone to prepare Sara's appeal.

We had realised that George Delf and Sara were against the use of psychiatric evidence. He felt that in Sara's case, there had been a very damaging use of expert psychiatric evidence at trial which was presented to show that she was in a 'fugue' state. Her defence was diminished responsibility. The prosecution countered this by building up a picture of her as a wild woman who had often threatened to kill her husband and who was in complete possession of herself when she plunged the knife into him. Financial greed was presented as a motive for the crime. Domestic violence was not used as a mitigating circumstance. Delf was therefore very reluctant to run any element of diminished responsibility again at the appeal. Sara agreed, designated psychiatry as 'witchcraft' and instructed her lawyers to consider only provocation.

At the time SBS felt that this was a huge mistake, and in retrospect it seemed an even bigger one. Sara should have left her lawyers free to explore all the options. The campaign also seemed very low-key. 'When we were sitting in the court of appeal, the atmosphere was very quiet. Fawzia and I thought we must never let this happen to Kiranjit when her case came up.' Delf did not want Sara's supporters to be campaigning visibly, picketing the court and packing the gallery. There was a lot of news coverage, as he was happy to organise publicity, but he was against a political campaign, and did not want to work with feminists.

Sara lost her appeal. The appeal court refused to widen the interpretation of the conditions under which provocation could take place. The classic definition of provocation was reaffirmed. This was devastating for Sara, but it was also a huge setback for our campaign. The appeal had been the first opportunity to put before the courts the arguments that had emerged about the flaws in the law. The defence had asked the appeal court to go back to the original statute, removing from the law the requirement that the loss of self-control had to be 'sudden' as well as 'temporary'. Counsel for Sara, Lord Gifford, had argued that a time-lag between the act of killing and the last act of provocation could be a 'slow-burn period', and not a cooling-off period. It was a very dangerous situation for Kiranjit, as we had pinned our hopes on running a provocation defence.

Cases like that of Joan Calladine, who in an interview for the *Dispatches* programme had described stabbing her drunken husband, had shown us that good defence lawyers can get their clients a suspended sentence if they are able to build up a convincing history of violence prior to the event. If the woman is seen to be truly a victim, the court has on occasion been able to show mercy in passing sentence. But the fear of opening the floodgates and giving women a 'licence to kill' remained, as did a reluctance to view provocation as a legitimate defence for women, particularly women like Sara who were seen as both defiant and self-possessed.

HUNGER STRIKE

Six days after Sara had been sent back to Bullwood Hall, Joseph McGrail was tried in Birmingham Crown Court for kicking his alcoholic wife to death. He received a suspended sentence, and left the court a free man. The judge said that he had been provoked.

Women's groups immediately mounted protests, and we saw a number of new campaigners on television. Some who had been campaigning for the release of women convicted of domestic murders were demanding to know why a man had been allowed to walk free after killing his wife. Sara's reaction was perhaps more consistent. She said that she understood the frustration of having to live with an alcoholic, and could understand why McGrail may have been driven to kill. But she didn't know why the same court that had sentenced her to life imprisonment should release McGrail. She announced that she was going to start an indefinite hunger strike.

Sara's hunger strike was a watershed for the campaign. It was that one single action which galvanised public opinion through the media which championed Sara's cause. It put enormous pressure on the Home Secretary to consider whether battered women who had killed should be serving such long sentences.

For Pragna, who was working with both Sara and Kiranjit, there were very particular dilemmas. 'I remember when I went to visit Sara, she said, "If you're thinking of telling me not to go on hunger strike, get out." It was a huge dilemma for us, and it was a dilemma which remains. I had the opportunity to talk to Gareth Peirce about it. A lot of her clients have been on hunger strike, and she was very helpful. She said that you must give them some hope with their legal case, give them a way out.'

The explosion of media interest was both exhilarating and bewildering. All sorts of people who had never shown the slightest enthusiasm for feminist causes suddenly began to write sympathetically about battered women who kill. Sara became the icon, the representative of all battered women in the eyes of the world.

It was at this stage that we met Julie Bindel and others whom we were to work with over the next few years. They had helped establish the Free Sara Thornton campaign, and were the ones usually asked by the media for comments about the law. SBS, on the other hand, was sometimes asked to comment on Kiranjit or the situation of Asian women. We were never asked about the law. This was frustrating, since it deprived us of a chance to express views on an area in which we had done a lot of work. We discussed this with Sara's supporters (who were to change their name to Justice for Women and broaden the scope of their campaign), and they agreed that the media should be referred to us on legal issues as well.

As Sara's hunger strike went on her supporters organised daily pickets outside Holloway Prison. At Bullwood Hall, Kiran said that she too wanted to go on hunger strike to support Sara. Pragna: 'Kiran said to me, "You give me the word. I'm willing to go on hunger strike, and there are other women, too, ready to go on hunger strike. Advise me."

'I just didn't know what to do. All I could say to her was, don't do it just yet. She gave me a statement about why she was going on hunger strike, which I said I would hang on to. I wouldn't release it until I'd discussed it with the group.

'We never did make that statement public, because she never

went on hunger strike. We were having so many discussions among ourselves about what to do. We felt that she and other women had every right to go on hunger strike and to give solidarity and support to each other. But it was very painful. We were even closer to Kiran than we were to Sara, and my feeling was that if she went on hunger strike then we must also go on hunger strike.

'I came back crying from that meeting. The sense of responsibility was overwhelming. How could we advise her to starve herself to death and carry on living our own lives? But we had to think of our role as advisers and as a campaigning group. What act of solidarity would be strong enough to convey the strength of our feelings?'

The underlying romantic thrust of SBS politics had sprung to the surface. It seemed to be a time for grand gestures rather than the mundane work of day-to-day campaigning. Although we were having to present a public face to the world, we became very introspective. Pragna: 'What was our relation to the women who were threatening to go on hunger strike? Should we support them, which as activists we were very inclined to do? As their advisers, was it our responsibility to put them off the idea? We recognised that prisoners have few other weapons, but by then Sara was on day twenty. We were terrified she would die.'

Pragmatism soon reasserted itself in our discussions, while tension caused hilarity. Hannana: 'We laughed when Pragna said we should go on hunger strike, because she was suggesting we should do it for two days a week, separated from each other, and that seemed very tokenistic.'

Pragna: 'I said that because I felt we had to do it. But then the question was, if we go on hunger strike, who will do the work? We'll be sitting there outside the prison, dying, and who will do all the mail-outs and the press releases. So we had to think about going on fasts in relays and all kinds of tactics that campaigners in other countries have used.'

In the end we did none of this. Sara was persuaded by Rohit

to bring a dignified end to her strike. She had not been released, but she had won an immense moral victory, not only for herself but for all battered women in prison for homicide.

It was only later that we heard a story which, if true, would indicate how near Sara had come to a complete victory. Apparently the then Home Secretary, Kenneth Baker, was sufficiently jolted by the uproar to consult experts on whether Sara should be released. In a scene worthy of *Yes Minister* he argued for release, while his civil servants urged caution. Her release would open the floodgates, it would set dangerous precedents and give women a licence to kill. Whether Baker thought Sara's release would serve the interests of justice or boost the popularity of a Home Office shaken by Tory failures on law and order and a number of miscarriages of justice, we will never know. We do know the outcome, though – the status quo prevailed.

WE'LL FREE ALL THE WOMEN, YES WE WILL

Unaware of the tremors we had already caused, SBS decided to keep up the momentum of the campaign by holding weekly pickets outside the Home Office, near St James's. Every Wednesday for six months a crowd of singing, shouting, whistling and stamping women gathered during the lunch hour, calling for the release of Sara Thornton, Amelia Rossiter and Kiranjit Ahluwalia. To the tune of 'What shall we do with the drunken sailor?', we sang 'What shall we do with Kenneth Baker?' and the theme song of the pickets, 'We'll free all the women, yes we will' (to the tune of 'She'll be coming round the mountain'). Women came in minibuses from as far afield as Newcastle and Wales, many of them from refuges. The pickets became a focus for campaigning among those who were concerned with issues of violence against women. For anyone who claimed the women's movement had collapsed by the mid-eighties, these pickets were testimony to the life of nineties feminism. And yet there were differences from earlier times. Men were not excluded – though they were always in a tiny minority (if they were there at all) – as we felt it important to include the families of the women should they want to participate.

For Meena this aspect of the campaign was cathartic, making worthwhile the sheer organisational grind which she largely handled for SBS: 'It was a lot of work, paying in money, collecting money, making sure that the campaign was sponsored. It's a hell of a lot of work, from handling the campaign finances to making banners and going out once a week outside the Home Office and shouting and screaming. Doing that work I didn't feel tired, because I really enjoyed it. I may have moaned now and then, but at the end of the day you know you've got to do it. If I hadn't enjoyed it so much it would have been difficult to put a lot into it.

'Some of the mail-outs and the banner-making – I remember we sat there, Pragna and Hannana weren't involved, and we were working until really late at night, and all of us, including the volunteers, were really enjoying ourselves. Rajdeep, Jas and others who came were really involved. They came along to volunteer, and there was a lot of work on the campaign so they got involved in it. That's why a lot of these other campaigns fail. They haven't made it enjoyable as well as trying to raise the issues. People say they enjoy our pickets more than any others that they go to.'

LEAVE TO APPEAL – A FOOT IN THE DOOR

In September 1991, Kiranjit was granted leave to appeal on the grounds of misdirection in the trial judge's summing-up. Rohit remained cautious, 'But the door that had been slammed shut at Sara Thornton's appeal had opened just a chink. It was sufficient to jam our foot into it. Before we put in the grounds I thought we had a 2 or 3 per cent chance, but when we were given leave to appeal in September 1991, I thought we'd increased our chances to 10–15 per cent.'

As we began to get more attention for our case, an unusual report appeared in the *Guardian* which dealt with the statistics of men and women sentenced for murder. It showed that women were likely to receive shorter sentences, and more non-custodial sentences, than men. Later, we found out how these statistics had appeared.

In October 1991 a Tory MP, Sir John Wheeler, had tabled a question in Parliament asking for information on defences to charges of murder, and how men and women were treated by the courts. The Home Office responded that women were nearly twice as likely as men to be indicted for the lesser charge of manslaughter. Women were also, according to these figures, more likely to be convicted of manslaughter on the grounds of provocation – 50 per cent, compared with 30 per cent of men. These figures had never been released to academics, who had tried to get them for years. The media didn't pick up the story, so the Home Office put out a press release three weeks later, rang the *Guardian* and got them to cover it. The statistics were published without any comment from campaigners or academics. Hannana: 'It was very damaging. A lot of the time the Home Office quotes the statistics as confirmation that women aren't being discriminated against.' We tried to persuade the media to feature a critical response to the statistics, but could not get anyone interested.

Susan Bandalli, an academic at Birmingham University, wrote, 'We could not let the statistics go unchallenged.' She helped us decode the statistics, and wrote a paper criticising the Home Office intervention as disingenuous and intended 'to undermine genuine concern in the country about the unfairness of the law at an unprecedented time when three women have found the courage and the lawyers willing to challenge it'. She pointed out that the statistics were misleading in several ways, including the way in which categories were inappropriately lumped together. Current and former partners were lumped together, so that it was impossible to tell whether men and women killed in the same circumstances. Men often pursue and kill former partners, whereas women tend to kill while living within a context of violence.

In an SBS paper circulated among MPs, we pointed out that the context of the debate on domestic violence in which the Home Office released this information was entirely ignored: 'There is no attempt to show how many women killed their partners following a history of battering and how many men kill within the context of battering their partners.' The numbers, rather than percentages, were telling. Between 1982 and 1989, 785 men killed their partner or former partner, compared to 177 women.

PROVOCATION AND SELF-PRESERVATION

Side by side with direct action in front of the Home Office were our attempts to look at ways of reforming the law. After studying the literature on the subject we decided to concentrate on amending the law of provocation. In discussions with MPs it emerged that our best chance of success in the near future lay in campaigning for relatively limited reforms. We were unlikely to succeed in any really thoroughgoing reform of the criminal law when a new Criminal Justice Act had recently been passed and the Law Commission had considered and rejected changes in homicide law.

We based our work on amendments to the law in New South Wales, Australia. There the notion of cumulative provocation, which we had raised as early as the first leaflet on Kiranjit, had been passed into law. The requirement for a 'sudden' loss of control was removed, with the recognition that a time-lag was not just a cooling-off period, but could be a boiling-over period. In effect, what we were trying to do was to go back to the definition of provocation in statute, which had been made much more restrictive by successive decisions of the court of appeal, most recently in Sara Thornton's case. Finally, the notion of the 'ordinary person' replaced the more technical concept of the 'reasonable person'.

We felt that these changes would be beneficial to battered women who were trying to get their history taken into account by the law. They would certainly have helped both Sara and Kiranjit. But we also believed that we should make the defence of provocation more available to women defendants.

We discovered that this was a highly controversial course of action. Many feminists who had been involved in campaigns to convict violent men who had killed their partners felt that a reform of the law of provocation was inherently wrong. Feminists have argued that provocation is constructed as a male defence, particularly in cases of adultery, or nagging or irritating behaviour. To widen the definition was to risk more men being able to take advantage of it, while the courts would remain hostile to women defendants.

Tensions in this area nearly led to a breakdown in the coalition that had built up between the Free Kiranjit Ahluwalia campaign and Justice for Women. Eventually we held a meeting to try to arrive at a compromise. It was decided that we would all argue for a reform of both the provocation law and the law of self-defence. The criticisms that we levelled at the former also applied to the latter. We would all work to amend the clauses which stated that self-defence was only applicable when the danger was imminent, and that the force applied had to be proportionate to the imminent threat. But we would also pursue strategies and legal changes that we thought appropriate.

Justice for Women felt that as reform of the existing defences did not really encapsulate the range of battered women's experiences, it would be better to try to formulate an entirely new law, and so they developed the notion of self-preservation. Initially it was a gender-specific defence. Later they were to moderate it as a partial defence to be used by women and children who had been victimised by sexual or domestic violence. They envisaged the concept of 'honest belief' as central to understanding why a woman should feel that she has reached a point where there is no way out of her circumstances – 'It's his life or mine.' While we agreed with the view that the existing defences were unsatisfactory, we felt there were a number of conceptual problems with the way in which 'self-preservation' was formulated. We believed that it would still be difficult to avoid producing medical evidence to show why and how a woman had decided to kill, especially if there had been no violence or provocative act for some days or even months. This would defeat the purpose of creating a new defence which avoided the need to show that battered women are always depressed and not of sound mind. It was also unclear as to how children acting to protect their mother or a sibling would fit the criteria. Whose perceptions of 'honest belief' – the child's or the mother's? – would be relied on? For instance, the concept of 'honest belief' has been used in rape cases by men who argued that they believed they had the consent of the victim. Could it be used legitimately in some cases and not in others? Another difficulty we had was that even though self-preservation was no longer gender-specific, it could only be utilised by women and children in the context of ongoing violence in the family. If we went down that route, then by logical extension there should be a race-specific defence to enable victims of racial violence to argue provocation. The list could be endless. The case of Satpal Ram, an Asian man who is currently contesting a life sentence for responding to a racist attack, is an example. At trial, his plea of provocation was rejected.

We believe that existing homicide laws should become inclusive rather than exclusive of other experiences. Perhaps the way forward is to ensure that the courts and the law look at the context in which an act of homicide takes place, rather than focusing only on the fatal act.

THE CAMPAIGN IN PARLIAMENT:
JACK ASHLEY'S BILL

In December 1991, we heard that the Labour MP Jack Ashley was going to introduce a Ten-Minute Rule Bill to change the law on provocation. We went to see him and offered to do a joint press conference, but he wanted to keep his distance from us. So we prepared a very detailed briefing on our proposed changes in the law and on the Home Office statistics, and circulated it to a large number of MPs. Ashley was very pleased with our briefing, and he mellowed a lot towards us. Since then he's always kept us informed, even after he went to the House of Lords. Ashley had a lot of influence and respect across the House, and that probably affected the reception of the Bill. He had already tabled an Early Day Motion, and Teresa Gorman and others had asked the Home Secretary questions on domestic violence.

On the morning the Bill was to be debated there was extensive press and radio publicity. The women on the picket outside Parliament were keyed up. It was a long time since the issue had received such extensive, sympathetic coverage. We knew that the Bill was highly unlikely to be passed, and that it could easily be killed off if someone objected. But this was the first time that the whole issue had been debated by Parliament. MPs must have been conscious of a profound change in public opinion since the campaign began. The public gallery was full of women waiting with a sense of anticipation, and the ushers were jumpy. The Chamber was packed, not, unfortunately, because of the Bill, but because Mrs Thatcher was due to make a rare appearance.

As Jack Ashley began to speak, Labour MP Dawn Primarolo got up to object that some members were chatting loudly to each other, ignoring his speech. Suddenly we saw the ushers pounce on some women in the gallery and drag them away. They were accused of being disruptive and were locked in the cells, only being released long after the debate was over, after repeated interventions on their behalf. The Bill went forward to a second reading because, unexpectedly, no one objected to it.

Ivan Lawrence, a Conservative MP, had been one of the most vocal opponents of the reform of the law on provocation, and had debated with both Pragna and Hannana on different television programmes. Yet he was silent when Jack Ashley presented his Bill. Later he wished Pragna luck in getting the case reopened, and as Chair of the Home Affairs Select Committee on domestic violence conceded that the law needed clarification. Things had come a long way from the start of the Parliamentary campaign, when we were told that the Law Commission had recently examined the question of homicide and concluded that no change was necessary. Since then the Women's Institute, with its considerable mobilising muscle, has adopted the SBS amendments. A temporary coalition to reform the law on provocation was formed by SBS, the Women's Institute, the Townswomen's Guild and Justice for Women, and co-ordinated by Harry Cohen, MP. In 1994 the coalition presented a huge petition of 45,000 signatures to Parliament.

AMELIA ROSSITER: CLASSIC PROVOCATION

When talking to journalists we always mentioned three women, all in the same prison: Kiranjit, Sara Thornton and Amelia Rossiter. After Sara lost her appeal, Amelia's was the next big case. Pragna: 'I used to ring her daughter a lot to check whether I could mention Amelia, but by the time the case came up they didn't want publicity. The family and lawyers wanted to detach her from the campaigns and the legal arguments we were deploying. I felt very hurt by this.' The case rested on classic provocation. The defence were arguing that this was a woman who killed in a moment of frenzy, unlike Kiranjit and Sara. Their legal strategy was to argue that Amelia fitted the classic definition of provocation, which is based on a sudden and temporary loss of self-control. They did not need to argue that the law should be changed for justice to be done to her. Her lawyer, Mike Fisher, who was interviewed for 'The Provoked Wife', did concede that it would be useful for the court to admit evidence of battering in the past.

The strategy succeeded, and Amelia was released from prison in April 1992.

PREPARING FOR THE APPEAL

By this time we had rehearsed our arguments in the media and at meetings up and down the country. In public we were still concentrating on campaigning for a change in the law on provocation, and the injustice done to battered women was firmly established in the public mind. But would that count in the court of appeal? The message we were getting was very contradictory.

As time wore on and the date of the appeal, July 1992, came closer, the legal team were still refining their final strategy. Receiving legal aid at last, they were able to commission more expert reports. Geoffrey Robertson, who had by now taken on the case, was sceptical of the likelihood of success on provocation alone. Sara Thornton's case appeared to have shut the door very firmly on any liberalisation of the classic definition.

In the months leading up to the appeal the defence had at its disposal five psychiatric reports on Kiranjit. They had started with Dr Weller, who had examined her while she was waiting for her first trial. His report then had indicated that she was suffering from endogenous depression. His first, unadduced report had led to leave to appeal being granted. All the psychiatrists agreed that Kiranjit had indeed been depressed at the time of the incident, a depression which began because of circumstances in her marriage and continued through her incarceration in prison, when she was afraid she might never get her children back. They faced head-on the problem of her changes of story, and the different accounts she gave of the events of that night.

By the end, the defence team were of the opinion that Kiran's actions before, during and after the incident could most coherently be accounted for by pleading both provocation and diminished responsibility. Fortunately the expert evidence was very strong on both counts. The defence developed two novel arguments. In the first they used the evidence to suggest that though there was a time-lag between the last act of provocation and the incident itself, this did not involve merely a slow build-up of rage, but an actual loss of self-control, as was required to prove provocation. As Dr Weller wrote: 'In what might be seen as a planned, co-ordinated and malicious response, but, in the light of her inability to retaliate at first, it was still within the resonances of the most recent provocation, piled upon the long series of humiliations and provocations that her remarkably cruel husband had heaped on her.'

Secondly, a report by Dr Gillian Mezey had examined Kiranjit's case in the light of the battered women's syndrome. Her evidence was used not to support a plea of diminished responsibility, but one of provocation. Kiranjit's lawyers argued that in order to judge whether she had acted as a reasonable person would have done, 'battering' would have to be included as one of her characteristics, which the trial judge had not done in his summing-up. Moreover, he had presented the jury with a closed list of characteristics which would have prevented them from independently considering any others that they thought were relevant. This amounted to a misdirection of the jury.

Thirdly, there was fresh evidence of diminished responsibility submitted to the court: Dr Weller's report, which had not been submitted at the first trial.

One of the grounds for appeal which we had decided to try to reopen was the question of Kiranjit's 'culture'. If the idea of battering required experts to explain its significance to jurors, how could an all-white, largely male jury arrive at an understanding of the 'reasonable Asian woman' without some explanation? There were issues that Kiran herself had stressed which we felt needed some comment to put them into context. The notion of *izzat* was perhaps the most important of these. But there were others, such as the use of fire to attack Deepak, her relationship with her family and his, their part in her marriage, and many other issues. As Rohit wrote: 'That she was Asian was of less significance than that her particular experience of her culture, and the resulting perception she would have of her options in and out of her marriage, would have constrained her seriously in her endeavours to find a solution' (*Criminal Law Review* 728, 1993).

We approached legal academics at the School of Oriental and African Studies. Jane Connors, who had extensive experience working on issues of violence against women in different cultures, wrote a report concentrating on the position of women in India, but ranging from the significance of fire in Indian culture to the ways in which marriage is regarded as an indissoluble contract across a wide range of class and regional boundaries.

Pragna also wrote an extensive report looking not just at Kiranjit's case but also using the collective insights of years of working at Southall Black Sisters. She had to tread very carefully in order to describe common aspects of Asian women's experience in this country without creating a new racial stereotype – the battered Asian woman: 'We were at pains to point out that all women experience violence in a cultural context, and that culture is not a phenomenon of more relevance to Asian women simply because it is different from the dominant culture. We had to tread a very careful tightrope. Whilst not wanting to construct Asian culture as some monolithic and static phenomenon (reinforcing the "problematic" and "pathological" model), we needed to spell out exactly how Asian women can be constrained by their families and communities.'

But raising the cultural context in which an act of homicide is committed brings its own problems. We had always protested against forms of cultural relativism. When Asian men used family honour as a justification for homicide, we had said that cultural background was irrelevant and could not be used as an excuse for leniency. Were we using the same arguments for Kiranjit? Pragna argued strongly that we were not: the balance of power within a relationship was an important factor to take into account. Nor were we using culture as an alibi, but trying to explain the way in which it acted as a constraint. We knew that women of many different backgrounds felt they had to preserve their marriages even when they suffered terribly within them. For an Asian woman like Kiranjit, who had married because of family pressure, it was reasonable to expect the family's backing in trying to end the marriage.

THE SOUTHALL MEETING:
TYING UP THE THREADS

On a hot June night in 1992, the Free Kiranjit Ahluwalia campaign came home to Southall. Rahila produced all the publicity for the meeting. We had spent two years tramping up and down the country, in university halls, to women's groups, trade unions, on the radio and on television. We had argued our case in Parliament. Now, two years after our exploratory beginnings in Crawley Town Hall, we were, at last, on our own home ground. As people arrived at the Dominion Centre in the heart of Southall, they saw videos of parts of the campaign, Kiranjit's story and a national demonstration against violence against women.

On the platform were old friends and new – Jo Richardson

MP, who had long supported our work and who, already in her final illness, had made a huge effort to come to the meeting; Piara Khabra, MP for Southall, benignly offered us his blessing and support for the campaign (who would have thought that only a few years before he had tried to get the women's centre closed down?); Sukhjit and Hannana, who had spoken at the very first meeting; and Julie Bindel, representing Justice for Women, with whom we had built up a strong relationship. Perhaps the most surprising participant was Gareth Peirce, rarely seen on public platforms, who was now Sara Thornton's lawyer and who has successfully worked on such celebrated recent cases of miscarriages of justice as the Birmingham Six and the Guildford Four. She warned us of the possibility of losing out in a system more concerned to take away rights than to grant them. It was likely that the law of provocation would change, but the threatened abolition of the right to silence would disadvantage women in the future. 'There are repeated losses going on in our system,' she said.

When Hannana spoke, she explored the way in which the Kiranjit campaign had broadened and redefined what constituted a miscarriage of justice – that it was not merely a question of innocence wrongly ensnared: a crime may have been committed, but not one that justified imprisonment.

The biggest difference since the original Crawley meeting was the presence of so many different campaigns. There were representatives of Abnash Bisla, whose husband walked out of court with a suspended sentence after he'd killed his 'nagging' wife, and of Vandana Patel, who was killed by her husband during a reconciliation meeting in a police station. There were representatives of those who had been imprisoned for homicide, including Janet Gardner, who was serving five years for manslaughter. Her children had been running a campaign to press for an early release. They were familiar with the Ahluwalias, whom they had met several times to discuss strategies, and they spoke from the floor. It was a long, sweltering meeting, translated throughout by the writer Rukhsana Ahmad. The fact that Kiranjit's appeal was due to come up in a month's time lent the proceedings a sense of urgency. We had not won yet.

THE COURT OF APPEAL

When Peter Taylor was appointed Lord Chief Justice, he came in with the reputation of a new broom wanting to bring sweeping changes to the judiciary – changes of image, such as getting rid of wigs, as well as ones of greater substance. He appeared to be conscious of the declining reputation of the judiciary after the collapse of the convictions of the major Irish cases, and of others such as Mark Braithwaite and Engin Raghip of Broadwater Farm.

As a sign of the change of style, the new Lord Chief Justice appeared on *Desert Island Discs*. We listened hopefully. He talked about the plight of battered women who kill, and said there were anomalies in the law. However, he suggested that it was up to Parliament to clarify the law. Our hope turned to apprehension. Would he be willing to use his position to create radically new case law?

We heard that he had reserved the hearing of Kiranjit's case to himself. What did this mean?

As the hearing approached, we were concerned that media interest, which had raged for a year, was beginning to dwindle. We were convinced that side by side with the legal preparations we had to keep up public pressure. So began a series of strategy discussions to try to attract media attention to Kiranjit. We looked for photo opportunities, tried to interest journalists in interviews by offering new angles and so on. Rahila appeared on the 'Comment' slot after the Channel 4 News to put our case to the public.

Public interest and sympathy for Kiran meanwhile continued

unabated. Petitions and donations kept coming in. One of the petitions which moved us most was signed by male prisoners, many of them Asian. They wrote not only to extend their support to Kiranjit but to acknowledge their own violence towards women in their families.

It was on a blazing hot day in July 1992 that Kiranjit's case finally came up for appeal. A huge picket assembled outside the law courts in the Strand. Shakila and Fawzia had written a new song, and everyone was in particularly good voice. There were placards and balloons, and the privileged had 'Free Kiranjit Ahluwalia' T-shirts.

Inside, the galleries were packed. Pragna was in front with the defence team. As the judges walked in, robed and bewigged, she looked around and thought, 'I can't believe it. We've finally got them to come and listen to our agenda.'

Early on in the arguments the Lord Chief Justice said, 'Make no mistake, this court is sympathetic to the case.' But as the complex legal arguments progressed, it became clear that we were not going to have an easy ride.

After the two-day hearing, which had been headlined in all the press, there was a lull as we waited for the judgement. A week later, the women assembled again. The judgement set aside Kiranjit's previous conviction as 'unsafe and unsatisfactory' on the fresh evidence of diminished responsibility. His Lordship acknowledged the impact of the campaign, and said: 'This is a tragic case which has aroused much public attention ... Had the evidence which has now been put before this court been adduced before the trial judge, different considerations may have applied ... There has been put before this court a significant number of reports of a psychiatric and similar nature, most of them obtained only recently ... we have been driven to the conclusion that without, it would seem, any fault on the part of the appellant, there may well have been an arguable defence which, for reasons unexplained, was not put forward at trial.'

But Kiranjit was still not free. A retrial had been ordered, and she was to remain in jail on remand.

Outside, the women were shouting, 'Free Kiranjit Ahluwalia, free her now!' As the news of the judgement filtered through, there was a sense of shock and outrage.

Expectations had been raised so high that the verdict smacked of defeat, although members of SBS had been well briefed that a retrial was a possible outcome. We were disappointed that Kiran would not leave the court with us, but we were also aware of the enormous effort it had taken to reach the court of appeal at all, and how very slim our chances had seemed at the beginning, more than two years ago. We went out and told the assembled press that we had won a great victory.

The extent of the legal victory was not plain until we had had time to analyse the judgement. We found then that although the appeal judges had rejected our arguments on provocation, we had still managed to introduce into the law three of the basic issues that we had raised. One was the notion of cumulative provocation. The history of violence may be taken into account. Secondly, there may be a time-lag between the provocation and the incident. Thirdly, the acceptance of battered women's syndrome as a characteristic of the accused opened up many possibilities in defending battered women who have killed.

However, as well as creating important precedents, we might have set a trap for ourselves. Battered women's syndrome may elicit sympathy for battered women, but it does not help establish the legitimacy of their experience. As both SBS and Rohit have argued, the experts will supplant the testimony of the woman herself, and it is her character rather than the conditions she finds herself in which are placed on trial. As Rohit and Donald Nicolson wrote in an article on the law of provocation and the implications of the Ahluwalia case: 'By focusing on the defendant's personality, attention is diverted from society's complicity in the killing and the situation which helped precipitate it ... To help juries understand the context of domestic violence, without medicalising and stereotyping battered women, lawyers need to press for expert evidence not just from the "psy" professions, but preferably also from those who work with battered women and if possible from battered women themselves.'

The campaign helped to remake Kiranjit's image from a wicked killer to a battered woman. In doing so we challenged the norms that she was expected to live by, but the image of Kiranjit herself remained, indeed was reconstructed as, quintessentially feminine.

Most of us would only begin to know the real Kiranjit as the months passed and she was able to resume a normal life. But the process of getting to know her started at the huge party in her honour in Southall a few days after her release. When she stood on the platform, flanked by Janet Gardner and another prisoner friend, Ida, she was greeted with an outpouring of joy from the women who had followed her fortunes since that first meeting in Crawley. Her story was so very nearly their story, her triumph was their triumph. Southall Black Sisters' champagne moment had finally arrived.

AFTERWORD

IN EARLY MAY 1993, Kiranjit moved into her new house with her children and started volunteering at the SBS offices, providing support and co-counselling for other women who were suffering as she had. The official solicitors appointed by the family court dealt with matters relating to property and children, and Kiran's previous house was finally sold at a loss. The building society did not pursue her for the difference. There were two insurance policies for Deepak from his Post Office job. One went to pay off part of the shortfall on the house, the other was used by the official solicitors to set up a trust for the children.

The issue of domestic violence had received such extensive coverage through her campaign and those of Sara Thornton, Amelia Rossiter, Janet Gardner and Emma Humphreys, that Kiran found herself being interviewed for radio, television or the press at least once a month. And yet when she considered employment, she did not feel confident enough to apply for jobs other than packing in factories or working at dry cleaners. She found that she was caught in a poverty trap. The wages offered for the hours she could work while the children were at school did not compensate for the resulting loss of welfare benefits. She has now started work at a women's refuge counselling and supporting other women suffering from domestic violence, and is earning a reasonable salary which has enabled her to give up income support.

Kiranjit has addressed a number of public meetings organised by the Women's Aid Network, Justice for Women, the Zero Tolerance campaign and others. She said: 'The pressure of freedom and of people's happiness for me made me ill. I had to talk again and again. It made me both depressed and light-hearted. It was not just my success: it was a success for every woman who had worked for me, who had petitions signed, who had shouted slogans. Speaking in front of five hundred people or more is no joke. When my name was mentioned, there would be such thunderous and continuous applause that I had to put my hand up to ask them to stop. When I talked about my experiences, I noticed that many women wept.'

She is a celebrity who is recognised in the street, but she dreads such attention until it turns out to be positive. When she was asked by her Chinese neighbour to look after her son when she was occasionally late back from work, she agonised about whether she should tell her about her past. She later discovered that her neighbour already knew, yet had entrusted her with her son. Kiranjit found this heartwarming. Her neighbour also typed up an excellent reference for Kiranjit to aid her search for employment. Gradually Kiran developed a supportive network of friends in the neighbourhood.

After her release, Kiranjit visited Sara Thornton a few times in prison. On these visits she met Mumsy. A second approach to win an appeal for Sara Thornton was made to the Home Secretary in September 1992, this time on the grounds of fresh evidence. It took the Home Secretary until August 1993 to reject the application, but Sara was at last given leave to appeal again. She was represented by Gareth Peirce. In December 1995 the appeal court ordered a retrial and Sara was released on bail. In May 1996, after a two-week-long hearing, she was convicted of manslaughter on the grounds of diminished responsibility and sentenced to the same number of years she had already spent in prison. She was free.

Janet Gardner received five years for manslaughter after killing her violent boyfriend in the middle of a frenzied attack on her. On appeal in October 1992, a year after she was sentenced, she was released and given a two-year probationary sentence. She spoke at the launch of Emma Humphreys' campaign and actively supports other women in similar situations.

When Emma Humphreys' appeal was being heard in June 1995, Kiran was shouting slogans outside the Royal Courts of Justice along with hundreds of other women. Emma had been convicted at the age of sixteen of murdering her violent lover. As she was a juvenile at the time, she was detained 'at Her Majesty's pleasure', without limit. After ten years in prison, however, she won her appeal and walked free. Her murder conviction was quashed and was substituted by a conviction for manslaughter. It was a strange reversal of roles for Kiran to participate in something which she had only been able to conjure up in her mind's eye when she sat through her own appeal inside the court.

Kiranjit, in common with other battered women who kill, is torn between the desire to brave the glare of publicity and support other campaigns, and her wish to forget the past. She is trying to concentrate on bringing up her children well, giving them all the attention they need. Their homework is getting harder, and Kiranjit has to resort to a dictionary to help them with it or get a neighbour in to help. Sandeep is at the top of his class in maths due to Kiran's efforts. Rajeev works harder than Sandeep, but they have both been awarded certificates for 'hard work'. They have been to a few family counselling sessions, but these have been suspended at the request of the children, who found them boring. On the face of it, they appear to be suffering no long-term damage from the events of their early life.

When Sandeep and Rajeev go to their grandmother's once a month and for half the school holidays, Kiran feels completely lost. They have become very close, and she feels she has not yet filled the hole left by their separation. They are very loving and become very concerned if Kiran is quiet. She reports that they feel chuffed when they see her on television or when she points out all the famous people she has met. Her relationship with Mamma is as cordial as can be expected. There have been arguments once or twice over access, and over the publication of this book, but the underlying bitterness on both sides is not allowed to surface. Suresh and Raju have visited Kiran in her new house. Suresh was married while Kiran was in prison, and he has one daughter. Neelu is also married. Kiran has not seen him or Manju since her release. Pummi and Paul now live in California. They have four children, two girls and two boys. Pummi and Kiran talk regularly on the phone.

In January 1995 Kiranjit's brother Bindhi died while Kiran and her children were on holiday in India. He was a diabetic, he had a wound in his right leg which wouldn't heal, he had heart problems and he eventually died of kidney failure. Kiran spent most of her time in the hospital with him. She had gone to India because she wanted her children to see how Diwali was celebrated, and was unaware of her brother's condition. She went on a thanksgiving pilgrimage with her family to the Gurdwara where the family had prayed for her release – a twenty-hour journey from Ahmedabad to a town, Hazoor Sahib, where there are fifteen or more Gurdwaras dedicated to the chief saints and prophets of Sikhism. The loss of Bindhi, her father-figure, has had a profound effect on her.

Tommy is married to his third wife, a Muslim. He has one daughter and is still living in Canada. Billoo and Surinder are doing business and happily married in Canada. Jyoti and Puppi have two daughters and one son. They are both working for the airline catering firm where Kiranjit worked, and are living in Crawley. Kiranjit is very close to them, and stays with them and visits Hansapur aunty and Chandrika when she takes the children to see their grandmother. Chandrika tragically lost her daughter to leukemia in 1996.

Joan is working full-time. Kiran still relies heavily on her for advice on a whole range of issues. Joan's husband Ron is quite ill, so Joan has her hands full.

Dev and Sukhjit still lead extremely busy lives, but they see Kiran and talk with her on the phone. Kiran feels she has a place with them should she ever need it. One of their three children was married just before Kiran went to India.

Southall Black Sisters won the Liberty Award for 1993 in recognition of its work with Kiranjit. Kiranjit's case has set such an important precedent that law students are set examination questions on provocation in the light of the Ahluwalia judgement. The massive increase in SBS's caseload as a result of post-Kiranjit publicity, the recruitment of new workers and the readjustments required by the changes led to a year of consolidation and fund-raising in 1994. SBS received pleas for assistance from both men and women in prison as far afield as Jamaica, where a man on death row thought he could avail himself of their help. There was an extremely positive response to the fund-raising initiatives which enabled SBS to carry out a number of youth projects and activities which it did not previously have the resources to do. After the Kiranjit campaign, SBS attracted the attention of quite a few wealthy individuals, among them Lady Sabiha, who offered advice. The intermediary who put Lady Sabiha in touch with SBS advised them to shed their 'feminist' image and take on a softer name like 'The Sheltering Tree'.

SBS gave evidence to the Home Affairs Select Committee on domestic violence and the one-year immigration rule which traps women in violent marriages. They are launching a campaign to change these rules, which allow women no independent status and no recourse to state funds.

Pragna Patel left SBS at the end of 1993, but she is still on the SBS collective and carries on being responsible for a variety of projects. As a result of her involvement with Kiranjit, she received a number of calls from probation officers asking for help with women who were in prison on homicide or infanticide charges. She continues her involvement with them on a purely voluntary basis. One of her recent successes is Kuldip Binning, an Asian woman who was convicted of murdering her baby. She had her conviction reduced to manslaughter and will be moved from prison to a supported, therapeutic environment. Pragna has had a baby daughter and has enrolled at a law college to become a solicitor. In 1993 she was nominated by one of the SBS women for the *Cosmopolitan* award for the community worker of the year. She was kept in the dark about the true nature of her meetings with *Cosmo* (as she would never have agreed to the nomination otherwise), believing that she was helping them with an article on SBS. When she won the award and had to attend a champagne breakfast at the Hilton and be dressed up and made up to grace the pages of the magazine, she was endlessly teased about her new role in life. In autumn 1995 she was invited to chair the high-level medical conference that she had attended during the Kiranjit days as catering assistant because the fees were too high. She has progressed from charwoman to chairwoman.

Hannana Siddiqui is still beavering on in the SBS tradition of long hours and low pay, producing a number of expert reports for solicitors in cases involving Asian women, some of which have been highly commended. Meena Patel went on to do a degree in psychology, side by side with her arduous workload at SBS, enlivening class discussion with her rich and varied experience of her women clients. SBS will soon have an in-house psychologist and an in-house solicitor, making it as cosily self-sufficient as possible.

Following hard on the heels of Emma Humphreys' successful appeal, Justice for Women worked on Sara Thornton's appeal. They are also working on the case of Josephine Smith, whose campaign was launched by Norwich Justice for Women. She was convicted of the murder of her violent husband in November 1993, her plea of manslaughter on the grounds of diminished responsibility being rejected at her trial. She was refused leave to appeal in 1994, and Justice for Women are preparing a lengthy statement in the search for fresh grounds.

Geoffrey Robertson, Kiranjit's QC, went on to uncover the arms to Iraq scandal. Andrew Nicol has taken silk and has worked with SBS on other cases.

And Rohit Sanghvi has steadfastly refused to specialise,

although he has had a number of successful, high-profile criminal appeals like that of Janet Gardner and Emma Humphreys. With a pioneering spirit and the persistence of a dog with a bone, Rohit has taken on some of the toughest cases – cases which push at the frontiers of established law, setting precedents and teasing out further refinements. He acted for Marie Shahir at her trial in 1994, when she was convicted of no intent manslaughter for stabbing her violent boyfriend. He also acted for Kuldip Binning at her successful appeal in 1995. In 1994 he was involved in a major case involving government regulations relating to the licensing of medicinal products, and in 1995 he represented pharmaceutical importers who had undermined the monopoly of drugs manufacturers by importing cheaper medicines from Spain. Both cases were referred to the European Court, and both were won resoundingly on every count, establishing two principles: the freedom of movement of goods within the European Community, and that consumers should be entitled to the cheapest medicinal products within Europe.

Meanwhile, back at SBS, we continue to sing one of our old favourites, sharpened up during the long and numerous pickets we have attended:

We'll be back, Justice Taylor, yes, we will.
You'll be sorry, Justice Taylor, yes, you will.
We'll be freeing all the women, freeing all the women,
Freeing all the women, yes, we will.

RESOURCE LIST

If you need emergency protection, call the police. If you need to go to a refuge, the following will refer you to an appropriate one.

London Women's Aid
52–54 Featherstone Street
London EC1Y 8RT
Tel: 0171 251 6537 (24 hours)

National Women's Aid Federation (England)
PO Box 391
Bristol BS99 7WS

Welsh Women's Aid
38–48 Crwys Road
Cardiff CF2 4NN
Tel: 01745 334767

Scotland Women's Aid (National Office)
12 Torpichen Street
Edinburgh EH3 8JQ
Tel: 0131 221 0401

Northern Ireland Women's Aid
129 University Street
Belfast BT7 1HP
Tel: 01232 249041/249538

For specialist help, you can also contact the following:

Southall Black Sisters
52 Norwood Road
Southall
Middlesex UB2 4DW
Tel: 0181 571 9595

Rights of Women
52–54 Featherstone Street
London EC1Y 8RT
Tel: 0171 251 6577

Justice for Women
55 Rathcode Gardens
London N8
Tel: 0181 340 3699

Sexing the Millennium

Linda Grant

'Linda Grant is on the side of women and sex, fearlessly making the case for passion . . . This is feminist writing at its imaginative best'
Joan Smith

Sex is under siege – sex is fighting back – sex has always been dangerous, to societies as well as individuals. It has always been the stuff around which utopias have been woven.

Charting the origins of sexual freedom in the anarcho-erotic sects of the English Civil War, through the hippie idealism of sixties counter-culture, to our present, postmodern bewilderment, *Sexing the Millennium* examines the intellectual, economic and technological movements that formed the sexual revolution, from the sixties to the present day.

In the age of AIDS, Madonna and Virtual Reality porn, the memory of the brief years when sex was free from the threats of both pregnancy and disease continues to shape our dreams. *Sexing the Millennium* affirms that the personal is still political. It calls for a new sexual revolution, which would at last liberate female desire from the thrall of male fantasy and allow women to pursue the passionate, erotic adventure of their own lives.

'Wise, witty – and wistful . . . I hope this warm book is as widely read and pondered as it deserves to be'
Angus Calder, *Scotland on Sunday*

What Do Women Want?

Luise Eichenbaum and Susie Orbach

Many women today feel that they pour love, commitment and understanding into their relationships, but that it is not returned in kind. He seems secure and independent, she feels insecure and clingy.

The truth is that men and women are *both* dependent. But his needs are catered to so well – first by his mother, then by his girlfriend or wife – that he doesn't know he has them, while her needs – for closeness and tenderness – are constantly rebuffed as he retreats from intimacy.

Susie Orbach and Luise Eichenbaum set out to explore this crisis in the relationships of men and women. They explain how men have learned to 'manage' their dependency needs very differently from women, and *why* women feel dependent and hungry for love. Finally they show why dependency on both sides is the essential core of any successful relationship.

ISBN 0 00 638252 5

The Courage to Live

Discovering Meaning in a World of Uncertainty

Dorothy Rowe

The way in which we perceive death shapes the fundamental pattern of our lives, the very core of our existence.

Fear death, and we live pessimistically in its shadow; learn to accept it, and life's possibilities open up as splendidly varied, infinitely exciting, precious beyond price.

Drawing on personal interviews and her deep insight into the practices of psychotherapy today, eminent psychologist Dorothy Rowe reveals how we structure our lives – how, out of the formless chaos of reality, we give meaning and purpose to our existence through the influences of different cultures, languages and beliefs.

With true warmth and humour, Dorothy Rowe challenges us to find our own ways of living with the uncertainty of death, encouraging us to embrace the freedom of a life without fear.

ISBN 0 00 637736 X

Jealousy

Nancy Friday

By the author of the bestselling *My Mother My Self*.

'Every page is readable, intelligent and full of insight and information. *Jealousy* is big in importance' *Washington Post*

Jealousy is an evil word. It is an emotion that gnaws away inside you, souring relationships, and if it is not controlled can ruin your life.

When Nancy Friday first discovered her own strong feelings of jealousy, she was horrified. Yet she found she was not alone, and that jealousy is at the heart of family life and the core of many relationships.

What makes you feel so bitter when:

Your best friend lands the job of your dreams?

Your mother confides in your sister rather than you?

You fear your partner has been seeing someone else?

A baby is born and disrupts family life as you know it?

Nancy Friday has used her own experiences and those of many men and women to strip bare this multi-faceted emotion. All too often we blame our jealousy on the target of our resentment, but Nancy Friday enables us to understand ourselves more deeply, and to recognize that jealousy is a misery we inflict upon ourselves.

ISBN 0 00 638250 9

Love Isn't Quite Enough

The Psychology of Male–Female Relationships

Maryon Tysoe

Finding out that love isn't quite enough is something most men and women do the hard way.

The traditional Western myth of romantic love has much to answer for. Both sexes can be devastated when they discover that, far from having the power of a psychological superglue, love is only one of many elements needed to sustain a relationship. Even those who are aware of – or reluctantly suspect – this are left floundering as to what other mysterious processes might be involved.

In *Love Isn't Quite Enough*, Dr Maryon Tysoe, widely admired social psychologist and journalist, has written an indispensable book for those seeking a better understanding of how relationships really work, why they fail and what we need to know to make them succeed. With characteristic wit and insight, she draws on a great deal of untapped psychological research to explore the route towards more realistic, and hence potentially more successful, relationships between the sexes.

'A wise, witty and highly readable book'   Dr Anthony Clare

ISBN 0 00 637766 1

My Mother/My Self

Nancy Friday

The No. 1 Bestseller

Why are women the way they are? Why, despite, everything, do we find so much of ourselves mysterious? Where do the dependence, the longing for intimacy, the passivity come from?

Drawing on her own and other women's lives, Nancy Friday shows compellingly that the key lies in a woman's relationship with her mother – that first binding relationship which becomes the model for so much of our adult relationships with men, and whose fetters constrain our sexuality, our independence, our very selfhood.

'Brilliant. Courageous. Moving. One of the most important books I have ever read about my mother, myself and my life.'

Washington Post

'An exhaustive examination.' *Company*

ISBN 0 00 638251 7